April 29, 2009

Humane Economics

NEW THINKING IN POLITICAL ECONOMY

Series Editor: Peter J. Boettke
George Mason University, USA

New Thinking in Political Economy aims to encourage scholarship in the intersection of the disciplines of politics, philosophy and economics. It has the ambitious purpose of reinvigorating political economy as a progressive force for understanding social and economic change.

The series is an important forum for the publication of new work analysing the social world from a multidisciplinary perspective. With increased specialization (and professionalization) within universities, interdisciplinary work has become increasingly uncommon. Indeed, during the 20th century, the process of disciplinary specialization reduced the intersection between economics, philosophy and politics and impoverished our understanding of society. Modern economics in particular has become increasingly mathematical and largely ignores the role of institutions and the contribution of moral philosophy and politics.

New Thinking in Political Economy will stimulate new work that combines technical knowledge provided by the 'dismal science' and the wisdom gleaned from the serious study of the 'worldly philosophy'. The series will reinvigorate our understanding of the social world by encouraging a multidisciplinary approach to the challenges confronting society in the new century.

Recent titles in the series include:

Markets, Planning and Democracy
Essays after the Collapse of Communism
David L. Prychitko

Governance and Economic Development
A Comparative Institutional Approach
Joachim Ahrens

Constitutions, Markets and Law
Recent Experiences in Transition Economies
Edited by Stefan Voigt and Hans-Jürgen Wagener

Austrian Economics and the Political Economy of Freedom
Richard M. Ebeling

Anarchy, State and Public Choice
Edited by Edward Stringham

Humane Economics
Essays in Honor of Don Lavoie
Edited by Jack High

Humane Economics

Essays in Honor of Don Lavoie

Edited by

Jack High

George Mason University, USA

NEW THINKING IN POLITICAL ECONOMY

Edward Elgar

Cheltenham, UK • Northampton, MA, USA

Published by
Edward Elgar Publishing Limited
Glensanda House
Montpellier Parade
Cheltenham
Glos GL50 1UA
UK

Edward Elgar Publishing, Inc.
136 West Street
Suite 202
Northampton
Massachusetts 01060
USA

A catalogue record for this book
is available from the British Library

Library of Congress Cataloging in Publication Data

Humane economics : essays in honor of Don Lavoie / edited by Jack High.
p. cm. — (New thinking in political economy)
Includes bibliographical references and index.
1. Lavoie, Don, 1951–2. Economics—Philosophy. 3. Hermeneutics. I. High, Jack C. II. Lavoie, Don, 1951– III. Series.
HB72.H825 2006
300.092—dc22

2006002683

ISBN-13: 978 1 84542 511 1
ISBN-10: 1 84542 511 1

Printed and bound in Great Britain by MPG Books Ltd, Bodmin, Cornwall

To Mary, John, Mark and Gabrielle

Contents

PART 5 CULTURAL STUDIES

PART 6 APPENDIX

Contributors

Peter J. Boettke, Department of Economics, George Mason University
Robert L. Bradley Jr., Institute for Energy Research, Houston, TX
Emily Chamlee-Wright, Department of Economics, Beloit College
Wayne J. Froman, Department of Philosophy, George Mason University
Jack High, School of Public Policy, George Mason University
Don E. Kash, School of Public Policy, George Mason University
Israel M. Kirzner, Department of Economics, New York University
G.B. Madison, Department of Philosophy, McMaster University
Deirdre McCloskey, College of Arts and Sciences, University of Illinois at Chicago
Mark S. Miller, Hewlett Packard Laboratories, Palo Alto, CA
David L. Prychitko, Department of Economics, Northern Michigan University
Virgil Henry Storr, Don C. Lavoie Research Fellow in the Program in Philosophy, Politics and Economics, Department of Economics, George Mason University
Bill Tulloh, School of Public Policy, George Mason University

Acknowledgements

This volume grew out of a conference held at George Mason University to honor Don Lavoie, a colleague who passed away in 2001. The University's President, Alan Merten, its Provost, Peter Stearns, and its Dean of the School of Public Policy, Kingsley Haynes, warmly supported the conference. Many colleagues besides those who contributed to the volume participated in the conference; Robert Axtell, Howard Baetjer, Clayton Coppin, Roy Cordato, Jim Finkelstein, Francis Fukuyama, Mark Gilbert, Steve Horwitz, Mark Jacobs, Richard Langlois, Axel Leijonhufvud, Ralph Rector, and Karen Vaughn helped to make the conference a fitting tribute. Financial support was generously provided by The Charles G. Koch Charitable Foundation, The Earhart Foundation, The Fund for American Studies, and the Wilbur Foundation. The President of The Fund for American Studies, Roger Ream, provided encouragement and sound advice. Jackie Montegut of the Fund coordinated the conference. To all of them, and to the contributors to this memorial volume, I extend my heartfelt gratitude.

The author and publisher wish to thank the following for kindly giving their permission for the use of copyright material:

Jack Birner and Pierre Garrouste, *Markets, Information and Communication* (London, UK: Routledge, 2004), pp. 21–46.

PART 1

Introductory

1. Humane economics: an introduction to the work of Don Lavoie

Jack High

Don Lavoie's published work encompasses a wide variety of subjects – socialism, hermeneutics, information technology and culture. At a glance, the subjects appear unrelated, perhaps even oddly juxtaposed. What has the impossibility of socialist calculation to do with hermeneutical philosophy or with cultural studies? What have any of these to do with computer programming or the Internet? Many who admired Lavoie's research on socialism found his work on methodology or cultural studies to be a misguided departure from his original insights. Those who found his writing on methodology or cultural studies to be persuasive looked upon his research into computers as a personal interest only. Yet a close examination of Lavoie's research reveals an underlying unity to his work. Moreover, this unity reveals a conception of economics that is quite different from mainstream economics of the post-WWII era. In Lavoie's view, economics is not a physical science but an interpretive one. By linking economics to hermeneutics, cultural studies and software development, Lavoie was attempting to demonstrate that economics is closer to the humanities than to physics. He was working towards a humane economics.

There are different ways of seeing the unity of Lavoie's research and its implications for economics. One way is through the audiences that he was trying to reach. Early in his career, Lavoie began a dialogue with Marxists. He was trying to show the value of marginalist economics to socialist ideals. To do so, he needed to show that economics was something more than the maximizing logic of neoclassical economics. Economic decisions, Laovie argued, were made by sentient persons embedded in historical and cultural processes. In fact, markets were an expression of values and culture. They were a means of helping individual persons realize their dreams and lead richer lives. This message naturally linked economics to philosophy and cultural studies.

Another way to see the unity of his work is to understand what Lavoie was trying to accomplish within the tradition of Austrian economics in which he worked. The Austrian tradition in economics contains two distinct strands of thought – an interpretive approach to human action developed primarily by Ludwig Mises, and an evolutionary approach to human institutions developed primarily by Friedrich Hayek. Intertwining these two strands of thought in one discipline was unusual. Lavoie (1993, p. 2) noted that:

> In most other parts of contemporary scholarship these two orientations, evolutionary and interpretive social science, are almost completely separated from one another.... Interpretive ideas arise from the humanities, and the approach is strongest in fields such as anthropology, philosophy, literary criticism, and history. Evolutionary thinking arises in the field of biology and is strongest in fields that see themselves as scientific as opposed to humanistic, such as computer science and ecology.

The connecting medium that joins these two strands together, said Lavoie, was a proper philosophy of science. 'I believe that in the work of philosophical hermeneutics', he wrote, 'can be found the kind of unifying framework which permits the [Austrian] school [of economics] to retain both its interpretive and its evolutionary ideas.'[1] Again, we see a vital connection between economics and philosophy.

Another way to see the unity of Lavoie's work, and its implications for economics, is through its emphasis on social learning. The creation and dissemination of knowledge in markets was a central point of contention in the socialist calculation debate. Lavoie realized early in his studies that the coordination of dispersed knowledge was not unique to markets. It existed in a variety of complex systems. In describing his research in the early 1990s, Lavoie wrote, 'I have been trying to show that there is an identifiable process of "social learning" at work within complex systems, whether those systems happen to be economies, discourses, or software systems.'[2] Social learning is a unifying thread that runs throughout Lavoie's research. He argued that an economics built around social learning would retain the valuable insights of the marginal revolution but would move economics away from equilibrium theorizing, which does not allow for discovery or creativity or open-ended dialogue, and toward the disciplines of biology and anthropology and history, which do. The unity of Lavoie's work and its implications for economics will emerge more clearly from considering his contributions to each of his distinct subjects in more detail.

SOCIALISM

A notable feature of Lavoie's work on socialism was its emphasis on the work of Karl Marx. Lavoie praised Marx for presenting 'a single, coherent, and remarkably consistent view of socialism', and for understanding the indivisibility of capitalist institutions. Marx understood that private property, division of labor, market exchange, money and banking, and profit seeking are necessarily linked. One could not simply pick and choose which of these elements one liked and discard the rest, as some socialists (Proudhon, for example) wanted to do. It was contradictory to advocate an economy that retained market exchange, money and banks but suspended interest and profits. Marx also realized that plan coordination under capitalism was necessarily imperfect. Lavoie expressed Marx's insight this way,

> Just from the fact that thousands of separate private-property owners independently direct their resources toward various projects through time, quite unaware *ex ante* of the many inevitable conflicts among their plans, we see that there necessarily must be disequilibrium. For Marx it is this alienation of producers from each other that makes any complete coordination inherently impossible.[3]

Marx's insight into the integrity of the market institutions and the impossibility of achieving a perfect consistency of plans, led to his advocacy of central planning. At one stroke, by organizing the whole of the market economy as a single factory is organized, society could eliminate private property in the means of production, exchange, money, money prices and profits, while at the same establishing a perfect coordination of plans. The power of Marx's argument resides in the logical consistency of eliminating all vestiges of the market and at the same time improving plan coordination. In the Marxian vision, society can dispense with market relations; socialism is a complete replacement for them.

The consistency and breadth of Marx's vision exerted a strong influence on Lavoie. Lavoie's first major works in economics, *Rivalry and Central Planning, The Socialist Calculation Debate Reconsidered*, and *National Economic Planning, What is Left*, were addressed to Marx's work. Lavoie's interpretation of the socialist calculation debate rested squarely on Marx's view of capitalism. Embracing the Marxian view of capitalism as an integral whole, which grew out of private property and competitive struggle, enabled Lavoie to stand the common interpretation of the debate on its head. The usual account of the debate ran like this: Marx advocated central planning as a remedy for the faults of capitalism. Ludwig von Mises argued that central planning was impossible. The market socialists, especially Oskar Lange, responded to Mises by demonstrating that central planning was indeed possible. Friedrich Hayek then conceded that central planning was possible, but developed a fallback argument that it was not practical. Oskar Lange replied that, with the advent of modern computers, central planning was more practical than ever; in fact, it would become comparatively simple.

If even Hayek's fallback position is untenable, then Lange had refuted the Austrian position.

Lavoie offered a rather different interpretation: Marx proposed a logically coherent alternative to the competitive processes of markets. Mises, relying on the theory of value developed during the marginal revolution, and therefore unavailable to Marx, demonstrated that Marx's alternative was not possible because, in the absence of market prices, central planners could not channel productive resources into their most highly valued uses. The market socialists, especially Lange and Abba Lerner, conceded that prices were essential, but then tried to combine markets and planning in illogical ways, just as socialists before Marx had done. Mises, Hayek and Lionel Robbins responded by pointing out the inconsistencies of the market socialists. In Lavoie's view, the market socialists retreated to the muddled view of capitalism that existed before Marx wrote. In this way Lavoie brought the weight of Marx to bear against market socialism.

Lavoie's study of Marx and Mises, which was an unusual combination in the post-WWII world of neoclassical economics, resulted from his own predilections and from his circumstances at New York University, where he pursued his graduate studies. His predilections were evident in the 1960s at Worcester Polytechnic Institute, where Lavoie majored in what was then a new and exciting discipline, computer science. By an odd chance he discovered Austrian economics. In the summer between his junior and senior years in college, he took a temporary featherbedding position on the railroad. He ostensibly operated a gate to let rail cars pass by, but by 1968 the gate was automated, so he had nothing to do but sit in the gate shack and stare at the tracks. He decided to put his idle time to use by studying some economics. He had already had one course, macroeconomics, as part of his college curriculum requirements. He disliked the class, learned nothing of value from it, and felt that he needed to fill this gap in his education on his own. He ran across Henry Hazlitt's *Economics in One Lesson*, which, given his earlier experience with economics, was about as many lessons as he wanted. However, he liked Hazlitt's book and decided to delve into the subject, beginning with the books in Hazlitt's bibliography. He started Friedrich Hayek's *Road to Serfdom*, but before he finished it, he picked up Mises' *Human Action.* Mises' ideas so captivated him, especially the book's first part, which locates economic theory within a broad philosophical context, that he spent the rest of his railroad job reading and re-reading Mises' treatise.[4]

After graduating from Worcester Polytechnic in computer science in 1973, Lavoie decided to pursue graduate studies in economics. He discovered that New York University was initiating an Austrian economics program under the direction of Israel Kirzner. NYU was a fortunate choice; in addition to Kirzner, who supervised Lavoie's research into the socialist calculation debate, Lavoie was able to study under Fritz Machlup and Ludwig Lachmann. All three of these eminent scholars exerted important influences on his thinking. NYU also offered a specialized field of study in Marxism. Lavoie studied Marx under James Becker and a visiting Japanese scholar of Marxism, Makato Itoh. It was in these courses that Lavoie developed his appreciation for Marx. Marx had the same broad outlook on society as Mises and Hayek. Marx's economics was embedded in explicit philosophical principles, which attracted Lavoie to economics in the first place, and was grounded in the competitive processes of business and politics. Also, as mentioned earlier, Marx appreciated the inherent integrity of the market system. It was Marx's mistaken theory of value, and his consequent lack of appreciation for the communicative aspects of markets, that led him into the errors of central planning. In Lavoie's eyes, these errors were understandable in light of the prevailing economic thinking of the mid-nineteenth century; if the labor theory of value were true, central planning would be possible, or at least would not be precluded by the inability to determine relative values.[5]

Lavoie's first book, *Rivalry and Central Planning*, was a sympathetic criticism of Marx. Lavoie criticized Marx, as had Mises and Hayek, for advocating a social system that ignored the communicative functions of prices.[6] But he appreciated the theoretical integrity of the Marxian system which, in Lavoie's judgment, was more coherent than the attempts at market socialism advocated by Oskar Lange and the market socialists. Lavoie's combination of criticism and appreciation found a ready audience. Boettke and Prychitko explore the influence of *Rivalry and Central Planning* in their chapter for this volume. They chronicle Lavoie's influence within the field of comparative systems. *Rivalry and Central Planning* was favorably reviewed even by those who disagreed with the ultimate conclusions. The book was frequently cited, and it persuaded two leading economists, Janos Kornai and Robert Helibroner, to conclude that the Austrian economists had been correct in their assessment of socialism. Lavoie's work also stimulated further research into socialism along Austrian lines, not least of which was conducted by Prychitko (on worker managed systems) and Boettke (on the Soviet experience) themselves.

Lavoie's work might have been even more influential had he paid more attention to the distorted incentives of socialist planners; the public choice aspects of central planning might have drawn a large and growing discipline into the debate. Lavoie did not ignore the incentives facing planners; he drew an interesting connection between knowledge and incentives. The impossibility of rationally allocating resources opens the door to arbitrary behavior, which is why militarism so often accompanies attempts to establish socialism. But Lavoie usually set aside incentives to concentrate on knowledge.[7]

Israel Kirzner's contribution to this volume argues that the knowledge problem is more fundamental than the incentive problem. Unless the knowledge problem is solved, there is no such thing as an incentive problem. Kirzner's argument stems from his insight that, in the purely socialist state, there is no economy. There are households and workers and land and equipment, but they are not a system. They are merely collections of individual persons and resources, in the way that iron filings on paper are an unordered collection until a magnetic force arranges them into a system. The impossibility of knowing how to properly arrange a vast collection of economic resources precludes the central planner from applying magnetic force, as it were; his ignorance prevents him from creating a system or order. Without an order within which to operate, there is no incentive problem facing the central planner. Of course, distorted incentives are very important in historical attempts to establish socialist states. The impossibility of creating a coherent order through fiat means that, in practice, central planners rely on market forces. They buy and sell goods in international markets, borrow from international lenders, and adopt technology and production techniques from capitalist economies. Attempts to create socialist economies in countries such as Russia, China, and many smaller countries have produced militarism, corruption, and enormous inefficiency. Inadequate knowledge and distorted incentives have combined to produce these results. Socialist experience is consistent with Kirzner's insight that, strictly speaking, a central planner does not face distorted incentives until he solves the knowledge problem.[8]

If markets and planning cannot be combined in arbitrary ways, as argued by Marx, Mises and Lavoie, then economists must study what happens when governmental policies attempt to combine the two. Mises argued that partial attempts at intervention would lead to unintended consequences that required undoing the original intervention or undertaking another, resulting in dynamic processes that lead either to socialism or free markets. Bradley examines this proposition by constructing a typology of the processes that intervention can take. Using his typology of cumulative processes and a wealth of historical examples taken from regulation of the energy industries, Bradley concludes that interventions often lead to cumulative processes, but sometimes reach a static equilibrium that persists for long periods. The cost-based regulation of utilities, for example, lasted for decades without engendering further regulation or deregulation. Bradley concludes that Mises identified a powerful tendency of intervention, but not an iron law.

HERMENEUTICS

Two parts of *National Economic Planning, What is Left?* deal explicitly with the philosophy of science. In chapter 3, entitled 'The knowledge problem', Lavoie draws out the similarities between the market process and the scientific process, in order to demonstrate that central planning would be as disastrous for markets as for science. Science, whether restricted to the physical sciences or expanded to include the social and biological sciences, is a form of social intelligence in which the sum of knowledge possessed by all scientists dwarfs the knowledge possessed by any individual scientist, however great. The enormous disparity between social knowledge and the knowledge possessed by a committee of planners was the central point of Mises, and later Hayek, in the socialist calculation debate. Scientific knowledge is arrived at by the interaction of a community of scholars committed to pursuing the truth. Similarly, economic knowledge is arrived at by a community of businessmen committed to pursuing profit, that is, to employing resources so that their value in existing uses is greater than their value in alternative uses. Scientific discoveries are made by scientists pursuing hunches based on their understanding of nature, just as new combinations are introduced into economic life by entrepreneurs pursuing hunches based on their understanding of the market. Scientific hunches depend on explicitly stated scientific principles, but also on inarticulate knowledge that scientists are as yet unable to put into words. In the same way, entrepreneurial hunches depend on articulate knowledge that a budding entrepreneur could express to a venture capitalist, but also on inarticulate knowledge of an industry or technology that the entrepreneur could not express. In order to pursue their hunches, scientists must be free to act on their own judgment, devoting their intellectual resources to lines of inquiry that they consider worthwhile, just as entrepreneurs must be free to invest in those lines of commerce that they consider most promising. Lavoie wrote, 'Coercion obstructs the flow of knowledge in the market process for the same reason it obstructs it in the scientific community.'[9]

In the appendix to *National Economic Planning*, Lavoie briefly defends scientific method as a social process against the demands of scientific knowledge imposed by positivism. Positivism, Lavoie points out, founders on the rock of logical consistency. That is, the two main requirements of positivism, logical completeness and extensive empirical confirmation, do not themselves justify positivism as a proper method of science. Lavoie invokes Gödel to argue that such completeness is impossible; a formal system must rely on considerations outside the confines of its axioms and deductions to judge whether its axioms are contradictory or its conclusions are relevant. Lavoie makes this point in order to explain why the Austrian position in the calculation debate, including Lavoie's own explication of it, is not a formal proof of the sort demanded by neoclassical economics. Lavoie writes, 'The main tools of this argument are not formalistic and mathematical but descriptive and analogical. To many economists this form of argument already condemns it as unscientific. It is partly in order to anticipate and counter this charge that I embark on this epistemological reconstruction.'[10]

G. B. Madison clearly sees that Lavoie's study of philosophy informs his view of the socialist calculation debate. He writes,

> [o]ver and beyond the details of the socialist calculation debate ... what I found most interesting is that he should have referred to this classic debate not as the 'calculation problem' but as the 'knowledge problem.' His interest in this matter was philosophical–hermeneutical; his basic concern was the nature of 'knowledge' itself and how it comes to be generated....Summing up his position, he stated: '[T]he whole case against planning that is being developed here is rooted in a critique of objectivist theories of knowledge'.[11]

It might appear from Lavoie's published work up to 1985 that his interest in philosophy stems from a desire to expand and buttress his arguments in the calculation debate. This view, however, unduly narrows his interest in philosophy. His early interest in economics, as recounted above, was stimulated by the way in which Mises justified the social sciences. Lavoie was attracted to economics as much for philosophical reasons as for economic ones. He seriously considered earning his doctorate degree in philosophy rather than economics, but was dissuaded from this by friends who were concerned about his financial prospects in philosophy. Although he entered the doctoral program in economics at New York University, philosophy was a parallel interest, which he was able to pursue in tandem with economics. As mentioned above, he studied Marx's *Grundrisse*. He worked with Fritz Machlup, who had written extensively on economic method and was familiar with the German *verstehen* tradition. Israel Kirzner's first work, *The Economic Point of View*, was an outstanding example of interpretive philosophy. Lavoie attended the seminars of Ludwig Lachmann, who introduced him to the philosophical writings of Wilhelm Dilthey, Edmund Husserl, and Max Weber. He worked with a new faculty member at NYU, Mario Rizzo, and fellow graduate student Richard Ebeling. Rizzo had a particular interest in Alfred Schutz, a student of Husserl, and Ebeling introduced Lavoie to the work of Hans Georg Gadamer and other hermeneutical writers. Philosophy was in the air of NYU's economics department during the 1970s, and the atmosphere nurtured Lavoie's philosophical interests. His study went from Mises and Marx to early hermeneutics and phenomenology (Dilthey and

Husserl and Schutz) to Polanyi and Kuhn and the growth of knowledge philosophers, to the modern hermeneutics of Gadamer and Ricoeur.[12]

Hermeneutics is defined as the art and science of interpretation. In Lavoie's words, it is 'essentially a philosophy of understanding, which elucidates how it is that one person comes to understand the actions or words, or any other meaningful product, of another' (Lavoie, 1993). Hermeneutics had its origins in the interpretation of text, particularly Scripture. In its modern development by Ricoeur, Gadamer, Madison and others, text is used broadly, as a metaphor, really, to include natural and human events. Lavoie extended this philosophical tradition by conceiving of the economy as a vast, complex text that is continually being written and read by consumers, workers, managers and investors. Less metaphorically, the economy is a complex system of actions whose meanings and effects are not self-evident. Only by properly interpreting the intentions of others, and communicating their own, can the actors in this network mutually adjust so as to attain their ends. The market is a hermeneutical process of communicating and interpreting intended actions in the pursuit of individual goals.[13]

If the economy is a complex system that requires interpretation by those who participate in it, then economics is the study of these interpretations. It is doubly hermeneutical, in that the economist interprets the operation of a system that is itself actuated by interpretations. Although we must recognize that a catallaxy is driven by interpretations, this does not mean that an economist takes the economic agents' interpretations as the final word. Investors, executives and consumers may or may not be correct in their actions and expectations, and even where they are correct, they may exert effects that were no part of their intentions. The study of spontaneous order, or emergent order as it is called today, has been at the heart of economics since Adam Smith. The fact that objects of our study already have an interpretation of what is going on does not make the economist a mere recorder of intentions; she has her own responsibility to develop and defend her own explanations.[14]

There is yet a third layer of interpretation involved in economics. Most academic education and publishing involves reading the work of other economists. We attempt to understand, criticize and extend their ideas. Here we are interpreting interpretations of interpretations. The first level interpretations are those of the entrepreneurs, investors, and others who interpret the signals of the market; the second level interpretations are those of the economists who theorize or historicize about the market; the third level interpretations are those of economists who evaluate the second level interpretations. This third level interpretation is especially important for economists who write about the history of economic doctrines, and about the proper methods of economics, which great economists since Nassau

Senior and John Stuart Mill have done. This third level interpretation has been forcefully advanced by Deirdre McCloskey, whose Socratic dialogue, 'The Rosenberg', was particularly critical of those philosophers of science who freely offered their advice on how to study economics without bothering to learn how practicing economists actually conduct their studies.[15]

Lavoie's hermeneutical approach led him to offer rules for the study of economics. First, economic theory should include first-level interpretations in its theoretical constructs. The proper interpretation of changes in a complex system is an important undertaking that economists should acknowledge in their theories. We should not remove judgment and foresight from economics by assuming perfect knowledge. Recognizing the difficulties of first-level interpretation roots our theory in realistic decision-making, whereas assuming perfect knowledge cuts theory from its human moorings and makes humans into lightning calculators of utility, more akin to machines than men. Lavoie was critical of relying on theoretical ideas that squeeze out the richness of human interpretation from economic activity. Even theoretical constructs such as rational expectations admit only a thin and brittle kind of interpretation into economic theory. As Ralph Rector has convincingly demonstrated, the rational expectations of macroeconomics are not fully rational in the human sense of that term.[16]

Lavoie offered a second rule for the conduct of economic research, viz., that economists should undertake empirical studies that elucidate human interpretation. He did not deny that statistical studies, the usual form of empirical work in economics, could be useful, but statistics by themselves do not get close enough to the mental processes, decisions and actions of economic agents. Understanding the life-world of economic actors requires up-close empirical studies of the sort conducted by historians and anthropologists. Lavoie thus re-established a link to narrative economic history that had been a part of economics since Adam Smith, but which has been in progressive decline since the ascendance of neoclassical economics in the 1940s. Lavoie helped to organize an empirical workshop at George Mason University led primarily by historian Clayton Coppin. Out of this workshop came numerous studies that exemplified the kind of empirical research advocated by Lavoie. This workshop also established ties to the work of other narrative historians, many of whom were the business historians at Harvard University – Alfred Chandler, Tom McCraw, Richard Tedlow, Richard H.K. Vietor – but which also included the noted food and drug historian James Harvey Young. Up-close empirical studies became a common feature of dissertations written under Lavoie at George Mason University.[17]

Don Kash's 'Innovation of Cardio-Imaging Technology at Hewlett-Packard and HP/Philips' illustrates the values of up-close empirical work enumerated by Lavoie but also illustrates many of the themes of Lavoie's research. The episode recounted by Kash is one of innovation and rivalry. Hewlett-Packard's interest in both ultrasound imaging and magnetic resonance imaging was motivated by the desire to lead the market in imaging heart diseases. The research and development was motivated by foresight and guided by tacit knowledge; there was no existing market demand when Hewlett-Packard developed ultrasound for imaging the heart, yet the researchers believed that a market would develop if the technology was effective. The responsibility for technological advance resided in teams of scientists rather than executive suites, an organization that enabled researchers to take advantage of their experience and tacit understanding. Cultural and organizational issues were paramount in the collaboration between Hewlett Packard and Philips. The two firms found it difficult to establish trust at the working level because of different corporate philosophies, different languages, and differences in the organization and carrying out of everyday work. A telling example of the differences occurred when researchers at Hewlett-Packard requested the latest drawings on magnetic resonance imaging and received drawings of outdated technology. The Hewlett-Packard team took this as evidence of distrust, when in reality the Philips manager sent over what he thought were the latest drawings. The manager did not have access to the latest research because of the culture of secrecy and 'need-to-know' information flows at Philips. In the open, sharing environment of Hewlett-Packard, a senior manager would have always had access to the latest technology. Secrecy of the sort routinely practiced at Philips was inconceivable to the engineers of Hewlett-Packard and led to much misunderstanding. The culture of openness and decentralized decision-making at Hewlett-Packard resulted from the values of the founders. They did not want to be a hire and fire shop; they wanted to 'be in business for the long haul, to have a company built around a stable and dedicated workforce'. The subjects illustrated by Kash's chapter – rivalry, entrepreneurship, tacit knowledge, culture and values – were subjects that formed the heart of Lavoie's research. Little wonder that Lavoie extolled the virtues of up-close empirical work.

A third rule of economic research that Lavoie did not propound, but certainly practiced, is humility. As McCloskey argues in her contribution to this volume, humility is not debasement. Rather it is seriously listening to the arguments of others, especially those whose conclusions cast doubt on your own. Lavoie never tired of doing this. He spent his career persuading other economists that their discipline needed fundamental change, that its scope was too narrow, that its methods were inappropriate, that its conclusions were too often irrelevant to the pressing problems of economic life. He argued that a hermeneutical approach to studying social processes would yield better insight into human economy. Yet he was never arrogant or rude. He advocated free markets in a way that seriously engaged socialists. He advocated hermeneutics in a way that engaged positivists and other philosophers of science. He advocated the importance of cultural studies in a way that engaged those who were suspicious of it. He seriously considered the arguments opposed to his, presented the opposition's best case, and contended against it. Collectively, these traits make up McCloskey's meaning of humility. As she said of Lavoie, 'Don was humble – it was his most startling personal quality in a profession not known for exhibiting it.'[18]

Lavoie's application of hermeneutics to economics supported the distinctive features of Austrian economics, with its emphasis on process, complexity, ignorance, uncertainty, entrepreneurship, rivalry and rational discursive methods. All of these features were captured in, or justified by, his notion of interpretation and he often spoke of an 'interpretive economics'. However, his hermeneutics sometimes led to somewhat different conclusions or emphases than those of his teachers. Lavoie did not draw the sharp distinction between the natural sciences and the social sciences that we find in Mises. In Lavoie's view, both sciences were interpretive and neither relied upon the standards of positivism in practice. Lavoie did not deny a difference between natural and social science – natural science worked with a single level of interpretation while the social sciences worked with a double one – but both realms arrived at knowledge through a dedicated community of scholars, each committed to the values of science and contending for their version of the truth. Nor did Lavoie draw such a sharp distinction between history and theory as Mises did, again because he saw the social processes that produced historical and theoretical knowledge as similar.

Hermeneutics influenced not only Lavoie's economics, but also his view of the social sciences generally. These influences are nicely presented in Madison's chapter. On the connection between hermeneutics and democracy in Lavoie's work, Madison writes (p. 152), 'Economic democracy, then, is to be conceived of in terms of the hermeneutical principle of freedom of discourse; so conceived, economic democracy is precisely what permits the creative discovery process to operate in the economic arena, just as it does in the cultural and political arenas.' The social institutions that underlay the market require cultivation, as do the institutions that underlay productive dialogue. And while Lavoie's commitment to liberty predated his knowledge of hermeneutics, he certainly found that philosophy conducive to his way of thinking. Madison says (pp. 146–7), '…freedom was always the leading value in the phenomenological tradition, in both Husserl's transcendental phenomenology and in the existential phenomenology that developed out of it. Gadamer summed up very well the hermeneutical position in this matter when he stated: "There is no higher principle of reason than that of freedom.'"

INFORMATION TECHNOLOGY

When he began his graduate studies in economics, Lavoie had hoped to put his background in computers to use in his new subject matter. One of his interests in computers was artificial intelligence. For his senior project at Worcester Polytechnic, he had programmed a computer to write music in the mode of Bach. He was struck by how easy it was to get a computer to follow mechanical rules, but how hard it was to get it to do anything the least bit subtle. Although the computer followed all the rules, no one would have mistaken the resulting music for a Bach chorale. His experience with computers made Lavoie deeply suspicious of Lange's claim that computers would make central planning feasible; he knew that computers had none of the sophistication of human judgment and intuition. Nevertheless, he did think that computers might help us to understand complex evolutionary processes through simulations.[19]

He toyed with the idea of creating a computer simulation of the market process for his dissertation at NYU, but decided that it was too difficult and too risky. He again considered attempting simulations a decade later when Ralph Rector, a graduate student at George Mason with a computer background, approached him about the subject. Again Lavoie concluded that the subject was too risky for a dissertation. But the subject did not go away. A few years later another graduate student, Bill Tulloh, discovered that a group of computer scientists were using Austrian economics to help them solve software engineering problems. Dubbed the high-tech Hayekians, this group introduced Lavoie to a new branch of artificial intelligence, called emergent intelligence, that made modeling economic processes seem feasible. For the first time, Lavoie, along with graduate students Bill Tulloh, Howie Baetjer, and Kevin Lacobie began to model economic processes. More importantly, they became acquainted with others, most notably Axel Leijonhufvud, Robert Axtell and Joshua Logan, who were also pursuing this line of research.[20]

Although Lavoie never developed simulations of economic processes very far, he and his students integrated economics and information technology in other respects. Howie Baetjer, for example, made an important contribution to capital theory by studying software as a capital good that consists almost entirely of knowledge. He took software as a paradigmatic case to emphasize the knowledge component of all capital goods. He argued that capital goods are best understood as embodied knowledge, not least of which is the knowledge of how one capital good is linked to others in a complex structure of production. Another integration was the use of economic concepts to analyze computer software. Building on the work of the aforementioned high-tech Hayekians, Lavoie, Tulloh and Baetjer, along with Richard Langlois, another able economist with a background in computers, produced a study predicting that object-oriented programming would eventually dominate the field. The arguments were strikingly similar to the arguments of the socialist calculation debate among economists. Computer programs were becoming too complex to be constructed by a single programmer. To cope with the increasing complexity, bits of code would have to be encapsulated within modules whose boundaries would be protected from interference from other bits of code. In other words, modules of computer code are assigned something akin to property rights in human society. In addition to establishing property rights, programmers have to establish rules by which the modules of code interact to achieve the desired results. In other words, programmers establish a complex order by creating a division of labor among modules of code and instituting a constitution or rule of law to which all modules submit.[21]

Bill Tulloh and Mark Miller, in their contribution to this volume, point to another similarity between software and markets. When software designers encapsulate code into distinct modules, they have to consider how the modules will interact with one another. The points at which modules interact are called abstraction boundaries. Programs with good abstraction boundaries permit existing modules to interact smoothly, but they also permit the program to be improved, which means that the program will still operate smoothly when new modules are added or existing ones are modified. Given the large number of modules and interactions in modern programs, devising proper abstraction boundaries is far from trivial. Tulloh and Miller point out that human societies have similar interfaces. The social equivalents of abstraction boundaries are organizational boundaries. Organizations not only specialize in production but also create interfaces that enable them to coordinate their specialized activities. These interfaces require shared meanings, which influence how specialization evolves in social life. Everyone knows what can be found inside hardware stores, or post offices, or Episcopal churches. As social creatures, we have learned that individual instances of each general type will enable us to fulfill specific kinds of needs. This kind of knowledge is so familiar to us that we take it for granted. We do not run to the post office to restore our souls, nor drive to a church for pipes and wrenches. But these shared meanings have not always existed. They were established by entrepreneurs who wanted to take advantage of a division of labor, and who realized that, in order to do so, they would have to communicate to others what a particular division of labor meant to those that might use it. Creating and modifying abstraction boundaries is a ceaseless process of communication that is usually overlooked in our economic theory, but which is a vital part of our economic life. Solving the knowledge problem in software and in markets requires similar institutions for similar reasons: the need to divide knowledge and coordinate plans.[22]

The area of information technology to which Lavoie devoted the greatest amount of his time was teaching. He experimented with two learning platforms: hypertext, for which he used a program called Folio Views, and groupware, for which he used Lotus Notes. He actively explored electronic learning with students and faculty in 1994, perhaps earlier, and he had courses operational by 1995. Over the next few years he and student colleagues developed two online learning environments. With Lotus Notes, they modified the software so that it could be used for teaching case studies. Marketing, macroeconomics, international policy and strategic management, all of which used cases from the Harvard Business School, were taught using this platform. Because the case discussions were asynchronous, the courses included students from different time zones without inconvenience. Because the discussions did not require video or streaming techniques, neither fast technology nor advanced computers were required. With Folio Views he taught courses in Austrian economics and in Comparative Economic Systems. Lavoie included written lectures among his material, but the emphasis was on student interaction with texts and with each other. Because the courses dealt primarily with text and were asynchronous, students from around the world took the courses. The hypertext environment that Lavoie developed, and its effectiveness as a teaching tool, are well described in Virgil Storr's contribution to this volume. Storr has the advantage of having taken one of Lavoie's courses using Folio Views, so we get an insider's view. With both groupware and hypertext, the most important characteristic of Lavoie's online courses was interaction. Lavoie emphasized from the beginning that the power of these electronic tools was not the distances that they were able to cross (he disliked the term 'distance education'), but the ways in which they could make texts come alive; navigation through electronic texts was easier than paper texts, and commentaries were easier to write and criticize.

In addition to describing the hypertext course, Storr also draws connections between hermeneutics and hypertext. His main thesis – that the power of hypertext resides in its power to help us seriously engage texts in ways that are already familiar to us – fits nicely with Lavoie's background in hermeneutics. Storr leaves little doubt that Lavoie's interest in hermeneutics attracted him to hypertext. For someone who saw the growth of knowledge as a social process, a dialogue in which we engage the ideas of one another, hypertext was worthy of close attention as a teaching tool. Lavoie embraced hypertext for that most hermeneutical of reasons: it opened up opportunities for dialogue that did not exist with speech and paper by themselves.

Although most of his work with groupware and hypertext was devoted to teaching, Lavoie also reflected on the wider significance of these technologies to the economy, especially the ways in which they could enhance performance. He did so by extending the ideas of Israel Kirzner. In true hermeneutical style, Lavoie conceived the entrepreneur as someone who interprets texts, where text is used broadly to mean socially constructed meaning.

> The Kirznerian entrepreneur is properly understood to be thoroughly immersed in the already linguistically constituted world, where the social relation *par excellence* is not market exchange but the exchange of words.... You could say that markets simply add whole new kinds of texts, prices, profits, contracts, advertising, etc. to the conversation. (Lavoie, 2004, p. 23)

In this linguistic world, the task of the entrepreneur is to profit by correctly discerning the meanings of the market texts and adding his own commentary. Once we conceive of the entrepreneur as an interpreter of market texts, the importance of communication technology is self-evident. '[C]rucial to these articulation processes,' wrote Lavoie, 'are the institutional and technological circumstances in which market participants act.'[23]

If '[p]ermeating the market process are millions of efforts to communicate meaning', then hypertext and groupware can enhance economic performance by enhancing communication. Both kinds of software enable market participants to interact in ways that are more productive than interaction by means of dialogue or text. Hypertext enables users to take different cuts at the text, to slice it in many different ways. This helps users of complex texts to orient themselves, to navigate with greater ease, and to uncover subtle relationships in the text that might otherwise be overlooked. Just as dissection gives the biologist a better understanding of the structures of living organisms, so hypertext gives entrepreneurs an improved understanding of the structures of markets. Groupware enables users to combine features of both written text and spoken dialogue. Text's strength, a fixity that facilitates sustained and consistent attention, is combined with dialogue's strength, the rapid interplay of give and take. With groupware, we get a hybrid form of communication that combines the strengths of speech and writing. The two technologies together, Lavoie argued, are bound to improve communication, entrepreneurship and performance. He concluded that, '[w]e make ourselves wealthier by making ourselves better understood.'[24]

CULTURAL STUDIES

Entrepreneurship also provided an entryway into cultural studies for Lavoie. Rather than confining himself to the effects of culture on tastes, Lavoie delved into the effects of culture on economic discovery and coordination. He defined culture broadly: culture is the significance that we attach to events through the mediation of language. Were it not for shared meanings, it would be impossible for modern civilization, with its complex division of labor, to evolve. Moreover, shared meanings make it easier for entrepreneurs to anticipate the wants of others and to coordinate actions to mutual benefit. Lavoie was especially critical of Crusoe economics, which ignores the rich set of cultural practices through which Crusoe and Friday cooperate to mutual advantage.[25]

But entrepreneurship was only an entryway into cultural studies. Lavoie was really interested in how the whole complex of values and meaning shape the market process. Chamlee-Wright, who worked closely with Lavoie in this area, calls his approach foundational. He saw culture as forming a branch of inquiry called cultural economy, in much the same way that politics forms a branch of study called political economy. Cultural norms will influence the direction of market processes. In fact, these norms will determine whether market processes can even be established, as experience in the former Soviet Union has shown. This research agenda is particularly relevant for the developing world – countries in Africa, the Middle East, and Asia. Foreign policies toward those countries that do not take account of cultures are bound to produce unintended and often undesirable results.[26]

Combining culture and economics enabled Lavoie to continue his conversation with the political left. He saw progress in the increased respect that some Marxist scholars paid to commercial culture. Rather than being treated as victims of a false consciousness instilled by manipulative capitalists, workers and consumers in a market economy are recognized as being active participants who express values and add meaning to their lives. More importantly, Lavoie pointed out that markets are not the dry, abstract maximizing machines of modern theory. Economic activity is as spiritual as art or drama or religion. It expresses our values, hopes and achievements, and it is marred by our cynicism, failures and frauds. Markets display the grandeur and pathos that characterize all great human institutions – our families, our friendships, our schools, our religions and our legislatures. In drawing our attention to the spiritual side of markets, Lavoie was speaking as much to neoclassical economists as he was to Marxists; in fact, he believed Marxists would be at least as open to the spiritual dimensions of markets as the mathematical modelers would be.[27]

CONCLUSION

We can now summarize the unifying themes that run throughout Lavoie's work. The overarching theme is the importance of social intelligence to economics. The discrepancy between individual and social intelligence is of course the central issue of the socialist calculation debate, but Lavoie explained that it has a much wider significance. Scientific discourse also creates a division of knowledge and the same distinction between individual and social knowledge. So does software design and engineering. The rise of object-oriented programming was an increased division of knowledge and coordination which enabled programmers to pack much more intelligence into a program than any single programmer could possess. Culture, too, has this characteristic of social intelligence. The meanings expressed in a large social group are far greater than those that can be represented by a small group. A culture, like an economy, is impoverished if an elite class is permitted to force its viewpoint on the larger community.

Lavoie's second theme, closely related to the first, is that certain kinds of institutions or practices are better at creating social intelligence than others. We might call this theme the primacy of liberty, or, to use an old-fashioned word, of voluntaryism. This principle is most evident in the socialist calculation debate. Voluntary interaction, based on right of several property, is essential to create the price structure that entrepreneurs use to formulate their plans. Without property and exchange, specialized producers cannot create the knowledge structure necessary to sustain a complex economy. In intellectual discourse, including science and philosophy, freedom to pursue the truth, even where it conflicts with accepted wisdom or party politics, is the analog of property in the economy. If research is conducted only by a central committee, or if political officials dictate history, social intelligence is compromised. Science and philosophy, like the economy, function best when voluntary communities pursue their own judgments in ways that each thinks best. Of course, liberty does not preclude error in science any more than it precludes mistakes and losses in markets. Scientific progress requires more than freedom; it requires appropriate values and methods. Lavoie articulated the values and methods that he deemed appropriate to economics (see below), but they all depend on the existence of freedom. Property rights are also a component of information technology as developed by Lavoie. The design and development of software requires the same kind of freedom as other forms of inquiry, of course, but property rights also enter software design in another way that is somewhat unusual. Object-oriented programming, which enables software designers to encapsulate code in specialized modules, requires something like property rights to be established among the modules. Specialization and coordination in software programs require that code respects boundaries just as specialization and exchange in markets requires that humans respect property. Although property rights among modules of code possess none of the moral force that made rights such an important part of the intellectual history of Europe and its offshoots, defining and enforcing boundaries is an essential part of software, and it appears that building something like consent into these boundaries will be necessary to eliminate the costly damage caused by worms, viruses and spyware. Rights in society have a different connotation than they do in software, but they are important in both realms. Rights also have a different status in hermeneutics and cultural studies than they do in economics. In economics, the analysis of the market presupposes the existence rights. Economics studies the consequences of the 'simple system of natural liberty', to use Adam Smith's phrase. Economists have had much to say that is useful concerning the effects of different kinds of property regimes, from communal to private, but the bulk of economic analysis takes rights as given. Hermeneutics and cultural studies, on the other hand, have as one of their main tasks the explanation of rights. These disciplines ask how rights emerge from the meanings and activities of everyday life. They ask how dialogue and values produce and sustain the complex set of rights and duties that underlie modern social life.[28]

A third theme that runs throughout Lavoie's work is that economics ought to be a humanistic discipline. He referred to this as interpretive economics, by which he meant that economics is more closely tied to history, anthropology, sociology and philosophy, especially ethics and epistemology, than it is to physics or mechanics. Economics is a human science and hence more closely allied with the humane disciplines than with the physical disciplines. We see this argument developing early in his career. He felt compelled to justify his arguments against central planning by turning to the philosophy of science. He knew that a work of discursive reasoning, one that paid close attention to the original participants in the socialist calculation debate, was likely to be dismissed because it did not present its ideas in the form of a mechanical model or test its ideas using multiple regression analysis. He further knew that the perfectly competitive model, which was expressed mechanically by Oskar Lange, Abba Lerner and others, was obscuring Mises' essential insight, which rested on an observation about human understanding, an insight that did not lend itself to mechanical reasoning. To justify his approach, Lavoie turned to Michael Polanyi, Thomas Kuhn, and the growth of knowledge literature, as well as to the *verstehen* tradition within German philosophy. This led Lavoie to post-modern philosophy, hermeneutics in particular, and provided him with the ideas he needed to ground economics in a general philosophy of human understanding, thus binding economics to the humanities. To be sure, Lavoie's research program connected economics to its past. From Smith, Marx and Mill through Marshall, Menger, Veblen and Knight, to Mises, Schumpeter, Keynes and Hayek, most great figures in economics have produced work that is fundamentally connected to philosophy, history and sociology. But Lavoie's focus was on the future. He pinned his hopes on advances in post-modern philosophy, in cultural studies, and in information technology. He felt that these disciplines would eventually influence the mainstream of economics, pulling it toward the humanities. It is still too early to tell whether his judgment will be vindicated. The resistance within the economics profession is strong and is showing only faint signs of weakening. But social change can occur with breathtaking speed. When Lavoie began arguing that socialism was not feasible, there were few signs that the Soviet system was about to give way, yet it gave way rapidly once *glasnost* began. Only time will tell whether the economics profession is about to undergo its own *glasnost*, and if it does, whether it will mark a period of rapid advance. If the next generation of economists does integrate economics with the humanities, part of the credit will go to Lavoie, who has shown us a promising way forward.

NOTES

1. Don Lavoie, 'Statement of my research', (1993). Interpretive action and the evolution of institutions in Austrian economics are both traceable to the founder of the Austrian school, Carl Menger. See Carl Menger, 'On the origins of money', (1892).
2. Lavoie, 'Statement of my research', (1993, p. 1).
3. Don Lavoie, *Rivalry and Central Planning* (1986a), p. 36. Schumpeter is another example of someone who opposed socialism yet admired Marx's economics despite its faults. See Joseph Schumpeter, *Capitalism, Socialism and Democracy* (1975), pp. 21–44.
4. This episode and much else in Lavoie's intellectual development was related to me in a series of interviews that I conducted after I learned in the late Spring of 2001 that he had pancreatic cancer. I taped the interviews, and The Fund for American Studies, located in Washington, DC, had them transcribed.
5. Interview with author, 16 June, 2001. Lavoie thought Marx's philosophical ideas, as presented in the *Grundrisse*, were necessary for understanding *Das Kapital.* Lavoie had a particularly high regard for Japanese scholars of Marx, especially the Uno school. The ideas and import of the Japanese economist Kozo Uno are presented in Thomas T. Sekine, 'Uno-Riron: A Japanese Contribution to Marxian Political Economy', (1975). For Lavoie's appreciation of Marx's economics, see Don Lavoie, 'Some strengths in Marx's disequilibrium theory of money', (1983); Don Lavoie, 'Marx, the quantity theory, and the theory of value', (1986b).
6. Lavoie, *Rivalry and Central Planning* (1986a). This work was a revision of his doctoral dissertation, written under the supervision of Kirzner.
7. See Don Lavoie, 'Computation, incentives, and discovery: the cognitive function of markets in market socialism', (1990a); Don Lavoie, *National Economic Planning: What Is Left*? (1985), pp. 76–7. Lavoie also recognized that militarism could bedevil capitalist economies. See Jeffrey R. Hummell and Don Lavoie, 'National Defense and the Public Goods Problem', (1990).
8. Brian Caplan, for example, argues that the Soviet system collapsed largely because of distorted incentives. See Brian Caplan, 'Is socialism really "impossible?"' (2004). For a

rough monetary measure of the inefficiency of central planning, see Jack High, 'The roles of entrepreneurship in economic growth', (2004).

9. Lavoie, *National Economic Planning: What Is Left?*, (1985, p. 84).
10. Ibid. p. 88.
11. G.B. Madison, 'Hermeneutics and liberty: remembrance of Don Lavoie', Chapter 7, this volume.
12. I do not know the particular order in which Don progressed through the philosophical literature. From interviews, I am certain that he started with Mises. I know that Lachmann introduced him to the *verstehen* philosophers that influenced Mises, and I know that Richard Ebeling, a fellow graduate student at NYU, introduced him to Hans Georg Gadamer. At George Mason University, Lavoie, along with an extraordinary group of graduate students, read Gadamer, Paul Ricoeur and Richard Rorty; Jacques Derrida and other deconstructionists; Ludwig Wittgenstein, Martin Heiddeger and others in phenomenology. Near the end of his life, Lavoie was also reading Hannah Arendt, a student of Heiddeger, and the American pragmatists, especially John Dewey. In all of these philosophers, he saw relevance to understanding the market order.
13. Don Lavoie, *Economics and Hermeneutics* (1990b), p. 1.
14. Don Lavoie, 'The accounting of interpretations and the interpretation of accounts: the communicative functions of "the language of business"', (1987, p. 594).
15. See Don McCloskey, *Knowledge and Persuasion in Economics* (1994), pp. 247–64. Arjo Klamer, *Conversations with Economists: New Classical Economists and Opponents Speak out on the Current Controversy in Macroeconomics* (1983) is an excellent example of third-level interpretation. The *locus classicus* of third-level interpretation is Joseph Schumpeter, *History of Economic Analysis* (1954).
16. Don Lavoie, 'Hermeneutics, subjectivity, and the Lester/Machlup debate: toward a more anthropological approach to empirical economics', (1990c), where he writes:

    > Whether understanding the meanings operative in everyday life is taken to be below them (and best left to undergraduates) or above them (and best left to angels), economists seem to agree that their scientific discourse of economics should dissociate itself from the everyday discourse of the economy. I would like to turn the tables on such economists by arguing that, precisely because they are dissociated from the life-world, they are already dangerously out of touch with the real world they think they are investigating. Theories of discourse such as hermeneutics might be seen not as a threat to the economist's realism but as a way to bring economists into closer contact with reality, of bringing theory and empirical work into a closer relationship with one another.

    Ralph Rector, 'The economics of rationality and the rationality of economics', (1990).
17. The goal of the empirical work was to integrate economic theory and history, in the belief that connecting the two subjects would improve both. For examples of research that resulted from the empirical workshop, see Jack High, *Regulation* (1990); Clayton A. Coppin and Jack C. High, *The Politics of Purity: Harvey Washington Wiley and the Origins of Federal Food Policy* (1999). For examples of dissertations, see Peter Boettke, 'The political economy of Soviet socialism,1918–1928' (1989); David Prychitko, 'The political economy of workers' self-management: a market process critique' (1989); Steven Horowitz, 'The private basis of monetary order: an evolutionary approach to money and the market process' (1990); Emily Chamlee-Wright, 'The cultural foundations of economic development: a study of urban female entrepreneurs in Ghana, West Africa' (1993).
18. Deirdre McCloskey, 'Humility and truth in economics', Chapter 9, this volume.
19. Alan Aho, Don Lavoie and James Paprocki, 'MUSIM – simulation of music composition using GASP', (1975).
20. See Don Lavoie, 'The Origins of "the Agorics Project"', (1990d). This note and an accompanying article, Don Lavoie, 'High-tech Hayekians: some possible research topics in economics of computation', (1990e) have been reprinted in Jack Birner and Pierre

Garrouste, *Markets, Information and Communication: Austrian Perspectives on the Internet Economy* (2004).

21. Howard Baetjer Jr, 'Software as capital: lessons for economic development from software engineering' (1993); Lavoie, Tulloh and Baetjer, 'High-tech Hayekians' (1990), pp. 101–103; Don Lavoie et al., 'Component software: a market perspective on the coming revolution in software development' (1993).
22. Tulloh and Miller draw much of the economic background for their article from Ludwig Lachmann, who was influenced by the *verstehen* tradition of Max Weber.
23. Don Lavoie, 'Subjectivism, entrepreneurship and the convergence of groupware and hypertext', (2004), pp. 23, 25.
24. Ibid., pp. 26, 41. Lavoie draws on the history of communication and the work of pioneers in the field of groupware and hypertext to make his arguments. Prose stylists have also emphasized that what makes for good speech does not necessarily make for good writing and vice versa. See Robert Graves and Alan Hodge, *The Reader over Your Shoulder* (1961), pp. 25–8.
25. Don Lavoie, 'The discovery and interpretation of profit opportunities: culture and the Kirznerian entrepreneur', (1991), Lavoie, 'Subjectivism, entrepreneurship and the convergence of groupware and hypertext', (2004), pp. 33–52.
26. Emily Chamlee-Wright, 'The development of a cultural economy: foundational questions and future direction', Chapter 10, this volume.
27. Don Lavoie and Emily Chamlee-Wright, *Culture and Enterprise* (2000), pp. 29, 130.
28. See Don Lavoie, Howie Baetjer and Bill Tulloh, 'High-tech Hayekians', in Jack Birner and Pierre Garrouste, *Markets, Information and Communication*, p. 102, who write, 'For the various subroutines [of computer code] to operate effectively, they need a certain amount of autonomy….Or, we might say, the subroutines' 'rights' to what is 'theirs' need to be respected. The analogy to property rights is very close.' On computer security, see William Tulloh and Jack High, 'From sobig to so what: toward a rights-based approach to protecting cyberspace', (2003). On the relationship between hermeneutics and liberty, see Tom Palmer, 'The Hermeneutical View of Freedom', (1990), pp. 299–318, and G.B. Madison's contribution to this volume (Chapter 7). An able group of economists has examined the economic origins of property. For examples, see Carl Menger, *Principles of Economics* (1976), pp. 97–8; Harold Demsetz, 'Toward a theory of property rights', (1975); Harold Demsetz, 'Toward a theory of property rights II: the competition between private and collective ownership', (2002).

REFERENCES

Aho, Alan, Don Lavoie and James Paprocki (1975), 'MUSIM – simulation of music composition using GASP', Proceedings of the 1974 Winter Simulation Conference of the Association for Computing Machinery, **2**.

Baetjer, Howard Jr (1993), 'Software as capital: lessons for economic development from software engineering', George Mason University.

Birner, Jack and Pierre Garrouste (2004), *Markets, Information and Communication: Austrian Perspectives on the Internet Economy*, London and New York: Routledge.

Boettke, Peter (1989), 'The political economy of Soviet socialism, 1918–1928', George Mason University.

Caplan, Brian (2004), 'Is socialism really "impossible?"', *Critical Review*, **16** (1): 33–52.

Chamlee-Wright, Emily (1993), 'The cultural foundations of economic development: a study of urban female entrepreneurs in Ghana, West Africa', George Mason University.

Chamlee-Wright, Emily (2006), 'The development of a cultural economy: foundational questions and future direction', in *Humane Economics*, edited by Jack High, Cheltenham, UK and Northampton, MA, USA: Edward Elgar.

Coppin, Clayton A. and Jack C. High (1999), *The Politics of Purity: Harvey Washington Wiley and the Origins of Federal Food Policy*, Ann Arbor: Univeristy of Michigan Press.

Demsetz, Harold (1975), 'Toward a theory of property rights', in *The Economics of Legal Relationships*, edited by Henry G. Manne, St Paul, Minn: West Publishing Co.

Demsetz, Harold (2002), 'Toward a theory of property rights II: the competition between private and collective ownership', *Journal of Legal Studies*, **31**, June.

Graves, Robert and Alan Hodge (1961), *The Reader over Your Shoulder*, New York: The Macmillan Company.

High, Jack (1990), *Regulation*, Ann Arbor: University of Michigan Press.

High, Jack (2004), 'The roles of entrepreneurship in economic growth', in *Entrepreneurship and Regional Economic Development*, edited by Henri de Groot, Peter Nijkamp and Roger Stough, Cheltenham, UK and Northampton, MA, USA: Edward Elgar.

Horowitz, Steven (1990), 'The private basis of monetary order: an evolutionary approach to money and the market process', George Mason University.

Hummell, Jeffrey R. and Don Lavoie (1990), 'National defense and the public goods problem', in *Arms, Politics and the Economy: Historical and Contemporary Perspectives*, edited by Robert Higgs, New York: Holmes and Meier, pp. 37–60.

Klamer, Arjo (1983), *Conversations with Economists: New Classical Economists and Opponents Speak out on the Current Controversy in Macroeconomics*, Totowa, NJ: Rowman & Allanheld.

Lavoie, Don (1983), 'Some strengths in Marx's disequilibrium theory of money', *Cambridge Journal of Economics*, **7**: 55–68.

Lavoie, Don (1985), *National Economic Planning: What Is Left?*, Cambridge, Mass.: Ballinger Publishing Co.

Lavoie, Don (1986a), *Rivalry and Central Planning*, Cambridge: Cambridge University Press.

Lavoie, Don (1986b), 'Marx, the quantity theory, and the theory of value', *History of Political Economy*, **18** (1): 155–70.

Lavoie, Don (1987), 'The accounting of interpretations and the interpretation of accounts: the communicative functions of "the language of business"'. *Accounting, Organization and Society*, **12** (6): 594.

Lavoie, Don (1990a), 'Computation, incentives, and discovery: the cognitive function of markets in market socialism', *The Annals of the American Academy of Political and Social Science*, **507**: 72–9.

Lavoie, Don (1990b), *Economics and Hermeneutics*, London: Routledge.

Lavoie, Don (1990c), 'Hermeneutics, subjectivity, and the Lester/Machlup debate: toward a more anthropological approach to empirical economics', in *Economics as Discourse: An Analysis of the Language of Economists*, edited by Warren Samuels, Boston: Kluwer Academic Publishers, pp. 167–70.

Lavoie, Don (1990d), 'The origins of "the Agorics Project"', *Market Process*, **8**, Spring: 116–19.

Lavoie, Don (1991), 'The discovery and interpretation of profit opportunities: culture and the Kirznerian entrepreneur', in *The Culture of Entrepreneurship*, edited by Brigitte Berger, San Francisco: ICS Press.

Lavoie, Don (1993), 'Statement of my research', unpublished manuscript, Fairfax, VA: George Mason University, pp. 1–8.

Lavoie, Don (2004), 'Subjectivism, entrepreneurship and the convergence of groupware and hypertext', in *Markets, Information, and Communication*, edited by Jack Birner and Pierre Garrouste, New York: Routledge.

Lavoie, Don, and Emily Chamlee-Wright (2000), *Culture and Enterprise*, London: Routledge.

Lavoie, Don, Howard Baetjer Jr and William Tulloh (1990), 'High-tech Hayekians: some possible research topics in economics of computation', *Market Process*, **8**, Spring.

Lavoie, Don, Howard Baetjer Jr, William Tulloh and Richard Langlois (1993), 'Component software: a market perspective on the coming revolution in software development', in *Strategic Technologies Series*: Patricia Seybold Group.

Madison, G.B. (2006), 'Hermeneutics and liberty: remembrance of Don Lavoie', in *Humane Economics: Essays in Honor of Don Lavoie*, edited by Jack High, Cheltenham, UK and Northampton, MA, USA: Edward Elgar.

McCloskey, Deirdre (2006), 'Humility and truth in economics', in *Humane Economics*, edited by Jack High, Cheltenham, UK and Northampton, MA, USA: Edward Elgar.

McCloskey, Don (1994), *Knowledge and Persuasion in Economics*, Cambridge: Cambridge University Press.

Menger, Carl (1976), *Principles of Economics*, New York: New York University Press.

Menger, Carl (1892), 'On the origins of money', *The Economic Journal*, **2** (6): 239–55.

Palmer, Tom (1990), 'The hermeneutical view of freedom', in *Economics and Hermeneutics*, edited by Don Lavoie, London: Routledge.

Prychitko, David (1989), 'The political economy of workers' self-management: a market process critique', George Mason University.

Rector, Ralph (1990), 'The economics of rationality and the rationality of economics', in *Economics and Hermeneutics*, edited by Don Lavoie, London: Routledge, pp. 195–235.

Schumpeter, Joseph, (1954), *History of Economic Analysis*, Oxford: Oxford University Press.

Schumpeter, Joseph (1975), *Capitalism, Socialism and Democracy*, New York: Harper and Row.

Sekine, Thomas T. (1975), 'Uno-Riron: a Japanese contribution to Marxian political economy', *Journal of Economic Literature*, **13** (3): 847–77.

Tulloh, William and Jack High (2003), 'From sobig to so what: toward a rights-based approach to protecting cyberspace', in *CIPP*, George Mason University. Fairfax.

PART 2

Socialist calculation

2. Calculation, competition and entrepreneurship

Israel M. Kirzner

The first major contribution of Don Lavoie's remarkable career as a scholar was surely his superb doctoral dissertation, later published as *Rivalry and Central Planning: The Socialist Calculation Debate Reconsidered* (1985). In this contribution, Lavoie's reconsideration developed the penetrating insight that Mises' critique of the possibility of rational calculation under socialist central planning proceeded from that same Misesian theoretical vision which saw the competitive market process as a *fundamentally* entrepreneurial one.

The present chapter seeks to explore this insight further. This exploration will proceed, in part, by commenting on a footnote in Lavoie's book.[1] In that footnote, Lavoie cited an objection to certain aspects of Mises' thesis which had been raised by Professor Buchanan. Buchanan had contended that the Austrians, Mises and Hayek, had focused on a less fundamental difficulty for central planning (the difficulty of calculation), instead of on the more important difficulty, that of motivation.

> Even if the socialist state should somehow discover an oracle that would allow all calculation to be made perfectly ... efficiency in allocation will emerge only if ... men can be motivated ... to make decisions in accordance with cost criteria that are different from *their own* ... This amounts to saying that even if the problems of calculation are totally disregarded, the socialist system will generate efficiency in results only if men can be trained to make choices that do not embody the opportunity costs that they, individually and personally, confront.[2]

Buchanan was pointing out that we must expect central planners to be motivated to see the relevant alternatives *that face them as individuals*, rather than those that are relevant to the society which they are ostensibly serving.

Lavoie's footnote responded to this criticism by expressing his own conviction that the Misesian 'problem of knowledge' is 'more fundamental' than Buchanan's 'problem of motivation'. In Lavoie's words:

> One could reverse Buchanan's argument and say that even if socialist managers could somehow, as he puts it, be 'converted into economic eunuchs... to make decisions in accordance with cost criteria that are different from their own', the central difficulty of obtaining the relevant information would still remain. Even fully motivated planners would not know how to plan rationally.[3]

In other words, the difference between Buchanan and Lavoie has been reduced to a difference concerning which of the two problems should be considered more 'fundamental'. Lavoie adduced no grounds for his own preference, in this regard, over Buchanan's.

The present chapter seeks to go somewhat beyond Lavoie's response. Our further exploration of the interface between the economics of socialist calculation and the economics of the process of entrepreneurial competition will permit us to argue, I believe, that there are analytical grounds for maintaining that the Misesian 'problem of knowledge' is indeed anterior to Buchanan's problem of motivation. Unless one could imagine that Mises' calculation problem has somehow been solved, questions of motivation, we shall see, cannot even begin to be asked. In fact, it will turn out somewhat paradoxically, these 'analytical grounds' can themselves be held to be rooted in certain other passages to be found in Buchanan's own rightly celebrated scholarly contributions. A superficial reading of this paper may suggest that this response to Buchanan's critique of the Austrians is its central purpose. I would like to emphasize that this is not the case. Our response to Buchanan's criticism is in fact merely an *illustration* of the central insight sought to be identified in the paper. This central insight, having to do with the very foundations of Austrian 'welfare theory', emerges from a careful appreciation of the 'welfare-economics' context of the socialist calculation debate.

THE SOCIALIST CALCULATION DEBATE AND THE ECONOMICS OF WELFARE

This writer has elsewhere[4] pointed out that the inter-war socialist calculation debate is to be credited with advances both in the mainstream economics of welfare, and in the Austrian understanding of the social usefulness of the market economy in terms of the *coordinative* process which the market promotes. Abba Lerner's *The Economics of Control* (1944) is a classic example of the way in which mainstream twentieth century welfare economics grew out of the debate. Similarly Hayek's celebrated 1945 paper 'The use of knowledge in society' (reprinted in his 1949 *Individualism and Economic Order*) represents a pivotal juncture in twentieth century Austrian thought; it was in that paper that Hayek's 'knowledge problem' was brought explicitly to the fore. It was the explicit identification of this Hayekian knowledge problem which made it clear that Austrians could not be part of the dominant mid-century tendency in mainstream economics to treat society as an entity seeking 'to allocate its resources' (in the same way in which Lionel Robbins had, in 1932, articulated the nature of individual economizing behavior as the allocation of scarce resources among competing ends). It was this Hayekian insight that crystallized the Austrian rejection of mainstream welfare economics, and which led to subsequent Austrian explorations into the normative meaning of the Misesian competitive–entrepreneurial market process. Certainly this 1945 paper of Hayek's is the obvious product of a decade of work in which Hayek had been grappling with a variety of attempted socialist refutations of Mises' demonstration of the inherent impossibility of central planning (due to the impossibility of economic calculation in the absence of the market).

For mainstream welfare economics the economic debate between the proponents of socialism and those of the market economy revolved around the question of which of these two systems can be expected to generate a more efficient allocation of society's given resources, in terms of that society's given arrays of consumer preferences. But Hayek's work, culminating in his 1945 paper, made explicit what had up until that time only been implicit in the work of Mises and other Austrians, viz., that (not only because of the generally well-recognized difficulties surrounding the interpersonal comparison of utilities, but more importantly) because of the problems arising out of the dispersed nature of knowledge in society, it is (except at the metaphorical level) simply *meaningless* to talk of a society 'allocating its resources' as if to maximize its 'total' welfare.

In fact, when one examines Mises' classic statements[5] concerning the impossibility of central planning, one discovers that he never did directly assert that *a society* is economically 'better off' under a market system than under a centrally planned system. He simply pointed out that under a market system the decision makers (and, in particular, the entrepreneurs) *are* able to calculate by using market prices, while under a socialist system the central planners had no market prices (for resource services) with which to work, and were, therefore, simply *un*able to calculate. Mises seemed to take it for granted that the reader would then understand how the market system functions to coordinate, and thus to render, to some extent, mutually consistent, the calculative decisions of all market participants, while the impossibility of calculation by would-be central planners inevitably spelled the inherently chaotic nature of the socialist economy. But, at least in his statements dealing directly with the problems of socialist calculation, he did not make direct 'welfare comparisons' between the two systems.

Indeed, reflection must render it evident – if perhaps in a way surprising – that such a direct 'welfare' comparison cannot in fact be made. The would-be socialist central planner *is* (at least in theory) seeking efficiently to allocate society's resources – that is, to allocate them in a manner which 'maximizes' the satisfaction of those goals which the planner deems relevant for 'society' (and with the ranking of importance of these competing goals, which the planner has adopted). The standard notions of efficiency in allocative choice are certainly relevant to the task of the would-be central planner. His very undertaking takes it for granted that society is to be treated, in effect, as a decision-making entity – with the central planner assigned the technical function of determining the particular pattern of resource allocation to be decided upon. Success in this undertaking would mean that society has been efficient in 'its' allocative function. Mises' argument was not only that such success is out of the question, but also that there is simply no way in which such success can even be systematically attempted. However, Mises did seem to be measuring the possibility or impossibility of successful planning under socialism by the measuring rod which, by the very definition of central planning, is the relevant one, viz., allocative efficiency as seen from the perspective of a single entity, the 'society' in regard to which central planning is being undertaken. But such a measuring rod is, it should be clear, quite inappropriate for any assessment of the 'economic success' (or failure) of a market economy. A market economy is by definition made up of a multitude of independently-made individual decisions. In such a context to talk of decisions made 'by society' is, at best, to engage in metaphor. 'Society' does not, as a simple matter of fact, choose; it does not plan; it does not engage in the 'allocation of resources'; it does not have ends; it does not have means; to talk of society facing 'its' allocative, economizing problem is, strictly speaking, to talk nonsense. And it was Professor Buchanan who was one of the first explicitly to point this out.

BUCHANAN AND THE ILLEGITIMACY OF THE IDEA OF SOCIAL 'ALLOCATION'

In his remarkable 1963 Presidential Address to the Southern Economic Association[6] 'What should economists do?' Professor Buchanan sharply criticized economists for having illegitimately transferred the notion, emphasized by Lionel C. Robbins (*The Nature and Significance of Economic Science, 1932*), of the allocation of scarce resources among competing multiple ends, from the context of the individual (where the notion is valid and important) to that of society (where the notion has no validity at all).[7] Buchanan cited Milton Friedman, for example, as defining economics as 'the study of how a particular society solves its economic problem'. But this formulation (which was, already at the time of Buchanan's address, taking over virtually every principles textbook on the market) is an illegitimate transferral of what Robbins had articulated strictly at the individual level. The economists whom Buchanan was criticizing 'are wholly concerned with the allocation of scarce resouces among competing ends or uses', with respect to 'social welfare functions'. Buchanan insisted that 'theirs is not legitimate activity for practitioners in economics'[8] as he defines the discipline. Buchanan talks of a 'bridge between personal or individual units of decision and "social" aggregates'. This bridge, he points out, is 'most difficult to cross'; his 'whole plea' to economists is: 'stay on the side of the bridge where you belong'[9]. On *that* side of the bridge, Buchanan was arguing, one simply cannot talk of 'the economic problem which faces society'.

THE ECONOMICS OF SOCIALISM AND BUCHANAN'S BRIDGE

Our point here can be made briefly; it is an obvious, almost a trivial, one. Any discussion of the possibility of economic calculation under socialism, must take it for granted that Buchanan's bridge *has* been crossed. What the central planner seeks to do is precisely to solve the allocation problem held to be faced by society. Buchanan wished to define the science of economics in 'catallactic' terms,[10] that is as the science of interpersonal exchanges. Of course such a definition rules out the economics of pure socialism (under which, by definition, there are no private exchanges at the level of input services.) Was Mises, in his exploration of the 'economics of socialism' (by demonstrating the impossibility of socialist planning), then illegitimately extending the realm of economics beyond the boundaries which Buchanan wished to see in place? Would Mises really maintain that economists *can* cross Buchanan's bridge, and endorse the simple aggregation of individual objectives and constraints so as to be able to talk meaningfully of the allocation problem 'facing society'? To anyone familiar with Mises' consistent insistence on the principle of methodological individualism, a positive answer to this latter question is simply unthinkable. Do we not then, in reading Mises, face a dilemma? I believe the solution to this apparent dilemma is a straightforward one: by demonstrating the impossibility of socialist economic calculation, Mises was doing more than proving the impossibility of rational central planning; he was in fact also proving that the very *objective* of socialist planning, that of efficiently allocating a 'society's' resources among 'its' multiple competing goals, is, strictly speaking, a *meaningless* objective. His demonstration, so far from violating

Buchanan's guidelines for economists, constituted a case study illustrating the *validity* of Buchanan's insight (on the basis of which he promulgated those guidelines) that the bridge between 'individual units of decision' and 'social' aggregates *cannot* be crossed. Mises' foray into the economics of socialism was a thoroughly iconoclastic one; it showed that the only valid theorem possible in that field of inquiry was the theorem demonstrating the *non-existence* of the field! Buchanan (of the Southern Economic Association Presidential Address) could not have asked for more. Let us develop our argument somewhat more explicitly.

ON THE ECONOMIC PROBLEM

Many years ago I heard (or read) a semi-humorous remark about the discipline of economics which resonates, and which has somehow stuck in my memory. The remark was to the effect that economics is able to instruct decision makers on *how to avoid trying to run in two opposite directions at the same time*.

This remark surely sees the central idea in normative economics as revolving around the notion of *consistency* among decisions. Such consistency is, of course, fundamental to the very meaning of a *plan*. A plan consists of a series of steps which have been calculated to achieve aimed-at objectives; these steps must not be mutually frustrating. A plan which calls for simultaneously running in two directions is simply incoherent. Economic thinking, the above semi-humorous remark maintains, is peculiarly suited to pointing out to would-be decision makers that the various steps they are considering may in fact be mutually frustrating; they may be attempts to run in two directions at the same time. Achieving efficiency in the allocation of resources is simply the achievement of consistency among the components in one's pattern of resource expenditures. A shopper's decision to buy an additional quantity of beef is inefficient if that beef is purchased at the cost of a quantity of fish which the shopper values more highly than she does the beef. To genuinely value the fish more highly than the beef, and then to buy the beef rather than the fish, is to seek to run in two directions at the same time. All this is what we seek to instill into our freshmen students of economics, in the very first lecture.

But if the economic problem consists in avoiding the hazards of indeed trying to run in two directions at the same time, we must surely identify who is facing this economic problem; *who* is tempted to run in two directions at the same time? Certainly each individual potential decision maker, each individual formulating a plan for his activities over the next few minutes, or few days, or few years, must be aware of the need to achieve mutual consistency, coherence, among the various elements of his plan. Yet, mindful though we may be of the difficulty (or impossibility) of crossing 'Buchanan's bridge', it is difficult to avoid the recognition, as one contemplates different areas in the beehive of economic activities in a society, that some of these activities are, surely, 'inconsistent' with activities being engaged in elsewhere in the beehive. The automobile industry may be rapidly expanding at the very same time that the availability of gasoline to this society has been sharply reduced; medical schools may be training an increased number of specialists in fields of medicine for which the need is rapidly declining; and so on. We do think that such situations may be, from a social perspective, incoherent; and we do ask how the economic organization in a society might reduce or eliminate the likelihood of such incoherencies.

So that, having thoroughly accepted the Hayek–Buchanan rejection of the Milton Friedman formulation cited above, of economics being the study of how a society solves its economic problem, we do, nonetheless, think of a *society as if it were* somehow running in two directions at the same time. Have we, in so doing, contradicted ourselves? Are *we* running in two directions at the same time?! Several passages in Hayek show how we are not only *not* contradicting ourselves, but that the *apparent* contradiction illustrates a profoundly important truth – often completely overlooked in modern mainstream economics.

THE NOTION OF SOCIETAL EFFICIENCY – WITHOUT CROSSING BUCHANAN'S BRIDGE

In his celebrated (and, in fact, revolutionary) papers on the place of knowledge in a society's economy, Hayek made observations which open our eyes to a remarkable circumstance. When the market achieves a single price for a commodity, he wrote in 1945, it has brought about 'the solution which (it is just conceptually possible) *might have been arrived at by one single mind* possessing all the information which is in fact dispersed among all the people involved in the process'[11]. In other words, a properly functioning market system tends towards the achievement of that pattern of resource allocation which a would-be socialist central planner would have sought to achieve (and which Mises had shown to have been impossible for that central planner to have achieved). In his earlier (1937) paper on knowledge, Hayek had made a similar observation. There he wrote of how a market might, without central direction, spontaneously bring about 'the combination of fragments of knowledge existing in different minds [thus achieving] results which, if they were to be brought about deliberately, would require a knowledge on the part of the directing mind which no single person can possess'. In this way, Hayek was pointing out, 'the spontaneous actions of individuals will, under conditions which we can define, bring about a distribution of resources which can be understood *as if it were made according to a single plan*, although nobody has planned it'.[12]

Now to talk, even hypothetically, of the distribution of resources in a society being understood as if made according to a single plan, is, in effect to assert that that society *can* be treated as an entity confronted by 'its' allocative economic problem. Yet certainly, by the date of his 1945 paper, Hayek was thoroughly convinced that the task of calculating the optimal allocation of a society's resources (of achieving that pattern of allocation such 'that the marginal rates of substitution between any two commodities or factors must be the same in all their different uses') is 'emphatically *not* the economic problem which society faces'.[13] The dispersed character of relevant knowledge in a society means that the 'economic problem of society' is not 'how to allocate "given" resources – if "given" is taken to mean given to a single mind...' but rather the problem 'of the utilization of knowledge which is not given to anyone in its totality'.[14] Yet, as we have seen, this seminal insight did not prevent Hayek from speaking, in that very same paper, of the solution to the problem facing, in effect, a single planner for the entire society. What Hayek seemed to have realized was that if all the dispersed bits of knowledge *could* be concentrated in a single mind, then, for that mind we could talk meaningfully of the attainment of social efficiency, in the sense of avoiding running in many different directions at the same time. We would *not* need to cross Buchanan's bridge in order to be able to talk meaningfully in these terms. To be able to engage in the quest for Paretian optimality one needs, not to cross the bridge of 'social aggregation', but to transcend the gulf created by dispersed knowledge. *Without* aggregating objectives, *without* aggregating available resources, we *would* – if Hayek's 'knowledge problem' could be spirited away – talk meaningfully of a society as a single entity for which considerations of consistency ['efficiency'] are relevant. We can now appreciate, I believe, an aspect of Mises' demonstration of the impossibility of central planning which seems not to have been recognized. But let us first review briefly the notion of *coordination* in Austrian normative economics.

COORDINATION AND EFFICIENCY

One certainly does not have to be an Austrian economist in order to understand that markets fulfill the social function of tending to coordinate independently-made individual decisions.[15] But Austrian economics has been characteristically consistent in the development of the idea of coordination as the primary, if not the sole, criterion for normative discussion in economics.[16] It was not by chance that Dr. Gerald P. O'Driscoll entitled his pioneering (1977) study of Hayekian economics, *Economics as a Coordination Problem*. Much earlier Mises had written, 'The coordination of the autonomous actions of all individuals is accomplished by the operation of the market'.[17] The notion of coordination does not, of course, presume the possibility of treating society as a single entity. But it does enable us to recognize the possibility of spontaneous cooperation among independently acting individual members of society. Surely all the 'invisible hand' insights of economics since the eighteenth century, consist of the recognition that, in the market, actions of individuals interact in a way which achieves outcomes which these individuals, if isolated from one another, could never have achieved. It is this idea of coordination which enables us to speak of the 'social' benefits effected by markets – without crossing any Buchanan bridge. If automobile industry executives are making plans to increase the production of cars at the same time that oil industry executives are planning to reduce their supply of gasoline, this may reflect a coordination failure. If the number of patients planning to seek medical help for obesity is declining at the same time that medical schools are expanding teaching and research in the obesity field, these decisions may not seem to be well coordinated. The idea of coordination and discoordination does enable us, despite all the methodological individualism in the world, to transcend the level of individual efficiency, and to talk of efficiency (or its absence) at the level of society. It is possible to talk of a society as if it were seeking to run in two directions at the same time. To do so does *not* require us to violate Buchanan's guidelines for the definition of economics; it does not require us to see society as an entity confronted by an allocation-of-scarce-resources problem. What we must now recognize, however, is that *our ability to treat society as an entity for which coordination-efficiency considerations are relevant, depends on the possibility of economic calculation in that society*. This is the central insight, mentioned (but not identified) in the opening section of this chapter, which it is the objective of this chapter to identify and to emphasize.

CALCULATION AND COORDINATION

Mises showed that, because the socialist economy does not generate market prices for resource services, would-be socialist planners cannot calculate. A socialist society must then consist of large numbers of individuals who are indeed controlled by a central authority whose commands they must obey – but whose individual objectives, individually-possessed scraps of local information, and individual abilities to contribute to potential social cooperation, must necessarily remain systematically uncoordinated. The central planner is simply and absolutely unable to ensure that the various commands (which issue from his attempted central plan) are not, in fact, ordering different segments of the economy to attempt to achieve mutually inconsistent and incoherent objectives. Although we can, from the perspective of assumed omniscience thus assert that the central planner's commands are necessarily incoherent, we must, *for that very reason*, also recognize that (once we recognize the abject ignorance which must in fact envelop any would-be central planner) we can no longer talk of coordination (or discoordination) *at all* in regard to the socialist economy. We cannot sensibly talk of the socialist economy attempting to run in two directions at the same time (or of its not so attempting) – since such an economy *must* consist of discrete individuals between whom no meaningful system of social cooperation can exist. A multitude of economically discrete individuals may constitute a unified entity from the perpective of tribal values, of military considerations, or from other 'sociological' perspectives, but from the perspective of economic science *they remain discrete individuals*. There *is* in the socialist society no entity in regard to which we can talk of its activities being coordinated or not. Of course we can and do point out that any attempted central *plan* for a socialist society must lack coherence and coordination among its elements. It is precisely this that is meant by the assertion that central planning is impossible. But what we have seen now is not merely that the impossibility of economic calculation under socialism renders the idea of a central plan impossible. We have now seen that the impossibility of economic calculation under socialism prohibits us from thinking of the socialist society as an economic entity – that is, as an entity for which it is meaningful to say that it is or is not seeking to run in many directions at the same time. Without the possibility of calculation, society is something for which the notion of coordination-efficiency is simply irrelevant. We may say that the plan drawn up by a would-be central planner consists of mutually inconsistent elements, and therefore is not a plan at all. But, precisely because it is thus not possible to plan for a society, that society must, from the economic perspective, necessarily remain a multitude of discrete individuals – not an economic entity at all.

PARADOX AND PARADOX

We saw earlier that Hayek had pointed out that it is exclusively in the non-centrally-planned (that is, in the market) society, that we can sensibly talk of the successful achievement of the resource-allocation pattern that might (conceivably) have been the objective of a central plan. In the socialist economy, for which such a central plan is presumably the objective, such a plan can, for reasons identified by Mises and Hayek, *not* be attained. But precisely in the market economy, where individuals are free to undertake their own separate (possibly mutually contradictory) projects, it *is* possible to see how the forces of entrepreneurial competition can propel such individual plans into a mutually coherent pattern – one that would have been the objective of a central plan under socialism. This fascinating paradox is the heart of the Mises–Hayek position in the socialist calculation debate. We can now recognize that a closely similar paradox emerges in regard to the very possibility of treating a society as an efficiency-relevant entity.

In a market society, the price system enables us to recognize possible situations in which the activities of its individual members are not coordinated. The price system enables us to understand how powerful market forces are at work, in such a system, to identify and to eliminate such states of discoordination. In other words, although the individual members of a market society act independently and autonomously, we can meaningfully treat the totality of these individuals as an economic entity. If automobile executives are expanding the output of cars while oil company executives are reducing refinery capacity, we can meaningfully say that this economy is 'attempting' to run in two directions at the same time.

But in the socialist society, we have seen, we are simply (and paradoxically) unable to talk in this fashion. Precisely in the society organized to marshall society's resources in a unified and centrally-planned fashion, it is, as we have seen, impossible to talk sensibly of that society's constituting a single economic (that is, efficiency-relevant) entity.

As a result of the central planner's inability to calculate, it is certainly possible for the socialist plan to call for a scale of automobile production that is inconsistent with refinery capacity set forth in the same plan. We may certainly, then, consider this an incoherent plan. But we will not, except at the metaphorical level, describe this plan as one in which society is attempting to run in two directions at the same time. We will not do so for the fundamental reason that, under socialism, the term 'society' has no economic meaning, other than as constituted by a multitude of discrete individuals. It is the necessary incoherence of all conceivable socialist plans which inexorably implies the disintegration of any economic sense for the term, 'society'.

BUCHANAN'S OBJECTION AGAINST MISES – AN ANSWER FROM BUCHANAN

We noted at the outset of this chapter that Lavoie had cited Professor Buchanan's objection to the Austrian emphasis on calculation as the source of the problem undermining the possibility of socialist central planning. The more fundamental difficulty, Buchanan had argued, was that we cannot expect human central planners to be motivated to make decisions on the basis of cost considerations that are different from their own. Even if Mises–Hayek problems of calculation could be imagined away, central planning would not attain efficiency (as defined from the perspective of the *social* importance to be attached to alternative objectives). We saw that Lavoie pointed out that, while this is certainly the case, the reverse observation could also be made. Even if central planners *were*, somehow, trained to be motivated solely by socially-relevant considerations, the calculation difficulties pointed out by the Austrians would still remain. I believe we are now in a position to see how the Austrian problems of knowledge and calculation must, on analytical grounds, be recognized (in assessing the possibility of central economic planning) as anterior to Buchanan's motivational grounds (valid though these latter grounds certainly are). And what enables us to see this is Buchanan's own 1963 critique of mainstream definitions of the economics discipline.

As we have seen earlier in this chapter, Buchanan's presidential address to the Southern Economic Association sharply criticized the mainstream view that economics is the discipline which studies how society solves its (allocative) economic problem. He pointed out that such a perspective illegitimately assumes that there is meaningful content in economics for 'social welfare'.[18] It assumes that 'society' is 'the entity that confronts the economic problem about which we, as professional economists, should be concerned, the entity, presumably, whose ends are to count in the appropriate calculus of margins'.[19] In other words, Buchanan was arguing that considerations of methodological individualism make it strictly impossible to treat 'society' as such an economizing entity.

But if this is the case – and it certainly is – then what are we to make of the very *notion* of central planning? If we are not to see 'society' as an entity to which the notion of an economic allocation problem is relevant, how can we even talk of attempting to formulate a central plan? Clearly, by showing how, in the absence of market prices for resources, a would-be central planner could not calculate, and thus could not plan, Mises was, from his own starting point, in effect simply re-affirming Buchanan's insight that we cannot treat society as an economizing entity. To put it in terms already proposed earlier in this chapter, Mises' theorem in the field of socialist economics was a theorem which proved the field to be non-existent. While, as we saw in the preceding section of this chapter, in a market society the price system permits us to treat the totality of the individuals in the society as an economic entity (to which coordination-efficiency considerations are relevant), the impossibility of socialist economic calculation requires us to see the socialist society as nothing more than a multitude of discrete individuals. It is this which requires us to recognize that the Austrian calculation problem (for the possibility of central planning) is anterior to Buchanan's 'motivational' problem. The latter problem shows us how, if we already assume that socialist society faces 'its' resource-allocation problem, motivational considerations must frustrate central planning attempts at successfully addressing the task of resource allocation. The Austrian economic calculation problem, on the other hand, shows us how, in a socialist society, the very objective of treating that society as an entity for which efficiency (that is, consistency) considerations are relevant, crumbles in our hands as soon as we seek to grasp it. Valid as are the questions which Buchanan's 'motivational' problems raise for socialist planning, those questions cannot in fact begin to be asked at all – because of the Austrian calculation considerations.

A critic may perhaps object that we are arguing as if, because a heavy metal weight happens to be too heavy to be lifted, one is to conclude that there is therefore no weight 'there' at all to challenge would-be weight-lifters. Surely, the objection may be raised, the circumstance that a socialist society is unable to tackle its economic allocation problem, does not justify our claiming that it faces no allocation problem at all. (And therefore, perhaps, one might argue, with Buchanan, that the more important reason for the failure of central planning is the 'motivational' problem.) But the analogy of the weight too heavy to be lifted, entirely misses the point; the appropriate analogy is a quite different one. Think of an array of tiny gold-colored beads arranged (without any string running through them) in a perfect circle on a sidewalk. Because these beads are so small and so close to one another, a casual observer walking on the sidewalk may mistake them for a gold ring. The observer then, let us imagine, tells his small child, who is with him, to pick up the gold ring and give it to him. Now this request is futile, of course, not because the child may possibly not be motivated to obey it (which is certainly possible), but, more 'fundamentally', *because there is no ring*; any attempt by the child to 'pick up' the ring must fail; in fact, not only must it fail, it must fail *by demonstrating to us* that there is no ring here at all, only discrete gold-colored beads. To attempt to solve socialist society's allocation problem is to demonstrate that there is no such societal problem; there are only discrete individual members of this 'society'.

ENTREPRENEURIAL COMPETITION AND THE NOTION OF COORDINATION-EFFICIENCY IN THE MARKET SOCIETY

The paradox that it is precisely the freedom of independently-acting competing entrepreneurs which is responsible for those regularities in markets which economic science explains, has often been noted. The very possibility that, out of the actions of many individuals, anything resembling economic *law* might emerge, results, not from these individuals being constrained to obey central commands, but precisely from their freedom of any central directives. What we have emphasized in this chapter is the related and parallel paradox that it is precisely the freedom of independently-acting competing entrepreneurs which (by generating the system of market prices, only on the basis of which they are individually able to 'calculate') permits us to talk of the possibility of coordination-efficiency as regards 'society'. It is only the price system in the market society which permits us to say that an increase in automobile production is inconsistent with a decline in oil refinery capacity. (It is after all *conceivable* that the previous refinery capacity was far greater than needed; only considerations of price can definitively stamp these two industry changes as mutually inconsistent.) It is the price system which permits individuals to calculate the prospects of pure profit in alternative projects. And it is, as we know from elementary economic theory, only the pure profitability of a prospective project which permits us to say that the pursuit of that project is coordinative, in the sense that it reveals the prior existence of market discoordination, which successful execution of that project will have corrected. Thus it is the very freedom of the individual participants in the market system to act, in regard to their property and persons, as they choose (which freedom, of course, is the basis for the price system) that is responsible for the possibility of treating society as an entity to which consistency-efficiency considerations are relevant. But while this result is certainly replete with the spice of paradox, it can for that very reason offer us deeper insight into the nature of entrepreneurial competition.

The entrepreneur, after all, is alert to pure profit possibilities. Such possibilities exist where incumbent producers have failed correctly to exploit available opportunities for serving consumers more adequately. To the outside observer the patterns followed up until now by existing producers are the 'normal', settled, ways of doing things; to them the invading entrepreneur is the iconoclast who disrupts the settled pattern of events. To such outside observers, fresh entrepreneurial activity is the unpredictable wild card, following no regular pattern, which continually but spasmodically churns the market and prevents us from realizing stable, law-like regularities in market outcomes. It is for this reason that mainstream economics, in its search for the underlying regularities submerged beneath the roiling surface waves churned up by unpredictable entrepreneurial innovation, found it necessary to filter out all entrepreneurial activity from its (equilibrium) models of markets.[20]

But for Austrian economists matters appear quite differently. From their perspective what the entrepreneur does is not to be seen as the abrupt injection of *inherently* disruptive, unpredictable courses of action into an otherwise near-stable, orderly environment. Rather what the entrepreneur does is – with all the surprise and unpredictability of what he does – to *reveal* potential *contradictions* in the activities of incumbent producers in *apparently* stable industries. Industry **A** has for years been producing with resources whose alternative uses are in Industry **B** (and in which these resources have relatively high value). This circumstance will have helped determine the market price of the products of Industry **A**. A brash new entrepreneur innovates with new methods of production (or of delivery, or of retailing, or of organization, or whatever) such that the resources required for production and delivery in Industry **A** can be drawn from Industry **C**, where their value is, let us imagine, sharply lower (than the corresponding resources which, in the 'settled' state of Industry **A**, had been diverted from possible use in Industry **B**). This brash new entrepreneur sets Industry **A** into turmoil. His apparently disruptive activity may indeed be gloriously creative and innovative; it may indeed be surprising in its novelty – and may have been, for these very reasons of creativity and novelty, totally unpredictable. But this activity has revealed the illusive quality of the earlier apparently tranquil and settled state of the industry. Production in Industry **A** has now been revealed to have been inefficiently costly. It has been the *apparently* disruptive activity of the innovative entrepreneur which has in fact uncovered the contradictions and the inconsistencies inherent in earlier patterns of production.

It is because *all* successful entrepreneurial activity can be seen as identifying and unmasking such pre-existing contradictions, that Austrian economics sees entrepreneurial competition as *fusing the disparate activities of individual market participants into a meaningful global, societal entity*. Only because the market offers freedom and scope for entrepreneurial creativity, originality and innovation, is it, in our disequilibrium world of dispersed information and constant exogenous change, meaningful to think of a market society as a whole in consistency-efficiency terms.

MISES, RIVALRY AND CENTRAL PLANNING

What Lavoie's reconsideration of the socialist calculation debate accomplished, was to teach the profession that Mises' critique of socialist planning can only be appreciated against the background of Mises' understanding of the competitive-entrepreneurial character of the market process. What we have sought to do in the present chapter is to make explicit what is in fact already implicit in Lavoie's work. That is, we have seen, how the very notion of what is 'economically good for a society', can only consistently be parsed in the context of freedom for entrepreneurial competition.

Mises made no direct 'welfare comparisons' between socialism and capitalism because, at one level, no such comparison can be made. The socialist planner *seeks* to address Milton Friedman's 'economic problem facing society'; certainly no such allocative-efficiency problem can be formulated for capitalism, at all. On the other hand, however, we have noted the almost directly opposite conclusion. When one focuses, not on society's resource-allocation pattern, but upon the possibilities for coordinative efficiency, upon the extent to which society as a whole may be guilty of attempting 'to run in opposite directions at the same time', then it is only under capitalism that the presence or absence of such guilt can be meaningfully talked of. Under socialism, we have seen, the notion of a society being a single entity subject to consistency-efficiency questions, evaporates as soon as such questions begin to be formulated.

NOTES

1. Don Lavoie, *Rivalry and Central Planning, The Socialist Calculation Debate Reconsidered*, (1985), p. 102n.
2. James B. Buchanan, *Cost and Choice, an Inquiry in Economic Theory* (1969), pp. 96ff.
3. Don Lavoie, *Rivalry and Central Planning*, (1985).
4. See Israel M. Kirzner, 'The Economic Calculation Debate: Lessons for Austrians' (1988), see especially pp. 111–15.
5. For English-language versions of Mises' 1920 and 1922 statements, see respectively: (a) Ludwig von Mises, 'Economic Calculation in the Socialist Commonwealth', (1935); (b) Ludwig von Mises, *Socialism: An Economic and Sociological Analysis* (1936), pp. 113–35.
6. Buchanan's address was subsequently published in the *Southern Economic Journal*, **30** (January 1964), pp. 213–22; it was also republished as the title essay in James M. Buchanan, *What Should Economists Do?* (1979) (to which all subsequent page references will relate).
7. As noted above, similar insights had been introduced earlier in F.A. Hayek, 'The use of knowledge in society', (1945), pp. 519–30; reprinted in F.A. Hayek, *Individualism and Economic Order*, (1949), pp. 77–91.
8. Buchanan, *What Should Economists Do*?, (1979) p. 23.
9. Ibid.
10. Ibid. p. 23ff.

11. F.A. Hayek, 'The Use of Knowledge in Society', in *Individualism and Economic Order* (1949), p. 86 (italics added).
12. F.A. Hayek, 'Economics and knowledge', Economica, IV, 1937, pp. 33–54; reprinted in Hayek, *Individualism and Economic Order*, (1949), p. 54, (italics added).
13. *Individualism and Economic Order*, (1949) p. 77; italics in the original.
14. Ibid. pp. 77–8.
15. For examples illustrating this see, Milton Friedman, *Capitalism and Freedom* (1962), p. 12; Axel Leijonhufvud, *Information and Coordination, Essays in Macroeconomic Theory*, (1981).
16. For further discussion of the coordination criterion in Austrian economics, see Israel M. Kirzner, *The Meaning of Market Process*, (1992), chapter 11; Israel M. Kirzner, *The Driving Force of the Market, Essays in Austrian Economics*, (2000), chapter 7. For the centrality of the coordination criterion in Lavoie's work, see *Rivalry and Central Planning*, (1985), pp. 54n, 111, 172–3. For a comprehensive survey of Austrian thought in regard to welfare economics, see Roy E. Cordato, *Welfare Economics and Externalities in an Open Ended Universe, A Modern Austrian Perspective*, (1992).
17. Ludwig von Mises, *Human Action, a Treatise on Economics*, 3rd edition, (1966), p. 725; the first edition of *Human Action* was published in 1949.
18. Buchanan, *What Should Economists Do?*, (1979), p. 22.
19. Ibid.
20. On this point see Israel M. Kirzner, *Discovery and the Capitalist Process*, (1985), pp. 3–4.

REFERENCES

Buchanan, James B. (1969), *Cost and Choice, an Inquiry in Economic Theory*, Chicago: Markham Publishing Co.

Buchanan, James M. (1979), *What should Economists do?*, Indianapolis: Liberty Press.

Cordato, Roy F. (1992), *Welfare Economics and Externalities in an Open-ended Universe, a Modern Austrian Perspective*, Boston, Dordrecht, London: Kluwer Academic Publishers.

Friedman, Milton (1962), *Capitalism and Freedom*, Chicago: University of Chicago Press.

Hayek, F.A. (1945), 'The use of knowledge in society', *American Economic Review*, **XXXV**(4), pp. 519–30.

Hayek, F.A. (1949), *Individualism and Economic Order*, London: Routledge and Kegan Paul.

Kirzner, Israel M. (1988), 'The economic calculation debate: lessons for Austrians', *Review of Austrian Economics*, **2**, reprinted in Israel M. Kirzner (1992), *The Meaning of Market Process, Essays in the Development of Modem Austrian Economics*, London: Routledge.

Kirzner, Israel M. (2000), *The Driving Force of the Market, Essays in Austrian Economics*, London: Routledge.

Lavoie, Don (1985), *Rivalry and Central Planning, the Socialist Calculation Debate Reconsidered*, Cambridge: Cambridge University Press.

Leijonhufvud, Axel (1981), *Information and Coordination, Essays in Macroeconomic Theory*, New York: Oxford University Press.

Lerner, Abba (1944), *The Economics of Control*, New York: Macmillan.

Mises, Ludwig von (1935), 'Economic calculation in the socialist commonwealth' in F.A.Hayek (ed.) *Collectivist Economic Planning*, London: Routledge and Kegan Paul.

Mises, Ludwig von (1936), *Socialism: an Economic and Sociological Analysis*, London: Jonathan Cape.

Mises, Ludwig von ([1949] 1966), *Human Action, a Treatise on Economics*, 3rd edn, Chicago: Contemporary Books.

O'Driscoll, Gerald P. (1977), *Economics as a Coordination Problem*, Kansas City: Sheed Andrews and McMeel.

Robbins, Lionel G (1932), *An Essay on the Nature and Significance of Economic Science*, London: Macmillan.

3. Don Lavoie's contributions to comparative economics

Peter J. Boettke and David L. Prychitko

INTRODUCTION

We both came to George Mason University to pursue graduate study with Don Lavoie almost twenty years ago. We worked closely with Don throughout our graduate careers, and wrote our dissertations under his direction. Our dissertations were, in fact, motivated to a considerable extent by professional reactions to Lavoie's own dissertation, *Rivalry and Central Planning.*[1] Both of us were led to Lavoie through our reading, while undergraduates, of his 1981 essay on the standard interpretation of the socialist calculation debate. As students from different undergraduate schools, and for different reasons, we were both persuaded by the Austrian argument about the problems with socialism as a politico-economic system. This position went against the grain. During the early 1980s, intellectual opinion in the field of comparative economic systems was clear and simple – the Austrians and Marxists were wrong. The truth, it was maintained, rested neither on the extreme of laissez faire markets or socialist central planning, but instead lay in middle ground of a regulated market economy with an extensive welfare state. To be sure, the policy world by this time (with Thatcher and Reagan) had moved in a pro-market direction, but the majority of intellectuals reacted with disbelief and often disdain for those who advocated market solutions to public policy problems. Economists (or at least a significant subset) were almost the only intellectuals who seemed to approve of the Thatcher/Reagan revolutions. Nevertheless, many economists insisted that while socialism may have an inferior incentive system, socialism could perform as well as, if not better, than capitalism – at least in theory – if those incentives could be aligned appropriately. Of course, aligning those incentives was a Herculean task.

We had both become convinced that this assessment was wrong, that the Austrians were indeed correct that socialism (strictly speaking) was not only inefficient, but impossible, and that the attempt to achieve socialism in practice was a disaster for many. It made no sense that others did not see this; the argument and the evidence seemed so clear. Lavoie's essay laid out to us why the majority of scholars thought that the Austrians were wrong, and also demonstrated why it was they, not Mises and Hayek, who misinterpreted socialism.

Lavoie's 1981 essay possessed two characteristics that would be evident throughout his career – erudition and radicalism. To our young and impressionable minds, reading his 1981 essay was awe-inspiring. Lavoie seemed to have read everything there was on the subject of the calculation debate. His command of the Austrian side was obviously thorough, but so was his understanding of his opponents. Lavoie had the ability to 'get on the other side of an argument', as we say, and he wrote in a respectful manner about his opponents. Lavoie's work did not have the screaming quality of some libertarian writers. Yet, at the same time, Lavoie did not shy away from the conclusions to which his careful reading had led him – Knight, Lange, Lerner, Dickinson, Durbin, Schumpeter and Bergson were wrong. Mises, Hayek and Robbins were right. Moreover, this was not simply a question of idle academic interest, but the resolution of a scientific dispute that impacted the lives and welfare of millions of people. It was this combination of a deep commitment to scholarship and a passion for a free and peaceful society that characterized Lavoie's work and teaching. So it made sense for us to leave our comfortable homes in Chicago (Dave) and the New Jersey shore (Pete) to study in a new PhD program with an assistant professor just barely out of graduate school himself. The next four years (1984–1988) were amazing years for us as we studied closely with Don, learned from him, argued with him, became his friend, and in the process embarked on a long and fruitful collaboration. Other contributors to this volume, we are sure, will comment on Lavoie's overall system of thought, so we will restrict our discussion to his contributions to comparative economic systems. First, we shall provide a short history of the dispute over capitalism and socialism. Second, we shall discuss the dominant professional opinion in the pre-Lavoie period. Third, we shall discuss the impact of Lavoie's books and subsequent work in changing the professional discourse. Finally, we shall address the influence of Lavoie's work during the post-communist period.[2]

A SHORT HISTORY OF COMPARATIVE ECONOMIC SYSTEMS

Classical liberal political economists promised a social system of exchange and production that would simultaneously achieve individual autonomy, generalized prosperity, and peaceful social cooperation. It is probably fair to say that, empirically, the countries that followed the liberal agenda achieved these results to a large extent. However, the doctrine of liberalism was vulnerable to the socialist criticisms concerning social justice and exploitation. The voice of socialist critics became emboldened in the late 19th and early 20th centuries. The highest form of capitalism, it was argued, was the imperialism practiced by Britain and other capitalist countries. As such, capitalism will breed war … necessarily. In addition, the internal logic of capitalism was such that it would suffer from periodic crises … necessarily. The events of the first decades of the 20th century seemed to confirm the socialist critique of capitalism as war and depression ravaged the western world. Socialism was, indeed, viewed as a viable alternative – an alternative that promised peace, prosperity and social harmony.

After his return from active duty during World War I, Ludwig von Mises penned forceful challenges to the socialist agenda. In *Nation, State and Economy* (1919), Mises demonstrated the failure of war socialism as an efficient economic organization. Next, in 1920, Mises published his famous essay on economic calculation. This was followed up with a book-length critique entitled *Socialism: An Economic and Sociological Analysis* (1922). Mises' strategy was that of immanent criticism: temporarily to avoid moral questions regarding the ends socialists sought, while analyzing the effectiveness of socialist means. Mises argued that socialist means could not satisfy the ends sought.

The reason was straightforward. Even if we grant socialism the most favorable assumption regarding the planners' (and the workers') motivation to promote the public good, it would be impossible for them to engage in the kinds of rational economic calculation required for advanced material production. They would unwittingly fall victims to economic chaos and waste.

Socialism sought to replace the institutions of private property with collective property and comprehensive economic planning. Mises argued that such an arrangement could not succeed; without private property in the means of production, there could not be a market for the means of production. Without a market for the means of production, there could not be any money prices for them. And, without money prices reflecting the relative scarcities of the means of production, there will be no way for economic planners to calculate the best uses of these scarce means. The distinction between technological possibilities and the economic use of resources is crucial to Mises' argument. Economic calculation is vital to the coordination of plans within a market economy precisely because it is the filter through which people are able to sort through the numerous technologically feasible projects and discover the economically feasible projects. We could, using one of our favorite examples, build railroad tracks out of platinum. In markets we have the freedom to do so, and, moreover, platinum tracks are consistent with the laws of physics and sound engineering. Why, then, aren't platinum tracks the norm? In fact, why aren't they even the exception? Expected profit and loss calculations provide the answer – it would be terribly unprofitable to invest in such a venture. That is what entrepreneurs need to know. From the economist's standpoint, the knowledge transmitted by the market prices of platinum and its substitutes, the prices of the services supplied by freight lines, and so on, suggest that there are more economical uses of platinum elsewhere. The market price for platinum (and other potential inputs) informs us about relative scarcity and its demand in alternative uses. The profit and loss statements signal to us our effectiveness at reading these market prices as guides for the actions we take.

Mises argued that socialism was unworkable because it abolished an effective price system, one that is tied to the relative scarcity of goods and services. This challenge set off a debate in the German language economic literature and a few English language responses by economists, such as Fred Taylor and Frank Knight. The German language arguments primarily focused on deriving schemes that would provide the requisite incentives and information but that were generated by institutions other than private property and freedom of contract. The English language arguments, on the other hand, tended to focus on the static optimality conditions within an economic system. The debate, however, was not really engaged at this stage. All this would change when F. A. Hayek edited *Collectivist Economic Planning* in 1935. In this collection, Hayek would reprint Mises' classic 1920 essay, as well as other critics of socialism, including a 1908 article written by an Italian economist – Enrico Barone – that demonstrated that the complex calculations required would exceed the ability of human beings to plan the system rationally.

Oskar Lange and Abba Lerner took up the task of developing a socialist alternative that would meet Mises' and Hayek's objections and thereby realize the socialist aspiration of providing a society which was more efficient and just than capitalism. They used the latest in neoclassical microeconomic theory to argue that socialism could replicate the efficiency results of standard equilibrium models. In the simplest representation of their model, the Central Planning Board (CPB) would give instructions to state owned enterprises that would mimic the optimality conditions of Walrasian general equilibrium. By focusing on static equilibrium, Lange and Lerner were able to show that, if the CPB deployed marginalist principles, the problem of economic calculation could be overcome. The CPB would discover the equilibrium prices of consumer goods and instruct socialist firms to gear their output at the point where the CPB price would equal marginal cost while minimizing average total costs. Lange himself stated (half-mockingly) that the leaders and economic planners of future socialist societies would have to acknowledge Mises' great insight concerning the necessity of utilizing prices within the planning of a socialist economy. But through the use of shadow prices, the model of market socialism would not only replicate the efficiency results of the market economy, it would *outperform* capitalist economies because it would overcome cyclical fluctuations, imperfect market structure, and the injustice of an unequal distribution of income.

Mises, Hayek and Lionel Robbins criticized the Lange/Lerner solution, but the vast majority of economists thought Mises had overstated his claim and that Hayek and Robbins offered little more than a practical warning about the difficulties of economic planning. Knight, for example, would argue that socialism was undesirable for political reasons, but he maintained that, as far as economic theory was concerned, socialism was viable.[3] Hayek, it turned out, made a tactical error in reprinting Barone's article in his 1935 volume. Barone's argument, like Pareto's, was one limited to the complexity of the mathematical calculations required to coordinate an advanced economy. This argument would be superseded by the development of computer technology. In fact, as Lange would say years after his original piece,

> Were I to write my essay today my task would be much simpler. My answer to Hayek and Robbins would be: so what's the trouble? Let us put the simultaneous equations on an electronic computer and we shall obtain the solution in less than a second. The market process with its cumbersome *tâtonnements* appears old-fashioned. Indeed, it may be considered as a computing device of the pre-electronic age (1967, 158).

In fact, a standard interpretation emerged long before Lange wrote these words, one that maintained that Mises had already been defeated by the earlier work of Barone and Pareto. They had shown, it was contended, that socialist planners could theoretically engage in rational economic calculation by using the mathematical representation of a competitive general equilibrium system. Bergson's (1948) survey of the field embedded this understanding of the debate in the minds of professional economists for at least two generations.

One of the most interesting things about the socialist calculation debate is that for years both parties claimed victory. It wasn't simply a matter of pig-headedness. Mises and Hayek could claim victory because many theorists would admit that the problems of socialism were problems of dynamics and not statics, thereby conceding the main point in Mises' and Hayek's interpretation. As far back as the 1920s, Mises argued that the problems of socialism were problems of dynamics, not statics (1922, 173–94).[4]

But in the years since, the nature of what constituted 'theory' had been transformed, yet the critics who admitted this point could nevertheless insist that under static conditions in a world of full and complete information, economic calculation under socialism was possible. Mises and Hayek agreed, but suggested that economic theory should not concentrate on the static conditions of equilibrium. The real issue is the dynamic processes of adjustment that are initiated by changes in tastes, technology, resource availability and knowledge.

In addition to shifting the meaning of the term 'theory', we should also highlight two other factors in the great debate: ideology and methodology. It must always be remembered that for two generations of economists trained on the heels of the Great Depression, 'the market economy' was deeply suspect. Keynes had successfully argued that markets were unstable and required government management to operate effectively. The step from macroeconomic management to rational planning was a short one for many economists to take. The idea of laissez-faire was considered old-fashioned. In addition, economists adopted a form of positivist methodology that demanded that all scientific statements must be submitted to empirical test. New techniques of statistical testing which reinforced this positivist bias were developed.

The Mises–Hayek economic arguments about the functional significance of private property rights in engendering the requisite incentives, information and innovation within an economic system were largely lost on the economists trained in the 1950s and 1960s. Mathematics replaced the study of history and institutions. In this environment not only was it difficult to explain the subtle nature of market processes, but next to impossible to get across the interconnectedness between economic and political freedom, as emphasized by both Mises and Hayek. However, during the 1960s, a new institutional economics was starting to arise with the development of the fields of public choice, law and economics, property rights economics, and the new learning in industrial organization. Ironically, while many of the originators of these fields were intellectually closely allied with the Mises–Hayek perspective, they tended to be methodologically opposed to their non-formalistic approach. As a result, as these fields developed they often moved in an alien direction, well away from their original intellectual affinities. Detailing that detour in the intellectual evolution of new institutionalism would be for another time, but the fact remains that except for the work in property rights economics, the integration of new institutionalism into the study of comparative economic systems was slower than in other economic literature.

The literature in comparative systems was divided into two camps by the 1970s: a theoretical literature that worked on optimal planning models along the lines of material balances, linear programming, or input–output analysis, and an empirical literature that worked on estimating growth rates for the Soviet Union and comparing those with the growth rates achieved in capitalist economies. Except for a few outliers, such as G. Warren Nutter, Paul Craig Roberts, and Svetojar Pejovich, the insights of Mises and Hayek were lost.

Into this intellectual climate of opinion stepped Murray Rothbard (1976), Karen Vaughn (1980) and Peter Murrell (1983), whose articles challenged the standard interpretation. Don Lavoie followed with *Rivalry and Central Planning* (1985a) – a book-length treatment of the theoretical issues that surrounded the inter-war English language debate over economic calculation in a socialist economy.

COMPARATIVE ECONOMIC SYSTEMS AFTER 1985

The impact of Don Lavoie's *Rivalry and Central Planning* was not insignificant and can be measured objectively in terms of citations, indirectly in terms of change in opinion among leading figures in the field, and more subjectively in terms of its influence on new research. A quick electronic search on the Social Science Citation Index records 109 citations to Lavoie's book. Reviews of *Rivalry* appeared in *The Economic Journal*, *American Political Science Review*, *Economica* and *Journal of Economic Literature*. Not all reviewers praised the work, but none condemned it. The work is described even by critics as 'stimulating and well-argued' (Aldrich 1987, 537), leading 'the neoclassical economist to a better understanding of the competing paradigms' (Bonin 1987, 752), and 'absorbing and very clearly written' (Bideleux 1986, 564). Peter Murrell (1987, 337) states simply that 'Lavoie's book is the most complete record written to date of this debate'.

In addition to the clarity of the argument, Lavoie had the fortune of good timing on two fronts. First, by the mid-1980s the formalist and positivist methods of economists were being called into question by a variety of economists and philosophers. McCloskey's *Rhetoric of Economics* was also published in 1985 and effectively summarized the philosophical literature, one that demonstrated that what economists thought was scientific actually lacked the argumentative foundations it presupposed, and, carefully addressing the actual practice of economics, showed that, despite their efforts, economists could not help but rely on a practice which by their own accounting would need to be viewed as unscientific. McCloskey's *Rhetoric of Economics* accomplished for the philosophy of economics what Feyerabend's *Against Method* accomplished for the philosophy of science. McCloskey argued that economists should stick to their knitting and be more self-aware of the rhetorical devices they deploy persuading their colleagues. McCloskey's unmasking of the true nature of the vibrant intellectual discussion in economics had the effect of knocking down a peg or two those who believed they practiced SCIENCE, while pulling up many others who had previously been dismissed as pursuing non-science (including in this group Austrian economists). What timing. Lavoie's message that the Mises–Hayek argument was dismissed when it should have been engaged more seriously entered the discussion during this emerging sea-change in the philosophy of economics.

Another factor, arguably more important than the change in philosophical perspective, is that socialism started to crumble in the mid to late 1980s.[5] The Solidarity movement and subsequent military crack-down in Poland discredited the idea of a workers' state and the political ideals it was supposed to represent in practice; and the rise of Gorbachev in 1985 and the introduction of *perestroika* exposed the failure of socialism as an economic system. Socialism turned out to be politically oppressive and economically inefficient. This was the position of the Austrians in the debate – a debate that they supposedly lost. As these facts became widely apparent, Lavoie explained how the Austrians did not lose the debate. Thus the theoretical and the empirical analysis of socialism were once again united.

Lavoie's thesis also enjoyed support from Janos Kornai and Robert Heilbroner. This, too, was crucial. Kornai (1986, 1727) argued that Lavoie 'rightly points out that in the neoclassical debate about socialism, the emphasis shifted one-sidedly to the issue of computing correct price signals. What got lost was the crucial Mises–Hayek–Schumpeter idea regarding "rivalry"'. As Kornai went on to argue, according to this understanding of the market process, actors make use of specific knowledge and opportunities and the market is in a state of constant flux in which victory brings rewards and defeat brings penalties. Translating this into his own work, Kornai argues that it is the Mises–Hayek–Schumpeter understanding of the dynamic market process that is most consistent with the notion of the hard budget constraint. The neoclassical model that underlies Lange's analysis does not even contemplate the requisite institutions and conditions.

The contradictions evident in the practice of socialism had cemented Kornai's position as a leading figure. Robert Heilbroner has been one of the leading public intellectuals in economics since the 1950s. Heilbroner, whose politics fall on the 'left' of the political spectrum, is often aligned with John Kenneth Galbraith. Yet in 1990, Heilbroner had publicly stated that 'It turns out, of course, that Mises was right' (Heilbroner 1990a, 92). This statement, made in an article in *The New Yorker*, signaled the end of the hope among public intellectuals that socialism could be a viable economic system. Heilbroner's essay is less dramatic than that statement might imply in that he did not 'convert' to being a laissez faire advocate in the wake of his admission that Mises was right on the problems with socialism. In fact, in a more subtle treatment of the issues at stake in the *Journal of Economic Literature*, Heilbroner argues that the victory of Mises–Hayek is due to their superior vision, not their analysis. That is, they did get it right, but for the wrong reasons. We do not want to dispute Heilbroner here,[6] but rather to highlight that, when it comes to discussing the socialist calculation debate, Heilbroner refers to Lavoie's *Rivalry and Central Planning* as providing an 'excellent review' of the crucial issues (Heilbroner 1990b, 1100, fn. 5).

Receiving this sort of endorsement from both Kornai, a leading theorist, and Heilbroner, a leading public intellectual, precisely at a time when history seemed to be turning against socialism, led to Lavoie's book getting a serious reading by his fellow economists and political economists. The field of comparative systems was about to experience something like a paradigm shift, and Lavoie had helped recapture the lost insights of Mises and Hayek.[7]

But a close reading of Heilbroner's (1990b) article demonstrates that the fundamentals of Lavoie's insight were not completely absorbed. Most readers thought that incentives were the key problem with socialism in practice. Comprehensive planning, if done by political eunuchs, could work. The planner as eunuch could indeed solve the problems of informational complexity and perform economic calculations. What Lange and Lerner misunderstood, said Heilbroner, was that individuals within the planning bureaucracy will not be able to step outside of their personal situation enough to make decisions independent of their private interests. Poor incentives killed socialism, not calculation problems.

The distorted pattern of incentives that exists under any socialist scheme represents a first-cut criticism. Both Mises and Hayek clearly recognized this point. But their argument went deeper than the success-indicator and other incentive problems that students of the Soviet economy identified during the Cold War. First, given the ideological nature of the dispute between socialism and capitalism, neither Mises nor Hayek wanted to be in a position of impugning the motivation of the planners for fear that their argument would be dismissed as ideologically motivated. Instead, they chose to argue that even if planners were rightly motivated and trained, they would still not have the knowledge required to make the necessary calculations. In short, they argued that the calculation problem held even under the best of assumptions about motivation. Second, and this is the point that was clearly missed (and still is), Mises and Hayek argued that the knowledge required to engage in rational economic calculation is concrete and contextual, and not abstract and theoretical.[8] In other words, the informational inputs to economic calculation are institution-specific and do not exist outside the context of a private property market economy. As Lavoie summarized it, 'the key point of the calculation argument is that the required knowledge of objective production possibilities would be unavailable without the competitive market process' (1985a, 102).

The problem of economic calculation within a socialist commonwealth[9] was not one of motivational shortcomings nor the mathematical complexity of the task, but resided in institutional demands of socialism and the interconnectedness of institutions and the dissemination of certain forms of information. In the limit, railroad tracks would be built from platinum. How do we know that platinum should not be used in making railroad tracks? Again – the *institutions* of a private-property, market-based economy inform us: platinum's relatively high price signals that it can employed in a better use and that to utilize it in the building of railroad tracks (given existing tastes and technology) would not be economical. But we only know that because of the institutions of relative prices and profit and loss accounting. Without these institutions, which are derivative of the broader institutions private property and freedom of contract, there would be no economic anchor. Socialism, by definition, precluded these institutions and attempted to substitute for them collective property, administered pricing and economic planning. These alternative institutions could not perform the requisite economic calculation to ward off endemic waste. Socialism suffered not only an incentive problem, but an epistemic problem that would prevent it from being workable even under the most favorable assumptions about the motivation of planners. Even the fantasy of the New Socialist Man could not solve the knowledge problem.

An additional insight from Mises–Hayek, and highlighted by Lavoie, is that, because economic planning under socialism could not be accomplished in an economic manner, it would be accomplished by meeting political objectives. The economic failings of socialism, in other words, were directly linked to the political problems of discretion and the abuse of power. Planned economies were militarized economies. The link between the knowledge problem and the political problems of socialism were clearly articulated in Lavoie's *National Economic Planning: What is Left?*, where he states that 'Planning does not accidentally deteriorate into the militarization of the economy; it *is* the militarization of the economy' (1985b, 230, italics in original). The theory of economic planning was based on feudal and military organizations, and the practice of planning is in reality nothing but the militarization of the economy. Attempts by those on the intellectual left to graft a humanitarian project unto this economic program were doomed to disappointment from the beginning.

In the end, the upshot of the Mises–Hayek position is that socialism is not reformable because the problem is not in the system of incentives or bureaucratic red-tape – which are admittedly significant in themselves – but resides instead in the nature of the system itself. The only way to improve socialist economies is to abandon the socialist project and transform them into capitalist economies.

AFTER THE COLLAPSE, WHAT IS LEFT?

It has become commonplace to refer to the collapse of the communism in East and Central Europe in 1989 and the former Soviet Union in 1991, along with the Great Depression of the 1930s, as one of the two most significant economic events of the 20th century. It has been over a decade since the 'autumn of nations', and the transition has proven more difficult than expected. Many critics believe this has discredited the notion of laissez-faire economics that was triumphantly touted in the late 1980s and 1990s. Disdain is probably the kindest term one could use to describe what some political economists now think of the so-called 'Washington consensus' of privatization, low inflation, balanced budgets, and open international trade (see Stiglitz 2002). We would argue that both the advocates of the Washington consensus and the critics have failed to grasp the radical implications of the socialist calculation debate to which Lavoie's recasting should have led.

Over the past decade, the community of economists has moved gradually from an emphasis on 'getting the prices right' to 'getting the institutions right' to a recognition that none of this is possible unless 'the right attitudes and beliefs underlie the institutional changes'. Aligning incentives is right, but we cannot align incentives unless we can figure out how the actors within that specific cultural context represent those incentives in their own hearts and minds.[10] Recognizing this has probably taken economists longer than it should have. But critics are wrong to argue that there is another way to prosperity other than private property, freedom of pricing, low or zero inflation, fiscal restraint and open international trade. The examples of state-led development have proven to be vulnerable to rent-seeking and political opportunism, and to mis-measurement of economic growth.[11]

The intellectual debate over the viability of the socialist model has focused on the alignment of incentives rather than the problems of knowledge and economic calculation (see Bardhan and Roemer 1992, 1994, and Shleifer and Vishny 1994). Both Israel Kirzner's (1997) and Bruce Caldwell's (1997) articles attempted to buck this trend and instead focus the attention of economists on the Austrian theory of the entrepreneurial market process and the notion of competition as a discovery procedure that underlies Lavoie's recasting of the contributions of Mises–Hayek in the socialist calculation debate. These issues, however, are less formally tractable than incentive alignment and as a result have been dismissed as interesting but incapable of assessment (see Stiglitz 1992, p. 6: 24–6).

The McCloskey methodological 'revolution' that originally aided the reception of Lavoie's articulation of the Mises–Hayek message in the mid- to late-1980s was short-lived in economics, as the scientific bias is strongly inbred in economists during their formative training, and the techniques of modern game theory have permitted discussion within a formal structure of economic outcomes which previously defied formalization.[12] In addition, the difficulties with the introduction of market reforms in former communist economies has had the effect of discrediting the market romance that the Austrians are often accused of adhering to by their critics.[13] Both the methodological and ideological honeymoon that Lavoie experienced in the 1980s is now over.

At the same time, more economists and political scientists than ever before are concerned with institutional, cultural and narrative subjects.[14] Austrian economists now find themselves in an awkward situation in the area of comparative systems. On the one hand, the questions that economists in this tradition have long asked, and the conclusions that they reached, are being recognized more widely than at any time since the 1920s. On the other hand, the analysis that generated those answers by the Austrians is being passed over in favor of a version of institutional and information-theoretic economics that is at times alien to the approach pioneered by Mises–Hayek. Something valuable is lost in the translation.

The current professional tension between institutionalism and formalism provides, therefore, a great opportunity for Austrian economists. For example, one area that has been underplayed is the institutional configuration of the radical political economy project presented by Lavoie (1985b, 211–45). The libertarianism that has been presented to the former communist countries has often appeared either sterile and uncaring, or simplistic and immoral. The political decentralization that Lavoie envisioned as the basis for an alternative radicalism for the 21st century represents a more dialogical model of libertarianism, one that can inspire the imagination of intellectuals and activists alike.[15] As Lavoie argued:

> We must not, however, let the decay of planning as an ideal for the Left destroy our hopes for radical change. What is wrong with that form of radicalism which aspires to the planned economy as its utopia is not the simple fact that it was a radical movement, that sought to inspire popular support by its appeal to an imagined alternative kind of social organization. What is wrong with it is that its specific utopia happens to be completely unworkable if carried to its logical conclusion, and essentially reactionary if not (1985b, 231).

Our task in the post-communist world (and post 9/11 world) is to explore the alternative institutional arrangements that would constitute a workable social organization that abolishes the exploitation of others through state power and realizes the benefits of a free economy in terms of increased standards of living for the population. Peace and prosperity was the rallying call of 19th century liberals, and it is still the social agenda for radical libertarians. The goal of a political economy of free people should be to enable those people to live flourishing lives. It was this demand for serious scholarship that aspired to a relevant radicalism that is Lavoie's most enduring contribution to a generation of students of his work.

CONCLUSION

Don Lavoie's *Rivalry and Central Planning* (1985a) challenged the received paradigm in comparative political economy in the 1980s. We have argued that this work significantly redirected the literature in the field, a direction that was favorable to the insights of Mises–Hayek. While we admit that his direct influence on the professional conversation was short-lived, we have argued that the theoretical and practical insights contained in *Rivalry and Central Planning*, and its companion volume, *National Economic Planning: What is Left?* (1985b), can still serve as a corrective to the errors of omission – with regard to the contextual nature of knowledge and the problem of power in the attempts to resurrect workable models of market socialism – and as an inspiring vision of a new radicalism that strives for a peaceful and prosperous world. Lavoie's legacy is one of committed teaching, serious scholarship, and a love of liberty. In a tragically all too brief life, Don Lavoie was able to instill in his students the sheer joy of living the life of the mind. Hopefully they, and their own students, will continue to carry that torch.

NOTES

1. Tom Bottomore challenged Lavoie's interpretation of Soviet history, which prompted Boettke to write a thesis that explored Soviet economic history (see Boettke 1990); Robert Bideleux challenged Lavoie's understanding of workers' self-managed systems, leading Prychitko to write a thesis that examined the theory and practice of workers' self-management (see Prychitko 1991). In addition to our work in Austrian economics and the history of political economy, we have continued research along the lines established in our respective theses (see Boettke 1993, 2001; and Prychitko 2002, Prychitko and Vanek, eds, 1996).
2. Perhaps also of interest, Prychitko (forthcoming) provides a complete and edited set of notes taken from Lavoie's 1985 graduate course on Comparative Economic Systems at George Mason University, a course which coincided with the publication of *Rivalry and Central Planning* and *National Economic Planning: What is Left?*

3. See Boettke and Vaughn (2002) for a discussion of Knight's conception of economic theory and the problems of socialism.
4. Schumpeter's own attempt at modeling market socialism grew critical of the Lange–Lerner 'solution' because it remained a static analysis. Schumpeter tried to acknowledge the problem of time and capital coordination in ways that Lange–Lerner barely anticipated. Unfortunately, Schumpeter, too, couldn't capture the heterogeneous problems of capital coordination, and seemed content to employ the traditional Keynesian aggregative framework. See Prychitko (2002, pp. 162–3).
5. We say arguably because individuals have a tremendous capacity to process new information in a manner which does not challenge their existing beliefs. Just because Soviet socialism failed, there is no immediate reason why that failure should be interpreted in light of the criticism leveled against socialism in general made by Mises–Hayek and Lavoie.
6. See Boettke (1992) for a response to Heilbroner on the relationship between vision and analysis in economic thought.
7. Lavoie's main contributions in *Rivalry and Central Planning*, which were accepted to varying degrees, were: (1) his insistence on the coherence of Marx's system, which refuted attempts to show a conflict between the young and old Marx, and how Marx's negative analysis of capitalism linked to the positive image of socialism he held; (2) his clarification of Mises' argument on the problems of socialism, showing that Mises' argument was never about static equilibrium, but about properties of dynamic adjustment; (3) his clarification of the Austrian paradigm and how it diverged from neoclassical economics with its emphasis on competition as a process of rivalry and entrepreneurial discovery; and (4) his demonstration of the interconnectedness under attempts to rationally plan an economy of the knowledge problem in economic coordination and the problem of the abuse of power within the politics of socialism.
8. Hayek's work, especially his later work on spontaneous order, emphasized the tacit domain of our knowledge. But it must be stated that Lavoie, building on the work of Michael Polanyi, emphasized this tacit domain more than any other scholar within the Austrian tradition and attempted to place it within the broader context of the nature of knowledge and communication. See Lavoie (1985b, 51–92; 247–65). Lavoie's turn toward hermeneutic philosophy can be explained largely by reference to the emphasis he placed on the questions of knowledge, its discovery, use and conveyance.
9. This argument is restricted to a certain clear meaning of what is meant by socialism. In the early part of the 20th century, this was clear – social ownership of the means of production and the substitution of production for direct use for production for exchange (means) with the purpose of achieving social harmony (to overcome class conflict) and increased material production (to move from the Kingdom of Necessity to the Kingdom of Freedom). As the 20th century progresses, socialist intellectuals often changed the means (as they proved ineffective), yet kept the name socialism. The calculation argument was directed at the earlier meaning of the socialist social system of production.
10. Lavoie's last book, co-written with Emily Chamlee-Wright, addresses the issue of cultural representations of incentives and enterprise (see Lavoie and Chamlee-Wright 2000). In this work, Lavoie and Chamlee-Wright are quite critical of cultural conservatives and champion an economically informed version of multiculturalism. While neither of us are cultural conservatives, the criticisms leveled by Lavoie and Chamlee-Wright miss the mark sometimes, due to the empirical fact that, while people can (and should be free to) live and organize their economic affairs in a variety of ways, very few ways are consistent with long term economic growth and generate generalized prosperity. Whatever disagreements we may have with the presentation, we must admit that the emphasis on cultural representation is a leading topic to address in transitional political economy.
11. We would contend that the Asian crisis revealed the moral hazard problems associated with the strong links between business, government and the banking system. Also, the problems of corruption that are reported in these economies indicate the difficulties associated with opportunism. Finally, the mis-measurement issues arise due to calculating the value of inputs and not outputs – this is the same problem that plagued Soviet

economic growth accounting and it reflects the 'conspicuous production' that characterizes state-led development efforts.

12. Boettke (1996, 1997 and 1998) has argued that this trend in modern economic thought is highly undesirable and has produced a form of 'formalistic historicism' that is damaging to progress in economic science. The substantive propositions of economics no longer claim generalizability, but are limited to particularizations. On the other hand, the form in which those propositions are stated has obtained a generalizable status – propositions in economics must be stated formally, or they are not considered propositions at all. For example, some economists reduce Ronald Coase's discussion of transaction costs from the 'Coase theorem' to the 'Coase conjecture'.
13. In the debate over the interpretation of the post-communist record, critics of market reform refer to the discrediting of neoclassical economics and then often cite Mises and Hayek as prominent examples. The irony of this is often too much to comprehend coherently since it was the neoclassical preoccupation with equilibrium conditions that blinded them to the insights of Mises–Hayek in the 1930s–1970s.
14. The leading economist in this regard is Douglass North. However, we should also note the economic literature in law and finance, geographic advantage, institutional quality, colonial heritage, and norms and conventions.
15. One such effort has already been published by Christopher Sciabbara (2001).

REFERENCES

Aldrich, J. (1987), 'Book review of Don Lavoie, *Rivalry and Central Planning*', *Economica*, **54** (216) November.

Bardhan, P. and John Roemer (1992), 'Market socialism: a case for rejuvenation', *Journal of Economic Perspectives*, **6** (3) Summer.

Bardhan, P. and John Roemer (1994), 'On the workability of market socialism', *Journal of Economic Perspectives*, **8** (2) Spring.

Bergson, A. (1948), 'Socialist economics', in Howard Ellis (ed.), *A Survey of Contemporary Economics*, Philadelphia, PA: Blakiston Co.

Bergson, A. (1967), 'Market socialism revisited,' *Journal of Political Economy*, **75** (October).

Bideleux, R. (1986), 'Book review of Don Lavoie, *Rivalry and Central Planning*', *Economic Journal*, **96** (382) June.

Boettke, P. (1990), *The Political Economy of Soviet Socialism: The Formative Years, 1918–28*, Boston: Kluwer Academic Press.

Boettke, P. (1992), 'Vision and analysis in modern political economy', *Journal of the History of Economic Thought*, **14** (1) Spring.

Boettke, P. (1993), *Why Perestroika Failed: The Politics and Economics of Socialist Transformation*, New York: Routledge.

Boettke, P. (1996), 'What is wrong with neoclassical economics (and what is still wrong with Austrian economics)?', in Fred Foldvary (ed.), *Beyond Neoclassical Economics*, Cheltenham, UK and Northampton, MA, USA: Edward Elgar.

Boettke, P. (1997), 'What went wrong with economics,' *Critical Review*, **11** (1) Winter.

Boettke, P. (1998), 'Formalism and contemporary economics', *Critical Review*, **12** (1–2) Winter–Spring.

Boettke, P. (2001), *Calculation and Coordination: Essays on Socialism and Transitional Political Economy*, New York: Routledge.

Boettke, P. and Karen Vaughn (2002), 'Knight and the Austrians on capital and the problems of socialism', *History of Political Economy*, **34** (1) Spring.
Bonin, J. (1987), 'Book review of Don Lavoie, *Rivalry and Central Planning*', *Journal of Economic Literature*, **25** (2) June.
Caldwell, B. (1997), 'Hayek and socialism', *Journal of Economic Literature*, **35** (4) December.
Feyerabend, Paul (1975), *Against Method*, London: New Left Books, p. 339.
Hayek, F.A., ed. (1935), *Collectivist Economic Planning*, London: Routledge.
Hayek, F. (1944), *The Road to Serfdom*, Chicago: University of Chicago Press.
Hayek, F.A. (1948), *Individualism and Economic Order*, Chicago: University of Chicago Press.
Heilbroner, R. (1990a), 'Analysis and vision in the history of modern economic thought', *Journal of Economic Literature*, **28** (3) September.
Heilbroner, R. (1990b), 'Reflections: after communism', *The New Yorker* (10 September).
Kirzner, I. (1997), 'Entrepreneurial discovery and the competitive market process', *Journal of Economic Literature*, **35** (1) March.
Kornai, J. (1986), 'The Hungarian reform process', *Journal of Economic Literature*, **24** (4) December.
Lange, O. (1967), 'The computer and the market', in C.H. Feinstein (ed.), *Socialism, Capitalism and Economic Growth*, Cambridge: Cambridge University Press.
Lavoie, Don (1981), 'A critique of the standard account of the debate', *Journal of Libertarian Studies*, **5** (1) Winter.
Lavoie, Don (1985a), *Rivalry and Central Planning*, New York: Cambridge University Press.
Lavoie, Don (1985b), *National Economic Planning: What is Left?*, Washington, DC: CATO Institute.
Lavoie, Don and Emily Chamlee-Wright (2000), *Culture and Enterprise*, Washington, DC: CATO Institute.
McCloskey, D. (1985), *The Rhetoric of Economics*, Madison, Wisc.: University of Wisconsin Press.
Mises, Ludwig (1919 [1983]), *Nation, State and Economy*, New York: New York University Press.
Mises, Ludwig (1920), 'Economic calculation in the socialist commonwealth', in F.A. Hayek (ed.), *Collectivist Economic Planning*, London: Routledge.
Mises, Ludwig (1922 [1981]), *Socialism: An Economic and Sociological Analysis*, Indianapolis: Liberty Press.
Mises, Ludwig (1949), *Human Action: A Treatise on Economics*, Chicago: Henry Regnery.
Murrell, P. (1983), 'Did the theory of market socialism answer the challenge of Ludwig von Mises?', *History of Political Economy*, **15** (1), Spring.
Murrell, P. (1987), 'Book review of Don Lavoie, *Rivalry and Central Planning*,' *American Political Science Review*, **81** (1), March.
Prychitko, D.L. (1991), *Marxism and Workers' Self-Management: The Essential Tension*, Westport, CT: Greenwood.
Prychitko, D.L. (2002), *Markets, Planning, and Democracy: Essays after the Collapse of Communism*, Cheltenham, UK and Northampton, MA, USA: Edward Elgar.
Prychitko, D.L. (forthcoming), 'Don Lavoie's graduate lectures on comparative economic systems, George Mason University, Fall 1985', *Research in the History of Economic Thought and Methodology*.

Prychitko, D.L. and Jaroslav Vanek (eds) (1996), *Producer Cooperatives and Labor-Managed Systems*, 2 vols, Cheltenham, UK and Northampton, MA, USA: Edward Elgar.

Rothbard, Murray N. (1976), 'Ludwig von Mises and economic calculation under socialism', in Laurence S. Moss (ed.), *The Economics of Ludwig von Mises: A Critical Reappraisal*, Kansas City: Sheed and Ward.

Sciabarra, C. (2001), *Total Freedom*, State College, PA: Penn State University Press.

Shleifer, A. and Robert Vishny (1994), 'The politics of market socialism', *Journal of Economic Perspectives*, **8** (2), Spring.

Stiglitz, J. (1992), *Whither Socialism?*, Cambridge, MA: MIT Press.

Stiglitz, J. (2002), *Globalization and Its Discontents*, New York: Norton.

Vaughn, Karen (1980), 'Economic calculation under socialism', *Economic Inquiry*, **18** (October).

4. A typology of interventionist dynamics[1]

Robert L. Bradley Jr.

> The proliferation of new forms of government interference into the market is certain to present many new challenges for the analyst in the future. ... But I believe all these will prove susceptible to the Misesian critique of interventionism and ... [to] a general typology into which any interventionist policy can be classified. (Don Lavoie, 1982: 180)

Twentieth-century Austrian economics identified government intervention in the market economy, like the market economy itself, as a *process* (High, 1991b). Ludwig von Mises is credited with this development (Ikeda, 1997: 1–3; Kirzner, 2001: 176–81). Mises, appreciating the natural workings of the market economy, saw interventionism as inappropriate, unstable, and likely to grow until faced with the all-or-nothing choice between total repeal and total control ([1952], 1980). Mises' student, F.A. Hayek, similarly noted that 'the close interdependence of all economic phenomena makes it difficult to stop planning just where we wish', and 'beyond a certain degree, the planner will be forced to extend his controls until they become all-comprehensive' (Hayek, 1944: 105).

The *Mises interventionist thesis* was restated by Don Lavoie:

> Attempts to violently manipulate the outcomes of [the market] process lead to reactions that the intervener can neither specifically predict nor effectively prevent. Efforts to make the initial intervention work as designed must take the form of ever-wider and more obtrusive interventions, which are in further conflict with the workings of the market mechanism. In the end the interventionists must either extend their activities to the point where the process has been completely sabotaged or they must abandon their quest to control the market. Any 'middle way' between the extremes may, of course, be advocated but would consist in a series of haphazard shocks to the system (Lavoie, 1982: 180).

Sanford Ikeda in the Misesian tradition described the 'micro-crises' of sequential endogenous intervention: 'Perceived problem in a → intervention in a → problems in a & b → intervention in b → another problem in a → another intervention in a → problems in a, b, & c → more intervention in a, b, & c → crisis in a → etc.' (Ikeda, 1997: 133).

The Mises interventionist thesis in the above reincarnations provides a foundation for understanding the mixed economy in theory and practice. This chapter builds upon that foundation by adding a process-oriented typology of interventionism. A typology by Murray Rothbard (1962: 766–68; 1970: 11–12), dividing government actions into *autistic* (government → individual), *binary* (government ↔ individual), and *triangular* (government ↔ two individuals), was a static classification, not a step-by-step examination of the interventionist process.[2] Yet Rothbard spoke of the 'direct and indirect' effects of intervention and its disruption of 'interconnected' markets (1970: 12; 1962: 826). Rothbard also ([1971] 1997: 205) praised Mises for explaining how 'an intervention generates unintended consequences and difficulties', leading to ever more difficult choices to expand or repeal the intervention. Rothbard describes Mises' 'cumulative . . . logic of intervention' as 'ecological' but does not develop the concept himself. Rothbard's analysis of the history of government intervention in money and banking, however, employs Mises' interventionist thesis ([1963], 1990: 88–89).

Economists outside of the Austrian tradition have independently reached the basic insight of the Mises interventionist thesis – the propensity of inappropriate government intervention to expand in an ill-fated attempt to achieve economic rationality. Alfred Kahn (1971, vol. 2: 28–29) spoke of the 'historical principle' of 'one interference with competition necessitat[ing] another and yet another'. James McKie (1970: 9) described the 'tar baby effect' of government intervention continually reacting to the 'compensating variation' of entrepreneurs. Other regulatory economists have similarly interpreted this dynamic (Bradley, 1996a: 1770–71).

A DYNAMIC TYPOLOGY

Elsewhere, I have put forward a dynamic typology to interpret the history of interventionism in US energy markets (Bradley, 1996a, 1996b, 1996c).[3] This typology, which is also applicable to non-energy intervention, including the welfare state's 'transfer dynamics' (Ikeda, 1997: 40), can be employed for prediction *ex ante* or historical analysis *ex post*. The examples herein mostly refer to energy, an active area of interventionism at all government levels for over 150 years.[4]

A. General Categories

Three classifications can capture and qualitatively describe virtually all interventions in a market: *dormant vs. causal*, *non-initiating vs. initiating*, and *initiating vs. consequent (cumulative)*. The interrelationships of each are illustrated in Figure 4.1.

Dormant vs. causal

The first classification of an interventionist dynamic identifies a regulation as being either dormant or causal to market decision-makers. A *dormant intervention* does not impact the market – either because the market would act in the manner prescribed by the regulation anyway, or because the regulation does not apply to actual or anticipated conditions. *Causal intervention*, by contrast, impacts the decision-making of market participants.

A dormant regulation could be a dead letter still on the books that is irrelevant, non-operable, or not enforced. An example of a *superfluous* regulation is a law in San Francisco left over from the horse-and-buggy era regulating the amount of horse manure that can be deposited on street corners (Bradley and Fulmer, 2004: 48). An example of a *latent* regulation is a 'price gouging' law, intended for times of natural disaster, that may go long periods without having an effect. But it is potentially active (causal), unlike superfluous regulation, discussed below. An example of an *ignoble* regulation is one that impinges on everyday voluntary actions but is violated with impunity such as some state-level morality codes.

A distinction between dormant and causal intervention was recognized early in the history of economic thought by Adam Smith, who differentiated between 'useless' and 'hurtful' regulation regarding a protective monopoly for domestic producers against importers. If the domestic good was naturally cheaper, the intervention was 'useless'; if the home product was more expensive, the monopoly grant was 'hurtful' (Smith [1776], 1981: 456).

An intervention can be causal in one direction and dormant in another. Regulation 'x' may be seen as applying to area 'a' but not 'b'. This is relevant to a regulatory process since dormant intervention can become causal. For example, a novel interpretation of a 'dormant' statute can make it effective. In 1953, for instance, a proposed natural gas pipeline interconnection between a Canadian and US firm near Niagara Falls was blocked by a rival project pursuant to Canada's Navigable Waters Protection Act. The private action was upheld by Canadian authorities, although it was considered frivolous and legalistic by critics. As intended, the regulation worked as a stop-gap measure for its beneficiaries until a federal license system was enacted by Parliament that formally regulated (and in this case, blocked) the planned interconnection (Kilbourn, 1970: 42). With broad statutory interpretation – and an activist judiciary – laws such as this lie in waiting.

Cause-and-effect in a typology of interventionism comes from the mind of the economic decision-makers, which can make dormant regulation causally effective on closer inspection. The *potential impact* of an otherwise dormant intervention is crucial. With a price gouging law, dormant is really causal if *expectations* incite sellers and buyers to hold less precautionary inventory. In Adam Smith's example, useless protectionism may actually be hurtful if it incites domestic merchants to be less efficient or discourages investment in the export business of the foreign country. Another example is a mandated price ceiling that is normally above the market but could come into play during a price spike, such as for wholesale electricity produced in California. Potential price constraints affect the economics for building new capacity in this example, especially peaking plants, which operate only for the highest-priced hours of the year.

As these examples show, there is less dormant and more causal intervention than often meets the eye. The paucity of dormant regulation reflects the fact that virtually all intervention is intended to affect market behavior, although it often has unintended consequences.

Non-initiating vs. initiating

A dormant intervention is an end in itself and not subject to dynamic analysis outside of its antecedent history. It may finally be repealed, but there is little else to be analyzed outside of any potential it has to 'come alive'. Causal intervention, on the other hand, has economic consequences subject to additional analysis.

A *non-initiating intervention* is one that does not engender subsequent intervention. An example would be a prohibition against smoking near gas pumps at a service station. Such regulations might be subject to reinterpretation or could be marginally altered, but such revision would be self-contained and unlikely to inspire add-on or corrective action. These stationary statutes, which may be repealed, are qualitatively different from an *initiating intervention* that inspires further government activism.

As with dormant intervention, non-initiating intervention is rarer than is first realized. A quiet-but-causal intervention is really initiating if it contributes to intervention in another jurisdiction or time period, as discussed below.[5] There might also be an *indirect effect* whereby an otherwise non-initiating intervention inspires the political or market decision-makers to increase or reduce interventionism elsewhere. Psychologically, interventionism begets interventionism (Ikeda, 1997: 176; Higgs, 1987: 261). The converse could also be true; deregulation can drive further deregulation as seen with the US transportation industries in the 1980s that were based on common economic precepts (Winston, 1998).

Initiating vs. consequent

An initiating intervention spawns further intervention in the economy. In all cases, the ensuing intervention can be traced back to the initiating intervention, which by definition is also a causal intervention. A dormant intervention, on the other hand, cannot be initiating without first becoming causal, as shown by the linkages in Figure 4.1.

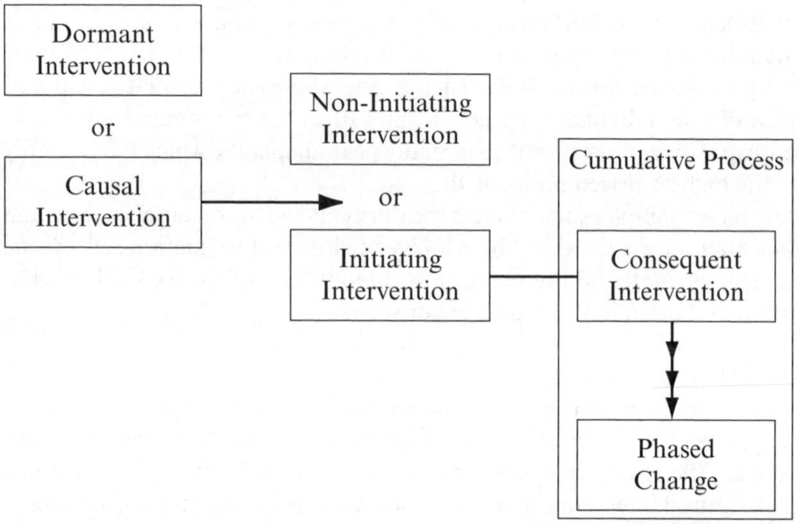

Figure 4.1 Interventionist typology

The complexity of the cumulative process makes it the most consequential to the economy and challenging for the analyst to trace and describe. [6]

B. Cumulative Process

An interventionist statute or administrative regulation therefrom can be *expansionary*, *contractionary*, or *both* at any point in the cumulative process (Figure 4.2). Alternatively, a consequent intervention can endure in its original form or be revised in a relatively neutral (non-contractionary and non-expansionary) way.

Expansionary

Consequent intervention can be divided into *phases*, with the first general expansion being Phase I, the second Phase II, and so on. The chronological sequence can occur over a short or long time sequence and involve new jurisdictions. Public utility regulation of manufactured gas distribution in the last century, for example, was a cumulative process to 'plug regulatory gaps' that would spread from localities to states and finally to the federal level – federally, first to regulate interstate natural gas transmission and then to

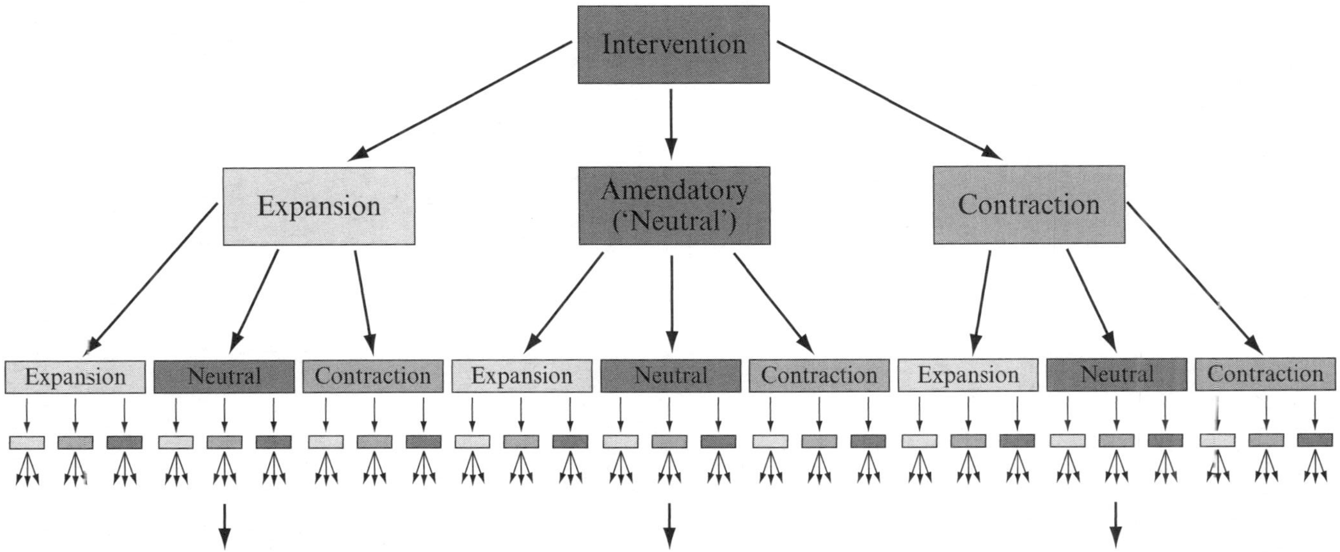

Figure 4.2 Interventionist dynamics possibilities map

regulate natural gas production dedicated to interstate commerce (Bradley, 1996b). Federal wellhead regulation itself would go through multiple phases – a cumulative process within a cumulative process.[7] While commodity prices were finally deregulated in the early 1990s, a new phase of public utility regulation began for interstate gas transmission firms – mandatory access at 'non-discriminatory' rates and terms of service (Bradley, 1996b: 16–19). The cumulative interventionist process that began with manufactured (coal) gas in the 19th century continues with natural gas into the 21st century.

Accounting and related managerial regulation was a cumulative process within public-utility-regulated industries. Initial regulation in the late 19th and early 20th century at the local and state level inspired opportunistic business strategies to maximize profits and accounting strategies while avoiding public scrutiny. Authorities, in response, implemented new accounting and reporting requirements, which inspired new business strategies, then new regulation, and so on.[8] C.O. Ruggles, professor of public utility management at Harvard University, described the march of managerial oversight by public authorities:

> There has been a steady growth in commission jurisdiction over more types of utilities, and greater authority over the managerial affairs of the utilities. This latter tendency was apparent as early as 1890 ... but it is doubtful if anyone at that time could have anticipated the extent to which internal operations of utilities would be made subject to actual regulation by utility commissions. . . . Increased attention was focused especially on such matters as the power to change contract rates, to issue terminable or indeterminate permits, to control depreciation rates, to approve consolidation and mergers, and to authorize the construction of electric transmission lines (Ruggles, 1937: 56).

The step-by-step dynamics of public-utility regulation and utility accounting practices, many unsound (May, 1943: 297), is a fertile area of process analysis.

Contractionary

Deregulation or *dis-intervention* (Ikeda, 1997: 139) is an unwinding process that can occur *incrementally* with the removal of cumulative expansions or *totally* with the repeal of the initiating intervention upon which the cumulative intervention rests. Contraction can begin immediately after the intervention takes effect or occur, more commonly, after a prolonged expansionary process.

Incremental deregulation is unlikely to play the tape in reverse. Decision-makers would be likely to remember the expansionary phase as unstable and prone to revision. Economic circumstances and political constituencies would have changed. More likely, the dis-interventionist path will occur in fewer steps than the expansion did – and maybe in just one step. Phased wellhead deregulation of natural gas prices between 1978 and 1993 followed a different (although intricate) course from the jurisdictional buildup of price controls between 1940 and 1954 and administrative revision from 1954 to 1978 (Bradley, 1996b: 12–18). Petroleum deregulation in 1981 instantaneously eliminated many programs for producers, refiners, transporters, resellers, and distributors that had been introduced and extensively revised between 1973 and 1980 – the Maximum Petroleum Price Regulation, Old Oil [Refinery] Entitlements Program, Small Refiner Bias, Supplier-Purchaser Rule, Buy-Sell Program, and Crude Oil and Petroleum Product Reseller Rules (Bradley, 1996a: 508–10, 1689–90, 1786–89, 1861).

The contractionary progress can begin from isolated liberalization in a centrally planned economy. *Perestroika* in the former Soviet Union is an example of creeping liberalism, although later developments proved how unstable the progress was (Boettke, 1993).

Mixed expansionary/contractionary

Consequent intervention, as mentioned, can contain expansionary and contractionary parts. 'Managed deregulation' under the Natural Gas Policy Act of 1978 extended interstate price controls to intrastate wellhead gas for the first time. This expansion of intervention was joined by price decontrol, immediate and phased, for certain gas categories (Bradley, 1996b: 15). The most recent phase of public utility regulation concerning natural gas, as mentioned, included commodity deregulation coupled with mandatory open-access requirements on interstate pipelines.

Comprehensive, industry-wide legislation can contain many threads of intervention and dis-intervention. The 373-page Energy Policy Act of 1992, 'a constellation of energy and environmental regulatory minutiae and pork for all energy sources and technologies' (Bradley, 1993: 1), concurrently relaxed regulation for certain energy activities. Judgment is necessary amid the myriad regulatory, subsidy and tax provisions to determine whether the overall effect represents less or more intervention than before – and whether the package creates more or less momentum toward regulation in the future.

Macroeconomic

The cumulative process has a *macroeconomic* dimension if the interventions are important enough to materially affect the aggregate statistics of employment, output and income. An example is an economy-wide initiating intervention such as a central-bank credit expansion triggering a wave of government action and reaction. If inflation creates an unsustainable boom, the intervention inspired by the ensuing contraction (public works, wage edicts, tariffs, securities regulation, and so on) is consequent intervention that can have a macroeconomic impact. The policy activism surrounding America's Great Depression, first under Hoover and then FDR, is a classic example (Rothbard, [1963], 2000).

The microeconomic has touched on the macroeconomic with petroleum regulation in the United States. During World War I and World War II, and again in the 1970s, rising prices from expansionary monetary policy led to price and allocation controls on petroleum (along with many other goods), a classic cumulative scenario (Bradley, 1996a: 466–86, 1786–87). In some cases, resulting shortages had repercussions across industrial sectors since energy was such a vital input. Shortages of natural gas and gasoline in major metropolitan areas in the 1970s closed factories and disrupted transportation with ripple effects on major parts of the structure of production. In 2000/2001, electricity shortages hampered production and productivity in major metropolitan areas of California, the world's fifth largest economy.

Jurisdictional/geographical

Many regulations have traveled from state to state and then been federalized to expand coverage and promote uniformity. Examples include rate and entry regulation for railroads, trucks, financial securities, oil pipelines, manufactured/natural gas distribution, and electricity distribution (Bradley 1996a: 1788). Each represented an expansion of the cumulative process. However, the net effect can be judged contractionary if the federal one-size approach eases compliance or is less interventionist than the state regulation it replaced.

The cumulative process can link domestic to international policy. The US Mandatory Oil Import Program of 1959, which set effective quotas on crude oil and oil product imports, particularly hurt Venezuela, the leading exporter to the United States. In response, Venezuela led the negotiations that resulted in the formation of the Organization of Petroleum Exporting Countries (OPEC) in 1960 (Bradley, 1989: 67–68). Parochial intervention by the US that created, in effect, a domestic producer cartel led to the creation of an international oil-state producer cartel. *Retaliatory* action is a not uncommon cumulative process given an initiating international trade restriction.

Intermittent (non-sequential)

The cumulative process is temporally sequential in the large majority of cases. But there can be instances of interventions being related after an interim noninterventionist period. Government energy planning is an example. World War I provided a precedent for New Deal planning, and both episodes inspired World War II planning. Bureaucratic planning during the brief Korean conflict occurred for little other reason than it was done in World War II (Bradley, 1989: 29–30; Bradley, 1996a: 234, 248, 1780–81). Each of these planning episodes occurred after a period of decontrol.

Another example of psychologically related, intermittent intervention[9] concerns 'pro industry' regulation that turned into 'anti-industry' regulation. Wellhead oil regulation and tax policy benefited the southwest oil states at the expense of the northeast consuming states from the 1920s through the 1960s due to the political balance of power. With energy price spikes and shortages in the 1970s, the northeast exacted political revenge by obtaining legislation that imposed price ceilings and other unfavorable regulation on major parts of the oil industry (Bradley, 1996a: 1855, 1860). To some extent, the political ill-will generated by pro-industry interventionism made subsequent anti-industry intervention cumulative.

C. Mises Interventionist Thesis

Ludwig von Mises saw interventionism as a powerful, inexorable force in the market economy. In Mises' words ([1952] 1980: 28): 'Intervention cannot be considered as an economic system destined to stay. It is a method for the transformation of capitalism into socialism by a series of successive steps.'

The Mises interventionist thesis can be viewed as a subset of our typology. It is the initiating/consequent case that results in total intervention in a sector (micro case) or general economy (macro case) – or a crisis-inspired repeal of the government action at any stage to establish, or reestablish, a free market situation as seen in Figure 4.3.

The Mises formulation has partial, not total, empirical applicability.[10] Intervention can be relatively innocuous and stable whereby the government action endures without significant expansion or contraction. Mises' 'slippery slope' argument that leads from interventionism to socialism (Kirzner, 2001: 178) is inconsistent with some, or many, real-world examples of interventionism (Butler, 1988: 86–88).

State-level public-utility regulation of different industries over the last century offers many examples. Some electric utilities were municipalized in response to problematic regulation – a localized example of Mises' thesis. Some electric municipalities were privatized – another all-or-nothing example congruent with the Misesian framework (Bradley, 1996c: 67–68; 72–73). But in many states cost-based regulation endured for decades without crisis and with limited revision. This was particularly true in many energy industries in the 1950s and 1960s.

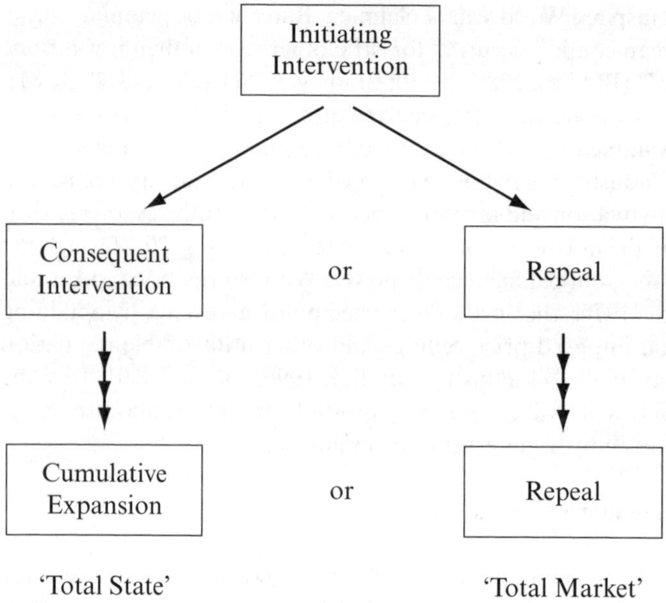

Figure 4.3 Mises interventionist thesis

Industry-wide, the breakdown of federal railroad regulation in the US led to a nationalization order in 1917 (Bradley, 1996a: 977). Growing government intervention in the coal industry of the United Kingdom led to performance problems and nationalization in 1917 and 1946 (Haynes, 1953; Dintenfass, 1992). The UK nationalizations were later followed by denationalization but not decontrol as the Mises' interventionist thesis might suggest. Mises' logic of interventionism comes into play as prominent examples, not an iron law.

The Mises interventionist thesis can be employed to identify a *critical mass* whereby a crossroad is reached between total regulation and total decontrol. But a crisis can lead to new halfway measures. In California, for example, rules governing mandatory transmission access and spot market sales for electricity have been redesigned in response to a performance crisis. Emergency measures increased intervention in 2001 after elements of deregulation within a regulatory framework were introduced in 1998 (Sweeney, 2002).

Some socialists who originally saw interventionism as 'a step toward socialism' discovered that the middle-way, however unstable in its parts, was well ensconced between capitalism and socialism. Gabriel Kolko wrote (1970: 203):

> Socialists everywhere failed to understand the [US] political-economic process they were living through ... was pragmatic, haphazard and hardly comprehended by even its most sophisticated advocates. Nothing in socialist theory, much less *laissez faire* and marginal economic theory, prepared socialists for the possibility that a class-oriented integration of the state and the economy in many key areas would rationalize and strengthen capitalism.

D. Interventionist Learning

Mises' formulation emphasized intervention as a series of steps with the unintended consequences of each intervention leading to a decision for complementary intervention or total repeal. This general description, while accurate in many instances, does not account for *interventionist learning* where the initiating intervention can include *complementary intervention* and become, incrementally at least, a more stable regime. A price control statute, for example, can include allocation controls given an anticipated need to address shortages created by the (causal) price ceiling. Since 'to every government action the private sector reacts or accommodates, and the government further reacts as the private sector "talks back" to the government' (Shultz and Dam, 1977: 8), there is opportunity for intervention to anticipate and capture, at the outset at least, part of the gaming to come.

Complementary intervention can bypass some of the would-be cumulative process by front-loading intervention. In the limit, 'perfect' regulation would anticipate and eliminate all the trial and error of a cumulative process. The economic results may be less desirable than a free market situation, but from the viewpoint of regulators and regulated it might be the most desirable (or least undesirable) outcome. However, front-loaded intervention is likely to simply create a new base for a cumulative process given the prevalence of error, surprises and plan revision.

Figure 4.4 illustrates two scenarios where intervention is front loaded, one with a reduced cumulative process and one where the (would-be) process is comprehensively implemented in the opening period.

These two illustrations assume that the regulatory process can be known before its time, a debatable proposition. But the general point is valid – seasoned intervention can incorporate up front what less mature intervention would grope to embody over time.

CONSEQUENCES: INTENDED AND UNINTENDED

Ikeda (1991: 291) has identified three different aspects of an interventionist dynamic. One aspect is the general economic process, presented above. A

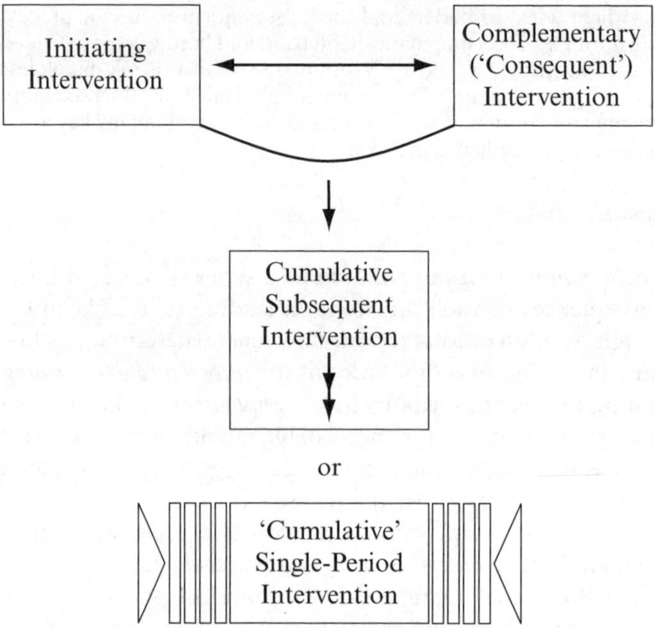

Figure 4.4 Front-loaded interventionism

second is the political motivation, the 'why' behind interventionism, which is examined in the next section of this chapter. A third area is the intended and unintended consequences of intervention, the subject of this section.

The *intended consequences* of an intervention are of interest to the social scientist in order to understand the causal relationship between intention and result. A match of the two equates to success for the involved officials and, on the private side, political entrepreneurs.

Unintended consequences have been a hallmark of interventionism due to complexity of policy-making where 'everything is related to everything else' (Shultz and Dam, 1977: 7). Yet interventionist learning can be expected to increase from greater experience and knowledge by the many stakeholders in the process – regulators, politicians, lobbyists, entrepreneurs, social scientists and the public. The 'unintended' would increasingly turn into the *foreordained collateral* for a more informed debate.

Three categories within unintended consequences can be distinguished: *predictable*, *unpredicted* and *unpredictable* (Bradley, 1996a: pp. 1790–92). The predicable consequences of an intervention are those that can be reasonably foreseen from an understanding of interventionism – such as the implementation of allocation regulation following price regulation.

Even if the price controllers profess surprise at the resulting shortages and the need to manage them, the social scientist can claim to know that this should have been a reasonable expectation.

Other unintended consequences may be less predictable *ex ante* but understandable *ex post*. 'We should have known' might characterize examples as the unpredicted but predictable. Oil protectionism by the United States, as mentioned, inspired the formation of OPEC. Wellhead price controls on crude oil during the 1970s created an oil trading boom in which price-controlled oil was sold back and forth, driving its price up to 'monopolistic' world price. Such gaming defeated the aims of regulators despite their best efforts to prevent it (Bradley, 1996a: 1803–04). Shortages of natural gas in the 1970s caused by price regulation shifted electricity generation toward coal – and thus had the unintended effect of increasing air pollution emissions (Bradley, 1996a: 1267). The rise of regulatory accounting in the public-utility-regulated industries contributed to unsound accounting practices in non-regulated industries (May, 1943: 296–97). All of these examples create potential for interventionist learning to do better next time in analogous situations. In this way, *ex post* understanding leads to *ex ante* prediction.

The deeper the cumulative process, the more unintended and unforeseen the regulatory process becomes. At some point the unforeseen turns into the unforeseeable; the total surprise that is so unique that it is beyond what could have been learned through past experience. An example was a major outbreak of legionnaires' disease in 1983 from bacteria that survived in water that was not heated sufficiently in response to a federal energy conservation mandate (Plouffe, 1983: 769). The complexity of human interaction combined with the tacit nature of much of our knowledge means that external mandates can bring about results that are not merely unforeseen, but unforeseeable.

POLITICAL MOTIVATION

The primary impetus for an intervention into the market economy may be external or internal. An *external intervention* is one that is imposed on an industry from political-sector reformers.[11] The intervention may have some industry support, but such support is secondary to the purely political momentum for the intervention. The political impetus could be from general voter sentiment, factual findings, or lobbying by influential non-industry groups.

An *internal intervention* is driven by vested business lobbying. Such interventions would not have been enacted by reformers without such well-defined support (Kolko, 1963).[12] In the US energy industry, the large majority of interventions have been internally solicited rather than externally imposed (Bradley, 1989, 1996a, 1996b, 1996c). Six categories of internal intervention can be presented in order of their frequency in the oil and gas market (Bradley, 1996a: 1820–51).

1. *Self-horizontal intervention* where a regulation or subsidy is obtained by the firm(s) for all members in its (their) industry for its (their) competitive advantage. Public utility regulation of electricity and manufactured/natural gas is an example. In both cases, certain leaders persuaded a majority of their industry brethren that the benefits of franchise protection would outweigh the costs of rate regulation. The industry activists also persuaded the public and political authorities that natural monopoly regulation was for the social good (Bradley, 1996a: 851–58; 1996b: 3–4; 1996c: 61–72).
2. *Vertical intervention* in which firms obtain regulation of upstream suppliers or downstream customers for competitive advantage. An example is mandatory access to oil or gas pipelines instigated by producers, marketers, and/or end users.
3. *Horizontal intervention* where a regulation is secured by the instigating firms for competitive advantage over one or more rivals. An example is import restrictions sought by domestic producers against importing companies that typically had domestic oil output as well, such as with oil tariffs in the 1930s and oil import quotas in the 1950s (Bradley, 1989: 37–57).
4. *Inter-industry intervention* where a regulation or subsidy is obtained by firms in one industry for competitive advantage at the expense of firms in another industry. An example is inter-modal regulation when railroads successfully lobbied for federal trucking regulation to reduce the competitive advantage of less regulated trucking (Bradley, 1996a: 1779). Another example of interventionist trespassing was a natural gas pipeline company working on behalf of its gas-using copper smelter customers to obtain a tariff on imported copper. The resulting tariff reduced imports, increased domestic smelter utilization, and aided gas demand to benefit the politically active pipeline (Mangan, 1977: 86).
5. *Self-intervention* where a regulation or subsidy is obtained by the instigating firm for itself but not its competitors. The 1979–80 federal bailout of Chrysler Corporation at the expense of relatively healthy Ford and General Motors is such an example. A private antitrust suit filed by a firm against its competitors or suppliers is another example.
6. *Self-vertical intervention* where a regulation or subsidy is obtained for competitive advantage by a firm for itself and for upstream suppliers or downstream customers for competitive advantage. I have not identified

an example in this category, but it is included to complete the possibility frontier.

Interventions that were originally driven externally may come to be internally supported. For example, wellhead price ceilings on crude oil were imposed during President Nixon's price control program in 1973 from a governmental desire for lower oil product prices. Oil refiners then came to support the ceilings to control the cost of their key raw material (Bradley, 1996a: 1841).

A dynamic analysis of political entrepreneurship can uncover new reasons for interventionist support during a cumulative process. An internal intervention could become unpopular with the industry that put it into place and continue on the strength of other industry support or become wholly an external (reformer-driven) intervention. Not only is the original motivation, but *later motivation* crucial for understanding the political considerations behind interventionism.

An intervention can have *both* internal and external roots and/or current support. The analyst must weigh each of the two to understand which one predominates or, in some cases, understand how both are equally important.

Administrative regulation is a vital part of the dynamics of external and internal interventionism in a cumulative process. Regulators by the force of their personality and skill can propel the cumulative process toward more or less interventionism. A typology of *regulatory personalities* based on oil and gas interventionism has been forwarded with six categories (Bradley, 1996a: 1864–66):

- *Professional regulator*, who welcomes activism as a way of life and public calling;
- *Naïve idealist*, whose good intentions toward the powers at hand may be marred by negative experiences and even disillusionment;
- *Opportunist*, who sees interventionism as a means to greater ends of power, income and prestige;
- *Pro-industry regulator*, who combines a propensity to regulate with a bias for the regulated industry;
- *Anti-industry regulator*, who combines a preference for regulation with a bias against the regulated industry; and
- *Pragmatic regulator*, who unlike the opportunist is not wed to the powers at hand but becomes indoctrinated toward regulatory activism.

One category that is missing from the list is one that has come into its own in recent decades – the *pro-market regulator* who works to minimize his or her authority and permitted responsibilities to allow greater scope for market forces.

These classifications can change over time with any particular individual. A regulator could be a blend of the above ideal types. A dynamic analysis must also account for regulatory learning among and between individuals or agencies to understand how, for example, intervention in another industry or country influences 'home' regulation.

It is the job of the applied economist or historian to best describe the regulatory personality at work in a particular situation and add categories of description as the evidence warrants.

A RESEARCH AGENDA

The economics and politics of interventionism is a fertile field for social science research. Great swaths of regulation, taxation and subsidization remain to be analyzed using the above typology – or a more refined one. Such research could map the myriad interventions and identify the weak and strong links among them.[13] With a sufficient data base, descriptive generalizations can be made. How much intervention in an economy at any point is initiating versus consequent? Restated, how *mature* is the interventionist process in an industry, across industries, or economy-wide? How might an interventionist process in one industry affect another industry either deliberately or accidentally?

What is the pattern of cumulative intervention between self-revision, expansion and contraction? What interventionist learning has taken place over time within and between industries and sectors? How might forthcoming intervention be different based on prior experience?

This chapter has focused on regulation. How does the cumulative process differ between regulation, taxation (including monetary inflation), and subsidization? What interaction can be identified between these forms of intervention?

How does government grow? Is the growth of government the result of cumulative intervention in normal times or driven more by 'crisis' intervention that creates a wartime–peacetime dynamic, as posited by Robert Higgs (1987: 18)? What similarities and differences are there between emergency and non-emergency interventionist dynamics?

Why are some interventions relatively stable and others not? Is it inherent in the type of intervention, determined by the regulatory personalities at work with their private-sector counterparts, or the result of exogenous factors?

Turning to the private sector, could a dynamic typology be constructed for entrepreneurial error and plan revision to better understand market processes? And could initiating and consequent/cumulative intervention apply to non-economic self-evolving (undesigned) orders that are subject to major change ('intervention')? For example, a factor in the bankruptcy of Enron in 2001 can be traced back to a decision by the company's board of directors to waive a company-wide conflict-of-interest provision for their chief financial officer (Fusaro and Miller, 2002: 135). Can this entrepreneurial error be understood as either an initiating intervention or part of a cumulative process from prior management or board actions that also perverted norms? Or is there a qualitative difference between coercive intervention in the marketplace by government and 'intervention' in voluntary social orders?[14]

Interventionism in predominantly market economies is ripe for analysis since government-engineered processes can be compared and contrasted to market ones. The above typology can also be used in reverse to understand the dynamics within planned economies where initiating entry of market entrepreneurship can create cumulative deregulation (dis-intervention).

A methodological note is in order. The range of possibilities and special cases outlined above mirrors the panoply of subjective, causal motivations driving the interventionist process. Accordingly, the different categories of this dynamic typology are *qualitative*, making historical judgment necessary to identify initial categories and evaluate linkages as strong or weak, direct or indirect, sequential or intermittent, microeconomic or also macroeconomic, and regional, national or international.

Purposeful human action makes a *quantitative* typology of interventionism difficult and problematic. *Scale* is not a determining factor. Local nondescript regulation that is initiating can be considered part of a cumulative process just as the major revision of a national price control program can. The historian, however, may sharply differentiate between the two.

CONCLUSION

The dynamics of interventionism presented herein is firmly within the Austrian School tradition. Its causality is anchored on the subjective evaluations of economic actors as interpreted by the social scientist. The categories prominently account for future change and *expectations* of future change, not just current relationships.

The typology recognizes *regulation as a process* rather than a state of affairs outside of a few limiting cases (dormant intervention, non-initiating intervention). It recognizes a *learning process* whereby intervention can become more sophisticated (albeit perhaps no more beneficial) over time. A typology inspired by Mises' (incomplete) interventionist thesis can capture and simplify some important elements of interventionism for greater historical understanding – and predictive power going forward. And with a greater appreciation of dynamic interventionism in its intended and unintended variants, the public policy process can become better informed – not so much for greater front-loaded intervention but for greater reliance on voluntarism, market order, and civil society, a conclusion that Don Lavoie's enduring work points toward.

ACKNOWLEDGEMENT

Robert L. Bradley Jr. wishes to thank Jerry Ellig, Richard Fulmer, Robert Higgs, Jack High, and Sanford Ikeda for helpful comments.

NOTES

1. While this chapter focuses on regulation, the typology can apply to the other major forms of intervention – taxation, including inflationary monetary policy, and subsidization.
2. See the critical evaluations of Rothbard's typology in Lavoie (1982: 177–80) and Ikeda (1997: 245–47). As Ikeda states (1997: 31), 'Interventionism, as a system, is more than a set of relations between the market and government, it is a social process.'
3. Some terminological changes have been adopted in this chapter versus my earlier work. The new (old) terms are: dormant (superfluous) intervention; causal (effective) intervention, non-initiating (dormant) intervention, initiating (malignant) intervention, and consequent (cumulative) intervention. Cumulative intervention is now used to cover the entire range of active intervention from initiating to consequent and phased consequent. I am indebted to Sanford Ikeda for his input with these revisions.
4. Don Lavoie, a member of my dissertation committee with the manuscript that resulted in Bradley 1996a, noted the perverse and sometimes unintended consequences of energy regulation (Lavoie, 1985: 134, 166).
5. Pp.72–73.
6. The institutional economist Thorstein Veblen used the term *cumulative* in a parallel sense to my usage above. Substituting 'intervention' for 'individual' and 'agent', the following statement by Veblen (1919: 74–75) can apply to interventionism: 'The economic life history of the individual is a cumulative process of adaptation of means to ends that cumulatively change as the process goes on, both the agent and his environment being at any point the outcome of the last process.' W.J. Baumol (1972: 380), as another example, has stated, 'a number of cumulative processes serve to compound the problems of the city; perhaps these dynamic relationships constitute the critical component of those difficulties.'
7. In such cases, *cumulative initiating interventions* appear where a self-contained series of revisions, expansions, or both flow from a previous expansion of intervention. Again, analytical judgment, not a rigid formula, determines what these categories and time periods are.
8. Discretionary accounting strategies could be used to reduce stated profitability or enlarge the capital account (rate base) on which an allowed rate of return was allowed. Mergers and internal contracting could shift profits from the regulated side to the unregulated

side. A lack of reporting requirements could hamper the ability of regulators to effectively regulate (Bradley, 1996b: 5; Bradley, 1996c: 79–87).

9. Historian William Appleman Williams (1961: 21) observed, 'It should be obvious that ideas persist for a long time after their immediate relevance is gone, and therefore may act as independent variables in later circumstances'.
10. The fact that the Mises' formulation has been 'lost in the wilderness' (Ikeda, 1997: 2) was due to a lack of empirical investigation by Mises and his followers. Other economists, as mentioned above, advanced Mises' insight of interventionist dynamics more than his followers – at least until the 1990s. An exception is Robert Higgs (1987: 258), who critically surveyed the literature on government-growth theory to find that 'each fails to depict the *process* whereby the United States developed its Big Government'.
11. Public-sector intervention can come from the legislative, judicial or executive branch of government. A government municipality would also be considered part of the public sector.
12. Intervention from the private sector would be instigated by a firm (firms) or industry (industries).
13. For such an effort with detailed energy regulation, see Bradley (2006).
14. The 'intervention' in Enron's case was non-coercive but later led to fraudulent activity, a separate but related issue.

BIBLIOGRAPHY

Baumol, W.J. (1972), 'The dynamics of urban problems and its policy implications' in Maurice Peston and Bernard Corry (eds) *Essays in Honour of Lord Robbins*, London: Weidenfeld and Nicolson, pp. 380–91.

Boettke, Peter (1993), *Why Perestroika Failed: The Politics and Economics of Socialist Transformation*, New York: Routledge.

Bradley, Robert (1989), *The Mirage of Oil Protection*, Lanham, MD: University Press of America.

Bradley, Robert (1993), 'Energy choices and market decision making' pamphlet, *Studies in Market-Based Energy Policy, No. 3*, October, Houston: Institute for Energy Research.

Bradley, Robert (1996a), *Oil, Gas and Government: The US Experience*, Lanham, MD: Rowman & Littlefield.

Bradley, Robert (1996b) 'The distortions and dynamics of gas regulation', in Jerry Ellig and Joseph Kalt (eds) *New Horizons in Natural Gas Deregulation*, Westport, CT: Praeger, pp. 1–29.

Bradley, Robert (1996c), 'The origins of political electricity: market failure or political opportunism?', *Energy Law Journal*, **17** (1), 59–102.

Bradley, Robert, and Fulmer, Richard (2004), *Energy: The Master Resource*, Houston: Institute for Energy Research.

Bradley, Robert (2006), 'Interventionist dynamics in the US energy industry', *Advances in Austrian Economics*, **8**, 301–34.

Butler, Eamonn (1988), *Ludwig von Mises: Fountainhead of the Modern Microeconomic Revolution*, Brookfield, VT: Gower Publishing.

Dintenfass, Michael (1992), *Managing Industrial Decline: The British Coal Industry between the Wars*, Columbus: Ohio State University Press.

Fusaro, Peter, and Miller, Ross (2002), *What Went Wrong at Enron*, Hoboken, NJ: John Wiley & Sons.

Hayek, F.A. (1944), *The Road to Serfdom*, Chicago: University of Chicago Press.

Haynes, W. Warren (1953), *Nationalization in Practice: The British Coal Industry*, Boston: Harvard University Graduate School of Business Administration.

Higgs, Robert (1987), *Crisis and Leviathan: Critical Episodes in the Growth of American Government*, New York: Oxford University Press.

High, Jack (1991a), 'Introduction', in Jack High (ed.) *Regulation: Economic Theory and History*, Ann Arbor: University of Michigan, pp. 1–17.

High, Jack (1991b), 'Regulation as a process: on the theory, history, and doctrine of government regulation', in Richard Ebeling (ed.), *Austrian Economics: Perspectives on the Past and Prospects for the Future*, Hillsdale, MI: Hillsdale College Press, pp. 261–79.

Ikeda, Sanford (1991), 'Commentary' to Jack High 'Regulation as a process: on the theory, history, and doctrine of government regulation', Richard Ebeling (ed.), *Austrian Economics: Perspectives on the Past and Prospects for the Future*. Hillsdale, MI: Hillsdale College Press, pp. 291–301.

Ikeda, Sanford (1997), *Dynamics of the Mixed Economy*, New York: Routledge.

Kahn, Alfred (1971), *The Economics of Regulation*, 2 vols, New York: John Wiley & Sons.

Kilbourn, William (1970), *PipeLine: TransCanada and the Great Debate, A History of Business and Politics*, Toronto: Clarke, Irwin & Company Limited.

Kirzner, Israel (1985) 'The perils of regulation: a market-process approach', *Discovery and the Capitalist Process*, Chicago: University of Chicago Press, pp. 119–49.

Kirzner, Israel (2001), *Ludwig von Mises: The Man and His Economics*, Wilmington, DE: ISI Books.

Kolko, Gabriel (1963), *The Triumph of Conservatism*, New York: The Free Press.

Kolko, Gabriel (1970), 'The decline of American radicalism in the twentieth century', in James Weinstein and David Eakins (eds) *For a New America*, New York: Random House, pp. 197–220.

Lavoie, Don (1982), 'The development of the Misesian theory of interventionism', in Israel Kirzner (ed.) *Method, Process, and Austrian Economics*, Lexington, MA: Lexington Books, pp. 169–83.

Lavoie, Don (1985), *National Economic Planning*, Cambridge, MA: Ballinger Publishing Company.

Mangan, Frank (1977), *The Pipeliners*, El Paso: Guynes Press.

May, George (1943), 'Accounting and regulation', *Journal of Accountancy*, October, 295–301.

McKie, James (1970), 'Regulation and the free market: the problem of boundaries', *Bell Journal of Economics*, Spring, 6–26.

Mises, Ludwig von ([1952], 1980), 'Middle-of-the-road policy leads to socialism', *Planning for Freedom*, South Holland, IL: Libertarian Press, pp. 18–35.

Plouffe, Joseph et al. (1983), 'Relationship between colonization of hospital buildings with *Legionella pneumophila* and hot water temperatures', *Applied and Environmental Microbiology*, September, 769–70.

Rothbard, Murray ([1962], 1970), *Man, Economy & State: A Treatise on Economic Principles*, Los Angeles: Nash Publishing.

Rothbard, Murray ([1963], 2000), *America's Great Depression*, Auburn: Ludwig von Mises Institute.

Rothbard, Murray ([1963], 1990), *What Has Government Done to Our Money?*, Auburn: Ludwig von Mises Institute.

Rothbard, Murray (1970), *Power & Market: Government and the Economy*, Menlo Park, CA: Institute for Humane Studies.

Rothbard, Murray ([1971], 1997), 'Ludwig von Mises and the paradigm for our age', in Rothbard, *The Logic of Collective Action I: Method, Money, and the Austrian School*, Cheltenham, UK and Lyme, USA: Edward Elgar, pp. 195–210.

Ruggles, C.O. (1937), *Aspects of the Organization, Functions, and Financing of State Public Utility Regulation*, Boston: Harvard University Graduate School of Business Administration.

Shultz, George, and Dam, Kenneth (1977), *Economic Policy Beyond the Headlines*, New York: W.W. Norton.

Smith, Adam ([1776], 1981), *An Inquiry into the Nature and Causes of the Wealth of Nations*, Indianapolis: Liberty Fund.

Sweeney, James (1992), *The California Electricity Crisis*, Stanford: Hoover Institution Press.

Veblen, Thorstein (1919), *The Place of Science in Modern Civilisation and Other Essays*, New York: B. W. Huebsch.

Williams, William Appleman (1961), *The Contours of American History*, New York: World Publishing.

Winston, Clifford (1998), 'US industry adjustment to economic deregulation', *Journal of Economic Perspectives*, Summer, pp. 89–110.

PART 3

Information technology

5. Institutions as abstraction boundaries

Bill Tulloh and Mark S. Miller*

INTRODUCTION

The exploration of the knowledge problem – the ability of an economic system to generate and sustain a complex structure of production based on an extensive division of knowledge – formed a central theme of Don Lavoie's research. His critique of central planning and investigations into the nature of knowledge led him to emphasize the indispensable role of the market process in solving the knowledge problem.[1] Only the market process can harness the diverse knowledge of millions of people into an evolving pattern of cooperative relationships that serves an ever increasing variety of individual purposes.

According to the critique of central planning developed by Mises, Hayek, Lavoie and others, central planners lack the knowledge necessary to successfully plan production and calculate economic tradeoffs. Central planners do not have access to the tacit and contextual knowledge that individuals use in planning their activities, nor do they have access to competitive price and profit signals that are required for calculating tradeoffs among the myriad uses of scarce means. The effective use of knowledge, Lavoie argues, requires a decentralized solution – a solution provided by the market process.

For the market process to make effective use of knowledge, it must solve two problems: 1) it must divide knowledge to capture gains from specialization, and 2) it must coordinate the separate plans of market participants to secure gains from cooperation. Gains from specialization arise when 'people can use other people's knowledge to their own advantage without themselves acquiring it' (Vaughn, 1999, p. 133). Specialization economizes on knowledge production by reusing proven solutions. Specialization increases knowledge production by encouraging the discovery of new solutions; knowledge, as Brian Loasby reminds us, 'grows through division' (Loasby, 1999, p. 50).

Each increase in specialization 'necessitates additional coordination somewhere in the social structure' (High, 1986, p. 117). Specialized activities must be combined with complementary activities, and individual plans based on time- and place-specific knowledge must be coordinated with those of others (Hayek 1937, 1945). The market process must do more than just coordinate plans based on dispersed knowledge that exists at a point in time; it must also adapt these plans to new knowledge constantly being created in the pursuit of further gains from specialization and cooperation.

The market process solves the twin problems of the division and coordination of knowledge through abstraction. Abstraction modularizes knowledge. Abstractions, by selectively hiding information, enable market participants to make use of a complex network of specialized knowledge without needing to acquire the knowledge themselves. As one computer scientist (Turbak, 2002, p. 4) describes it:

> Abstraction is ubiquitous in the modern world and we depend on it for functioning in our day-to-day lives. We are able to use a wide array of machines and devices (e.g. cars, telephones, stereos, computers) without having to understand the details of how they work. Supermarkets, department stores, and utilities are purveyors of abstractions; for the most part, we do not need or want to know how a loaf of bread is baked, how a piece of clothing is made, or how our electricity, water, and gas are produced.

To facilitate cooperation, abstractions must be made meaningful to others so that they can use them for their own purposes. Programmers call the process of carving up knowledge into meaningful units creating abstraction boundaries. An abstraction boundary captures a specialized solution to a type of problem and packages it for reuse. The abstraction boundary hides the details of how the solution is implemented from potential users, while providing them with the information they need to apply the solution to their particular problem. Programmers use abstraction to divide programs into modules that can be combined with other modules through well-defined interfaces (the boundaries) to create complex behavior.

Abstraction boundaries enhance cooperation by reducing the cost of using the solutions.[2] Abstraction boundaries limit what clients need to know about solution providers, and what solution providers need to know about their clients. The boundary defines what the solution is, but not how it is provided, nor why it is used. Clients, by orienting their plans to the boundary, can ignore implementation details which are likely to change.[3] Providers, meanwhile, are free to change how they provide the solution so long as they continue to provide the type of solution defined by the boundary. Abstraction boundaries enable both solution providers and their clients to coordinate and adapt their particular plans based on the abstract plans embodied in the boundary.

By borrowing concepts from software engineering, we are drawing on work done during the late 1980s and early 1990s by Lavoie, the current authors and others. The Agorics Project explored the relationships between object-oriented concepts from software engineering and the market institutions of property and contract.[4] As Lavoie remarked, 'In particular, the concepts surrounding the idea of "modularity" have proven valuable in rethinking the nature of property rights and evolutionary change in market systems.' (Lavoie, 1994, p. xi). The recognition that software developers faced a knowledge problem analogous to that of markets and that they had independently evolved solutions that resemble market solutions suggested that this would be a fruitful line of research to increase our understanding of both systems.

We argue that the commonality of solutions is no mere coincidence, but a consequence of underlying principles for organizing complex adaptive systems. The concepts of abstraction and modularity that underlie the object-oriented approach to organizing a complex software system also underlie the market process approach to organizing a complex structure of production.[5]

The Austrian vision of the market process can be enhanced by recognizing the role that abstraction boundaries play in dividing knowledge and coordinating plans. Hayek's (1973, 1976) account of an abstract order based on abstract rules provides a framework for understanding abstraction boundaries, but fails to acknowledge their role. What Lachmann (1971) calls secondary institutions – the day-to-day institutions towards which people orient their actions – fills the gap, capturing what we mean by abstraction boundaries. Abstraction boundaries also shed light on how markets deal with the problem of institutional coherence and change (Lachmann 1971, 1979, 1991). By facilitating orderly change, abstraction boundaries coordinate plans through time. Following Lavoie, we argue that abstraction boundaries emerge as part of the market process; they are best viewed as negotiated categories resulting from the dynamic process of exchange and dialogue.

BETWEEN ABSTRACT RULES AND CONCRETE PURPOSES

Friedrich Hayek, in particular, emphasizes the fundamental importance of abstraction. Abstractions, he explains, 'are a means to cope with the complexity of the concrete which our mind is not capable of fully mastering' (1973, p. 29). What he calls 'the primacy of the abstract' (1978), is deeply woven into his vision of the market order, visible in many diverse strands of his thought. The primacy of the abstract stems from his work on the mind, begun while he was his twenties and later elaborated and presented in *The Sensory Order* (1952b). His theory of the mind informs numerous aspects of his work including the limits to understanding complex phenomena, his concept of spontaneous order, and the importance of abstract rules of conduct. While Hayek paints a complex picture of the multi-faceted role of abstraction, he does not seem to recognize the role of abstraction boundaries. Abstraction boundaries, we argue, emerge as a natural complement to his discussion of abstract orders based on abstract rules.

Hayek presents the mind as a system of classification. We do not first perceive the world in its detailed particulars and then build up more abstract representations. To the contrary, our ability to perceive particulars depends on pre-existing abstractions which we use to classify our various sense perceptions. Perception must be viewed as an act of classification; we perceive only certain abstract properties of objects, not concrete details. As Heinrich Klüver elaborates, 'What we perceive are never unique properties of individual objects, but always only properties which the objects have in common with other objects. Perception is thus always an interpretation, the placing of something into one of several classes of objects.' (Hayek, 1952b, p. xviii).

As Hayek makes clear, the classifying of objects does not proceed based on a simple one-to-one mapping of observed objects into mental categories. It is rather the 'product of superimposition of many "classifications" of the events perceived according to their significance in many respects' (1978, p. 36). Each classification triggers a response in terms of a kind of action; we respond to a certain class of events with a disposition to a certain kind of action. It is only through the superimposition of many classifications and dispositions that a particular action is specified: 'both the specification of a particular experienced event and the specification of a particular response to it are the result of a superimposition of many such dispositions' (Hayek, 1978, p. 40).

Specification by superimposition, Hayek claims, is the 'best description of the mechanism for the operation of … the primacy of the abstract, because each of its causal determinants decides only one of the attributes of the resulting action' (1978, p. 48). The specification of action through the superimposition of multiple dispositions enables the individual to make use of knowledge of typical aspects of a situation while adapting the response to the unique aspects. The various dispositions serve as adaptations to the typical features of the environment. By superimposing many dispositions, we are able to generate unique responses to novel situations.

Hayek, especially in his later work, presents a vision of the market order that is remarkably similar to his account of the sensory order. Both mind and market are examples of what Butos and McQuade (2002) describe as knowledge-generating orders – orders where the knowledge generated consists of classifications meaningful in the context of that order. They argue that 'it is strictly incorrect to say that the market gathers up "divided" individual knowledge and makes this information available to many others .... Instead, the market takes, as input, knowledge in the individual sense ... and classifies this, producing a totally different kind of knowledge.' (1999, p. 29).

Classifications provide knowledge that others can use. They abstract from detailed particular circumstances and purposes to provide reusable knowledge of general circumstances that can be applied to multiple purposes. They enable individuals to economize on knowledge by substituting abstract knowledge of the class for specific knowledge of the instances. Hayek's work suggests that these classifications exist at multiple layers and adjust continuously to changing circumstances and accumulated experience. This multi-layered view of the knowledge-generating properties of the market order stands in contrast, however, to the stark distinction Hayek seems to draw between the roles that abstract rules and concrete purposes play in creating that order.

Hayek argues that the emergence of the extended order of cooperation (1989) rests on the gradual change from a society organized around the common pursuit of a limited number of concrete purposes to a society organized around adherence to a common set of abstract rules of conduct that coordinate a countless number of diverse purposes.[6] Rules of conduct are abstract in the sense that they abstract from the concrete purposes and circumstances. They abstract from particular circumstances of time and place to capture certain general circumstances that have proven useful for the pursuit of many diverse plans. Abstract rules are purpose independent: they serve no particular purpose, but improve the chances for success of a large number of different purposes.

Actions based on abstract rules generate an abstract order. Abstract orders are formed spontaneously, not by deliberate arrangement. They are based on abstract relations serving multiple purposes, not concrete relations serving a single purpose. By serving multiple purposes, the complexity of abstract orders is 'not limited to what a human mind can master' (1973, p. 38). The abstract order exists independently of any particular member; the order persists through the abstract relations that define it. Hayek (1973, p. 39) tells us that abstract orders

> ... consist of a system of abstract relations between elements which are also defined only by abstract properties.... The significance of the abstract character of such orders rests on the fact that they may persist while all the particular elements they comprise, and even the number of such elements, change. All that is necessary to preserve such an abstract order is that a certain structure of

relationships be maintained, or that elements of a certain kind (but variable in number) continue to be related in a certain manner.

Abstract rules enhance the ability of individuals to predict the actions of others. They increase predictability by delimiting protected domains of actions. Domains of action provide a place where individuals can plan based on their particular knowledge. They provide a space where individuals can make use of their resources free from interference by others. Abstract rules must do more, however, than just prevent plan interference by delimiting protected domains of actions. They must provide us with a way to connect these separate domains into cooperative relationships. Hayek (1973, p. 99) tells us that:

> What is required if the separate actions of the individuals are to result in an overall order is that they not only do not unnecessarily interfere with one another, but also that in those respects in which the success of the action of the individuals depends on some matching action by others, there will be at least a good chance that this correspondence will actually occur. But all rules can achieve in this respect is to make it easier for people … to form that match; abstract rules cannot actually secure that this will always happen.

While Hayek highlights the importance of matching complementary actions, he provides us with little guidance on how the matching process takes place. His distinction between purpose-independent rules and purposeful action suggests that coordination occurs at the level of concrete purposes and plans. The attempt to match concrete plans directly with other concrete plans, however, leads to plan failure as circumstances change. In the face of change, people must constantly adapt their plans in unforeseeable ways. Concrete plans are highly brittle in the face of such changes. All plans, however, need not share the same level of concreteness; plans may differ in their degree of specificity. Abstract plans that encompass a range of specific purposes, are likely to be more robust in the face of changing circumstances. By capturing the abstract aspects of many individual plans and embodying them in market institutions, market participants can enhance their ability to coordinate their plans through time. The matching process occurs not through direct matching of concrete plans but through matching of abstract plans embodied in institutions.

The problem with Hayek's treatment of abstract rules, one might say, is that it is too abstract. He does not explain how these abstract rules are specified into concrete actions that coordinate plans. While he highlights the importance of judge-made law in delimiting domains of action, he fails to provide an account of how market participants through their everyday actions convert abstract rules into institutions that facilitate the matching of complementary activities. The boundaries defined by abstract rules must do more than separate activities where they conflict. They must also combine activities where they complement. Hayek's account leaves a large gap in how this occurs; it leaves a gap between abstract rules and concrete purposes. What is missing is the role that market institutions play in filling the gap by classifying useful knowledge and facilitating the matching process required for its reuse.[7]

SECONDARY INSTITUTIONS AS ABSTRACTION BOUNDARIES

Ludwig Lachmann, in his 1971 book, *The Legacy of Max Weber*, discusses the role that market institutions play in coordinating plans. Like Hayek, he highlights the fundamental role played by property, contract, and the rule of law in shaping the market order. Unlike Hayek, he moves beyond abstract rules to discuss the specific institutions of the market order, which he calls secondary institutions. Secondary institutions 'gradually evolve as a result of market processes and other forms of spontaneous individual action' (1971, p. 81). They are the familiar institutions of day-to-day life: the restaurants, the banks, the post offices, the stock exchanges, and so on.[8]

These concrete institutions embody abstract plans. They fill the gap between purpose-independent abstract rules and specific concrete purposes. A plan, Lachmann tells us, 'is but a generalization of purpose' (1971, p. 33). It abstracts the multiple purposes, means, and obstacles pursued by an individual into a comprehensive framework for action. Similarly, a secondary institution is but a generalization of plan, it abstracts from the multiple plans of various individuals to provide a common point of orientation. As Lachmann explains, 'If the plan is a mental scheme in which the conditions of action are coordinated, we may regard institutions as it were, as orientation schemes of the second order, to which planners orient their plans as actors orient their actions to a plan' (1971, p. 50).

Secondary institutions serve as means of orientation that help coordinate action in society. By orienting our plans towards these institutions, we make use of a vast amount of knowledge without the need to acquire it in detail. Lachmann (1971, p. 50) gives the example of a post office.

> Whether we post a letter, wait for a train, or draw a cheque, our action is in each case orientated towards a complex network of human action of which we know enough to make it serve our ends, though we may know next to nothing about the internal working order of these institutions. We know of course that such an internal working-order exists, but in our everyday life take no interest whatever in its details. We know very well that the Post Office works according to

> a general plan, but such knowledge as we have about it is usually quite irrelevant to the achievement of our purpose in posting a letter. Only a few aspects of this general plan, perhaps the times of collection and delivery of mail, need be of concern to us.

By drawing our attention to the aspects of an institution with which one interacts, Lachmann is presenting what software designers refer to as an abstraction boundary – the interface between actors. The abstraction boundary captures the abstract plan common to the various actors. The actors coordinate their actions to the boundary, not to the detailed plans of the other actors. As Lachmann notes, the postal customers need concern themselves with only a few aspects of the post office's plan. These few aspects form the abstraction boundary. The post office communicates these aspects to the postal customers, who rely on these details in forming their own particular plans.

The abstraction boundary defines a division of knowledge. Instead of each of us having to deliver our own letters and packages, we can rely on the specialized services of a post office. We no longer deliver our own mail because some entrepreneur, forgotten to history, recognized a profitable division of labor and created an abstraction boundary.[9] The entrepreneur 1) recognized an abstraction – the commonalities in the separate plans of people delivering their own letters, 2) drew a boundary around the abstraction defining the service of mail delivery, and 3) encapsulated the implementation of these services behind the abstraction boundary while convincing others that it would serve their purposes to use this new service.[10] The post office, by reusing its specialized knowledge across many instances of mail delivery, is able to capture economies of specialization. Postal customers benefit when the cost of their using a post office to deliver a letter is less than the cost of their delivering it themselves.

Institutions as abstraction boundaries are not the same as organizations. An abstraction boundary is the interface that lies between actors, such as that between postal customers and the post office. The post office as an organization differs from post office as an abstraction boundary. The post office as an abstraction boundary represents a particular kind of provider–client relationship. The post office as an organization implements the services defined by the abstraction boundary. The boundary defines how the post office as an organization relates to other elements of the more comprehensive order of which it is part. A concrete post office instantiates the abstract interface and implements the delivery services. It is part of a larger postal system that encompasses additional entities such as delivery vehicles, warehouses, sorting machines and tracking facilities. From the point of view of the postal customer, however, the implementation detail is hidden behind the abstraction boundary of the post office.

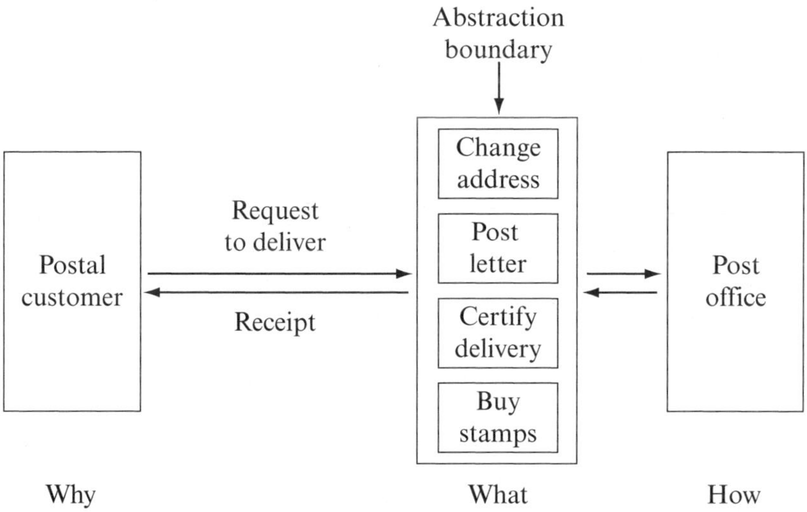

Note: Adapted from Carrano & Prichard, 2001.

Figure 5.1 Abstraction boundary for post office

The abstraction boundary of the post office separates the relationship into distinct actors; it forms the interface between a postal customer requesting delivery of a letter and a post office that fulfills that request. The boundary describes the vocabulary used in the dialogue between a post office and its customers: post my letter, change my address, certify delivery, and so on.[11] The abstraction boundary also defines what it means for a post office to be an instance of the type post office. Objects of the same type share the same interface. The abstraction boundary embodies and reifies what it means to be an object of a particular type. It defines what services can be expected from a post office, while distinguishing this type of service from other types of services.[12]

ABSTRACT PLANS SERVING ABSTRACT PURPOSES.

The abstraction boundary enables what software designers refer to as separation of concerns; it separates:

- *why* a customer wants to mail a letter (the concern of the postal customer) from,
- *what* it means to mail a letter (the mutual concern of the parties) from,
- *how* a letter gets delivered (the concern of the postal system).

The post office does not need to know that Alice wants to invite Bob to a birthday party, or that Carol wants to send her monthly payment to the power company. The boundary abstracts from the details of the customers' plans to focus on the common attributes of transporting a sealed envelope to a specified address. Similarly, the postal customer does not need to know how the commitment to deliver a letter will be implemented. They do not need to know that the mail will be delivered using a tractor-trailer truck if the address is within 500 miles, or delivered by airplane if the address is more than 500 miles away. Both parties, however, need to know the 'what', that is, the specific steps needed to post the letter. This is the boundary.

By abstracting on the one side from the specific purpose of a request, and on the other side from the specific way the requested action is implemented, the abstraction boundary enables a large degree of flexibility on both sides. The post office can accommodate a large range of specific reasons for mailing a letter, including ones not yet known. At the same time, the post office is free to try to discover better ways of delivering letters. The entities obtain this flexibility because of the stability of the boundary. The abstraction boundary, by capturing the mutual concerns of both parties while abstracting from their particular purposes, is able to remain relatively stable in the face of change. The stability and familiarity of the category of a post office makes it easy, for example, for someone visiting a new town to locate a new instance of the type post office and mail a post card home even without any prior knowledge of that particular post office.

The creation of an abstraction boundary converts a specific relationship into an abstract relationship. A specific relationship directly links a particular solution to a particular purpose. An abstract relationship links a type of solution to a type of purpose through an abstraction boundary. A relationship is abstract when the common services defined in the boundary can be used for multiple purposes, and provided by multiple providers. The abstraction boundary limits what the parties need to know about each other; it allows the provider to treat as common a diverse set of clients, and the client to treat as substitutes a diverse set of providers.

An abstract relationship combines both reusability and polymorphism. Reusability occurs when a single solution can be reused for multiple purposes. Polymorphism occurs when multiple providers can serve a single purpose. Reusability generalizes across the purposes of the various clients (the

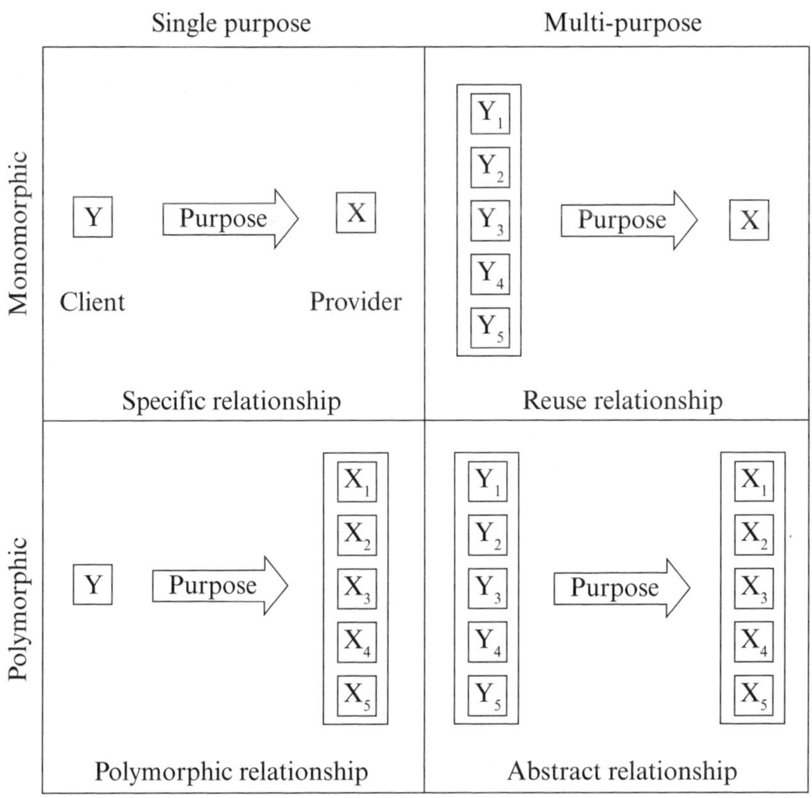

Figure 5.2 From specific to abstract relationships

particular whys) to focus on the aspects they share in common. Polymorphism generalizes across the implementations of the various providers (the particular hows) to focus on the common services that they provide. Polymorphism enables clients to substitute one provider for another so long as they provide the same type of service; it shields the clients not only from how the services are provided, but also from who provides the service.

Lachmann's post office example highlights the advantages of moving from specific to abstract relationships. Organizing around specific relationships is neither economical nor adaptable. We would not expect to see mail delivery organized around specific relationships on a large scale: a post office specializing in delivering Alice's birthday cards to her grandmother, or a post office specializing in delivering Bob's payment to the gas company. By abstracting from the various purposes, a provider can reuse the common mail delivery solution for multiple purposes.

By abstracting from the particular implementations, clients can substitute different providers of those services, based on their more exact requirements. Wirfs-Brock and McKean (2002, p. 3) use the example of mail delivery to make this point to programmers.

> Objects that play the same role can be interchanged. For example, there are several providers that can deliver letters and packages: DHL, FedEx, UPS, Post, Airborne. They all have the same purpose, if not the same way of carrying out their business. You choose from among them according to the requirements that you have for delivery. Is it one-day, book rate, valuable, heavy, flammable? You pick the mail carrier that meets your requirements.

Abstraction boundaries play an important cognitive role by classifying various activities into types of activities, and by making these classifications accessible to others. The boundary takes an abstraction and makes it concrete. It reifies the abstraction by articulating it in the design of the interface – in its contracts, in its store designs, in its customer-facing procedures, and in the design of its products. The abstraction boundary is the invention of the possibility that two entities can interact in a particular way; without the boundary the abstraction is too intangible to be useful.

In the market context, abstraction boundaries often take the form of transaction boundaries. The abstraction boundary increases the potential for gains from trade by reducing the costs for people seeking a particular kind of trade. An abstraction boundary increases the chances that a particular kind of trade will happen by limiting the types of transactions that can occur through the boundary. There are all sorts of potential gains from trade that may exist between a particular postal customer and a particular postal worker. For example, the postal customer may be in the market for a used car, and the postal worker may be looking to sell his old one. However, this kind of transaction is not permitted through the boundary of the post office. The post office enables the realization of some of the potential gains from trade between postal customers and the postal workers, while ignoring a vast number of other potential gains from trade. By doing so, it increases the chances that many more postal customers and post offices will realize the gains from posting a letter. The abstraction boundary serves as a meeting place for people seeking a particular kind of gain from trade; it provides a familiar place to which people seeking a type of transaction can orient their plans.[13]

The concept of abstraction boundary can also help us answer Lachmann's question of 'How is the need for coherence and permanence reconciled with that for flexibility in the real world?' (1971, p. 90). Secondary institutions provide stability with flexibility. Lachmann uses the metaphor of a hinge. He writes, 'one is tempted to think of the institutional order as an array of hinges: the institutions within each hinge can move a good deal, if within limits, but the hinges themselves cannot.' (1979, p. 253). Abstraction boundaries play the role of the hinges, enabling flexibility on both sides of the boundary. Relatively stable abstraction boundaries permit a wide range of changes in purposes and implementations through the separation of concerns. Changes on either side of the boundary will not upset plans so long as the interface does not change.

Abstraction boundaries can coordinate existing plans while supporting new requirements through what programmers call subtyping. A subtype extends the scope of an existing abstraction boundary by adding additional behaviors. Since a subtype must fulfill all of the obligations defined by its supertype, it can be substituted in place of its supertype without upsetting the expectations of existing clients for that type. This enables what Lachmann calls the widening of institutions.[14] We can adapt to change 'not by the creation of a new institution, nor by replacing an old by a new, but by "widening" an existing institution in such a way that it can serve new interests without upsetting the plans which have thus far made use of it.' (1971, p. 91).

PROGRAMMING AS PLAN COORDINATION

As Lachmann's post office example suggests, programming can be usefully analyzed in terms of the Hayekian notion of plan coordination. Programs perform actions: plans are specified by the programmer at design-time; plans are executed by the computer at run-time.[15] In order to cope with the intellectual complexity of large programs, programmers divide a program into separate modules, each embodying its own plan of action. The challenge facing programmers can therefore be seen as one of plan coordination; programmers must coordinate the plans of the various modules to ensure the harmonious working of the overall system.

Most software bugs result from plan interference. Breakdown occurs because of coordination failure between parts of the program. Actions taken by one module destroy the assumptions used by another module in planning its actions. Hidden dependencies between modules render assumptions unstable and plans mutually incompatible. For example with procedural programming, the plans of two subroutines may conflict because they unknowingly share the same data. Subroutine A performs a calculation and stores the resulting data for future use. Meanwhile, subroutine B performs its operation overwriting A's data. Subroutine A retrieves the data for further processing, not realizing that it has been modified by B – leading to unexpected results and potential system failure.

The history of software development can be seen as an ongoing development of techniques – embodied in programming languages and development methods – to cope with the challenges of plan coordination through time.[16] Centrally planned approaches to software development broke down in the face of increasing complexity, forcing programmers to introduce a division of labor into their programs. Attempts to divide labor according to the principles of procedural programming enabled programmers to build more complex programs, but were subject to massive plan failure when program requirements changed. Procedural programming, which divided the tasks into subroutines while keeping program data in common, could not easily adapt to changing circumstances. Object-oriented programming improved on procedural programming by dividing both the tasks and the data; it combined the data with the procedures that act on it. By eliminating the dependencies caused by shared data, it provided greater flexibility in adapting to change.

Object-oriented programming divides a program into separate objects that are each instances of a particular type. An object combines a set of related behaviors (its methods) with its private data (its state). The object's type is defined by its set of methods. An object's state – its particular circumstances of time and place – is said to be encapsulated because only its methods have the ability to access or modify that state. Other objects cannot directly access the internal state of another object; they must send a request to the object asking it to perform a particular action.[17]

The move from procedural programming to object-oriented programming can be seen as a move from concrete plans to abstract plans. Objects do not coordinate their actions with the specific plans of other objects; they coordinate their actions to the abstract aspects of those plans. An object's interface abstracts from a specific plan to a kind of plan. Object-oriented programming, or more generally the move to encapsulation, message passing, and polymorphism, is essentially trying to move from plan coordination to pattern coordination (O'Driscoll and Rizzo, 1985), where what is meant by patterns is abstracted plans. It does this by re-discovering the virtues of property rights and contract.[18]

Hayek's explanation of the primary virtue of property rights for organizing large scale economic activity parallels the rationale for encapsulation in object-oriented systems: to provide a domain (an object's encapsulation boundary) in which an agent (the object) can execute plans (the object's methods) that use resources (an object's private state), where the proper functioning of these plans depends on these resources not being used simultaneously by conflicting plans. By dividing up the resources of society (the state of a computational system) into separately owned chunks (private object states), we enable a massive number of plans to make use of a massive number of resources without needing to resolve a massive number of conflicting assumptions.

Objects must collaborate to fulfill their responsibilities. They collaborate by sending messages requesting other objects to perform an action. Message passing distributes the responsibility for performing the work of an application across many objects. Each object is responsible for performing services or knowing information useful to others (Wirfs-Brock and McKean, 2002). The object receiving the message is responsible for determining how to respond to the message. The object's interface defines the set of messages to which it will respond. The interface represents a contract between the object making requests and the object providing the requested service.[19] The contract provides 'a list of the requests that can be made of the server by the client. Both must fulfill the contract: the client by making only those requests it specifies, and the server by responding only to those requests.' (Wirfs-Brock and Wilkerson 1989, p. 72).

Object-oriented programming reduces plan interference by encapsulating the computational state of a system into separate objects. It increases plan coordination by combining objects through message passing. Message passing increases the adaptability of the system by basing the interaction between specific objects on the abstraction boundary – the abstract relationship between types of objects. Collaboration between concrete plans occurs through the coordination of abstract plans.

The run-time composition of objects by message passing stands in contrast to the design-time organization of abstraction boundaries into a type hierarchy. The type hierarchy defines a static relationship between types, organizing them from more general supertypes to more specific subtypes. The run-time interaction of objects consists of the dynamically formed relationships among specific objects.[20] Programmers can enhance the ability of the program to adapt to unforeseen change by 'programming to an interface and not an implementation' (Gamma et al., 1995, p. 18). By programming to an interface, the programmer orients the behavior of an object to the abstract plans of other objects, not to the concrete plans of specific objects. Objects with different concrete plans can be substituted for one another at run-time without requiring the programmer to rewrite and recompile the program. Market participants, similarly, gain adaptability by orienting their plans to an interface and not an implementation. Programmers and market participants benefit from orienting their plans to stable boundaries, not frequently changing concrete plans.

Programmers create the abstraction boundaries of the program at design-time. The major creative act of programming is to look at some large set of computational activity and to discover boundaries in it – to find distinctions that enable programmers to see commonalities or patterns. The distinction reveals commonalities – among providers on one side and clients on the other – that were previously unnoticed. Once the commonality or pattern is recognized, programmers attempt to find a way to package it, so that they can embody the usefulness of that part of the computational space into a module that other programmers can use.

The perspective of programming as plan coordination also sheds light on the role of the entrepreneur. It suggests that the role of the entrepreneur is to create and adapt abstraction boundaries. Programming to abstraction boundaries adds flexibility at run-time. The boundaries, however, remained fixed; interaction occurs between objects with fixed boundaries. The abstract plans are fixed by the programmer in advance; they do not change during run-time.

Several software designers have proposed moving to market-oriented programming as a way to increase run-time flexibility.[21] Market-oriented programming introduces price signals into a program. Price signals allow objects to dynamically trade-off the scarce computational resources used in carrying out their plans. Objects are alert to opportunities presented by changes in price, and thus are able to dynamically shift from one plan to another. All of the adaptation of plans, however, must still take place within the divisions created by the programmer; the system still does not have creativity in the sense of being able to create new divisions. New abstractions are created outside of the system. It is the programmers, the human beings, who create new abstraction boundaries; the evenly rotating carrying out of plans is something we get the computer to do.

Our distinction bears a resemblance to the one that Buchanan and Vanberg (2002) make between creative and reactive choice. Creative choice creates alternatives from which other individuals choose; reactive choice is choice among the alternatives presented. Abstraction boundaries define what alternatives are available. New alternatives are created by changing the abstraction boundaries. Objects at run-time can react to the alternatives presented to them by the existing abstraction boundaries, but they normally cannot change the boundaries to create new alternatives.[22]

LAVOIE AND THE RE-CATEGORIZATION OF THE MARKET ORDER

By recognizing the role of the software designer in creating abstraction boundaries, we highlight an important difference between abstraction boundaries in software and those in markets. In markets, there is no programmer standing outside the economy ready to change the boundaries; there is no exogenous source of change. Changes to abstraction boundaries occur as part of the ongoing market process. Market participants are engaged in the process of drawing and redrawing abstraction boundaries. Abstraction boundaries emerge as negotiated categories that help orient plans.

The software design process is highly collaborative; software designers engage in a process of dialogue – with each other and with prospective users of the system – in order to discover abstraction boundaries.[23] The importance of dialogue in creating abstraction boundaries should not be surprising. As Hayek tells us, 'We learn to classify through language, with which we not merely label known kinds of objects but specify what we are to regard as objects or events of the same or different kinds.' (1989, p. 15).

Don Lavoie (1990b, 2003), in particular, has emphasized the creative role of dialogue in markets. He draws on the work of Gadamer (1989) to emphasize the emergence of new meaning from the spontaneous ordering process of dialogue – a process writ large in the spontaneous ordering process of the market. Lavoie argues that, 'Markets are an extension of language, and they work through concrete acts of articulation, whether oral or written or electronic. You could say that markets simply add whole new kinds of texts, prices, profits, contracts, advertising, etc., to the conversation.' (2003, p. 12). He goes on to urge that, 'Among the institutional forms that Austrian economists ought to pay attention to are the articulation processes and the resulting texts through which human actors communicate their meanings.' (2003, p. 16).

We suggest that we ought to pay attention to these institutional forms because they represent the process by which abstraction boundaries evolve and the means by which they are formed. Market articulations are attempts to create shared categories of meaning that enable us to coordinate our actions. Abstraction boundaries, in order to serve as orientation points, must be articulated; they must be made concrete.[24] Articulation in dialogue – by words and by texts – creates a space where shared meanings can form. Articulation in markets – by contracts, by product designs, and by other marketing efforts – creates a space where shared categories can form. These shared categories serve as points of orientation that help coordinate plans. As Peter Lewin writes, 'Expectations and plans are, for the most part, fulfilled because of the existence in the social world of shared categories and standards that facilitate the synchronization and coordination of activities.' (1999, p. 34).

Lewin illustrates this point by examining the emergence of new categories of products. These categories emerge from attempts to articulate the purpose of new products – how they are similar, how they are different, and how they relate to other products. He (1999, p. 39) writes:

> We cope with the complexity in the world by converging on institutions. Thus once the arrival of new products, made possible by the development of a new technology, has been digested, new categories of classifications tend to be developed, into which these products are grouped. These categories emerge spontaneously out of individual attempts to communicate the attributes of the new products. A good example is the products of the computer industry. A whole range of products exist, whose workings remain a mystery to the vast majority of people, but whose purposes needed to be explained. Laptops evolved into notebooks, micro computers into desktops.... All these shorthands provide the increasingly informed public with a way to tailor their expectations when choosing between products.

Shared categories, the abstraction boundaries of the market, emerge from the interaction of entrepreneurs and their potential customers. They emerge from the attempt by entrepreneurs to define what services their products can provide; and the attempt by their customers to express what services they desire. Entrepreneurs orient their actions to existing categories: they mimic current categories by imitation; they modify them by differentiation; and they try to create new ones through innovation. Successful categories, those that persist, reflect not just the action of entrepreneurs, but also the responses of potential customers. Potential customers express their requirements through various means, through negotiation, through novel uses of products, through responses to market research, and ultimately through their purchase or failure to purchase the entrepreneur's offering. The resulting categories become embodied in the design of products, in the design of secondary institutions, and in the grouping of product and institutional types into more general categories that help orient people's actions. Shared categories emerge from the market process of dialogue and exchange.[25]

Lavoie argues that 'entrepreneurship should be conceptualized as a social process of mutual orientation' (2003, p. 6). He argues that 'Our ability to coordinate with one another may depend on our capabilities for mutual orientation, to see not the things themselves, but to see how one another are seeing things.' (2003, p. 2) The focus on mutual orientation suggests that we shift our attention to how market participants articulate and share meanings, and how they negotiate shared categories that orient their actions.

In recasting entrepreneurship as mutual orientation, Lavoie generalizes the account of the entrepreneur provided by Lachmann.[26] Lachmann (1956) presents the function of the entrepreneur as one of combining heterogeneous capital goods into a specific production plan which must fit into a complex capital structure. Lachmann emphasizes both the need to specify a concrete use, and the need to fit the particular use into a complex web of complementary capital goods.[27] As we have seen, abstraction boundaries are the key to flexibly combining complementary activities. The process of 'specifying' and 'fitting' requires both the discovery of an abstraction and the creation of a boundary that allows it to connect to complementary activities. Entrepreneurs must look beyond existing categories to specify new solutions, yet at the same time fit the new solution into a pattern of complementary activities. The entrepreneur oriented to the existing categories reads a situation anew, identifies a problem or opportunity, specifies a solution and fits the solution into a complementary web of activity so that the plans of others can be easily reoriented to the new categories.

Entrepreneurs and marketers look beyond existing boundaries to identify commonalities currently hidden behind those boundaries. By creating new distinctions (new abstractions), entrepreneurs are identifying both what should be treated as similar and what should be treated as different. They re-categorize existing shared categories in order to capture overlooked commonalities, or to separate overlooked differences. Entrepreneurs create value by creating new distinctions: where two similar things are being treated as different, there are gains to be had from removing the differences; where two different things are being treated as similar; there are gains to be had from removing the similarities.

Israel Kirzner's (1992) theory of entrepreneurship as arbitrage provides an example of one way that entrepreneurs can capture gains from removing differences. The entrepreneur notices that two similar goods are being treated as if they were different; two instances of the same type of good are selling for two different prices. The alert entrepreneur, by buying low and selling high, can profit from removing this difference. The entrepreneur helps re-categorize the undervalued good by bringing it to the attention of those who value it more.

Arbitrage, however, is not the only source of potential gains from noticing commonalities; recognizing commonalities can also lead to economies of scale and scope. Langlois (1999) argues that economies of scale and scope result primarily from the reuse of knowledge.[28] Economies arise from abstracting out the common aspects of a solution and reusing them across multiple instances. He gives the example of multiplex cinemas: cinema owners gain economies of scale by reusing the services of ticket windows, lobbies, restrooms, snack bars, and management across multiple individual theaters. The common features of stand-alone cinemas were abstracted out, and packaged for reuse by the theatres in the multiplex.[29]

Gains can also be had by recognizing differences where others see similarities. Fred Smith (2002), for example, when starting Federal Express (now FedEx) recognized that shippers and recipients of small packages differed in the value they placed on the timeliness and reliability of delivery.

He recognized that customers who value speed and reliability (for example those who need spare parts to keep expensive capital equipment running) would be willing to pay for guaranteed overnight delivery. Standard approaches to package delivery abstracted from these differences, treating them all the same. By looking past the existing boundary, Smith was able to discern differences in why people wanted package delivery services. By identifying a new commonality among these differences (desire for guaranteed overnight deliver), he was able to create a new abstraction boundary defining this new type of service.[30]

Just recognizing the new abstraction, however, was not enough. Federal Express had to create new capital combinations, and fit them into an evolving capital structure. Airplanes were purchased and flight routes were organized into a then novel hub-and-spoke configuration. Air delivery was combined with delivery trucks to provide door-to-door service. New interfaces that defined this new type of service were created and marketed to both shippers and receivers of packages. The creation of the new abstraction boundary of overnight delivery required a reconfiguration of the capital structure involved in providing that service. The change in abstraction boundary generated a new structure of cooperating objects involved in providing guaranteed overnight delivery. By hiding these changes from the customers, the abstraction boundary made it easy for customers to adapt their plans.

As the FedEx example suggests, abstractions boundaries, by virtue of being abstract, provide a source for endogenous change. Abstractions, by emphasizing commonalities and suppressing differences, create opportunities for changing the boundaries. When the differences being hidden are unimportant, there is no incentive to change the boundary; when the differences being hidden start to make a difference, there is an incentive for the boundary to change. An abstraction necessarily hides the diversity of the various instances of the particular type. As long as those differences can be ignored for the purpose at hand, the abstraction boundary will be dynamically maintained by the system. When certain types of purposes and characteristics being hidden behind the abstraction become identifiably important, the abstraction boundaries will need to adapt to accommodate them.

The pervasiveness of the creation of new abstraction boundaries is illustrated by the role of marketing: marketers look across existing boundaries to better understand the 'whys' of their customers and potential customers. It is marketing's job to identify commonalities that may be hidden behind existing boundaries, and to identify new ways of servicing these commonalities. Marketing theorist, Wroe Alderson (1957), argues that marketing involves trying to match segments of heterogeneous supply to segments of heterogeneous demand. Marketers try to create offerings that provide value to a particular market segment. The market segment identifies a group that shares certain requirements in common despite their underlying diversity. Marketers design new products and services that serve these common needs, while at the same time trying to identify opportunities for further segmentation and differentiation.

Marketers, however, must go beyond the creation of offerings matched to the needs of particular market segments. They must also invest in creating secondary institutions that reduce the costs of transactions. Secondary institutions reduce the transaction costs associated with a type of transaction. Streit and Wegner (1992), also drawing on Lachmann, call these 'the sunk costs of transactions'. They emphasize that the costs incurred to create an interface for a particular type of transaction are sunk costs from the perspective of a particular transaction occurring through the interface. They write, 'The costs of making economic agents familiar with institutions become the sunk costs of transactions as soon as the corresponding knowledge is used repeatedly. What remains as a source of current transaction costs is the task of adapting or supplementing the institutional framework to make it fit individual transactions.' (1992, p. 138).

From this perspective, the essential role of marketing is making markets – both creating a type of product or service, and creating secondary institutions to facilitate transactions of that type. Market institutions provide the customers 'with readily-usable knowledge about how to make particular classes of transactions' (Loasby, 2000, p. 306). They are attempts to lower the information costs (Dahlman, 1979; Streit and Wegner, 1992) associated with a type of transaction. The particular shape of market abstraction boundaries will be influenced by the nature of those information costs – the cost of discovering with whom to transact, of informing others of exchange opportunities, of comparing options, of negotiating terms of trade, and of policing and monitoring compliance. Streit and Wegner give the example of negotiation costs: 'quite a number of internal [secondary] institutions have evolved precisely to reduce this highly uncertain cost component, e.g. standardized contracts, and general conditions of sale.' (1992, p. 137). Marketing efforts are investments in creating secondary institutions that generate informational externalities designed to lower the current costs of transactions. Secondary institutions by reducing these costs for a class of transactions, remove the need for individuals to incur these costs for each specific transaction.

Alderson (1957) makes a similar point with his distinction between fully negotiated transactions and routine transactions. Fully negotiated transactions are unique or non-recurring transactions, which involve bilateral negotiations between the parties. Routine transactions are recurring transactions of a particular type: 'transaction routines apply to classes of transactions that are judged to be essentially similar in their purposes and in the means of carrying them out' (Alderson, 1957, p. 297). With fully negotiated transactions all transaction costs are current; with routine transactions many of the transaction costs are sunk. Investments in secondary institutions reduce the costs of routine transactions; previous marketing activities and institutions replace the need to negotiate every feature of each transaction.

Abstraction boundaries bring the benefits of separation of concerns, but they also provide an incentive for providers to look across the boundary for unmet needs, and an incentive for customers to express needs that are not being met. The potential for gains from reconfiguring the boundaries always exists. The abstraction boundaries are necessary to coordinate actions and to match segments of supply to segments of demand. Yet the essential diversity being hidden behind the abstraction provides an incentive for the discovery of new commonalities, and the creation of new abstraction boundaries to service them. The particular form of market abstraction boundaries will be shaped by the nature of the solution as well as the transaction costs associated with that type of solution. By ignoring the role of entrepreneurs and marketers in creating new products and new secondary institutions, economists do themselves a disservice. They miss an important source of endogenous changes to abstractions and their boundaries.

CONCLUSION

We are embedded in a world of abstraction boundaries; their very familiarity renders them largely invisible. We shop at instances of the type grocery store, we mail letters at instances of the type post office, and we live in instances of the type house purchased through instances of standardized mortgage contracts which are in turn bundled and sold on instances of the type secondary mortgage market. While we always interact with concrete instances, it is the abstract boundary that enables us to coordinate our plans and adapt to changing circumstances.

Abstraction boundaries represent abstract plans that fill the gap between abstract rules and concrete purposes. The abstraction boundary enforces a separation of concerns: it separates particular implementations of a solution from particular uses of the solutions. Abstraction boundaries convert specific relationships into abstract relationships: they enable the reuse of solutions by multiple clients, and the provision of solutions by multiple providers. By orienting their actions to the abstract plan defined in the boundary, the parties on both sides of the boundaries can more easily coordinate and adapt their particular plans. Abstraction boundaries enhance coordination by making it easier to separate plans where they conflict, and combine them where they complement. By abstracting from the particulars on both sides, boundaries provide a point of stability in the face of change. This abstractness, however, also provides an incentive for people to look beyond existing boundaries and create new ones that may better serve needs hidden by the boundaries.

Secondary institutions, understood as abstraction boundaries, play an important but overlooked role in the market process. They are the chief means by which the market classifies knowledge into reusable solutions, and by which the market reduces the costs of reusing the solutions. They enable market participants to make use of a wide range of knowledge without the need to acquire it themselves. As such, they are indispensable for understanding how the market process solves the knowledge problem. Abstraction boundaries are the negotiated categories that emerge from what Lavoie calls the dialogue of the market. From the boundaries of the firm (Langlois 2002) to the emergence of new markets (Loasby 2000), new capital goods (Baetjer 1998), new products (McNulty 1984) and new product categories (Lewin 1999), the definition and redefinition of abstraction boundaries permeates the market process.

NOTES

* The authors thank Darius Bacon, Howard Baetjer, Jack High, Ken Kahn, Thomas McQuade, Nick Szabo and Lauren Williams for helpful comments.

1. Lavoie (1985b) provides an historical overview of the calculation debate which focused on the limits of comprehensive planning. Lavoie (1985a) extends this critique to non-comprehensive planning. Lavoie (1986), drawing on the work of Michael Polanyi, emphasizes the role of inarticulate knowledge. His subsequent investigations into the nature of the knowledge problem, influenced especially by the hermeneutic philosopher Hans Georg Gadamer, led him to focus on the interplay of articulate and inarticulate knowledge. See for example, Lavoie (1990b, 1991 and 2003).
2. Abstraction boundaries enhance productivity by bundling reusable solutions to common problems. The reusable solution embodies a resolved decision: 'the decision to use an abstraction replaces the decisions resolved by the abstraction. Abstractions increase productivity when the former decisions are more easily resolved than the latter.' (Cunningham and Beck, 1989, p. 17). Demsetz describes a similar process occurring in the market: 'A production process reaches the stage of yielding a salable product when downstream users can work with, or consume, the 'product' without themselves being knowledgeable about its production.' (1988, p. 159).
3. The separation of interface from implementation is known in software engineering as information hiding (Parnas 1972). Information hiding is a key principle for good modular design.
4. The name comes from the 'agoric systems' papers (Miller and Drexler 1988a, 1988b, and Drexler and Miller 1988) which applied Hayekian insights to coordinating software systems. The discovery of these papers by Tulloh inspired Lavoie to launch the Agorics Project as an interdisciplinary research effort between economists and software engineers.

The Agorics Project consisted of Lavoie and a group of his graduate students, including Bill Tulloh, Howard Baetjer and Kevin Lacobie, in collaboration with a number of software engineers, including Phil Salin, Mark S. Miller, Dean Tribble and Eric Drexler. See Lavoie (1990a) and Lavoie, Baetjer, Tulloh (1990) for an overview of the Agorics Project.

5. See Lavoie, Baetjer, Tulloh (1991a, 1991b), Lavoie, Baetjer, Tulloh and Langlois (1993), Cox (1996), and Baetjer (1998) for explorations of the relationship between object oriented programming and market processes. See Baldwin and Clark (1997), Langlois (2002), and Garud, Kumaraswamy, and Langlois (2002) for recent and complementary discussions on the role of modularity in markets.
6. Hayek (1988, p. 12) explains the nature of abstract rules: 'What are chiefly responsible for having generated this extraordinary order, and the existence of mankind in its present size and structure, are those rules of human conduct that gradually evolved (especially those dealing with several property, honesty, contract, exchange, trade, competition, gain, and privacy). These rules are handed down by tradition, teaching, and imitation, rather than by instinct, and largely consist of prohibitions ("shall not's") that designate adjustable domains for individual decisions.'
7. Vaughn (1999, p. 140) recognizes a similar gap in Hayek's account of the market order.
8. Lachmann (1971) seems to be groping for the right terminology: he distinguishes first between external and internal institutions, only to later switch to a distinction between fundamental and secondary institutions. See Horwitz (1998) for a criticism of Lachmann's distinction between external and internal institutions. Langlois (1986) provides an insightful analysis of Lachmann's theory of institutions.
9. We oversimplify to make a point, but this can be misleading. By presenting the creation of the abstraction boundary as the result of a single entrepreneurial act, we are ignoring the interaction between providers, customers and other interests that shape the evolution of most abstraction boundaries. This is particularly true of the gradual development of the postal system into its current familiar shape. As one commentator notes, 'Although the basic need for a system to exchange written communications has been felt by all human societies and has been met in many ways, the evolution of varied postal systems adopted by different societies through the centuries into the basically similar pattern of today's state monopoly service has been a long and difficult process.' (*Encyclopedia Britannica*, 2003)
10. Liskov (2001, p. xvii) identifies three steps that programmers use to create abstraction boundary: 1) abstraction – the programmer abstracts a common solution to a recurring problem, 2) specification – the programmer defines a boundary that captures the meaning of the abstraction in terms of the services it provides potential users, and 3) encapsulation – the programmer hides the details of how the services are to be provided behind the abstraction boundary.
11. Wirfs-Brock and McKean explain, 'An interface describes the vocabulary used in the dialog between an object and its customers: "Shine my shoes. Give me my shoes. That'll be five bucks please. Here is your receipt." The interface advertises the services and explains how to ask for them.' (2002, p. 12)
12. Type and interface are used by programmers as synonyms for abstraction boundary. They can be seen as emphasizing two related notions of abstraction: interface refers to what an object does abstracted from how it does it; type refers to what kind of object it is abstracted from concrete instances of that type. The two are related because we classify objects based on what services they provide; we classify what an object is, by what the object does. Compare Hayek who writes, 'People behave in the same manner toward things, not because these things are identical in a physical sense, but because they have learned to classify them as belonging to the same group, because they can put them to the same use or expect from them what to the people concerned is an equivalent effect.' (1952a pp. 44).
13. Abstraction boundaries serve as focal points for a type of transaction (Schelling, 1960).
14. Lachmann's widening is sometimes referred to as narrowing by software engineers. This apparent contradiction results from different perspectives. For software engineers, the

subtype is narrower than the supertype because it is less general: a smaller set of providers provide the more specific functionality of the subtype. For Lachmann the subtype is wider since the new services that are provided by the subtype serve a broader range of client purposes.

15. Run-time is what occurs when a program is run on a specific computer. Design-time is what occurs when a programmer designs and codes the program. A programmer writes source code (readable by the programmer) that embodies the design of the program. The source code is compiled into machine-readable code that is capable of being run on a particular type of computer. The user executes this code when running the program.
16. Software design provides a language for thinking about plan coordination. It provides a set of concepts for reasoning about the problem of dividing and recombining knowledge. This language is much richer than we are able to show here. It also exists in two important senses: 1) as a set of concepts for thinking about these distinctions, and 2) as programming language constructs for implementing these distinctions. As an engineering discipline, software design concepts must pass the empirical test of building better programs. For good overviews of these distinctions see Meyer (1997), Gamma et al. (1995), and Liskov (2001). The E programming language (Miller et al., 2000, www.erights.org) is an open source programming language that takes a rights-based approach to problems of plan coordination in programming.
17. In addition to types and objects, object-oriented programming has the concept of class. A class is a template for creating objects; it implements an object's methods, but not its state. For simplicity, we ignore this distinction in this chapter.
18. The similarity between object and market concepts has been widely recognized by software designers (Miller and Drexler 1988b, Cox 1996, Meyer 1997). For example, Bertrand Meyer writes, 'like an economist of the most passionate supply-side, invisible-hand, let-the-free-market decide school, we are interested in individual agents not so much for what they are internally as for what they have to offer to each other ... The economic analogy will indeed accompany us throughout this presentation; the agents – the software modules – are called suppliers and clients; the protocols will be called contracts, and much of object-oriented design is indeed *Design by Contract*.' (1997, p. 127).
19. Contract in this sense is another name for abstraction boundary, a standardized contract for a type of interaction. Meyer (1997) provides a narrower definition of object contracts which emphasizes the terms and conditions (assertions) required for an object to respond correctly to a particular request.
20. Gamma et al. caution, 'Trying to understand one from the other is like trying to understand the dynamism of living ecosystems from the static taxonomy of plants and animals and vice versa.' (1995, p. 22).
21. For example, Malone et al. (1988), Miller and Drexler (1988b), and Wellman (1996).
22. Evolutionary programming techniques can be seen as attempts to build creative choice into programs. See Baum (1999) for a market-oriented approach to evolutionary programming inspired by Hayek.
23. See Baetjer (1998) for a description of the role of dialogue in software development.
24. Articulations, while concrete utterances, are also necessarily abstract. Lavoie (1985a, p. 60) explains, 'nothing can be completely articulated, since the very process of articulation involves the abstraction from some real features of the entity or process that is being described'.
25. Lavoie writes, 'Entrepreneurship is not an individual act of perception ... it is an interpretive and communicative process involving efforts of different persons to communicate meaning about the future to one another. It is perhaps misleading to even present this coordinating process in terms of the activity of "the entrepreneur", the single individual who is more or less alert to opportunities. What we have here is a coordination process that is taking place among persons who are oriented towards the future.' (2003, p. 15).
26. See especially Lavoie (1991 and 2003). See also Spinoza, Flores and Dreyfus (1997)
27. Lavoie explains, 'Lachmann's work *Capital and Its Structure* depicts the entrepreneur as involved in trying to mesh her plans with those of the ultimate consumers, by in some sense "fitting" into an evolving structure of capital. This idea of fit is what Lachmann

called "complementarity". The process of economic production involves the continuous adaptation of heterogeneous parts of the capital structure to one another. It is in this context that he sees the essential role of the entrepreneur as one of figuring out how to specify particular ways of using heterogeneous capital goods that in principle can be used in a multiplicity of alternative ways. Lachmann identifies the key role of the entrepreneur in terms of deciding how to initially select (or later adapt) particular patterns of use of capital goods.' (2003, p. 8)

28. As Langlois (1999) points out, there is a blurry line between economies of scale and scope: scale economies result from the reuse of knowledge across many identical units; scope economies result from the reuse of knowledge across many similar units.
29. The emergence of online ticket vendors, such as www.fandango.com, shows how boundaries can also support polymorphism.
30. This is an example of subtyping. The type post office can be extended to meet more specific purposes. A subtype of post office can be created that includes the ability to post a letter with guaranteed overnight delivery. New instances of this subtype can be substituted to provide these new enhanced services. FedEx makes use of the postal customer's familiarity with the same general interface (delivering a sealed envelope to a specified address) to offer the innovation of overnight delivery, adding more specific services without upsetting those with more general plans.

REFERENCES

Alderson, Wroe (1957), *Marketing Behavior and Executive Action*, Homewood IL: Richard D. Irwin.

Baetjer, Howard (1998), *Software as Capital: An Economic Perspective on Software Engineering*, Los Alamitos, CA: IEEE Computer Society.

Baldwin Carliss Y. and Kim B. Clark (1997), 'Managing in an age of modularity', *Harvard Business Review*, September/October, pp. 84–93.

Baum, Eric B. (1999), 'Toward a model of intelligence as an economy of agents', *Machine Learning*, **35** (2), 155–85.

Buchanan, James M. and Viktor J. Vanberg (2002), 'Constitutional implications of radical subjectivism', *Review of Austrian Economics*, **15** (2/3), 121–9.

Butos, William N. and Thomas J. McQuade (2002), 'Mind, market, and institutions: the knowledge problem in Hayek's thought', in Jack Birner, Pierre Garrouste and Thierry Aimar (eds), *F. A. Hayek as a Political Economist*, New York, US and London, UK: Routledge, pp. 113–33.

Carrano, Frank M. and Janet Prichard (2001), *Data Abstraction and Problem Solving with Java: Walls and Mirrors*, Reading, MA: Addison-Wesley.

Cox, Brad (1996), *Superdistribution: Objects as Property on the Electronic Frontier*, Reading MA: Addison-Wesley.

Cunningham, Ward and Kent Beck (1989), 'Constructing abstractions for object-oriented applications', *Journal of Object-Oriented Programming*, July/August, pp. 17–19.

Dahlman, Carl J. (1979), 'The problem of externality', *The Journal of Law and Economics*, **22** (1), April, 141–62.

Demsetz, Harold (1988), 'Theory of the firm revisited', *Journal of Law, Economics and Organization*, **4**, pp. 141–6l.

Drexler, Eric and Mark S. Miller (1988), 'Incentive engineering for computational resource management', in Bernard A. Huberman, (ed.), *The Ecology of Computation*, Amsterdam: North-Holland, pp. 231–66.

Encyclopedia Britannica (2003), 'Postal system', *Encyclopedia Britannica Online*, 31 March, 2003, http://search.eb.com/eb/article?eu=115192.

Gadamer, Hans Georg (1989), *Truth and Method*, second revised edition, New York: Crossroad Publishing.

Gamma, Eric, Richard Helm, Ralph Johnson and John Vlissides (1995), *Design Patterns: Elements of Reusable Object-Oriented Software*, Boston: Addison-Wesley.

Garud, Raghu, Arun Kumaraswamy and Richard N. Langlois (2002), *Managing in the Modular Age: Architectures, Networks, and Organizations*, New York: Blackwell Publishers.

Hayek, Friedrich A. (1937), 'Economics and knowledge', *Economica* (4), February, pp. 33–54.

Hayek, Friedrich A. (1945), 'Use of knowledge in society', *American Economic Review*, **35**, September, pp. 519–30.

Hayek, Friedrich A. (1952a), *The Counter-Revolution of Science: Studies in the Abuse of Reason*, Glencoe, Illinois: The Free Press.

Hayek, Friedrich A. (1952b), *The Sensory Order: An Inquiry into the Foundations of Theoretical Psychology*, London: Routledge & Kegan Paul.

Hayek, Friedrich A. (1973), *Law, Legislation and Liberty, Vol. I: Rules and Order*, Chicago: University of Chicago Press.

Hayek, Friedrich A. (1976), *Law, Legislation and Liberty, Vol. II: The Mirage of Social Justice*, Chicago: University of Chicago Press.

Hayek, Friedrich A. (1978), 'The primacy of the abstract', *New Studies in Philosophy, Politics, Economics and the History of Ideas*, Chicago: University of Chicago Press, pp. 35–49.

Hayek, Friedrich A. (1979), *Law, Legislation and Liberty, Vol. III: The Political Order of a Free People*, Chicago: University of Chicago Press.

Hayek, Friedrich A. (1988), *The Fatal Conceit: The Errors of Socialism. The Collected Works of F. A. Hayek, Vol. 1*, edited by W. W. Bartley, Chicago: University of Chicago Press.

High, Jack (1986), 'Equilibration and disequilibration in market processes' in Israel Kirzner (ed.), *Subjectivism, Intelligibility and Economic Understanding: Essays in Honor of Ludwig M. Lachmann on his Eightieth Birthday*, New York: New York University Press, pp. 111–21.

Horwitz, Steven G. (1998), 'Hierarchical metaphors in Austrian institutionalism: A friendly subjectivist caveat', in Roger Koppl and Gary Mongiovi (eds), *Subjectivism and Economic Analysis: Essays in Memory of Ludwig M. Lachmann*, New York, US and London, UK: Routledge, pp. 143–62.

Kirzner, Israel M. (1992), *The Meaning of the Market Process: Essays in the Development of Modern Austrian Economics*, New York, US and London, UK: Routledge.

Lachmann, Ludwig (1956), *Capital and its Structure*, Kansas City: Sheed Andrews and McNeel Inc.

Lachmann, Ludwig (1971), *The Legacy of Max Weber*, Berkley, CA: Glendessary Press.

Lachmann, Ludwig (1979), 'The flow of legislation and the permanence of the legal order', Ordo, pp. 69–77, reprinted in Don Lavoie (ed.), (1994), *Expectations and the Meaning of Institutions: Essays by Ludwig Lachmann*, New York, US and London, UK: Routledge, pp. 249–60.

Lachmann, Ludwig (1991), 'Austrian economics: a hermeneutic approach', in Don Lavoie (ed.) *Economics and Hermeneutics*, New York, US and London, UK: Routledge, pp. 134–46, reprinted in Don Lavoie (ed.), (1994), *Expectations and the Meaning of Institutions: Essays by Ludwig Lachmann*, New York, US and London, UK: Routledge, pp. 276–90.

Langlois, Richard N. (1986), 'Coherence and flexibility: social institutions in a world of radical uncertainty', in Israel Kirzner (ed.), *Subjectivism, Intelligibility, and Economic Understanding: Essays in Honor of the Eightieth Birthday of Ludwig Lachmann*, New York: New York University Press, pp. 171–91.

Langlois, Richard N. (1999), 'Scale, scope, and the reuse of knowledge', in Sheila C. Dow and Peter E. Earl (eds), *Economic Organization and Economic Knowledge: Essays in Honour of Brian J. Loasby*, Cheltenham, UK and Northampton, MA, US: Edward Elgar, pp. 239–54.

Langlois, Richard N. (2002), 'Modularity in technology and organization', *Journal of Economic Behavior and Organization* **49** (1), September, pp. 19–37.

Lavoie, Don (1985a), *National Economic Planning: What is Left?*, Cambridge: Ballinger.

Lavoie, Don (1985b), *Rivalry and Central Planning: The Socialist Calculation Debate Reconsidered*, Cambridge: Cambridge University Press.

Lavoie, Don (1986), 'The market as a procedure for the discovery and conveyance of inarticulate knowledge', *Comparative Economic Studies*, **28**, Spring, pp. 1–19.

Lavoie, Don (1990a), 'Prefatory note: the origins of "The Agorics Project"', *Market Process*, **8**, Spring, pp. 116–19.

Lavoie, Don (1990b), 'Understanding differently: hermeneutics and the spontaneous order of communicative processes', in Bruce Caldwell (ed.), *Carl Menger and his Legacy in Economics, History of Political Economy*, annual supplement to volume 22, pp. 359–77.

Lavoie, Don (1991), 'The discovery and interpretation of profit opportunities: culture and the Kirznerian entrepreneur', in Brigitte Berger (ed.) *The Culture of Entrepreneurship*, San Francisco: Institute for Contemporary Studies, pp. 33–51.

Lavoie, Don (1994), 'Preface: the meaning of market process', in Peter Boettke and David Prychitko (eds), *The Market Process: Essays in Contemporary Austrian Economics*, Aldershot, UK and Brookfield US: Edward Elgar, pp. ix-xii.

Lavoie, Don (2003), 'Subjectivism, entrepreneurship, and the convergence of groupware and hypertext', in Birner, Jack and Pierre Garrouste (eds), *Markets, Information, and Communication: An Austrian Perspective on the Internet Economy*, New York, US and London, UK: Routledge, pp. 21–46.

Lavoie, Don, Howard Baetjer and Bill Tulloh (1990), 'High tech Hayekians: some possible research topics in the economics of computation', *Market Process*, **8**, Spring, 120–141, reprinted in (2004) Jack Birner and Pierre Garrouste (eds), *Markets, Information, and Communication: An Austrian Perspective on the Internet Economy*, New York, US and London, UK: Routledge, pp. 91–120.

Lavoie, Don, Howard Baetjer and Bill Tulloh (1991a), 'Coping with complexity: OOPS and the economist's critique of central planning', *Hotline on Object-Oriented Technology*, **3** (1), November, pp. 6–8.

Lavoie, Don, Howard Baetjer and Bill Tulloh (1991b), 'Order in complex systems: object-oriented programming and the economists' critique of central planning', unpublished manuscript.

Lavoie, Don, Howard Baetjer, Bill Tulloh and Richard Langlois (1993), 'Component software: a market perspective on the coming revolution in software', Patricia Seybold Group Special Research Report, Strategic Technologies Series.

Lewin, Peter (1999), *Capital in Disequilibrium: The Role of Capital in a Changing World*, New York, US and London, UK: Routledge.

Liskov, Barbara, with John Guttag (2001), *Program Development in Java: Abstraction, Specification, and Object-Oriented Design*, Boston: Addison-Wesley.

Loasby, Brian (1999), *Knowledge, Institutions and Evolution in Economics*, New York, US and London, UK: Routledge.

Loasby, Brian (2000), 'Market institutions and economic evolution', *Journal of Evolutionary Economics*, **10** (3), 297–309.

Malone, Thomas W., Richard E. Fikes, Kenneth R. Grant, and Michael T. Howard (1988), 'Enterprise: A market-like task scheduler for distributed computing environments', in Bernardo A. Huberman (ed.) *The Ecology of Computation*, Amsterdam: North-Holland, pp. 177–205.

McNulty, Paul (1984), 'On the nature & theory of economic organization: the role of the firm reconsidered', *History of Political Economy*, **16** (2), 233–53.

Meyer, Bertrand (1997), *Object-Oriented Software Construction*, 2nd edn, Upper Saddle River, NJ: Prentice Hall.

Miller, Mark S. and Eric Drexler (1988a), 'Comparative ecology: a computational perspective', in Bernardo A. Huberman (ed.) *The Ecology of Computation*, Amsterdam: North-Holland, pp. 51–76.

Miller, Mark S. and Eric Drexler (1988b), 'Markets and computation: Agoric open systems', in Bernardo A. Huberman (ed.) *The Ecology of Computation*, Amsterdam: North-Holland, pp. 133–76.

Miller, Mark S., Chip Morningstar and Bill Frantz (2000), 'Capability-based financial instruments', in Yair Frankel (ed.), *Financial Cryptography*, 4th International Conference, FC 2000 Proceedings, Lecture Notes in Computer Science, 1962, Springer, pp. 349–78.

O'Driscoll, Jr., Gerald P. and Mario Rizzo (1985), *The Economics of Time and Ignorance*, New York, US and Oxford UK: Basil Blackwell.

Parnas, David L. (1972), 'On the criteria to be used in decomposing systems into modules', *Communications of the ACM*, **15**, December, pp. 1053–58.

Schelling, Thomas C. (1960), *The Strategy of Conflict*, Cambridge, MA: Harvard University Press.

Smith, Fred (2002), 'How I delivered the goods', *Fortune Small Business*, October, online at http://www.fortune.com/fortune/fsb/specials/innovators/smith.html.

Spinoza, Charles, Fernando Flores and Hubert L. Dreyfus (1997), *Disclosing New Worlds: Entrepreneurship, Democratic Action, and the Cultivation of Solidarity*, Cambridge MA: MIT Press.

Streit, Manfred and Peter Wegner (1992), 'Information, transaction, and catallaxy, reflections on some key concepts of evolutionary market theory', in Ulrich Witt (ed.), *Explaining Process and Change. Approaches of Evolutionary Economics*, Ann Arbor: University of Michigan Press, pp. 125–49.

Turbak, Franklyn (2002), 'Big ideas', course notes from 'CS111: Introduction to Programming and Problem Solving', Spring 2002, on the web at http://cs.wellesley.edu.

Vaughn, Karen (1999), 'Hayek's implicit economics: rules and the problem of order', *Review of Austrian Economics*, **11**, pp. 129–44.

Wellman, Michael P. (1996), 'Market-oriented programming: some early lessons', in S. Clearwater (ed.), *Market-Based Control: A Paradigm for Distributed Resource Allocation*, River Edge, NJ: World Scientific, pp. 74–95.

Wirfs-Brock, Rebecca and Alan McKean (2002), *Object Design: Roles, Responsibilities and Collaborations*, Boston: Addison-Wesley.

Wirfs-Brock, Rebecca and Brian Wilkerson (1989), 'Object-oriented design: a responsibility-driven approach', *OOPSLA '89 Conference Proceedings*, ACM: pp. 71–75.

6. 'New' collaborative learning environments: the convergence of hermeneutics and hypertext

Virgil Henry Storr*

INTRODUCTION

Don Lavoie was the consummate teacher. He embraced the life of the mind, the world of ideas and philosophies and books with all of his being. And, he taught by example rather than by pronouncements, that being a scholar meant that you had to respect but not be bound by disciplinary borders, that being a teacher meant that you had to give generously not only of your ideas but of your time, and that being a student meant that you had to be an ardent and assiduous reader. Indeed, the anchor of Lavoie's pedagogic creed, to borrow a term from Dewey, was a belief that one of the best ways to learn was by meticulously questioning a text and then listening intently to what it and your fellow questioners had to say to you in reply.[1] Consequently, Lavoie (ever the good hermeneuticist) embraced those settings that facilitated this play of questions and answers. Although he was an excellent lecturer and enjoyed teaching in the traditional classroom, he thrived in the workshop, in the readings group, in the one-on-one conversation and in the hypertextual learning environment.

I have to confess that I did not go gently into the electronic classroom. Mine was a reluctance, shared, I believe, by almost all of Lavoie's students, to abandon the familiar world of books, to give up the intimacy, the security that comes from actually holding a monograph, to trade in the sensuality of reading and responding to the printed page for the awkwardness of reading combinations of pixels on a computer screen. I had tried to read lengthy documents on the web before and had always abandoned the project, opting instead for a hard copy and so was more than a little weary going into a course that demanded that I read several e-books. Heightening my anxiety was the notion, which often found its way from the writers on hypertext into Lavoie's lectures and discussions of the course, that hypertext is a dramatically different discourse technology from the kinds that we are familiar with (the hand written note, the telephone, the telegraph, the printed page, the book).

Hypertext is a kind of electronic text, where links are used to connect 'blocks' of text to one another in a manner that encourages the reader to determine her own path, as it were, into the text (rather than following the path suggested by the original author, as is traditional). As Theodor Nelson (1981: 0/2), who coined the term in the 1960s, explains, 'by hypertext I mean non-sequential writing – text that branches and allows choices to the reader, best read at an interactive screen. As popularly conceived, this is a series of text chunks connected by links which offer the reader different pathways.' But hypertext, goes the hype, is not simply a way of facilitating non-linear writing and reading. Instead, hypertext, according to these writers, will radically change (if it has not already changed) the way that we read and write. As Chartier (1995: 18) says,

> The revolution of the electronic text will also be a revolution in reading. … While earlier revolutions in reading took place without changing the fundamental structure of the book, such will not be the case in our own world. The revolution that has begun is, above all, a revolution in the media and forms that transmit the written word. In this sense, the present revolution has only one precedent in the West: the substitution of the codex for the volume – of the book composed of quires for the book in the form of a roll – during the first centuries of the Christian era.

This *hypertext hype* was not the only frightening thing that we found in our syllabi. The so-called 'course procedures' – the strangeness of our assignments, the way that we were going to be evaluated, having to read ten e-books in seven weeks – were also causes for concern.

The first day our Comparative Economic Systems class met we were each given a CD that contained all of our reading materials.[2] Lavoie explained to us that, unlike in our other graduate courses, there would be no problem sets to solve, no papers to write and no exams to sit. We were, instead, expected to read and comment extensively on 'about a book a week' and then hand over those comments to another student who would be doing the same thing. Only, everyone in the class would be 'tackling the reading in a different sequence'. My first assignment was a book on fascism. Others began with the Soviet System, Marxism or the Austrian critique of central planning. All of our reading and commenting was 'to be done at a computer screen' using the hypertext software (Folio Views) that came bundled with our electronic books, and our entire grade in the class would be based on our annotations. As Lavoie explained in the syllabus,

> Basically the idea is simply for you to read a book (or so) every week, extensively mark it up with marginal notes (and other sorts of markups which you will learn gradually during the semester), and pass it along to the professor and to another student, who will do the same. The annotations accumulate throughout the semester, so you can benefit from the comments of your fellow students.

The in-class lectures and discussions would necessarily focus on the broader themes of Comparative Economic Systems since everyone in the class would be focusing (in our homework reading assignments) on a different topic. Although the syllabus and that introductory lecture were littered with reassuring phrases, many of us, as you might imagine, left that first class more nervous than excited about the course.

Like most in my class, however, I quickly became comfortable with the process of reading and, eventually, writing hypertextually. And, *ex post*, I have become convinced of the virtues of this kind of learning environment (electronic books read collaboratively with the aid of a rich hypertext markup application). Why? What was it about our experience with hypertextual reading that made us embrace a way of reading and writing that we were initially so reluctant to attempt? Why, to get more to the motivation of this chapter, was Lavoie so enamored with hypertext?[3] I contend that it is the seldom stressed similarities between hypertext and previous discourse technologies and not their often exaggerated differences that won converts to hypertext's camp. Hypertext's attractiveness, I believe, has much more to do with how well it supports our reading in the ways that we do now – non-linearly, skipping chapters, exploring references and footnotes, flipping back to previously read chapters. Rather than viewing it as a discourse technology that radically transforms the way that we read and write, I propose that we view hypertext as a technology that decreases the cost of us reading and writing in ways that we are already comfortable with. Although different in many respects to the printed book, hypertext is not so different that it blows away our schema for how we read, interpret and ultimately understand texts. Indeed, reflecting on our experiences in hypertext yields some of the same insights that come out of philosophical hermeneutics, which seeks to understand how we understand texts.

THE CONVERGENCE OF HERMENEUTICS AND HYPERTEXT

Unfortunately, Lavoie did not have an opportunity to articulate for us how his hermeneutics informed his attraction to and his understanding of hypertext. Before discussing what he saw as hypertext's promise, it is therefore necessary to at least sketch out an account of how hermeneutics and hypertext might have converged in his system of thought.[4] The connection between the two is by no means obvious. Hermeneutics, on the one hand, seems to insist that we be almost reverential towards texts; we are encouraged to assume that every text we endeavor to read is complete/perfect and we must, tentatively at least, accept the validity of its claims (we must assume that it has something meaningful to say to us). Hypertext, on the other hand, obliterates any notion of a pristine text; erasing the borders of the text, removing the covers, if you will, from the book and discarding the table of contents. The notion of completeness, thus, seems inappropriate to this medium.

Noting that Jacques Derrida 'continually uses terms like *link (liaisons)*, *web (toile)*, *network (reseau)*, and *interwoven (s'y tissent)*', terms that would fit naturally into any discussion of hypertext and hypertextual systems, terms 'which cry out for hypertextuality', Landow (1997: 33; see also 1994) has tried to link hypertext to critical theory, specifically to aspects of Derrida's post-structuralist project.[5] According to Landow (1997: 2),

> the parallels between computer hypertext and critical theory are of interest at many points, the most important of which, perhaps, is that critical theory promises to theorize hypertext and hypertext promises to embody and thereby test aspects of theory, particularly those concerning textuality, narrative, and the roles or functions of reader and writer.

To my mind, Derrida's project is notoriously difficult to pin down, but it is clear that Derrida, as Landow (1997: 33) says, does consistently (if such a term can meaningfully be applied to Derrida) think hypertextually, emphasizing 'textual openness, intertextuality, and the irrelevance of distinctions between inside and outside a particular text'. For Derrida, there is *nothing outside the text*. 'The point,' Rorty (1977: 675) explains, 'is that we cannot merely by going linguistic … get outside of all our representations to a standpoint from which the legitimacy of those representations can be judged'. It is impossible to escape from a world of texts; texts are necessarily embedded in a context of other texts. The parallels with hypertext where discrete units of text are embedded in a network of other units are, thus, obvious. As Landow (1997: 33) writes, 'Derrida properly recognize[d] (in advance, one might say) that a new, freer, richer form of text, one truer to our potential experience, perhaps to our actual if unrecognized experience, depends upon discrete reading units.'

Although Landow's arguments concerning the convergence between critical theory and hypertext are well developed and are often quite compelling, there are aspects of Derrida's philosophy, aspects that do not necessarily come into play in Landow's utilization of Derrida but are nonetheless lurking in the background, which make it difficult for me to embrace his use of Derrida in this manner. Madison (1991) has offered a devastating critique of Derrida's deconstruction from a hermeneutical perspective. As he (1991:130) suggests,

> Deconstruction tends to issue in relativism, interpretive arbitrariness, because while it maintains [agreeing with hermeneutics] . . . that there is no meaning *present* in the text, one that it would be the task of interpretation simply to re-present (there is no original, fixed, hidden meaning to be uncovered), it maintains, at the same time, in accordance with its structuralist inspiration, that there is nothing but texts, that meaning is nothing but the interplay of signs which are themselves without intrinsic meaning.

For Derrida, then, every attempt to understand a text is necessarily a futile endeavor. If all texts are embedded in a web of texts that cannot be escaped, since everything is a text that merely points to another text (and so on and so on, ad infinitum), then understanding is impossible, there is simply no subject-matter to be understood. Derridean deconstruction thus reveals itself as a nihilistic endeavor.[6] Consequently, if hypertext and deconstruction had really 'converged' (as Landow asserts), then it would be impossible to talk about hypertextual reading in any meaningful sense. But, as we are well aware, it is possible to understand texts and hypertexts. And, although hypertext does embody some aspects of Derridean deconstruction, it does not embody his entire 'theory' (another word that is hard to apply to Derrida). There is *an entire world outside of hypertext*.

Hermeneutics, while offering many of the insights about textuality that are associated with deconstruction, escapes the nihilistic trap that has ensnared Derrida. As Madison (1991:131) writes,

> To the deconstructionist notion of undecidability should be opposed the quite different hermeneutical notion of *inexhaustibility*. In contrast to deconstruction, hermeneutics maintains that there is always the possibility of meaning, but, in contrast to logocentrism, it maintains that it is never possible to arrive at final meaning ... Unlike 'undecidability', 'inexhaustibility' points not to the eternal vanity of all human endeavor but rather to the limitless possibility of interrogation, expression, and understanding.

Hermeneutics holds open the possibility of understanding texts and has done much to explain what is actually going on when we find ourselves in a questionable situation (when we are confronted with a text) and try to understand it.

As such, I propose that hermeneutics, which appreciates the openness, intertextuality and the embeddedness of texts, is more useful for understanding hypertext and particularly hypertextual reading/writing than Derridean deconstruction. This, I suggest, can be easily demonstrated by reexamining the key aspects of hypertext in the light of hermeneutics, particularly its two most critical facets, linking and annotating.

The key element of hypertext is the link. Recall that hypertext is defined as 'a series of text chunks connected by links' (Nelson 1981: 0/2). Links are, as Landow (1997: 11) says, 'the element that hypertext adds to writing and reading'. Or, stated another way, 'electronic linking creates hypertext' (Landow 1997: 24). Although linking can take many forms, ranging in complexity from unidirectional links 'from lexia to lexia' to 'typed links ... which limit an electronic link to a specific kind of relationship', such as a counter-point or an example, the most common form of linking, which is found, for instance, on the web, is the link from a string (that is, a word, a phrase, a sentence) to an entire lexia (Landow 1997: 24). Indeed, the string-to-lexia link is the form of linking that most readily comes to mind when we think of hyperlinks. Often used to signal the reader that additional information is easily accessible (we only need follow the link), the string-to-lexia offers the hypertextual writer 'a simple means of orienting readers by permitting a basic rhetoric of departure' (ibid.).

String-to-lexia hyperlinks give readers the ability to follow different pathways through the text and give writers the ability to make explicit associations between texts; a concept that is referenced in one text can be formally associated and bound to a text that elucidates that concept. 'Electronic links', as Landow (1997: 3) explains, 'connect lexias "external" to a work – say, commentary on it by another author or parallel or contrasting texts – as well as within it and thereby create text that is experienced as nonlinear, or, more properly, as multilinear or multisequential.'

Hypertext thus embodies notions of both non-linearity and intertextuality; notions that find only a limited expression in other discourse technologies such as print media. As Bolter (2001: 35) describes,

> a hypertext consists of topics and their connections, where the topics may be paragraphs, sentences, individual words, or indeed digitized graphics and segments of video. A hypertext is like a printed book that the author has attacked with a pair of scissors and cut into convenient verbal sizes. The difference is that the electronic hypertext does not simply dissolve into a disordered heap, because the author also defines a scheme of electronic connections to indicate relationships among the slips.

And, the author also defines a set of electronic connections to indicate relationships between the text and other texts. Hermeneutics, I contend, can help us make sense of both the concepts of non-linearity and intertextuality in the context of hypertext.

Post-structural critiques of hermeneutics would seem to exclude this possibility. Indeed, it is precisely because Barthes, Derrida and others in the post-structuralist camp believe that hermeneutics is unable to contend with non-linearity, intertextuality and other aspects of the text as they see it that they reject hermeneutics (Risser 1991, 94). How, then, is hermeneutics able to make sense of hypertext? How can Gadamer, for instance, with his commitment to 'anticipating completeness' make sense of intertextuality where texts are never 'complete' and are continually pointing to other, perhaps contradictory, texts? This problem, however, with due deference to the post-structuralist, is only apparent.[7] Hermeneutics understands a text generally as anything that is open to interpretation but the question of what actually comprises a particular text makes sense only when that text is being read.

A text is reconstructed, its borders redrawn, its boundaries redefined, during the act of reading, and the markings that serve to describe the text are always tentative. That the text to be understood could be comprised of a series of related texts is, thus, not a problem for hermeneutics. Of course, it is in the process of reading that the reader determines the dimensions of the hermeneutic circle. Of course, it is in the process of reading that the reader decides what, in fact, is the appropriate whole.[8] Similarly, the possibility that two readers of the same lexia, although guided by different prejudices and so motivated by different questions, might enter at different points and construct different texts is also not a problem for hermeneutics. In hermeneutics, intertextuality and non-linearity find their meaning in the process of textual reconstruction.[9]

Linking and so textual reconstruction, however, are not unique to hypertext. Admittedly, hypertext makes it less cumbersome for authors to include links and easier for readers to consume them and so to read in a non-linear fashion. But, these processes are at play regardless of the medium. No active reader, for instance, treats the author's ordering of the text as sacrosanct. Indeed, just as a text can suggest to us meanings not intended by the author so too can it suggest to us a path through it that is unintended by the author. It is commonplace for readers to turn to the back of a book, look up a particular subject in the index and read only the relevant pages, thus driving off of the author's roadmap. Similarly, few of us read every book that we pick up from cover to cover. Almost all of us have skipped chapters, ignored sections that do not pique our interest and read chapters out of order, particularly during subsequent readings.[10] And, even in fiction, nothing prevents us from skipping to the back of the book to read the ending, if, for instance, we cannot stand the suspense of not knowing how it turns out.

Similarly, it is naive to assume that hypertextual authors do not suggest pathways into their texts. Although it is harder for writers in print media than it is for hypertextual authors to propose varied and multiple paths through a text, it is possible for writers in all media to propose alternatives. As even Bolter (2001: 35) concedes, 'In the medium of print, the writer may use the index to show alternatives'. Still, Bolter (ibid.) has a point when he concludes that, in print 'these alternatives must always contend with the fixed order of the book's pages'.[11] As he (ibid.) suggests, 'Although the canonical order of a printed book is defined by the pagination, and all other suggested orders remain subordinate, a hypertext need not have any canonical order.' But, we should also be aware that hypertext can allow writers, if they choose, to enforce their recommended pathways more rigidly than can print authors. Although we have always to contend with the order decided on by the author when reading a book, we are free to open the book to any page that we desire and to begin reading at any point on the page that we choose. In hypertextual environments, however, this ability can be (perniciously or unwittingly) curtailed. Almost everyone familiar with the web, for instance, has experienced the disappointment of being unable to find information on a website, even though we know that it is stored there, or the frustration of wanting to skip ahead in an article that we are reading and being forced, instead, to click through a series of pages. Indeed, the cost of reading ahead, of skipping back and forth, of locating specific information may be more costly in a hypertextual environment than it is in a printed book. To be sure, many of these frustrations will go away as the design of websites, in particular, and hypertextual systems, in general, improve. 'Lethargy rather than strategy' is often what is at play. But, it would be a mistake not to acknowledge that hypertext makes it possible for authors to make these kinds of moves on purpose. Authors could, for instance, decide to force us to contend with a particular page before allowing us to see another. The richer reading experiences that hypertext promises (the ability to follow different pathways through the text) could just as readily begin to limit our reading experiences.

In addition to allowing for alternative, non-linear readings, printed media (like hypertext) also permits authors to associate texts with one another. As Landow (1997: 4) states,

> The standard scholarly article in the humanities or physical sciences perfectly embodies the underlying notions of hypertext as multisequentially read text. For example, in reading an article on, say, James Joyce's *Ulysses*, one reads through what is conventionally known as the main text, encounters a number or symbol that indicates the presence of a foot- or endnote, and leaves the main text to read that note, which can contain a citation of passages in *Ulysses* that supposedly support the argument in question, or information about the scholarly author's indebtedness to other authors, disagreement with them, and so on. The note can also summon up information about sources, influences, and parallels in other literary texts. In each case, the reader can follow the link to another text indicated by the note and thus move entirely outside of the scholarly article itself. Having

> completed reading the note or having decided that it does not warrant a careful reading at the moment, one returns to the main text and continues reading until one encounters another note, at which point one again leaves the main text.

Writers in printed media can suggest links using footnotes, endnotes, references and quotations. The point being that there are effective, albeit cumbersome, ways to make explicit links in non-hypertext environments.

And, then there are the mental links and associations that readers make regardless of the medium, often not intended by the author. As we read, as we question a text, the text presents us with answers, suggests to us new questions and points us toward related texts that the author may not have in mind.[12] We make annotations in the margins of printed works or create popups in hypertext systems whenever we wish to record these ideas.

Although websites are certainly hypertextual environments, they support only a very limited hypertextual experience. From the very beginning, however, theorists had in mind much richer hypertextual environments, like Xerox's NoteCard or NextPage's Folio Views, where readers are permitted not only to activate links but to create them, to make annotations and to even, in some applications, modify the underlying text. As Landow (1997: 6) describes, 'A full hypertext system ... offers the same environment to both reader and writer. Therefore, by opening the text-processing program, or editor, as it is known, you can take notes, or you can write against my interpretations, against my text ... you can write a response and link it to my document.'[13]

Full hypertext systems, thus, allow readers, through markups, to carry on a conversation with the text and with subsequent readers of the text. In most of these implementations this is done through *popups* and *notes*; the reader is permitted to create a popup or note containing her commentary on the text (or her commentary on the comments of previous readers) and then associate that popup or note to a particular string in the text. This anchor, often appearing as a hyperlink, persists and is available on subsequent readings of the text to the initial reader qua commentator, as well as to others. The benefit of this kind of system should be obvious: a transcript of the dialogue that every reader has with the text is created and can subsequently be shared.

Gadamer has had a great deal to say about the dialogical character of reading, about the play of questions and answers that occurs whenever we try to read, that is, interpret and so understand a text.[14] As Gadamer (1976: 57) writes,

> The understanding of a text has not begun at all as long as the text remains mute. But a text can begin to speak. ... When it does begin to speak, however, it does not simply speak its word, always the same, in lifeless rigidity, but gives

> ever new answers to the person who questions it and poses ever new questions to him who answers it.

Reading for Gadamer is, thus, a process of inquiry, a dialogue, where questions are put to the written text and answers or questions are offered by the text in response.[15]

Descombes' (1991) distinction between *the interpretative text* and *the interpreting text* might prove quite useful here; particularly in helping us to understand exactly what is occurring when readers mark up a text. The *interpretative text* is simply a written text that is questionable, that must be interpreted. 'The basic condition for there being an interpretation of a given text,' Descombes (1991: 255) asserts, 'is that the text be replaced by yet another text, one which is in certain respects its equivalent, but for which one no longer needs still another interpretation.'[16] According to Descombes (ibid.), reading 'consists in exchanging an interpretative text for a second text which is not interpretative, and which is accepted in place of the first'. As he (ibid.) writes,

> It is not possible to speak of interpretation (or something resembling an interpretation) unless one can point to something playing the role of interpretative text, to something playing the role of the interpreting text, and to the conditions under which the second text is accepted in exchange for the first.

In a full hypertext system where markups are permitted it is especially easy to see which text plays the role of the interpretative text (the original text that was read) and which the role of the interpreting text (the annotated text that is created by the reader), but we should recognize that 'something playing the role of the interpreting text' is created whenever a text is read. Indeed, it is also possible for readers to create markups in non-hypertext media. We can, of course, make notes in the margin, underline texts to signal important passages, add sheets of paper with roughly recorded thoughts or write our comments inside the book's back cover (or make mental notes, for that matter).

Electronic hypertext systems, however, do permit these markups to exist in a form that can be easily shared with and consumed by others. Again, what hypertext does is not to radicalize the way that we read but instead to make the process of reading and particularly this process of annotating a text and allowing others to benefit from our annotations less cumbersome. Hypertext removes many of the difficulties that readers in print media encounter when they try to record their dialogue with the text; in hypertext systems, for instance, the size of the margins is limited only by the memory of the computer (and so is effectively unlimited for most purposes). Also, hypertext facilitates a dialogue over the text with past and future readers, a dialogue that would be much more difficult, though certainly not impossible, to have if readers and writers were restricted to traditional print media.

What then is the socio-economic significance of hypertext, given our appreciation of hermeneutics and our realization that hypertextual reading has much in common with more traditional forms? How should we view hypertext given this speculative account of the convergence of philosophical hermeneutics and hypertext in Lavoie's thought? What does it mean for reading and writing? Why have I stressed the similarities between hypertext and previous discourse technologies rather than highlighting its rupture from previous ways of reading and writing? Hypertext and previous discourse technologies, I contend, are simply more alike than they are different. There is no element in hypertext that does not find its counterpart, however imperfect, in the printed book. Linking and annotating, for instance, are possible in traditional printed media.

It is not that the advent of hypertext signaled a radical shift in the ways in which we would be able to interact with a text that explains its promise but, rather, it is because hypertext lowers the cost of our reading and writing in the ways that feel most natural. Linking and annotating are more costly to implement, for a variety of reasons, in printed media than in hypertext environments, and this 'higher cost' may even make some activities prohibitively expensive in non-hypertext contexts. Similarly, collaboration is often more awkward in non-hypertext environments; it is difficult simultaneously to maintain both a close proximity to the text and to have dialogue with past and future readers of the text. I have stressed the similarities between hypertext and other discourse technologies not to suggest that hypertext does not signal a change in the way we write and read (to be sure, it represents a qualitative change).[17] But, rather, I have stressed the continuity between hypertext and other discourse media because it is this continuity that explains why these systems have gained acceptance and so 'remediated' print (to borrow a term from Bolter).[18]

'The real payoff of electronic media,' Lavoie (2001: 49) explains, 'comes from tapping the advantages of the complex structuring of texts that had arisen in the aftermath of Gutenberg [and his printing press], but now in a context where multiple persons are involved in an interactive process with these structured texts.' Hypertext systems are *collaborative learning environments*.[19] It is on this point, regarding the potential of hypertext systems to improve the way that we work with texts, to learn from texts collaboratively, that Lavoie was so prescient. As Lavoie (2001: 49) wrote, hypertext's 'most important capability is that of permitting more complex kinds of structures in the texts through which we orient our plans with one another ... it is ... the ability to contextualize our articulations through the use of meaningful structures, that constitutes the real promise of these technologies'.

HYPERTEXT SYSTEMS ARE COLLABORATIVE LEARNING ENVIRONMENTS

Hypertext supports 'a kind of writing and reading in which there is a higher degree of interactivity both among the persons involved and between the persons and their text' (Lavoie 1997). Prior to hypertext or, rather, prior to the advent of hypertextualized groupware applications, discursive partners faced a series of tradeoffs depending on whether they opted for more or less synchronous forms of dialogue and more or less dynamic ways of talking.

In synchronous dialogues, like face-to-face conversations or telephone calls, the questions and answers that are characteristic of all dialogues take place in real time making immediate feedback possible. Asynchronous dialogues, like dialogues through the post or over email, slow down discourse, allowing individuals to respond to queries at their convenience and, so, allowing for more considered feedback. 'The point,' as Lavoie (1997) is quick to stress,

> is not to say one of these modes is good or bad. The crucial point … is to find the mode that is most appropriate to the situation at hand. In a world where we [can make] phone [calls] and [leave] voice mail we can accomplish more than we could in a world where we only had recourse to one or the other of these modes.

Discourse partners also have had to choose between fixed and dynamic ways of communicating. Fixed forms of dialogue, like written correspondence and scholarly debates in academic journals, have the advantage of preserving discourse, thus making it possible to include others in the dialogue or to return to conversation at a later point. Dynamic forms of discourse, like verbal communication, on the other hand, allow us 'to get immediate feedback and thus avoid going off in directions that do not work for the discourse partners' (Lavoie 1997).

Historically, all textual (fixed) forms of communication were, necessarily, asynchronous and it was difficult to fix/preserve synchronous dialogues (these were necessarily dynamic). Hypertext, however, 'breaks the paper technology's barrier that forces text to be asynchronous, opening up the possibility for synchronic textual dialogue' (Lavoie 1997). Similarly, with hypertext 'asynchronous activities can be more dynamic'. Stated another way, hypertext makes for more dynamic texts; textual dialogues can occur in real time, asynchronous dialogues can garner more immediate feedback. This is the crucial benefit of the collaborative learning environments that can now be constructed in hypertext.

Although Lavoie has not had a great deal to say in print about the way his hermeneutics informed his understanding of hypertext, he did have a great deal to say about the benefits that he perceived would accrue from using the collaborative learning environments that are now possible because of 'the convergence of groupware and hypertext'.[20] As Lavoie et al. (1999: 16) assert,

> From the standpoint of the future hypertextually-supported dialogue what we are doing now looks broken. Compare the way we read and write with the way we engage in verbal dialogue. Verbal discussions appear to have the possibility of a close relationship between what is being heard and what is being said. While the printing press was unquestionably an enormous advance in our ability to engage in discursive activities, it was a one-sided technological advance. It gave our 'voices' a permanence that our vocal chords alone could never achieve, and as a result it gave our 'ears' access to far more voices in the written texts of civilization. But it leads to an unfortunate 'alienation' of speaking from listening.

Asynchronous hypertext-supported dialogue has the potential to repair this rupture, to eliminate the 'unfortunate "alienation" of speaking from listening'. Specifically, Lavoie believed that these 'new' collaborative (hypertext-supported) learning environments have the potential to improve the learning process in the classroom.[21]

Lavoie et al. (1999) saw the readings group (traditionally conceived) and the intensive dialogue over a text or group of texts that it encourages as an effective way to learn a variety of subjects. Asynchronous hypertext-supported dialogue is, for a variety of reasons, seen as adding to this sort of learning process. How is learning improved by encouraging the social reading processes that occur in these kinds of dialogues? Why use these 'new' collaborative reading environments in the classroom?

First, as Lavoie et al. (1999: 34) assert, these systems 'facilitate the intimacy of the contact between the student and the texts'. Students are given and are expected to use an 'extensive set of markup tools' and are thus discouraged from lazily/passively reading the texts. For example, the ability to create links that will be visible to subsequent readers (be it themselves in subsequent passes, their professor or their fellow students), encourages students to think through the relationships between the text that they have before them and other texts. Similarly, the ability to anchor notes to particular passages or to particular phrases even, encourages students to challenge any paragraphs, sentences or words that they find questionable or objectionable. Students, in these environments, can put questions directly to the text, or can leave questions (as they are reading through the text) for future readers. They can also offer examples or clarifications. As Lavoie et al. (1999:33) explain, 'reading with an extensive set of markup tools like this brings us closer [to the text] and gets us involved in what is being said'.[22]

Second, hypertext-based collaborative learning environments allow readers to see how previous readers have read the text; we can follow the links that they have left in the text for us and we can respond to the questions that they have put to the text or to us. As Lavoie et al. (1999: 34) say,

> when we read using paper-based technology what we almost never encounter is how this text, which we tend to react to in our own idiosyncratic way, has been read by others. That is really not only interesting information about other readers, it is also important additional information about the text.

Different readers will focus in on different aspects of a text, will draw different implications, will notice different analogies to what is being said and will ask different questions. Having to contend with these differences, participating in this kind of dialogue over but in close proximity to the text, has the potential to radically improve our understanding of each other, but most importantly of the text and, so, its subject matter.

CONCLUSION

Lavoie had a habit of 'getting it' before the rest of us did. Prof. Karen Vaughn's account, for instance, of how Lavoie responded to the radical message that Lachmann delivered at the famed South Royalton conference is paradigmatic. Although both would eventually see much value in the message Lachmann delivered at the retreat, Prof. Vaughn (1994: 110) admits that she, like so many others, failed to appreciate Lachmann's contributions 'straight off'. As she confesses, 'I found Lachmann to be virtually incomprehensible. He was raising problems and issues that I had never considered before or even heard considered by anyone else.' Lavoie, on the other hand, was '"shaken up" by Lachmann right from the beginning'.

Lavoie possessed an intellectual courage that seemed to propel him down paths that frighten the rest of us; the implications of a thoroughgoing subjectivism (Lavoie 1990b, 1991b), the benefits of hermeneutical reflection (Lavoie 1987, 1990b and 1990c), the potential gains from intellectual trade with Cultural Studies (1991a, 1994 and with Chamlee-Wright 2001) and the usefulness of hypertext as a learning environment for business and for the classroom (2001 and with Nelson and Gilbert 1999) are just a few examples. Mises (1963: 139), whom Lavoie loved, has described a pioneer, a creative genius, as someone who 'clears a road through land hitherto inaccessible'. Lavoie was also a pioneer. It is now our task to catch up.

NOTES

* I thank several of my colleagues for their comments and suggestions on earlier versions of this chapter, particularly Jack High, Roman Kulchitsky, Bill Tulloh, Thomas Burke and Mark Steitz. The standard disclaimer applies.

1. As Gadamer ([1960] 1989: 368) suggests, 'it is more than a metaphor; it is a memory of what originally was the case, to describe the task of hermeneutics [that is, understanding] as entering into dialogue with the text.'
2. Comparative Economic Systems 'is the study of fundamental alternatives in public policy. It explores the systemic, evolutionary patterns in overall socio-economic institutional arrangements, and examines the manner in which knowledge is discovered, changed, and communicated in social systems' (Lavoie 1999: Course Syllabus).
3. One theory is that hypertext appealed to the 'techie' in Lavoie. To be sure, Lavoie had been a software developer, and the beauty of hypertext, I should confess, appeals to something base in all of us former programmers. But, natural attraction is not enough to explain his evangelism nor is it enough to explain how/why he was able to convert so many of us.
4. Particularly since Lavoie was such a deliberate and consistent thinker. His journey from comparative economic systems through hermeneutics to hypertext, and the stops along the way, was a trip characterized more by progressions and refinements than by ruptures and breaks with his past. Indeed, Lavoie's radicalism had everything to do with his willingness to take the next step. The progression from hermeneutics to hypertext was, thus, most likely an understandable next step.
5. Landow (1994: 1) has also tried to link hypertext to Barthes post-structuralism as well as to 'Julia Kristeva's notions of intertextuality, Mikhail Bakhtin's emphasis upon multivocality, Michael Foucault's conceptions of networks of power, and Gilles Deleuze and Felix Guattari's ideas of rhizomatic, "nomad thought".'
6. As Lavoie often complained, you are never quite sure that Derrida means what he says (for instance, that texts cannot be understood) because what he says often seems to call into question the very act of speaking. For an alternate view, see Froman's (1991) response to Madison (1991).
7. 'From a hermeneutic perspective,' Warnke (1987: 84), 'it might be argued that the conviction of coherence is necessary even if one is concerned with textual self-contradictions, since contradictions are contradictions only within, or of, a presumed general meaning. The presumption of unity thus does not preclude the discovery of points at which the text "deconstructs" itself; instead it is essential to it.' Indeed, Gadamer's use of the term 'completeness' is not meant to suggest that the text is somehow finished with firm borders erected around it but is, instead, meant 'as a counterforce to the potential arbitrariness and idiosyncrasy of textual interpretation' (Warnke 1987: 82). As Warnke (1987: 83) explains, 'the text must be approached as an internally consistent whole because it is this assumption of self-consistency that provides a standard for keeping or discarding individual interpretations of the text's parts. Conversely, if one denies that a given text is internally consistent from the start, one has no way of knowing whether its inconsistency is the fault of the text or one's understanding of it. For this reason hermeneutic efforts are directed at finding an interpretation that can both make sense out of the individual parts of a text and integrate them into a consistent whole.'
8. See, for instance, how Warnke (1987: 85) contends with Hirsch's suggestion that we can improve our understanding of a text 'by moving outside the text and referring to the [author's] intentions as gleaned from a knowledge of his life, typical concerns, beliefs and the like'. But, as Warnke (ibid.) explains, 'the solution fails to clarify how the kind of extra-

textual evidence to which he appeals is supposed to aid purely textual interpretation since one also needs an interpretation of this evidence and of its relations to the text. In other words, the extra-textual evidence to which Hirsch points can be itself considered from the point of view of the hermeneutic circle.' Extra-textual evidence once it is referenced (once the link is followed) becomes a part of the text being read and a new conception of the whole is formed. One of the values of this dialogue between hypertext and hermeneutics now comes into view. Reflecting on hypertext reminds us that 'what is the text to be understood?' is also at issue.

9. It should also be noted that the 'anticipation of completeness' is actually critical to working in a hypertext environment. When we encounter a string with a link associated with it, we have to anticipate that following that link will provide an answer to the question that is asked by the string. If we could not, in principle, assume this completeness we would not be able to proceed, reading hypertextually would be severely hampered. We would be reluctant to follow any links as we would have no clue of where it was taking us, we would be forced to jump out on faith, we would never be able to assume that following a link would, in fact, be beneficial to us.
10. Almost all of us have followed Francis Bacon's dictum (perhaps unwittingly) and recognized that, 'some books are to be tasted, others to be swallowed, and some few to be chewed and digested'. As McCloskey (2000: 103) confessed, '[she] rarely read[s] a nonfiction book cover to cover, though [she has] used many thousands.'
11. Consider, for instance, the typical university website. Frequently in such a setup you will see areas for students, for prospective students, for alumni and for faculty and staff. Often these are just 'wrappers' for the same information presented in a slightly different order and emphasizing different aspects of the data. It would be difficult to support this kind of process in a single printed book.
12. As Lavoie often remarked, 'it's not just that authors know more than they can say but that they say more than they can know.'
13. Word processing applications like Microsoft Word, I should note, are increasingly moving in this direction. The new version of Word, for instance, gives users the ability to add links and comments and to track changes made to the underlying document.
14. See, for instance, Gadamer (1976 and [1960] 1989).
15. It should be noted (particularly in light of our discussions of non-linearity) that the questions that we put to a text necessarily impact our pathway through the text, influencing the links that we will follow and those we will ignore. As Dewey ([1938] 1991: 112) says, 'Without a problem [read a formulated question], there is blind groping in the dark. The way in which the problem is conceived decides what specific suggestions are entertained and which are dismissed; what data are selected and which rejected; it is the criterion for relevancy and irrelevancy of hypothesis and conceptual structures.'
16. He is, of course, not suggesting that the meaning of the text becomes settled for all time. As Descombes (1991: 256) concedes, 'there is no question of denying that the interpretative text can itself be the product of an interpretation'. Again links between how hermeneutics describes understanding and how Dewey describes inquiry suggest themselves. As Dewey ([1938] 1991: 108) explains, 'inquiry is the controlled or directed transformation of an indeterminate situation into one that is so determinate in its constituent distinctions and relations as to convert the elements of the original situation into a unified whole'. That this unified whole may become the subject of a subsequent inquiry was, however, recognized from the start.
17. As Lavoie (2001: 51) concluded, 'Convenience is not ***mere*** convenience. Electronic texts can make it so easy to follow links of this kind that in effect the reader's experience undergoes a qualitative shift.'
18. By remediation, Bolter (2001: 42) simply means that hypertext is a way 'of improving on the older medium, or more precisely on the genres associated with the medium of print'.
19. To be sure, we can think of other *collaborative learning environments*: the classroom when it works, the corporate boardroom. But, working collaboratively on texts in these

contexts can often be quite difficult. Hypertext allows us to capture many of the benefits that come from working closely together without having to face many of the costs.

20. The convergence of hypertext and groupware was for Lavoie a critical step. As Lavoie (2001: 44) writes, 'One can imagine a hypertextual repository of texts as a tool for an individual person to use. One can also imagine a groupware environment where the shared information is flat, unstructured content, with none of the textual structuring associated with hypertext. But in practice each of these kinds of capabilities is almost always found combined to some extent with elements of the other. Groupware is more powerful precisely when it incorporates more hypertextual capabilities, and vice versa. Groupware begins in a sense with the notion of individuals working together in a networked environment, and asks what tools, including textual structures, might enhance their work. Hypertext begins at the other end. It starts from the context of an individual confronting a structured text, and soon comes to take up the interpersonal context of shared access to the text.'
21. Lavoie also believed that these environments could potentially help entrepreneurs generate real 'objective' wealth. See, for instance, Lavoie (2001) for a detailed presentation of that argument. As Lavoie (2001: 4) cautiously suggests, 'the contemporary workplace and marketplace are increasingly enhanced by information technology capabilities that are improving, both with and between organizations, our ability to orient ourselves to one another's meanings'. Although I will not be discussing this aspect of his work here, I will suggest (following Lavoie) that the advantages of hypertext-facilitated collaborative learning environments which lead to improved learning environments in the classroom, also make for improved learning environments in organizations and so help them to generate wealth.
22. 'It is important to see,' Lavoie et al. (1999: 33) argue, 'that the point of achieving intimacy with the text has not been primarily from a fascination with or reverence for the texts themselves, but to grapple with the subject-matter of the text.' As they point out, 'By engaging in very specific reactions to the wording, we deepen our familiarity with the text, we get away from the tendency to pass over the words lightly, keeping them at arm's length, and instead involve ourselves deep inside of what is said. The experience of reading with an extensive set of markup tools like this brings us closer and gets us involved in what is being said.'

REFERENCES

Boettke, Peter J. and Virgil H. Storr (2002), 'Post classical political economy: polity, society and economy in Weber, Mises and Hayek', *American Journal of Economics and Sociology*, **61** (1).

Boettke, Peter J., Don Lavoie and Virgil H. Storr (2004), 'The subjectivist methodology of Austrian economics and Dewey's theory of inquiry', in E. Khalil (ed.), *Dewey, Pragmatism and Economic Methodology*, London: Routledge.

Bolter, Jay David (2001), *Writing Space: Computers, Hypertext and the Remediation of Print*, Mahwah, NJ: Lawrence Erlbaum Associates.

Chartier, Roger (1995), *Forms and Meanings: Texts, Performances and Audiences from Codex to Computer*, Philadelphia, PA: University of Pennsylvania Press.

Descombes, Vincent (1991), 'The interpretative text', in H.J. Silverman (ed.), *Gadamer and Hermeneutics*, New York, NY: Routledge.

Dewey, John ([1925] 1929), *Experience and Nature*, Chicago, IL: Open Court.

Dewey, John (1929), *The Quest for Certainty: A Study of the Relation of Knowledge and Action*, New York: Minton, Balch & Co.

Dewey, John ([1938] 1991), *Logic: The Theory of Inquiry*, Volume 12 (1938) of *The Later Works, 1925–1953*, Carbondale, IL: Southern Illinois University Press.

Dewey, John (1973), *The Philosophy of John Dewey (Two Volumes in One): 1 The Structure of Experience, 2 The Lived Experience*, Chicago, IL: The University of Chicago Press.

Froman, Wayne J. (1991), 'L'ecriture and philosophical hermeneutics', in H.J. Silverman (ed.), *Gadamer and Hermeneutics*, New York, NY: Routledge.

Gadamer, Hans-Georg (1976), *Philosophical Hermeneutics*, Berkeley, CA: University of California Press.

Gadamer, Hans-Georg (1986), *The Relevance of The Beautiful And Other Essays*, New York, NY: Cambridge University Press.

Gadamer, Hans-Georg ([1960] 1989), *Truth and Method*, New York, NY: Crossroad.

Hayek, F. A. (1948), *Individualism and Economic Order*, Chicago, IL: The University of Chicago Press.

High, Jack (1990), *Maximizing, Action, and Market Adjustment: An Inquiry into the Theory of Economic Disequilibrium*, Muchen, Hamden: Philosophia.

Kirzner, Israel M. (1973), *Competition & Entrepreneurship*, Chicago, IL: The University of Chicago Press.

Kirzner, Israel M. (1979), *Perception, Opportunity, and Profit: Studies in the Theory of Entrepreneurship*, Chicago, IL: The University of Chicago Press.

Lachmann, Ludwig M. (1971), *The Legacy of Max Weber*, Berkeley, CA: Glendessary Press.

Lachmann, Ludwig M. (1977), *Capital, Expectations, and the Market Process: Essays on the Theory of the Market Economy*, Kansas City, Kansas: Sheed Andrews and McMeel, Inc.

Lachmann, Ludwig M. (1990), 'Austrian economics: a hermeneutic approach' in D. Lavoie (ed.), *Economics and Hermeneutics*, London, UK: Routledge.

Lachmann, Ludwig M. (1994), *Expectations and the Meaning of Institutions: Essays in Economics by Ludwig Lachmann*, London: Routledge.

Landow, George P. (1994), *Hypertext Theory*, Baltimore, MD: The Johns Hopkins University Press.

Landow, George P. (1997), *Hypertext 2.0: The Convergence of Contemporary Critical Theory and Technology*, Baltimore, MD: The Johns Hopkins University Press.

Lavoie, Don (1985), *National Economic Planning: What is Left?*, Cambridge, MA: Ballinger.

Lavoie, Don (1987), 'The accounting of interpretations and the interpretation of accounts: the communicative function of "the language of business"', *Accounting, Organizations and Society*, **12**: 579–604.

Lavoie, Don (1990a), *Economics and Hermeneutics*, London, UK: Routledge.

Lavoie, Don (1990b), 'Hermeneutics, subjectivity, and the Lester/Machlup debate: toward a more anthropological approach to empirical economics', in W. Samuels (ed.), *Economics as Discourse*, Boston, MA: Kluwer Academic Publishing.

Lavoie, Don (1990c), 'Understanding differently: hermeneutics and the spontaneous order of communicative processes', *History of Political Economy*, Annual Supplement to **22**: 359–77.

Lavoie, Don (1991a), 'The discovery and interpretation of profit opportunities: culture and the Kirznerian entrepreneur', in B. Berger (ed.), *The Culture of Entrepreneurship*, San Francisco, CA: ICS Press.

Lavoie, Don (1991b), 'The progress of subjectivism', in Mark Blaug and Neil de Marchi (eds), *Appraising Modern Economics: Studies in the Methodology of*

Scientific Research Programmes, Cheltenham, UK and Brookfield, US: Edward Elgar, pp. 470–86.
Lavoie, Don (1994), 'Cultural studies and the conditions for entrepreneurship', in T.W. Boxx and G.M. Quinlivan (eds), *The Cultural Context of Economics and Politics*, Lanham: University Press of America, Inc.
Lavoie, Don (1995), 'The market as a procedure for the discovery and conveyance of inarticulate knowledge', in D.L. Prychitko (ed.), *Individuals, Institutions, Interpretations*, Burlington: Ashgate Publishing Company.
Lavoie, Don (1997), 'Hermeneutics, hypertext, and the civil society: the big picture', Working Paper.
Lavoie, Don (2001), 'Subjective orientation and objective wealth: entrepreneurship and the convergence of groupware and hypertext capabilities', Working Paper (May draft).
Lavoie, Don and Emily Chamlee-Wright (2001), *Culture And Enterprise: The Development, Representation, and Morality of Business*, New York, NY: Routledge.
Lavoie, Don and Virgil Storr (2001), 'Distinction or dichotomy: rethinking the relationship between thymology and praxeology', Working Paper.
Lavoie, Don, Theodor Holm Nelson and Mark Gilbert (1999), 'The electronic readings group: generating annotation dialogue streams with hypertext markup tools', Working Paper.
Madison, G.B. (1988), *The Hermeneutic of Postmodernity: Figures and Themes*, Bloomington, IN: Indiana University Press.
Madison, G.B. (1990), 'Getting beyond objectivism: the philosophical hermeneutics of Gadamer and Ricoeur', in D. Lavoie (ed.), *Economics and Hermeneutics*, London, UK: Routledge.
Madison, G.B. (1991), 'Beyond seriousness and frivolity: a Gadamerian response to deconstruction', in H.J. Silverman (ed.), *Gadamer and Hermeneutics*, New York, NY: Routledge.
Madison, G.B. (1995), 'How individualistic is methodological individualism', in D.L. Prychitko (ed.), *Individuals, Institutions, Interpretations: Hermeneutics Applied to Economics*, Burlington: Ashgate Publishing Company.
McAleese, Ray (1989), *Hypertext: Theory into Practice*, Norwood, NJ: ABLEX Publishing Corporation.
McCloskey, Deirdre (2000), *How to Be Human: Though an Economist*, Ann Arbor, MI: The University of Michigan Press.
Mises, Ludwig von ([1934]1963), *Human Action: A Treatise on Economics*, 3rd revised edition, San Francisco, CA: Fox & Wilkes.
Nelson, Theodor H. (1981), *Literary Machines*, Self-published.
Prychitko, David L. (ed.) (1995), *Individuals, Institutions, Interpretations: Hermeneutics Applied to Economics*, Burlington: Ashgate Publishing Company.
Risser, James (1991), 'Reading the text', in H.J. Silverman (ed.), *Gadamer and Hermeneutics*, New York, NY: Routledge.
Rorty, Richard (1977), 'Derrida on language, being, and abnormal psychology', *The Journal of Philosophy*, **74**: 673–81.
Schutz, Alfred ([1932] 1967), *The Phenomenology of the Social World*, Evanston, IL: Northwestern University Press.
Vaughn, Karen I. (1994), *Austrian Economics in America: The Migration of a Tradition*, New York, NY: Cambridge University Press.

Wachterhauser, Brice R. (1994), *Hermeneutics and Truth*, Evanston, IL: Northwestern University Press.

Wachterhauser, Brice R. (1999), *Beyond Being: Gadamer's Post-Platonic Hermeneutical Ontology*, Evanston, IL: Northwestern University Press.

Warnke, Georgia (1987), *Gadamer: Hermeneutics, Tradition and Reason*, Stanford, CA: Stanford University Press.

PART 4

Philosophy

7. Hermeneutics and liberty: remembrance of Don Lavoie

G.B. Madison

In his life-work Don Lavoie embodied in an outstanding way a virtue often much praised but seldom practiced, that of interdisciplinarity. Don was a genuinely humanistic scholar whose interests ranged all the way from economics to political theory to philosophy to information technology. It was thanks to these wide-ranging interests of his that I in fact had the good fortune to make his acquaintance. Here's how it happened.

As a keen student of Austrian economics, Don had discovered something about the history of this discipline that had for the most part been forgotten: its philosophical background. Back in the 1920s, in the context of the informal discussions organized by Ludwig von Mises in Vienna (the so-called *Privatseminar* or *Mises-Kreis*), there had been a significant, ongoing interchange between Austrian economists and phenomenological philosophers, F.A. Hayek and Alfred Schutz in particular. Hayek at that time was concerned with the question of 'the method and philosophical character of the social sciences' (see Hayek 1992, p. 53), and Schutz, a student of Husserlian phenomenology, was very much concerned with providing Austrian economics with a suitable philosophical foundation.[1] (Schutz, it may be noted, was a younger contemporary of Hayek and had studied economics in Vienna with Mises and Friedrich von Wieser, the latter of which was one of Hayek's teachers.) This encounter between economics and philosophy was of a most interesting sort, but it was not destined to endure and to bear fruit at the time. Under the force of circumstances in the disruptive 1930s in Europe, the two disciplines drifted apart, just as did the principals in the dialogue.

The encounter itself might well have remained a forgotten chapter in the bygone history of ideas had it not been for Ludwig Lachmann. Although Lachmann studied under Werner Sombart in Berlin, he was heavily influenced by the writings of Mises, Max Weber and Wilhelm Dilthey. During World War II, Lachmann held an economics position at the University of Hull, and after the war took up a post at the University of Witwatersrand in Johannesburg. In the mid-1970s, he began splitting his time between Witwatersrand and New York University. Not only did Lachmann play a major role in the revival of Austrian economics in the United States from the mid-1970s to the mid-1980s that he taught at New York University, he also introduced a new generation of American economists to this forgotten phenomenological background of Austrian economics. Lachmann was in fact responsible for initiating a *second encounter* between economics and phenomenology by pointing out to his students the relevance to Austrian economics of more recent developments in the phenomenological movement, those now commonly referred to as *philosophical hermeneutics*. The study of market processes, Lachmann insisted, 'calls for treatment by a method inspired by the hermeneutical style, a method which defies the spirit of orthodox formalism' (Lachmann 1990, p. 145). The purpose of economic analysis is not so much *explanation* (*Erklären*) as it is *understanding* (*Verstehen*); ever since Menger, Lachmann wrote, 'the Austrian research effort...has been to *understand* and not merely give formal expression to, what men do in markets' (Lachmann 1986, p. 3). In the Hermeneutics Club he organized while at NYU, Lachmann stressed the need for economists to give careful consideration to, as he put it, 'general ideas' – over and beyond the standard requirements of the discipline of mastery in formalized, quantitative measuring techniques. Don Lavoie took these lessons to heart.

Convinced of the relevance of the 'general ideas' defended by hermeneutics to the study of market processes, Don set about acquainting himself in a most thoroughgoing fashion with the work of the two leading exponents of philosophical (or phenomenological) hermeneutics, Hans-Georg Gadamer and Paul Ricoeur. He even wrote to Gadamer directly, putting some questions to him about his work. This is how I first came to hear of Don. In the early 1980s, on the occasion of one of his visits to Canada, Gadamer mentioned to me that he had received a letter from an economist in the States by the name of Don Lavoie, and he said to me (like a good German professor to his assistant): 'You know what I think, Gary. Would you mind answering this gentleman for me?' So I did, as best as I could, and the rest, as they say, is history. A very fruitful relationship between hermeneutics and economics had begun to take shape.

Believing that the sad lack of conversations between economists and philosophers was something calling out to be remedied, Don went on in 1986 to organize under the auspices of the Center for the Study of Market Processes a pivotal conference at George Mason University entitled 'Interpretation, Human Agency, and Economics'.[2] Lachmann was the guest of honor at this conference, giving a talk on 'Economics as a Hermeneutical Discipline,' and it was for me a great and very rewarding occasion to meet not only Lachmann and, finally in person, Don himself, but also a number of Don's very bright students (Ralph Rector, Dave Prychitko, Pete Boettke, Steve Horwitz, and Matt Kibbe in particular).[3] Subsequent to the conference, Don put together a book containing some of the conference papers along with others he solicited afterwards. It took some dogged determination on his part, but this deftly edited book did finally see the light of day in 1990, although the economics editor at Routledge (where it finally found a home) requested that the title be changed from 'Hermeneutics and Economics' to *Economics and Hermeneutics.* Understandably so, no doubt, since the main intended audience of the book was the economics profession, and, as Don rightly said in his introduction to the volume, 'most economists have never even heard of hermeneutics' (Lavoie 1990, p. 1).

Thanks to Don's efforts, a number of economists have now heard of hermeneutics – though how many is an open question. I shouldn't think that even today the number would be all that great, but, not being myself an economist, I am not (unlike a Chicagoan of the George Stigler type [see for instance Stigler 1982]) particularly interested in doing quantitative measurements when it comes to the realm of ideas. What's important to know is that, by means of his unstinting labors in this field, Don did clearly demonstrate, for all those who had the ears to hear, the *philosophical* relevance of hermeneutics to economics (see, for instance, Lavoie 1994). He showed in a most convincing fashion how there exists, between Austrian economics and phenomenological hermeneutics, a kind of natural symbiosis or 'synergetic collaboration' (to borrow a phrase from Hayek [1988, p. 64]).[4]

A critical assessment of any science, natural or social – as regards its nature, its scope, its limits and the methodology most appropriate to it – is ultimately a matter of philosophical reflection, as the more sophisticated practitioners of science have always known. At a time when an uncritical, narrow-minded positivistic mentality (the 'physicalism' that Hayek inveighed against in the 1940s (Hayek 1979) – without much effect, it must be said) dominates the social sciences in general and economics in particular, this sort of philosophical–critical reflection is more urgent than ever. As Don once pertinently remarked, 'the often dubious philosophical assumptions economists carry around with them don't conveniently disappear just because they aren't brought up explicitly' (Lavoie 1988, p. 1).

In the absence of philosophical–critical reflection, it is, indeed, all too easy for working economists to fall prey to a certain cult of scientificity and to succumb to the allures of a form of mathematico-abstractive thinking which, for all its theoretical attractiveness, has oftentimes very little to do with the world inhabited by real-life, flesh-and-blood human beings (the lifeworld, as phenomenologists call it). There is nothing wrong, per se, with abstract, purely theoretical constructs like *homo economicus*, general equilibrium, Paretian optimality, rational expectations theory, or the efficient-market hypothesis, but there is, nevertheless, an inherent danger associated with them (see Lavoie 1986a). This is the danger of mistaking theoretical attractiveness for practical relevance, of, in a word, *forgetting* that constructs such as these are, indeed, *constructs*, that is, interpretations, and not objective representations ('pictures') of reality itself. It is, as Edmund Husserl said in his hermeneutical investigations into the origins of modern, mathematicized science, the danger of 'taking for true being what is only a method'.[5] When we lose sight of the nature and limits of theoretical-scientific understanding and allow ourselves to fall prey to, as Don referred to it, the 'vice of formalism', we run the risk of falling into a kind of sophisticated simple-mindedness.[6]

This is where philosophical hermeneutics comes into the picture. Hermeneutics is itself a theoretical undertaking; it is the philosophical attempt to work out a general theory of human understanding in all its forms; it is the systematic attempt to discern how understanding *in fact* works (that is, its nature and limits).[7] What many would no doubt consider to be the main tenet of philosophical hermeneutics in this regard is that all understanding is a matter of *interpretation*. Hermeneutics is the general theory of interpretation in all its forms (and is thus sometimes referred to as Interpretation Theory). Science is, of course, one way in which we creatively interpret the world in an attempt to make sense of it. Nature itself, as an early modern scientist, Leonardo da Vinci, said, is a kind of book (the *liber naturae*) which needs to be interpreted. And so likewise is the realm of human action, the proper object of the social sciences (Ludwig von Mises entitled his major work *Human Action* [1963] and referred to his approach to economics as praxeology, the study of *praxis* or action). As one hermeneuticist has said: 'Hermeneutics is concerned with the interpretation of any expression of existence which can be preserved in a structure analogous to the structure of the text. Taking it to the limit, the entirety of human existence becomes a text to be interpreted' (Pellauer 1979, pp. 112, 109). The relevance of hermeneutics to economics in this regard is that it has (implicitly, at least) a lot to say about how to read that 'text' which is an economy, that is, as Don put it, 'the price movements, or monetary institutions, or industrial organization of economies, each of which is the meaningful product of [human agency]' (Lavoie 1990, p. 2).

If economic science is a matter of making sense of the actions of human agents in the everyday economic lifeworld – relying in this endeavor, as Schutz pointed out, on ideal types such as the consumer, the businessman, the banker, the investor, and the Wall Street trader – then, like social or cultural anthropology as Clifford Geertz has described it (see Geertz 1973), it too is an interpretive, hermeneutical discipline. 'Modern economics,' as

Don said (Lavoie 1986a), 'is not so much a non-interpretive science as it is an interpretive one that has been striving to be otherwise in spite of itself....As with all the human studies, what economics needs most is a general transformation of our ways of thinking in the direction indicated by hermeneutical philosophy.' Economics ought not to be conceived of as an experimental science in search of nomological-deductive law but as an interpretive science in search of meaning, its proper object being those meaningful patterns of action that go to make of that order of human activity referred to as 'economic'. To speak in phenomenological terms, economics is a regional hermeneutics. Not only that. Hermeneutics can also take as its object what those who do this kind of interpretive work, that is, the tribe of professional economists, themselves do. What this amounts to is a kind of second-level interpretation: interpreting the interpretive activity of economists.

And this is where general hermeneutical theory is of especial relevance to economics from a methodological standpoint. For one thing, hermeneutics can, by reminding practicing economists of the *interpretive* (and metaphorical) nature of their theoretical constructs, help to keep them from falling prey to the naïve, positivistic scientism, the theoretical concept-fetishism I referred to above (mathematical 'model fetishism', as Don called it). (Even before the recent stock market crash, hermeneutical theory could have helped to moderate the theoretical zeal that some economists displayed for the efficient-markets hypothesis and which led them, against all evidence of the senses, to believe that speculative bubbles could not occur in an economy populated by rational, utility-maximizing creatures.) Hermeneutical theory can, in a word, help economists do better economics. I won't belabor this point, since it is one that has been more than amply made in the hermeneutical reflections on the practice of economists by Don McCloskey in his work on the rhetoric of economics (see McCloskey 1985 and 1994). The work of Don in this regard (carried on by Deirdre) is enough to refute some of the more malicious accusations that were made against Lavoie and the 'hermeneutical Austrians' (and, by implication, me as well) by some fellow Austrians to the effect that if philosophical hermeneutics was not purely and simply irrelevant to economics, it was, at the very least, highly pernicious.[8] All that these attacks demonstrate in the final analysis is that there are a lot of people out there who do not have, as Don rather nicely put it, 'a very sophisticated appreciation of hermeneutics'.

Be all that as it may, the philosophical–economic partnership between Don and me that got going via Gadamer was a great stimulus to my own thinking – not only in regard to economics but in regard also to philosophy itself. In retrospect, our encounter seems as if it were something that was destined to have become an integral part of my own *Denkweg* or *Dao*. What, as regards economics, Don said in the introduction to his *Economics and Hermeneutics* book certainly applied to me when I first met up with him: '[I]t is probably fair to say that very few hermeneutical writers have more than a passing familiarity with economics' (Lavoie 1990, p. 1). Having been invited a bit before then to give a talk at a meeting of the Mont Pèlerin Society hosted by the Fraser Institute in Vancouver, I knew a little about 'economics talk', but very little. Don changed all that for me. He impelled me to learn as much as I could about economics, just as he had learned so much about philosophy.[9] It is really with great pride that I see myself sometimes referred to in the literature as an 'Austrian scholar'. If I am now a legitimate Austrian scholar (as a number of my publications might suggest), this is something I owe to Don. The only reason I make these rather personal comments is because it testifies, as I said at the outset, to Don's great learning and his desire to break down barriers between disciplines – to, in a word, his belief in what Gadamer called 'conversation'. And on the philosophical side of the ledger, barriers were certainly overcome.

To talk in terms of information technology, a very interesting feed-back loop developed, thanks to my relationship with Don. This is the way it worked: as I mentioned, Don had started off by writing to Gadamer; I answered Don in Gadamer's name; which got me involved with Don and his circle of outstanding students. This in turn stimulated me to concentrate on economics as one area where hermeneutics could be 'applied' with interesting ramifications for the whole issue of political economy. Gadamer naturally always kept up on what I was doing, and at one point (when I had been invited to Frankfurt to give a talk to an august assemblage of Habermasian Critical Theorists)[10] Gadamer made it publicly known at that event that he fully supported me in my attempt to read Austrian economics (that is, economic liberalism) back into his own hermeneutics.[11] That was indeed, after many years, the closing of the loop that Don had initially opened. In other words, via the work Don had inspired me to do, he had brought Gadamer around to subscribing to the premises from which Don himself had started out. That's no mean accomplishment. When a young, American, assistant professor (as he was then) can have a big influence on the most famous living German philosopher, that is something that merits being noted.

At bottom, the thing that perhaps made all of this interesting communication possible, or which in any event greatly facilitated it, was Don's unswerving commitment to freedom (or liberty) in all its forms. The Ideal of Freedom, as Hayek referred to it, had always been a prime concern of mine[12] (though it took Don to show me how it applies in economics), and freedom was always the leading value in the phenomenological tradition, in both Husserl's transcendental phenomenology and in the existential phenomenology that developed out of it. Gadamer summed up very well the hermeneutical position in this matter when he stated: 'There is no higher principle of reason than that of freedom' (Gadamer 1981, p. 9). From a hermeneutical point of view, it is only in light of the rational principle of freedom that human history has meaning; indeed, from a hermeneutical point of view the entire record of history – of human agency – is to be interpreted or understood as 'the ever-to-be-renewed and the never-ending struggle' for freedom, which is to say, for 'the freedom of all'.[13]

Although I'm not aware of Don's actually saying so, I am inclined to think that this was a belief he held as well. In any event, it seems to me that the principle of freedom was the lens through which he viewed everything else. His overriding commitment to freedom was, I suggest, the underlying reason why he was so opposed to the on-going attempt (ever since the nineteenth-century) to make of economics a kind of social physics or Newtonian mechanics of human affairs and to what Nobel Laureate Amartya Sen has called the 'engineering' approach to economic issues (see Sen 1987, p. 4).[14] The main reason, I suspect, why Don was such an uncompromising critic of the 'panmechanistic' world-view (as Mises called it) that dominates mainstream economic thinking is because this theoretical-interpretive approach to things ('mechanicomorphism', as it has been aptly labeled, see Mittermaier 1986) leaves absolutely no room for acknowledging, let alone understanding, human freedom. If, as phenomenology maintains, the essence of human being is freedom, there is absolutely nothing *human* about that calculating utility-maximizer known as 'economic man', as that outstanding economist, Frank Knight, argued earlier in the last century (see, for instance, Knight 1982, pp. 246–7). What worth (as in the economic expression, 'What's it worth?') can economics have (one is inclined to ask) if, as a science, it ignores that which is most essential about the object it purports to study.

The fact of the matter is that freedom is not a mere variable in an economic calculation; it is, as Knight said, 'the meaning of human living'. And as one of Knight's students, James Buchanan, has said, the meaning of human being is 'becoming'. To a large extent, as Buchanan says, we are and will be that which, in our freedom, we make ourselves to be; we are 'artefactual' beings, products of our own making (see Buchanan 1979, pp. 94, 110) – a point also insisted upon by existential phenomenology. Thus, as Buchanan observes, human beings, as 'imagining' beings, do not value freedom simply for its 'instrumental' value, for the sake of maximizing present, known utilities. Indeed, as he says, 'individuals do not maximize anything that remains stable for more than the logical moment for analysis' (Buchanan 1979, p. 109). In a work of his with the revealing title, *What Should Economists Do?*, Buchanan wrote: 'Let us remove once and for all the instrumental defense of liberty, the only one that can possibly be derived directly from orthodox economic analysis. Man does not want liberty in order to maximize his utility, or that of the society of which he is a part.'[15] Precisely because, orthodox economics notwithstanding, life is shot through with *contingency*, *uncertainty* and *risk* and humans do not *know* what, in the *unforeseeable* future, they might want to become (and thus cannot have any 'rational expectations' in this regard), they value freedom or liberty *for its own sake*, as something which is a value 'in itself'. As I said on another occasion in speaking of the freedom-to-be (see Madison 1996): if freedom is a supreme value, it is not because it enables us, instrumental-wise, to achieve this or that particular goal, but simply because it enables us to be the kind of person we not only want, at any given moment, as a matter of fact, to be, but because it is the necessary condition for becoming the altogether different kind of person we might in the unforeseeable future just possibly might want to become.

Buchanan's argument in defense of liberty and against the mechanistic-deterministic mind-set that dominates mainstream economics is of a distinctly phenomenological-hermeneutical sort, and it is of vital importance when, in the realm of *praxis*, it comes to, as he says, 'promoting rather than holding back the good society of free and responsible men and women' (Buchanan 1979, p. 106). To speak of 'the good society of free and responsible men and women' is to speak in decidedly ethical terms. If the proper object of economics is human reality, and if human reality is the realm of freedom, then, it must be allowed, economics is not a natural-science type discipline but, as the founder of Austrian economics, Carl Menger, said, an 'ethical' science having to do with 'the ethical world', the realm of human or 'ethical phenomena' (see Menger 1985, p. 58). All of Don Lavoie's theoretical work in economics was fundamentally 'ethical', in that it was all guided by a practical, properly ethical concern. As he said in one of his earlier writings, 'We need to find a principled approach to social issues which will outline a clear goal of a peaceful, prosperous, and just society, and then seek consistent and feasible paths to its realization' (Lavoie 1985a, p. 16). His overriding concern was for freedom or liberty, which, for hermeneutics, is the highest of all political-ethical values. In everything he dealt with, Don was guided by this most supreme of ethical values, by the ideal of what he called 'a radically liberal society' (see Lavoie 1993).

It is this underlying practical concern which accounts for his unremitting hostility, on the theoretical level, to the idea of economic planning, of either a comprehensive or noncomprehensive sort.[16] The Austrian critique of the idea of economic planning, as instanced in the famous 'socialist calculation debate' of the 1930s, is that any such attempt at planning ignores the role that *monetary prices* play in an economy. As Hayek showed in his work on the philosophy of knowledge, in a market economy prices perform a *cognitive function*; when prices are determined by the free play of supply and demand, they communicate to economic actors vital information about the relative scarcity of goods and services, and they do this without, as Hayek was insistent on pointing out, anyone's having to know anything about the causes behind changes in relative scarcity. By means of this knowledge-conveyance and discovery process, the price system allows for the most efficient or profitable allocation of resources. The crucial point in all this, as Austrians have traditionally argued, is that there is simply no way that, in the absence of market generated prices, a planned or centrally controlled economy could determine (calculate) the 'right' price of anything. If socialism had ever managed to conquer the world, I'm sure the socialists themselves would have wanted to allow at least one country to remain free (say Luxembourg, for instance), just so that they would have had a means for knowing what prices they should attach to things.

Over and beyond the details of the socialist calculation debate and the role played by prices, which Don presented in a masterful way, what I found most interesting is that he should have referred to this classic debate not as the 'calculation problem' but as the 'knowledge problem'. His interest in this matter was philosophical–hermeneutical; his basic concern was the nature of 'knowledge' itself and how it comes to be generated (he had made of point of reading up on the 'growth of knowledge' literature, see Lavoie 1985b). Summing up his position, he stated: '[T]he whole case against planning that is being developed here is rooted in a critique of objectivist theories of knowledge' (Lavoie 1985a, p. 57). Knowledge, Don argued, is not merely an amoral ('value-free'), 'epistemological' affair having to do with the relation between an atomistic, Robinson Crusoe subject and an objective, determinate world. Knowledge is not the same thing as information or data and is never simply 'discovered' but is something that is always *produced* by individuals acting in concert and within the shared context of an interpretive framework of one sort or another. Contrary to one of the most tenacious of modernist (Cartesian) prejudices, knowledge is never merely, or even primarily, 'subjective' (existing within the confines of individual 'minds') but is something that is essentially *intersubjective* (existing, as it were, 'outside' of the individuals who make use of it). Any organized body of knowledge is *social* through and through (and, being social or 'intersubjective', it has an unavoidably ethical dimension). There exists a kind of *social intelligence* that transcends individual consciousnesses and that cannot properly be understood in purely individualist terms.[17] Society is of course composed of individuals and does not exist as an entity in its own right (contrary to what collectivists seem to think), but 'just as surely', as Don said, 'individuals are composed of society' (Lavoie 1994, p. 58). Opposing 'the individual' to 'society' (in such a way as to subordinate one of the terms to the other, as in the old individualism vs. collectivism debate) is, hermeneutics maintains, a legacy of metaphysical either/or thinking that needs to be overcome (see Madison 1995). I would be tempted to say that one of Don's most significant contributions to Austrian economics was precisely the way in which, his unshakable commitment to individual liberty notwithstanding, he managed to highlight the social dimension of human action,[18] helping in this way to counteract a way of thinking which, qua theory, not only gives rise to a faulty view of knowledge but which also, qua practice, has disastrous consequences when it comes to promoting what Buchanan referred to as a 'good society', viz., the atomistic, solipsistic individualism that dominates mainline economic thinking and to which Austrian theorists have not themselves been wholly immune.

From a hermeneutical point of view, the market process is to be conceived of not in physicalistic terms as a kind of 'allocation mechanism' that automatically (like some kind of physical equilibrating system) produces an 'efficient' distribution of resources but, rather, as a form of creative *play* (*Spiel*) in Gadamer's sense. In other words, the market process is to be understood not in terms of instrumental rationality (as it generally is, by critics and defenders of the market alike) but in terms of what hermeneuticists call *communicative rationality*. The market process is a *communicative process*, a 'conversation' or 'dialogue' by means of which acting persons manage, in the face of ignorance and uncertainty, to arrive at spontaneously generated agreements ('coordination'). The notion of spontaneity is crucial here. The market process is like a conversation in that in a genuine conversation no one, as Gadamer says, can know in advance what will 'come out' (see Gadamer 1975, p. 345). Herein lies the ultimate philosophical–hermeneutical justification for the free market. When the market process is conceptualized in terms of a 'conversation' (as Gadamer describes it), it is clear why it is meaningless to think that, in a command economy, prices could somehow be effectively 'pre-coordinated', that is, determined in advance of actual market transactions. A hermeneutical understanding of the notion of spontaneous order furnishes the ultimate argument against the idea of central planning.[19] For Don, the notion of spontaneous order was in fact a more fundamental notion than that of market process (see Lavoie 1994, p. 56). The market is simply one of the many complex orders of human cooperation of a spontaneous sort that go to make up the extended social order of communicative processes characteristic of a free society.

If, as hermeneutical theory has it, the economic realm of a free society is a communicative process, then, as a practical injunction, it follows that the communication or 'conversation' should be as free as possible. The 'radically liberal society' that Don envisaged (see Lavoie 1993) is one which promotes the freedom of the individuals of which it is comprised by according them a full range of rights and liberties – civil, political *and* economic. One very interesting aspect of Don's work in this regard is that it shows how one might, in a properly liberal manner, conceive of *economic democracy*. Don was never one to let leftists steal the show, so to speak, by claiming as their own notions that, properly understood, are thoroughly liberal (in the way, for instance, that today's anti-globalizers have attempted to appropriate for their own anti-liberal purposes the quintessential liberal notion of 'civil society'). Believing as he did that 'the ideals of democracy and markets are essentially complementary' (Lavoie 1993, p. 109), Don could see no reason why leftists should be allowed to take over the moral high ground and claim exclusionary rights to the notion of economic democracy.

It is of course true that any attempt to implement economic democracy in the way in which leftists understand it would render meaningless the most fundamental economic right of all, the right to private property. Nonetheless, being open as he was to worthwhile ideas from whatever quarter they might come, Don allowed that the leftists had a valid point. 'Democracy', he said, 'should apply to all of our lives and should not be narrowly conceived as a form of government.' Democratic principles should be 'extended throughout society and into the very production process of the economy' (Lavoie 1992, pp. 440, 436). The important thing in this regard is to *rethink* democracy in such a way that it conforms to the actual logic of the market economy.[20] To think, as leftists do, that markets could be made democratic simply by subjecting them to the direct control of a *government* claiming to be democratic is not only naïve but would be, as Don said, 'a throwback to pre-democratic thinking' (Lavoie 1992, p. 451).

How, then, ought democracy to be conceived, such that it would be appropriate to the nature of market processes – which, let us recall, is that of communicative rationality? Here is where Don turned to hermeneutics.[21] Democracy, he said, has not so much to do with mere voting as it does with 'the extent to which the prevailing attitudes of the participants are conducive to genuine dialogue' (Lavoie 1992, p. 439). With a view to Gorbachev's attempts at democratic reform, Don spoke in this connection of *glasnost*, openness: 'What I think we should mean by democracy is the distinctive kind of *openness* in society which the Soviet system crushed, and which began to recover under the banner of *glasnost*.' And as he went on to say: 'It seems to me that this openness and publicness, not some particular theory of how to elect the personnel of government, is the essence of democracy' (Lavoie 1993, p. 111). Inquiring into the 'core meaning' of democracy and into exactly what it is that makes a culture, a government and a market democratic, Don said in a way which makes one think immediately of Gadamer: 'Democracy ... can be usefully defined as that set of attitudes conducive to mutual understanding and an open-ended process of dialogue ... [A] good conversation is in many ways the model of what we mean by democracy' (Lavoie 1992, p. 440).[22]

Working with this understanding of democracy, the question then becomes that of how the notions of openness and dialogue can be applied not just to 'the way we exchange words with one another, but also the way we exchange goods and services' (Lavoie 1992, p. 436). I won't elaborate on this issue here, since it is really only a matter of cashing out the hermeneutical–dialogical model in terms that Austrian economists have traditionally used to describe the market process, conceived of as 'an open-ended process with its own systematic dynamic' (Lavoie 1992, p. 451). As, in other words, a creative discovery process.

Economic democracy, then, is to be conceived of in terms of the hermeneutical principle of freedom of discourse; so conceived, economic democracy is precisely what permits the creative discovery process to operate in the economic arena, just as it does in the cultural and political arenas. Voluntary transactions are the very essence of a market economy, and when the market is conceived of in hermeneutical–Austrian terms it becomes possible to spell out the kind of economic rights and liberties that are constitutive of economic democracy. Two of the most basic of economic rights (counting as fundamental human rights) are the right to acquire and dispose of property and the right to work, by which I mean the right freely to pursue, within the limits of the law, any line of economic activity to which one believes oneself suited – the right, in other words, of 'free entry in markets'. Economic rights are not rights as socialists conceive of them; they are not rights to hand-outs from the State or the right to live at someone else's expense (as Frédéric de Bastiat aptly said, 'Socialism is the attempt on the part of everyone to live at the expense of everyone else'). Like political and civil rights (or liberties), economic rights are 'formal' rights, rights to a certain kind of *freedom* (in the liberal or 'negative' sense of the term).[23] This, it should clearly be noted, is a freedom or liberty that is still denied to much of the world's population.[24]

There is a great, two-fold advantage to approaching the whole issue of economic democracy and economic rights in the way Don did: on the one hand, it serves, as I indicated, to rescue what are basically liberal ideas from leftists who seek to employ them for their own anti-liberal purposes. At the same time it allows for the possibility of a productive dialogue with those leftists ('social democrats', say) who strive to be open-minded and to adhere to the fundamental hermeneutical imperative of 'good will' and who do have something constructive to contribute to what Michael Oakshott called the 'conversation of mankind'. Hayek notwithstanding, even the notion of 'social justice' can be interpreted in a perfectly good liberal (that is, non-statist) manner.[25]

Although he was an ardent defender of the market economy, Don was not by any means a 'market fundamentalist', by which I mean that he did not defend the market for ideological reasons and did not believe that unfettered markets automatically operate in the most efficient and 'economic' of ways and always produce 'optimal' results. In a 'perfect' world of omniscient and perfectly rational agents that would no doubt be the case, but in actuality this world is not, and never will be, perfect.[26] Don did not defend the market economy simply because he thought it was, in economic terms, the most efficient system yet devised. Like Ben Rogge, his commitment to the market was basically of a *moral* nature.[27] He defended the market for the simple reason that, when all is said and done, no society can be truly *free* in which citizens do not also enjoy, in addition to political and civil liberties, the greatest possible degree of economic freedom. Don was a genuinely *political* economist whose guiding idea was liberty, and the great attractiveness, to my mind, of Don's way of dealing with issues in political philosophy and political economy was the way it was so thoroughly non-dogmatic and non-ideological in character. (In my experience, laissez-fairists of a dogmatic sort resemble nothing so much as doctrinaire Marxists.)

Of particular interest in this regard was Don's keen appreciation of the vital role played by cultural, political and legal *institutions* in a market economy. Don was never so naïve as to think that the market functions best when, as a laissez-fairist might say, it is 'left to its own devices'. Unlike some laissez-fairists, Don did not hold to a simplistic idea of freedom, confusing liberty with license, or freedom with anarchy and equating it with the *absence* of rules and regulations. Don knew perfectly well that, as Oakeshott put it,

> if effective competition is to exist it can do so only by virtue of a legal system which promotes it.... To know that unregulated competition is a chimera, to know that to regulate competition is not the same thing as to interfere with the operation of competitive controls, and to know the difference between these two activities, is the beginning of the political economy of freedom (Oakshott 1962, p. 559).

An important, though usually overlooked, point to keep in mind in this connection is one that Mises once made: 'The policy of Liberalism', he said, 'is the policy of the common good'; from a liberal point of view, that system known as 'capitalism' exists to serve primarily not the private interests of capitalists but the common good, and, as he further pointed out, capitalists themselves cannot be relied on to defend the capitalist system, since their purely private interests can actually be well served by socialist-type measures ('To fight on principle for the maintenance of an economy based on private property is not part of the programme of organized entrepreneurs') (Mises 1981, pp. 455–56). In the normal course of events, market participants do not always (sad as it is to say) pursue their own best interests (see Madison 1998a). They are as prone to bouts of 'irrational exuberance' as they are to 'infectious greed', such that a well-functioning market economy designed to promote the common good (which, in the long term, is in the interests of all) requires, as Hayek for his part observed, 'an intelligently designed and continuously adjusted legal framework as much as any other' (Hayek 1944, p. 39). There is absolutely no contradiction involved in maintaining that while the market is a *spontaneous* order (just as are the cultural and political orders of a democratic society), it is also one that requires *diligent cultivation.*[28] The trouble with any dogmatic laissez-fairism that is based on the 'dubious philosophical assumptions' (as Don would say) of atomistic individualism and rationalistic utility-maximization ('egoism') and that advocates a 'minimal state' is that it allows no scope for the rational cultivation of the institutional-communicative environment in which the market process operates.[29] '[E]mphasis on the spontaneous nature of the extended or macro-order', Hayek warned, 'could mislead if it conveyed the impression that, in the macro-order, deliberate organisation is never important.' Quite to the contrary, the spontaneous order of the market requires, according to Hayek, the appropriate 'governmental framework' if it is to flourish and continue to evolve in a desirable fashion (see Hayek 1988, p. 37).[30]

One of the basic tenets of hermeneutics is what could be called 'the primacy of the practical over the theoretical' (see Madison 2001, chap. 5). For hermeneutics, theory is not, as it is for rationalism, an end in itself and should never be allowed to dominate or substitute for actual practice in a *dirigiste* sort of way. Nevertheless, even though theory should always remain subordinate to practice, it does have a vital, constructive role to play as regards practice. Don summed up this whole issue very nicely when speaking of the Hayekean distinction between *cultivation* and *control*:

> Hayek's term 'cultivation' is useful to suggest that when we understand a complex order's general principles of operation we may be able to cultivate conditions in which that order can best operate. Attempts to directly control the detailed operation of such complex processes as scientific discovery, political discourse, industrial organization, or the distribution and level of employment, have failed, but this does not mean that we need to give up trying to improve on the workings of these processes. What we need to do is cultivate more appropriate conditions within which these uncontrollable processes are more likely to yield the kinds of beneficial results we desire (Lavoie 1988b, p. 1).

The role that hermeneutical theorizing – interpretation – plays in this regard is that of enabling us to discover 'a complex order's general principles of operation' ('the principle of the thing', as Hayek called it), that is, the inner dynamic or meaning-structure which is constitutive of any particular social order. Once we have done so, we are in a position to alter existing practices in such a way as, on the one hand, to eliminate factors which are contrary to the 'logic' of the order or system, and which thus result in malfunctionings of the system, and, on the other hand, to devise new, institutional structures which will allow the system to function in a smoother way and to 'evolve' further.

Although it is altogether misleading to speak of 'steering mechanisms' in regard to a market economy (as, for instance, a neo-Marxist like Habermas does; see, in this regard, Madison 2001, chap. 7, and Madison 2000) – since in such an economy there is no one in the driver's seat, its chief characteristic being that it 'steers itself' – there are times when any such economy stands in need of judicious regulatory overhaul. Even though a market economy is a spontaneous order (a 'self-ordering' system), it is something that requires always a great deal of cultivation. There are even times when a market economy needs to be deliberately created from scratch, as it were. This was, in fact, the task that the Freiburg school of Ordo-liberals, working in the tradition of Austrian economics, assigned themselves when they set out to create a market economy in the ruins of post-war Germany.[31] This was an attempt on their part to draw up an 'economic constitution' (*Wirtschaftsverfassung*) modeled on Madisonian political constitutionalism, the purpose of which was to institutionalize liberty in the economic realm in the same way as a political constitution does in the political realm (see Madison 1998, pp. 157–61). The German attempt to create a free market is highly interesting as regards the proper relation (as hermeneutics sees it) between theory and practice, since, like the political order crafted by Madison and his associates, the economic order devised by the German neo-liberals was a *deliberate* attempt to promote the *spontaneous* ordering of a free society.

Liberalism is synonymous with constitutionalism, and economic constitutionalism (as it might well be called) is as essential to the building and maintenance of a free society as is political constitutionalism. As the ancient defenders of liberty (for example, Cicero) knew, there can be no Liberty without Law; no society can be truly free that lacks the proper *institutional* framework – cultural, political, and economic – and the more complex a society is, the truer this is. The fact of the matter is that individuals can be the individuals they are capable of becoming – can, as Hayek would say, be individuals in the 'true' sense of the term (see Hayek 1976a) – only when they have the good fortune to exist within the appropriate cultural and institutional frameworks, in particular those provided by the liberal State (the rule of law) and democratic capitalism. The market system itself could not properly exist without *money*, and as Georg Simmel pointed out in *The Philosophy of Money* published originally in 1900 (1990), money is not a natural entity but is, like language itself, a cultural or *geistig*, institutional phenomenon (and is thus, like all things cultural, something whose value is in constant need of 'cultivation').[32] As Don argued, contrary to a view espoused by many laissez-fairists (and, indeed, by neoclassical economists in general), markets are not driven by narrow materialist interests and are neither apolitical nor acultural.

Don sometimes bemoaned the current state of the economics profession and the fact that, in contrast to economists of earlier generations like Mises and Hayek or Knight and Buchanan, economists today often have limited cultural horizons and display no great interest in 'general ideas'.[33] In his intellectual life Don did what he could to remedy this 'progressive narrowing and technocatization of economics' (Lavoie 1986a). He was a worthy figure in what I would call the great tradition of philosopher-economists, from Adam Smith on (Smith, it will be recalled, was a professor of Moral Philosophy at the University of Edinburgh). Don liked to think of himself as a 'radical', and that he was, if being radical means getting at the root issues and thinking things through in a radical way. He was radical not just in his commitment to liberty but also with respect to the philosophically sophisticated manner in which he sought to conceptualize it. Although he clearly had something of a libertarian streak in him (with respect to his residual hostility to 'government'),[34] he nevertheless succeeded in overcoming the simplistic understanding of liberty that many 'anarchists', libertarians, and laissez-fairists often display.[35] He was radical in his critique of neoclassical economics, and he was radical also in the way he sought to go back and revive the philosophical–phenomenological roots of Austrian economics.[36] His implementation of the interpretive turn in economics amounted in fact to, as he said, 'a radicalization of subjectivism, transforming it from being just one among several distinct and somewhat divergent methodological tenets into being the single integrative concept which underlies the whole methodology of the Austrian school' (Lavoie 1994, p. 61).

Back in 1940 a leading American economist, Frank Knight, published a lengthy critical review of a book by the economic historian T.W. Hutchinson (1938) which, in line with the emerging trend of the times, advocated an empiricistic, positivistic approach to the 'methodology or philosophy of economics' and which Knight found 'particularly irritating' (see Knight 1956, p. 151). In opposition to Hutchinson's antihumanist way of attempting to understand things human, Knight, who was sympathetic to the Austrians and who, being a philosopher in his own right, always stressed the importance for economic science and policy of 'a broad, general education in the cultural sense', stated that there was a need 'for an interpretative study (*verstehende Wissenschaft*) which ... would need to go far beyond any possible boundaries of economics and should include the humanities as well as the entire field of the social disciplines' (Knight 1956, p. 177). Perhaps one could sum up Don's intellectual achievements by saying that, in a time of narrow over-specialization, he embodied in a thoroughly commendable way the broad learning that Knight so admired and that he succeeded to a great extent in laying out the basic principles of the kind of far-ranging interpretive or hermeneutical analysis of human affairs that Knight had hoped for. Liberalism, as Don realized, is (and is likely to remain) an incomplete project,[37] but in his life-work Don Lavoie did a remarkable lot to advance the cause of what he called (see Lavoie 1993, p. 108, n. 8) a 'post-socialist', 'radical' liberalism – a truly genuine liberalism.

NOTES

1. See Hayek 1992, p. 32: 'Through Schutz we all became familiar with Max Weber and Husserl's phenomenology.'
2. For a detailed account of this conference, see Rector 1986.
3. For a sampling of the writings of some of these young scholars, see Boettke and Prychitko, eds. 1994 and Prychitko, ed. 1995.
4. What is most distinctive about Austrian economics is precisely that which it has in common with hermeneutics: an emphasis on *process* over stasis (for hermeneutics, understanding is essentially of a 'processual' nature; understanding or 'knowledge' is not to be understood as the search for a final, definitive 'truth'; understanding is a 'spontaneous order' process) and a privileging of 'meaning-analysis' (interpretation) over causal explanation. As Don once wrote: 'The Austrian school distinguishes itself from mainstream economics in two fundamental respects: it focuses on the economy as an ongoing process of change, as contrasted with the mainstream's preoccupation with static states [equilibrium], and it considers the economy to be a matter of cultural meaning, rather than mere quantitative regularities....[T]he Austrian school takes time and radical change very seriously, and cannot be satisfied with a theory that reduces social dynamics to a deterministic causal mechanism' (Lavoie 1990a, pp. 4–5).

   For a discussion of some of the more noteworthy affinities between Austrian economics and hermeneutics, see Madison (1994a). One way of summing up the far-ranging affinities between hermeneutics and Austrian economics would be to say that both abandon, as Lachmann says (1986, p. 5), 'equilibrium in favour of process analysis' (hermeneutics seeks to conceptualize the communicative-understanding process precisely *as* a process – of an open-ended sort – and not terms of 'ideal speech situations' and final end-states marked by 'consensus,' that is, perfect agreement).
5. Husserl (1970, p. 51). Cf. Frank Knight (1956, p. 177): '[N]o problem is purely economic except by abstraction from other and more important features of concrete human existence.'
6. See Lavoie (1994, p. 55): 'Formalism is the artificial severing of economic theory construction from application, in effect the separation of theory from contact with the lifeworld, with everyday reality as we know it. In neoclassicism it takes the form

of mathematicization, but formalism has its Austrian variants as well.' Don once characterized his efforts as an attempt to extend Lachmann's critique of formalism: '[W]hat I now believe is the chief obstacle to progress in contemporary economics [is] the overexalted respect for formalistic at the expense of interpretive modes of explanation' (Lavoie 1986, p. 193).

7. For an overview of the background and main tenets of philosophical hermeneutics, see Madison (1994b) and, for an argument to the effect that hermeneutics is a discipline of *universal* scope, Madison 1996a.
8. See for instance Gordon (1987). At Don's request, I replied to these misguided accusations in Madison (1988).
9. This learning I was able to put to good use in Madison (1998), a detailed study of the various orders, the economic in particular, that constitute a free society.
10. The text of this talk appears as chapter 7, 'Hermeneutical liberalism', in Madison (2001).
11. In Gadamer (1997), Gadamer remarks on the usage I make of economics to illustrate some basic themes in hermeneutics in the following way: '[I]n Madison's presentation [of the hermeneutical role played by prices in a market economy as elucidated by Austrian economics] it makes sense to me that the market economy presents a convincing analogy to communication in a dialogue. When Madison speaks of the language of prices he could equally well have talked of the balancing-out (*Sich-Einspielen*) of prices in the market event, and this corresponds exactly to my own concept of play (*Spiel*) and its model function in the linguistic event as well as in understanding art....In my eyes...it is convincing and important that in the field of the economic sciences one should...speak more of the experience of practice than of the regulative schemata of economic models.... The market event is indeed really like a good discussion: one cannot know in advance what will come out of it' (p. 367).

    Gadamer's last remark might be profitably compared with Buchanan's observations in this regard: '[T]here is no means by which even the most idealized omniscient designer could duplicate the results of voluntary interchange. The potential participants *do not know until they enter the process* [the 'game'] what their own choices will be. From this it follows that it is *logically impossible* for an omniscient designer to know, unless, of course, we are to preclude individual freedom of the will' (Buchanan 1985, p. 74). Note Buchanan's reference to *freedom*. As I shall argue in what follows, freedom or liberty is the supreme value for both hermeneutics and the liberal economics of Buchanan and the Austrians.
12. It was what led me to write *The Logic of Liberty* (Madison 1986), which Don subsequently reviewed in a critical essay (Lavoie 1988a).
13. Gadamer (1981, p. 9). For a discussion of the hermeneutical philosophy of history, see my 'Global Ontologies', (Madison 2002).
14. In regard to the 'physics envy' that has long afflicted economics, see Mirowski (1988 and 1989).
15. Buchanan (1979, p. 112). Buchanan remarks: 'I have done little more than stress what Frank Knight spent much time discussing, namely man's tendency to want better things, to become a better man' (p. 100). Humans, he says 'imagine themselves to be other than they are and...they take action designed to achieve imagined states of being' (p. 103).
16. See Lavoie (1985a), as well as his earlier 1985. For a succinct statement of Don's views in this matter, see Lavoie (1995).
17. Cf. Lavoie (1995, pp. 125, 127): 'Through the interaction of intelligent beings in a social context, the society as a whole attains a kind of "intelligence" that is far greater than the sum of its parts....In fact our knowledge is fundamentally premised on our being embedded in a social process about the working of which we have only the crudest conception.'
18. 'Action is social at its very roots, in the very ability to formulate plans' (Lavoie 1994, p. 58).
19. In what could be called a 'reverse' move, I have used the Austrian argument against central planning based on its analysis of the cognitive–communicative role played by prices to

illustrate some basic themes in hermeneutics – another example of what I referred to as the 'symbiotic' relation between hermeneutics and Austrian economics; see Madison (1994).

20. See Lavoie (1993, p. 106): 'Liberalism needs to reinterpret its notions of markets and democracy in such a way that they fundamentally fit with each other. The principles of political and economic liberalism can be understood in a manner that makes them essentially complementary, but this will require some profound changes in the way we think about both. Seeing democracy and markets as *essentially* complementary suggests the possibility that we do not need to balance them off one another, and that they can each be taken considerably further than we have yet taken them.'
21. Hermeneutics, as I have argued, provides the philosophical basis for a general Theory of Democracy; see Madison (2001).
22. Cf. Lavoie (1993, p. 111, n. 14): 'The idea of openness has been elaborated by hermeneutical philosophy in its account of the conditions for mutual understanding in everyday life, in the humanities, and in science.'
23. The right of 'free entry' means that artificial barriers should not be erected which prevent or hinder individuals from pursuing any line of economic activity for which they believe they have a talent and from which they believe they can gain a decent living and can improve their well-being. As James Madison very pertinently stated in this regard: 'That is not a just government, nor is property secure under it, where arbitrary restrictions, exemptions, and monopolies deny to part of its citizens that free use of their faculties and free choice of their occupations which not only constitute their property in the general sense of the word [i.e., their 'indubitable, unalienable, and indefeasible rights'] but are the means of acquiring property strictly so called' (James Madison 1999, p. 516).
24. See in this regard the very interesting work of the Peruvian liberal activist, Hernando de Soto, in particular de Soto (2000), as well as de Soto (1989).
25. The notion of 'social justice' is not, contra Hayek, a meaningless term from a liberal point of view, merely a socialist 'mirage'; see Hayek (1976) and, for a discussion of the matter, Madison (1998).
26. A central tenet in basic hermeneutical theory in this regard is that human understanding is *essentially* finite.
27. Cf. Rogge (1979, pp. 40–41): 'I attach relatively little importance to the demonstrated efficiency of the free-market system in promoting economic growth, in raising levels of living. In fact, my central thesis is that *the most important case for economic freedom is not its vaunted efficiency as a system for organizing resources, nor its dramatic success in promoting economic growth, but rather its consistency with certain fundamental moral principles of life itself*. . . .[T]he significance I attach to those moral principles would lead me to prefer the free enterprise system even if it were demonstrably less efficient than alternative systems, even if it were to produce a *slower* rate of economic growth than systems of central direction and control.' (emphasis in original.)
28. See in this regard Kornai (1992): 'The market coordination of the developed countries emerged spontaneously, but each step in its development was supported by legislation and legal practice. There are a great many refined legal regulations to protect decentralized private transactions, enforce the observance of contracts, ensure fair competition, remove the obstacles to free entry, provide orderly ways of "exit", and defend the rights of debtors and creditors' (p. 452). In the absence of laws and regulations whose purpose is that of guaranteeing the 'security' of economic agents, the kind of market that would tend to prevail would not be a freely coordinating market but, as the Russians would say, a *mafiya* controlled market.
29. Classical liberalism is the doctrine of the *limited* state, not the *minimal* state; the difference between the two notions is all-important.
30. Although Hayek was an unremitting critic of 'constructivist rationalism', he did not, contrary to what is often thought, advocate a laissez-faire, agnostic evolutionism but defended, rather, a 'rational liberalism'; see Vanberg (1994).
31. For information on the background role played by Hayek and the Austrian school in the construction of the German social market economy (*Soziale Marktwirtschaft*), see

the many references to these subjects in Peacock and Willgerodt (1989). Ludwig Erhard, Walter Eucken and Wilhelm Roepke, key players in this endeavor, were all members of the Mont Pèlerin Society founded by Hayek in 1947.

32. For an attempt to conceptualize money along hermeneutical lines, in terms of the communicative process and as a kind of language, see Horwitz (1992a and 1992b).
33. Cf. Lavoie (1986a): 'As each generation of students is sent out into the profession its composition of bland and narrow technicians as compared with reflective and open scholars shifts for the worse. In the 1930s the profession was led by such true scholars as Frank Knight, Joseph Schumpeter and F.A. Hayek. As we proceed to the subsequent generations we see an undoubted increase in the mastery of technique combined with an alarming shrinkage of scholarship. Those young economists most of us consider the best and the brightest of our profession are generally unabashedly ignorant of the history of their own discipline, are often uninterested in any other human sciences, and are apt to impart similar attitudes to their students. The publish or perish and tenure systems encourage the kind of quick maturation time of scholarship that is typical of mathematics but rare in the historical sciences. As each new generation of graduate students enters the profession the depth of historical knowledge declines as the required technical sophistication grows.'
34. Although it does not justify a libertarian or 'minimalist' theory of government, Public Choice Theory should nevertheless make us extremely skeptical about the claims of government bureaucrats and elected officials to be acting 'in the public interest'.
35. As Don remarked (Lavoie 1993, p. 116): 'Anarchism seems workable to its advocates only because they implicitly assume a certain democratic political culture will prevail.' In this regard it may be noted that Don was clearly not a libertarian of the Murray Rothbard type (who was himself vehemently opposed to Don's attempt at instituting the 'interpretive turn' in Austrian economics), of whom he wrote: 'It seems that for Rothbard and his followers, genuine political discourse is not even needed in order to *get* to the free society. Instead, it seems there needs to be what is essentially a religious-conversion experience. The definition of rights is not open to exploratory dialogue but presumed to have been accomplished once and for all in Rothbard's *Ethics of Liberty* (Atlantic Highlands, NJ: Humanities Press, 1982).' (Lavoie 1993, p. 118, n. 30).
36. Cf. Lavoie (1986a): 'Hermeneutics is in my view the missing link in the modern American Austrian movement. It reconnects Austrians to their roots in the German language from which their English language training in economics had been artificially disconnected.'
37. Referring to Fukuyama's 'end of history' thesis (see Fukuyama 1989 and 1992), Don stated: 'I want to insist that the liberalism that is triumphant [subsequent to the collapse of Socialism] is not what we in the West already have, but is an incomplete project. Liberalism has not realized its own political and economic aspirations. There is a great deal of history left to happen in the development of a *genuine* liberalism, that is, one which truly advances both democratic and market processes' (Lavoie 1993, p. 109).

REFERENCES

Boettke, Peter J. and Prychitko, David L., (eds) (1994), *The Market Process: Essays in Contemporary Austrian Economics*, Aldershot, UK and Brookfield, US: Edward Elgar.

Boettke, Peter J. (ed) (1994), *The Elgar Companion to Austrian Economics*, Aldershot, UK and Brookfield, US: Edward Elgar.

Buchanan, James M. (1979), *What Should Economists Do?*, Indianapolis: Liberty Press.

Buchanan, James M. (1985), *Liberty, Market and State: Political Economy in the 1980s*, New York: New York University Press.

de Soto, Hernando (1987), *The Other Path: The Invisible Revolution in the Third World*, New York: Harper and Row.

de Soto, Hernando (2000), *The Mystery of Capital: Why Capitalism Triumphs in the West and Fails Everywhere Else*, New York: Basic Books.

Fukuyama, Francis (1989), 'The End of History?', *The National Interest* (Summer).

Fukuyama, Francis (1992), *The End of History and the Last Man*, New York: The Free Press.

Gadamer, Hans-Georg (1975), *Truth and Method*, New York: Seabury.

Gadamer, Hans-Georg (1981), *Reason in the Age of Science*, Trans. Frederick G. Lawrence, Cambridge, MA: MIT Press.

Gadamer, Hans-Georg (1997), 'Reply to G.B. Madison', in L.E. Hahn (ed.), *Philosophy of Hans-Georg Gadamer*, Library of Living Philosophers, vol. 24, Chicago: Open Court.

Geertz, Clifford (1973), *The Interpretation of Cultures*, New York: Basic Books.

Gordon, David (1987), 'Hermeneutics versus Austrian Economics', Occasional Paper Series, Mises Institute.

Hayek, F.A. (1944), *The Road to Serfdom*, Chicago: University of Chicago Press.

Hayek, F.A. (1976), *Law, Legislation and Liberty*, vol. 2: *The Mirage of Social Justice*, Chicago: University of Chicago Press.

Hayek, F.A. (1976a), 'Individualism: True or False', in *Individualism and Economic Order*, London: Routledge and Kegan Paul.

Hayek, F.A. (1979), *The Counter-Revolution of Science: Studies on the Abuse of Reason*, 2nd edition, Indianapolis: Liberty Press.

Hayek, F.A. (1988), *The Fatal Conceit: The Errors of Socialism, The Collected Works of F.A. Hayek*, vol. 1. Chicago: University of Chicago Press.

Hayek, F.A. (1992), *The Fortunes of Liberalism: Essays on Austrian Economics and the Ideal of Freedom, The Collected Works of F.A. Hayek*, vol. 4. Chicago: University of Chicago Press.

Horwitz, Stephen (1992a), *Monetary Evolution, Free Banking, and Economic Order*, Boulder, CO: Westview Press.

Horwitz, Stephen (1992b), 'Monetary Exchange as an Extra-Linguistic Social Communication Process', *Review of Social Economy* **50** (2) (Summer), reprinted in Prychitko (ed.) (1995).

Husserl, Edmund (1970), *The Crisis of European Sciences and Transcendental Phenomenology: An Introduction to Phenomenological Philosophy*, Trans. David Carr. Evanston, 111.: Northwestern University Press.

Hutchison, T.W. (1938), *The Significance and Basic Postulates of Economic Theory*, London: Macmillan.

Knight, Frank H. (1956), '"What Is Truth" in Economics?', in *On the History and Method of Economics: Selected Essays*, Chicago: University of Chicago Press.

Knight, Frank H. (1982), *Freedom and Reform: Essays in Economics and Social Philosophy*, Indianapolis: Liberty Press.

Kornai, Janos (1992), *The Socialism System: The Political Economy of Communism*, Princeton, NJ: Princeton University Press.

Lachmann, Ludwig M. (1986), *The Market as an Economic Process*, Oxford: Basil Blackwell.

Lachmann, Ludwig M. (1990), 'Austrian Economics: A Hermeneutic Approach', in Lavoie (ed) (1990).

Lavoie, Don (1985), *Rivalry and Central Planning: The Socialist Calculation Debate Reconsidered*, New York: Cambridge University Press.
Lavoie, Don (1985a), *National Economic Planning; What is Left?*, Cambridge, MA: Ballinger Publishing.
Lavoie, Don (1985b), 'The Interpretive Dimension of Economics: Science, Hermeneutics, and Praxeology', Working Paper Series 1985–15, Center for the Study of Market Processes, George Mason University.
Lavoie, Don (1986), 'Eclideanism versus Hermeneutics: A Reinterpretation of Miseian Apriorism', in I. Kirzner (ed), *Subjectivism, Intelligibility and Economic Understanding*, New York: New York University Press.
Lavoie, Don (1986a), 'The Present Status of Interpretation in Economics: Bad News with a Glimmer of Hope', paper presented at the annual meeting of the Canadian Society for Hermeneutics and Postmodern Thought, May 26–27, University of Manitoba.
Lavoie, Don (1988), 'Editor's Notes', *Market Process*, **6** (1) (Spring).
Lavoie, Don (1988a), 'A Political Philosophy for the Market Process', *Market Process*, **6** (2) (Fall), reprinted in Boettke and Prychitko (eds) (1994).
Lavoie, Don (1988b), 'Editor's Notes', *Market Process* **6** (2)(Fall).
Lavoie, Don (ed.) (1990), *Economics and Hermeneutics*, London: Routledge.
Lavoie, Don (1990a), 'Introduction to F.A. Hayek's Theory of Cultural Evolution: Market and Cultural Processes as Spontaneous Orders', *Cultural Dynamics*, **3** (1).
Lavoie, Don (1992), 'Glasnost and the Knowledge Problem: Rethinking Economic Democracy', *Cato Journal*, **11** (3) (Winter).
Lavoie, Don (1993), 'Democracy, Markets, and the Legal Order: Notes on the Nature of Politics in a Radically Liberal Society', in Ellen Frankel Paul et al. (eds), *Liberalism and the Economic Order*, Cambridge: Cambridge University Press.
Lavoie, Don (1994), 'The Interpretive Turn', in Boettke (ed.) (1994).
Lavoie, Don (1995), 'The Market as a Procedure for the Discovery and Conveyance of Inarticulate Knowledge', in Prychitko (ed.) (1995).
Madison, G.B. (1986), *The Logic of Liberty*, Westport, CT: Greenwood Press.
Madison, G.B. (1988), 'Hermeneutical Integrity: A Guide for the Perplexed', *Market Process*, **6** (1) (Spring), reprinted in Boettke and Prychitko (eds) (1994).
Madison, G.B. (1994), 'The Primacy of Action and Its Scientific Consequences for the Hermeneutics of the Human Sciences,' in Vincent Shen et al. (eds), *Psychology, Phenomenology and Chinese Philosophy*, Chinese Philosophical Studies, vol. 6. Washington, D.C.: The Council for Research in Values and Philosophy.
Madison, G.B. (1994a), 'Phenomenology and Economics', in Boettke (ed.)(1994).
Madison, G.B. (1994b), 'Hermeneutics: Gadamer and Ricoeur', in Richard Kearney (ed.), *Continental Philosophy in the 20th Century*, Routledge History of Philosophy, vol. 8. London: Routledge.
Madison, G.B. (1995), 'How Individualistic is Methodological Individualism?', in Prychitko (ed.) (1995).
Madison, G.B. (1996), 'Being and Speaking', in John Stewart (ed.), *Beyond the Symbol Model: Reflections on the Representational Nature of Language*, Albany: SUNY Press.
Madison, G.B. (1996a), '"Hermeneutics" Claim to Universality', in L.E. Hahn (ed.), *The Philosophy of Hans-Georg Gadamer*, Library of Living Philosophers, vol. 24. Chicago: Open Court.

Madison, G.B. (1998), *The Political Economy of Civil Society and Human Rights*, London: Routledge.

Madison, G.B. (1998a), 'Self-Interest, Communalism, Welfarism', in Herbert Giersch (ed.), *Merits and Limits of Markets*, Berlin: Springer-Verlag.

Madison, G.B. (2000), 'Critical Theory and Hermeneutics: Some Outstanding Issues in the Debate' in L.E. Hahn (ed.) *Perspectives on Habemtas,* Chicago: Open Court.

Madison, G.B. (2001), *The Politics of Postmodernity: Essays in Applied Hermeneutics*, Contributions to Phenomenology, vol. 42, Dordrecht: Kluwer Academic.

Madison, James (1999), 'Property', in *James Madison: Writings*, New York: Library of America.

McCloskey, Donald N. (1985), *The Rhetoric of Economics*, Madison: University of Wisconsin Press.

McCloskey, Donald N. (1994), *Knowledge and Persuasion in Economics*, Cambridge: Cambridge University Press.

Menger, Carl (1985), *Investigations into the Method of the Social Sciences with Special Reference to Economics*, trans. Francis J. Noch, New York: New York University Press.

Mirowski, Philip (1988), *Against Mechanism: Protecting Economics from Science*, Totowa, NJ: Rowman and Littlefield.

Mirowski, Philip (1989), *More Heat than Light: Economics as Social Physics, Physics as Nature's Economics*, Cambridge: Cambridge University Press.

Mises, Ludwig von. (1963), *Human Action: A Treatise on Economics*, Chicago: Contemporary Books.

Mises, Ludwig von. (1981), *Socialism: An Economic and Sociological Analysis*, Indianapolis: Liberty Classics.

Mittermaier, Karl. (1986), 'Mechanomorphism', in I. Kizner (ed.), *Subjectivism, Intelligibility and Economic Understanding*, New York: New York University Press.

Oakshott, Michael (1962), *Rationalism in Politics and Other Essays*, London: Methuen.

Peacock, Alan and Willgerodt, Hans (eds) (1989), *German Neo-Liberals and the Social Market Economy*, New York: St. Martin's Press.

Pellauer, David (1979), 'The Significance of the Text in Paul Ricoeur's Hermeneutical Theory', in C.E. Reagan (ed.), *Studies in the Philosophy of Paul Ricoeur*, Athens: Ohio University Press.

Prychitko, David L. (ed) (1995), *Individuals, Institutions, Interpretations: Hermeneutics Applied to Economics.* Aldershot: Avebury.

Rector, Ralph A. (1986), 'Interpretation, Human Agency and Economics: A Report on the Recent CSMP Conference', *Market Process*, **4** (2) (Fall).

Rogge, Benjamin A. (1979), *Can Capitalism Survive?*, Indianapolis: Liberty Press.

Sen, Amartya (1987), *On Ethics and Economics*, Oxford: Blackwell.

Simmel, Georg (1990), *The Philosophy of Money*, trans. Tom Bottomore and David Frisby, London: Routledge.

Stigler, George J. (1982), *The Economist as Preacher and Other Essays*, Chicago: University of Chicago Press.

Vanberg, Viktor (1994), 'Hayek's Legacy and the Future of Liberal Thought: Rational Liberalism versus Evolutionary Agnosticism', *The Cato Journal*, **14** (2) (Fall).

8. Hermeneutics in economics: on the status of 'as-if' functions

Wayne J. Froman

David Hume began his essay 'Of Commerce' with the following observations:

> The greater part of mankind may be divided into two classes. That of the shallow thinkers who fall short of the truth; and that of abstruse thinkers, who go beyond it. The latter class are by far the most rare and I may add, by far the most useful and valuable. They suggest hints, at least, and start difficulties, which they want, perhaps, skill to pursue; but which may produce fine discoveries, when handled by men who have a more just way of thinking. At worst, what they say is uncommon; and if it should cost some pains to comprehend it, one has, however, the pleasure of hearing something that is new. As another is little to be valued, who tells us nothing but what we can learn from any coffee house conversation.[1]

Don Lavoie understood the point thoroughly. He did not hesitate when it came to delving into philosophical works of thinkers such as Martin Heidegger, Hans-Georg Gadamer, and Paul Ricoeur, who would at times stretch language, stretch ideas to the point that new light could be shed on what we heretofore could not see. Don Lavoie was convinced that Austrian Economics and Philosophical Hermeneutics had much to gain from working in tandem. In fact, he found it difficult to understand how people who study Austrian Economics could resist delving into crucial works in the development of philosophical hermeneutics during the twentieth century. The proportions of Don Lavoie's conviction in this regard should not be underestimated. It meant that economics need not remain limited by nineteenth and eighteenth century philosophical contexts from which it took shape. It meant that philosophical hermeneutics, and the philosophical field in which it came to the fore in the twentieth century, phenomenology, philosophical innovations that escape American awareness in large part, would have a purchase, so to speak, in a discipline, economics, that addresses matters of constant concern to everybody in the United States. In fact, it would mean that approaches in philosophy that challenge, as does Austrian Economics, entrenched behavioral and calculative habits of thought and practice would get more of a hearing. It also meant that the claims of philosophical hermeneutics regarding its appropriateness and advantages in the social sciences would have more solid ground on which to stand. All this by putting aside mutual suspicions and avoidances that characterize attitudes of economics, and of philosophy, each in respect to the other. What I propose to do in this chapter is to specify features of compatibility between Austrian Economics and Philosophical Hermeneutics and in the course of doing so, indicate a line of thought that is generated in the enclave between the two, to borrow a term from a phenomenologist who interacted directly with an earlier generation of Austrian Economists, namely, Alfred Schutz. I will set my sights by two references that Don Lavoie, who already entered this enclave, established there, first, the sense of the market as a dynamic of knowledge discovery, and second, the sense of the market as a dynamic of a linguistic nature, which is a reference that resonates strongly with the major preoccupation with language in a number of philosophical movements, as well as in a good number of other intellectual disciplines, during the past one hundred years. Finally, I will hint at the pertinence that this line of thinking has in regard to policy issues.

First, philosophical hermeneutics comes to the fore in phenomenology. The philosopher who inaugurated phenomenology in the twentieth century, Edmund Husserl, found that perceptual awareness or consciousness serves as the base for all other modes of awareness or consciousness, such as affective, theoretical and voluntaristic. Husserl's explorative analyses of perceptual consciousness were taken up and taken forward by the mid-century phenomenologist Maurice Merleau-Ponty. To my mind, Merleau-Ponty's late investigations of perception offer an especially helpful context for understanding how philosophical hermeneutics comes to the fore, and do so in a way that makes the compatibility with insights from Austrian Economics particularly evident. Consider a simple illustration. In seeing the side of something in the room, or in seeing the side of a building, I see each, except under certain very specific circumstances, as the side of that something in the room or as the side of the building. I do not see them as free-standing surfaces. In Merleau-Ponty's late investigations of perception, he pointed out that this amounts to a determination that my own visibility, my own position in the field of visibility, enters into my seeing. Here then we may speak of two circles, neither of which encompasses the other. There is the circle of visibility, on the one hand, and there is the circle of vision, on the other. Each is, in effect, dependent upon the other. What we call 'the phenomenon' actually makes its appearance by virtue of the displacement of the two, each with respect to the other. The phenomenon does not distort and does not hide something lying behind it. I see a side of something in the room, or I see a side of a building, not despite the displacement of these two circles one with respect to the other, but in fact by way of that displacement. For phenomenology, there is no going behind this context. For phenomenology, furthermore, to disregard this is to be less scientific, rather than more scientific, if 'scientific' refers to the rigor of one's thinking. The phenomenon, therefore, is not epiphenomenal, and phenomenology is not phenomenalism, which still defines phenomena in terms of the non-phenomenal that phenomenalism would reject. Moreover, very importantly, the phenomenon is decidedly not a psychological superimposition on a prior context. A fortiori, the phenomenological context is not a matter for a psychology that uncritically imports its categories from physical science. Phenomenology and Austrian Economics are firmly allied against natural scientific reductionism and its extreme form of calculative mathematical reductionism. When hermeneutics comes to the fore within phenomenology, in a manner that I will address shortly, it too will maintain an irremovable resistance to natural scientific reductionism as well as calculative mathematical reductionism. Hans-Georg Gadamer's point of departure for hermeneutics is that scientific methodology, when imported from the natural sciences, short circuits the phenomenon as well as interpretation and in doing so simply misses the subject matter of the social sciences or human studies. In this specific way, again, the application of scientific methodology turns out to be less rather than more scientific. In the book *Being and Time*,[2] which contains the ground-breaking work in philosophical hermeneutics in the twentieth century, and which is one of the very small number of twentieth century philosophical works that now outlive that century, Martin Heidegger wrote: 'mathematics is not more rigorous than historiology, but only narrower' (p. 195). By virtue of its narrowness, mathematics is constitutively incapable of attending to the subject matter of any one of the human studies. In order to illustrate what happens in economics when economics 'misses the phenomenon', and how this amounts to being less scientific, I will draw on James Buchanan's criticism of economists' appeal to 'independently existing functions' in addressing the dynamic of choice. To my mind, the culprit in missing what Buchanan identifies as 'choice' is precisely 'missing the phenomenon', in the phenomenological sense of the term:

> Individuals do not act so as to maximize utilities described in *independently-existing functions.* They confront genuine choices, and the sequence of decisions taken may be comprehended, *ex post* (after the choice), in terms of 'as if' functions that are maximized. But these 'as if' functions are themselves generated in the choosing process, not separately from such process. If viewed in this perspective, there is no means by which even the most idealized omniscient designer could duplicate the results of voluntary interchange. The potential participants *do not know until they enter the process* what their own choices will be. From this it

> follows that it is *logically impossible* for an omniscient designer to know, unless, of course, we are to preclude individual freedom of the will. … In economics, even among many of those who remain strong advocates of market and market-like organizations, the 'efficiency' that such market arrangements produce is independently conceptualized. Market arrangements then become 'means', which may or may not be relatively best. Until and unless this teleological element is fully exorcised from basic economic theory, economists are likely to remain confused and their discourse confusing.[3] (emphasis in original)

When phenomenologists attend to the phenomena, what do phenomenologists find? Let us return to perception for a moment. We recall how my position in the visible enters into my seeing. We recall how we may say of this that there are two circles, one of vision and one of the visible, dependent upon one another, and always displaced one with respect to the other. Now, there is no one-to-one correspondence between the two. As a consequence, the phenomenon that makes its appearance by virtue of the displacement of the two circles each with respect to the other, is characterized, to begin with, by what phenomenologists specify as an 'horizonal structure', internally as well as externally. The horizon of these horizons then, is how phenomenologists understand 'world'. Where economists are characterized as 'worldly philosophers', and 'worldly' is associated with 'scientific' specifically in contrast to extrapolative or speculative, then the conclusion must be that 'worldly' needs to be understood in its phenomenological sense. In short, economists should be understood as phenomenological philosophers. Importantly, just as was said in regard to phenomena, world here is not understood as an appearance of a sort that distorts or hides something lying behind it. World here is not epiphenomenal. It is not a question here of phenomenalism because phenomenalism takes its understanding of what phenomenal is from the sense of the non-phenomenal that it rejects. Crucially, world here is not a psychological superimposition on some prior context. There is no going back behind this. A fortiori, world here is not a matter for psychology that uncritically imports its categories from physical science. To understand economists as worldly philosophers in the phenomenological sense of world is not that far-fetched at all when one considers historically that David Hume's work was not only as important as it was for the 'worldly philosophy of economics', but according to Edmund Husserl, that work also anticipated phenomenology in significant respects.

The horizonal character of world, as described above, marks the meaning character of world. Meaning implies direction, as is indicated already by the word 'sense'. In addition, meaning implies that something is at issue or at stake. Meaning pertains to the 'whereunto' or the 'for-the-sake-of-which' of phenomena. As was already said of phenomena and of world, meaning is not reducible to a psychological superimposition upon a context that is there ready-made. At the same time, meaning is not discoverable data. Early on, in his work on perception, Merleau-Ponty had made the point that empiricist and intellectualist accounts of perception both suffer from the same problem in so far as they both rely on the notion of isolated units of 'sense information' that are then combined in one way or another to produce a perceptual field, when in fact, nobody has ever encountered such data. To illustrate, Merleau-Ponty drew on color perception and pointed out that we never encounter a red that is devoid of sense but rather what we find is a 'fiery red' or an 'alarming red' or a 'warm red'. The point is that interpretation is not *ex post facto*. To my mind, this accounts for the way in which the 'as-if functions' that are operative in the process of choice as described in the above-cited passage by James Buchanan, are intrinsic to the process. Ultimately, it accounts for why Austrian economics, I think, is right on the mark in maintaining the dynamic or the process character of the market phenomenon. Basically, when economics describes the market as a 'spontaneous order', it is the way in which interpretation, or 'as-if functions', are not *ex post facto*, but rather are intrinsic, that is specified by that phrase.

We are now in a position to discern first how philosophical hermeneutics makes its appearance within phenomenology, and then features of compatibility between philosophical hermeneutics and the understanding, in economics, of the market as a knowledge discovery process and as a linguistic dynamic. The ground-breaking text in regard to the appearance of hermeneutics within phenomenology is, as mentioned, Martin Heidegger's *Being and Time*. There we find Heidegger's description of how we are always already 'in-the-world', a description that reinforces what has already been said here about the way in which interpretation is not *ex post facto*. The explorative analysis of perception by Merleau-Ponty from which I have drawn in the discussion above is consistent with this description. Heidegger identifies three basic features of how it is that we are always already 'in-the-world'. The first feature is what Heidegger calls '*Befindlichkeit*,' from the verb '*sich befinden*,' establishing oneself, taking position, in effect, a feature of our being always already 'in-the-world' that matches up well with the interaction between my position in the visible, on the one hand, and my vision, on the other. Heidegger's description associates '*Befindlichkeit*' with affectivity and perhaps one could locate here the basic sense of pleasure and avoidance of pain that one finds in maximization accounts, although the description from Heidegger is a highly nuanced and subtle one. This affective element, this sense of 'dis-position', accords with the 'dis-placement' of the two circles of vision and visibility, each with respect to the other. The second feature identified is '*Verstehen*', understanding. Heidegger elaborates on the description of 'understanding' in specifying three factors that it comprises.

The first is '*Vor-haben*', 'fore-having', which Heidegger describes as the way in which we apprehend what we apprehend against a background. The second is '*Vor-sicht*', 'fore-sight', which Heidegger describes as the way in which we apprehend what we apprehend from a specific angle or line of apprehension. Again, these two features of 'understanding' match up well with the description of the interaction between my position in the visible, on the one hand, and my vision, on the other hand. The third and final feature of 'understanding' is '*Vor-begriff*', 'fore-conception', which emphasizes that the motion or dynamic of understanding has a direction toward conception and at the same time makes the point that this motion or dynamic, the motion or dynamic of interpretation, is prior to conception and in so far as it is, is intrinsic to our always already 'being-in-the-world'. It is *not* an activity in which we engage *ex post facto*. In fact, inasmuch as the motion or the dynamic of interpretation is intrinsic to our 'being-in-the-world', it marks, for Heidegger, our very freedom. The third and the final feature of our always already 'being-in-the-world' identified at this point is '*Rede*', discourse. By way of a celebrated illustration, Heidegger makes the point that discourse is intrinsic to our being-in-the-world. The utterance 'the hammer is heavy' cannot be reduced to the proposition alone. When uttered in an everyday context, 'the hammer is heavy' conveys something of the sense of one's being-in-the-world, something of the 'whereunto' or the 'for-the-sake-of-which' comes across in the resistance marked by the term 'heavy'. To reduce the utterance to a proposition is to mistake an *ex post facto* analysis of language for its character as intrinsic to our always already 'being-in-the-world'. Language is in the first place, disclosive. Language *shows*. The mark of its intrinsic character with respect to our always already being-in-the-world is how even as we speak, there is always that which is 'to-be-said'. To reinforce the sense in which the dispositional, disclosive and discursive interpretive dynamic is intrinsic to our always already being-in-the-world, in contrast to a dynamic that would be started after the fact, Heidegger emphasizes strongly that the three features of 'disposition', 'understanding' and 'discourse' are '*gleichursprunglich*', equi-original. There is no going back behind this dynamic.

Once the interpretive dynamic is understood as intrinsic to world as understood in a phenomenological sense, which is to say, as neither a psychological superimposition on a prior context, nor as a prior context that is hidden or obscured behind phenomena, we can understand the historical character of meaning as specified in hermeneutics. For this we turn to the critical description of interpreting a work of art as found in the first part of Hans-Georg Gadamer's primary work in philosophical hermeneutics, *Truth and Method*.[4] To understand a work of art, we proceed by way of already available 'pre-judgments' or 'prejudices' that are the accumulated precipitate of interpretation understood as the dynamics of tradition, which are now generalized functions or operators divorced or removed from their initial historical contexts, and in this sense are cultural in nature. Certain of the prejudices in this sense will facilitate understanding and others will hinder it. All in all, Gadamer finds that prejudices in this sense are crucial to the dynamic of understanding. To acknowledge this is to acknowledge that the dynamic at issue here is not one that is thoroughly within our control, and that is simply another way of saying that an *ex post facto* reconstruction of the dynamic cannot be mistaken for the dynamic itself. It is by means of the artwork's resistance to, and accommodation of, prejudices understood in this way that meaning is brought forward or comes to light. This meaning does not precede this dynamic as 'data' that is somehow deposited ahead of time in the work of art. Nor does the meaning lie in a context that is prior to this dynamic, in particular, in a prior intent of the artist who created the work. Still, this meaning is not in any way a superimposition on the artwork. The integral character of this meaning is the mark of the historical moment and this enables us to understand how Gadamer finds that understanding is in fact an event.

It is particularly important to understand that this does not amount to historicism, any more than the phenomenological understanding of the phenomenon amounts to phenomenalism. Historicism fails to acknowledge the difference between an *ex post facto* reconstruction of an historical context and the moment of that context. Consequently, historicism fails to understand the sense in which the historical is not characterized by closure. Hans-Georg Gadamer makes a critical distinction between 'historical consciousness' as understood by historicism, according to which historical understanding pertains to the special task of reconstruction of prior contexts that are, in effect, available as 'givens', and 'consciousness of effective history' that pertains to the always ongoing interpretive dynamic intrinsic to world understood in a phenomenological sense, which entails acknowledgement of the event character of understanding as described above.

I can now redeem my announcement at the start that I would set my sights by the sense in which the market can be understood as a knowledge-discovery dynamic. If, as Don Lavoie urged, hermeneutics is brought to bear in the understanding of market processes, what is designated here as 'knowledge-discovery' could be understood less in the sense of the uncovering of what lies hidden, and more in the sense in which what we become aware of by way of the interpretive dynamic as described in hermeneutics was not previously deposited in what gets interpreted.

Now, Gadamer finds that basically, the above-described interpretive dynamic is linguistic in character. This is rooted in Heidegger's findings that (1) linguistic utterances cannot be reduced to propositions alone, but rather that they convey something of the sense, the 'whereunto' or the 'for-the-sake-of-which', of our being-in-the-world, and (2) that discourse is intrinsic to that being-in-the-world and does not follow, so to speak, after the fact. What Gadamer brings out is the sense in which every proposition responds, in some way, to a question. Indeed, every conversation can be understood as a response to a question. The interpretive dynamic described in hermeneutics is not a matter of intuiting pre-given data, and at the same time it is not a matter of adequation to any prior context. It has an intrinsically interrogative character. The horizon question, so to speak, for philosophical hermeneutics, pertains to who it is that we are to become.

I can now redeem my announcement at the start that I would set my sights by the sense in which market processes could be understood as linguistic in character. If, as Don Lavoie urged, philosophical hermeneutics is brought to bear on the understanding of market processes, such processes could be understood as linguistic, not in a sense that would be analogous to the reduction of language to a subject matter that is exhaustively accessible to a propositional logic or calculus, nor in a sense proper to argumentation, which in one way or another is based on some notion of a prior context, but rather in the sense in which, as Austrian Economics knew from early on, these processes are a matter of what is unsettled, or in other words, an open question.

Having delineated a line of thought within the enclave taking shape between Austrian Economics and Philosophical Hermeneutics, it is appropriate that I ask whether this enclave has limits. The answer is yes. To my mind, the limits pertain to the contingency of market situations, which economists might well insist ultimately cannot be accommodated in an interpretive dynamic. For this reason, economics is indeed a social science even when it is not reductionistic in favor of natural science and mathematics. The philosophical practitioner of hermeneutics would do well to pay attention to this point. But, at the same time, absent the interpretive dynamic as understood in philosophical hermeneutics, a dynamic that is intrinsic to world understood phenomenologically in terms of the horizonal character of phenomena rather than in terms of psychological superimpositions or mere appearances that hide and obscure a prior context, it would appear difficult, if not impossible, for economics to understand how action undertaken by individuals in the market is compatible with the sense of the market as a 'spontaneous order'. The challenge, I find, is to understand how the contingency and the interpretive dynamic intrinsic to world in its phenomenological sense both pertain at once.Now to redeem one further promise, and that is the word about the significance to policy issues of the line of thinking here in the enclave between Austrian Economics and Philosophical Hermeneutics. The way in which, on the one hand, meaning figures in philosophical hermeneutics as the whereunto or for-the-sake-of-which intrinsic to the open horizon of world understood in its phenomenological sense, neither as a given prior context nor as a psychological superimposition, and the coercive element of the political, on the other hand, are antithetical each in respect to the other. It is not by accident that Don Lavoie, who championed the opposition by Austrian Economics to the designs of 'central planners', appreciated the insights of philosophical hermeneutics. To be sure, what this does not mean is that thinking the character of the political should be left aside any more than the acknowledgment that world is not a question of a prior context or a psychological superimposition would mean relinquishing rigor in thinking. On the contrary, Don Lavoie had of late turned to the work of the political thinker Hannah Arendt where he detected the means for recovering the character of the political in what had once been understood as political economy. This was a task that lay ahead when his work was ended. I conclude with this precisely because it is not the case that what is to be said, has been. On the contrary, in an address entitled 'In Praise of Philosophy', Merleau-Ponty wrote that the memory that respects those who are no longer with us as are those among whom we live, is not a memory that feels closer to those whom we lost only because they no longer put us in question as do those among whom we do live, but rather is that memory that maintains 'the accent of freedom in the incompleteness of their lives'. In this way, we understand that 'the same fragile principle makes us alive and gives to what we do a sense that does not wear out'. As it is the case in history, so it is the case in life, that where the truth lies in fact, need not be in one's having a final word.

NOTES

1. 'Of commerce' by David Hume in *Hume: Political Essays*, edited by Knud Haakonssen, Cambridge Texts in the History of Political Thought (Cambridge: Cambridge University Press, 1994), p. 93.
2. Martin Heidegger, *Being and Time* (New York; Harper, 1962), trans. John Macquarrie.
3. 'Order defined in the process of its emergence', in *Liberty, Market, and State: Political Economy in the 1980s* (New York: New York University Press, 1986) pp. 73–4.
4. Hans-Georg Gadamer, *Truth and Method* (New York: Seabury Press, 1975).

9. Humility and truth in economics

Deirdre McCloskey

> I beseech you, in the bowels of Christ, think it possible you may be mistaken. (Cromwell, letter to the General Assembly of the Church of Scotland, 3 August, 1650)

A humble person, according to one standard translation of Aquinas' *Summa Theologia* (c. 1270), 'in respect of that which is his own ought to subject himself to every neighbor, in respect of that which the latter has of God's' (IIa IIae, q. 161, a. 3, 'I answer that ...,' quoted in Pope (2002) in Pope, ed., p. 45). The formulation is no clearer in the Latin, but seems in context to mean that we should respect what God has created in other people. The sparks of perfection in people should be esteemed, 'That we may know the things that are given to us by God', as St. Paul put it (1 Cor. 2:12, quoted by Aquinas, c. 1270). Or, as Augustine put it (also quoted approvingly by Aquinas), 'We must not esteem by pretending to esteem, but should really think it possible for another person to have something that is hidden to us and whereby he is better than we are.'

To put it academically and economically, humility enjoins listening to one's neighbors for the sake of God's message within them. Shut up and learn something. The wisdom books of the Hebrew Bible are full of such advice, as in the proverbs of Solomon:

> Wise men lay up knowledge, but the babbling of a fool brings ruin near (*Proverbs* 10: 14).
> He who belittles his neighbor lacks sense, but a man of understanding remains silent (11:12).
> If one gives answer before he hears, it is his folly and shame (18:13).

Harry Truman defined an expert as 'someone who doesn't want to learn anything new, because then he wouldn't be an expert'. Such pride is the opposite of humility, the humility to listen and learn. The philosopher Amelie Oksenberg Rorty once expressed the habit, rare among academics eager to speak and reluctant to listen. What is crucial is

> Our ability to engage in continuous conversation, testing one another, discovering our hidden presumptions, changing our minds because we have listened to the voices of our fellows. Lunatics also change their minds, but their minds change with the tides of the moon and not because they have listened, really listened, to their friends' questions and objections. (Rorty 1983, p. 562)

Humility is part of the cardinal virtue of Temperance, which in turn is the internal balance essential for a good life. Humility answers among the Christian virtues to the pagan virtue of Great-souledness, which Aristotle admired so much. To be humble is to temper one's passions in pursuing as Aquinas put it '*boni ardui*', goods difficult of achievement. To be great-souled, part of the cardinal virtue of Courage, is to keep working towards such goods nonetheless (IIa IIae, q. 161, a. 1, quoted in Houser in Pope, ed., p. 311). We evidently need both: think of the balance of Hope and Temperance, and in particular Great-souledness and Humility, necessary to sustain good work in science and scholarship. We need as I like to say it – I learned the English from my high school driving instructor – to follow the motto, '*Indendete alte in gubernando*': Aim High in Steering. That's Great-souledness. But if we are not to end in foolishness we need also to listen, really listen.

The goods difficult of achievement need to be 'goods' in the non-economic sense in order for humility and great-souledness in pursuing them to be ethical: scholarly excellence in understanding actual economies, for example, or wealth used in proper stewardship, are *good* goods, and proper objects therefore of a paired humility and great-souledness in their pursuit. Humility resists presumption as Aquinas' Christian version of great-souledness resists despair (Sweeney in Pope, ed., p. 163).

To be prideful in the bad, unChristian sense is to will to defy God, which is to say to make *oneself* the object of striving, a very god, violating the first and second commandments. God is God, said the commandments, not little *moi*. Thus Satan is described in *Paradise Lost*:

> … he of the first,
> If not the first archangel, great in power,
> In favour and pre-eminence, yet fraught
> With envy against the Son of God, that day
> Honoured by his great Father, and proclaimed
> Messiah King anointed, could not bear
> Through pride that sight, & thought himself impaired.
> Deep malice thence conceiving and disdain
> Milton, *Paradise Lost*, V, 656–666 (the number 666, by the way, was known in numerology as the Devil's number)

Satan in Milton is a great speaker, which has led romantics to imagine that Milton was of Satan's party. But he is, as Milton shows most clearly in the Satan–Christ colloquies in *Paradise Regained*, utterly incapable of shutting up and learning something. His pride is the opposite of a proper humility and a proper great-souledness.

Stephen Cook explains that 'Humility should not be confused with humiliating self-abnegation before others' (Pope in Pope, ed., p. 45). That's Satan's repeated error: he thinks humility before God is self-abnegation, and Self after all is his god. He declares: 'Better to rule in hell than serve in heaven'. No, my dear Lucifer, wrong again. Humility is not undignified. Uriah Heep in *David Copperfield* is most 'umble, but of course has merely the semblance of the virtue: he esteems, or pretends to esteem, rank. True humility is democratic, looking for God's merit in any other. Heep does not honor God's truth in the least high ranking of us, which is to say that he embodies – Dickens' minor characters are always *embodying* some vice or error – the fallacy that rank and truth are identical. He defers unreflectively, as misled scholars will defer unreflectively to, say, Mises; but he does not *listen*, really listen to anybody.

In his *Autobiography* Benjamin Franklin makes a characteristic joke about the matter, noting of humility, 'I cannot boast of much Success in acquiring the *Reality* of this Virtue; but I had a good deal with regard to the *Appearance* of it' (1784, p. 159). Yet in fact – a point which applies to most of his self-descriptions, and is part of his craftiness in appearing humble – he understated his ethical achievement here. Franklin was well-known as never giving an answer before he had heard out the other person. He acted as though he had read and taken careful note of the motto on the city hall of Gouda in the Netherlands (1448), *Audite et alteram partem*: Listen even to the other side. A shocking idea. Franklin was a listener in an age of orators. In the Constitutional Convention he hardly spoke, not out of pusillanimous fear of failure – after all, this diligent man had stood before kings – but out of a proper and habitual humility towards his fellows. To be humble is in this sense from the Christian and doubtless other perspectives a proper respect for the opinions of humankind, because they sometimes contain God's own truth.

What all this has to do with our loving and beloved friend Don Lavoie is I think obvious to anyone who knew him. Don was humble – it was his most startling personal quality in a profession not known for exhibiting it. He was not 'umble: his respect for the opinions of humankind was not deference to mere rank. He was a democrat, small-d. He certainly did not lack accomplishments, so jokes such as 'You don't have an inferiority *complex* – you're *inferior*!' don't apply. Nor did he lack the great-souledness that Aquinas viewed as paired with humility. He ventured on great, hopeful projects, such as bringing the humanities to economics, seriously, or bringing computation to economics and its teaching, seriously. He satisfied the Aquinian definitions most exactly, down to having a *telos* as a believing Christian of approach in his activities to God.

But there is another sense in which Don's life and work illustrate the theme of humility in economics. I said that economists are not known for personal humility. That is certainly true. When a physicist some time ago attended a conference on chaos theory and economics he remarked that he had *once* thought that physicists were the most arrogant academics around.

Yet one approach to economics does at least *recommend* humility, scientifically speaking – not the Marxist economics I started with; not the Harvard neoclassical and Chicago-School economics I was trained in and practiced; but the Austrian economics that Don discovered young as a student of computer science and improved in all his work. Austrian economists have been telling the rest of us all along that the economic scientist cannot expect to outguess the businessperson. We have to listen to the mystery of entrepreneurship, not airily assume as my fellow neoclassicals tend to do that nothing whatever is to be gained by actually *conversing* with economic agents, because after all they are *completely* determined by the following Max U model. I said Don improved Austrian economics, and this is one way he did it, by asking for a hermeneutics of the economy in economics and listening for the hermeneutics inside the economy itself. I regard hermeneutics as the listening side of a speaking rhetoric, and Don agreed. We both felt that Austrian economics is the natural home for a humanistic approach to the economy, which acknowledges as economics after Smith has not, that humans are speaking and listening and interpreting animals. Smith believed that the propensity to truck and barter was based on the faculty of reason – so much for Max U and the Reason half of the Enlightenment project. But Smith added 'and the faculty of *speech*', which is the other, Freedom half.

What I'm saying is that the attachment to listening, really listening in Don's life was strictly paralleled by his belief in it as a characterization of the economy. Adam Smith was again better than his followers. Smith's butcher and baker are not merely Max U folk who treat the rest of the world arrogantly as a constraint. A market depends, does it not, on an imaginative engagement with the customers and suppliers, to guess at what they are thinking, to see God's spark in them? An alert businessperson 'subjects himself to every neighbor'. She listens and learns. Her goods are difficult of achievement, requiring great-souledness. It seems odd to say so in the year of Enron and company, but Don believed, as I do, that capitalism is as the Christian Fathers and the Angelic Doctor said of the best of humans, humble.

REFERENCES

Aquinas, St. Thomas (c. 1270), *Summa Theologia. Secunda Pars Secundae Partis*, questio 161. trans. Fathers of the English Dominican Province, 2nd edn, 1920, online edition 2000 www.newadvent.org/summa/316101.htm.

Franklin, Benjamin ([1784] 1964), *Autobiography*, L.W. Larabee et al. (eds) New Haven: Yale University Press for the American Philosophical Society.

Houser, R.E. (2002), 'The virtue of courage', in Stephen J. Pope (ed.), *The Ethics of Aquinas*, Washington, DC: Georgetown University Press, pp. 304–20.

Pope, Stephen J. (2002), 'Overview of the ethics of St Thomas Aquinas', in Stephen J. Pope (ed.), *The Ethics of Aquinas*, Washington DC: Georgetown University Press, pp. 30–53.

Rorty, Amelie Oksenberg (1983), 'Experiments in philosophic genre: Descartes' meditations', *Critical Inquiry* 9 (March): 545–65.

Sweeney, Eileen (2002), 'Vice and sin', in Pope, ed., *The Ethics*, pp. 151–68.

REFERENCES

[illegible]

PART 5

Cultural studies

10. The development of cultural economy: foundational questions and future direction

Emily Chamlee-Wright

> Profit opportunities are not so much like road signs to which we assign an automatic meaning as they are like difficult texts in need of a sustained effort of interpretation. Entrepreneurship is not only a matter of opening one's eyes, of switching on one's attentiveness; it requires directing one's gaze. When an entrepreneur sees things others have overlooked, it is not just that he opened his eyes while they have theirs closed. He is reading selected aspects of a complex situation others have not read. And this raises the question of what gives a predirectedness to the entrepreneur's vision, of why he is apt to read some things and not others. I submit the answer to this question is culture. (Don Lavoie, 1991: 46)

INTRODUCTION

Over the course of his academic career, Don Lavoie made significant contributions to fields as diverse as comparative economic systems, Austrian economics, organizational learning, philosophical hermeneutics and computer science. Yet a common thread ties all these various inquiries together. At the heart of each of his research interests was Lavoie's passion for understanding how social learning takes place – how society can achieve a level of intelligence and coordination that far surpasses the intelligence and abilities of any individual or group of individuals within society. As Lavoie developed his own understanding of this phenomenon through his study of economics, philosophy and hypertext technology, he became increasingly interested in cultural processes. Lavoie argued that economists ought to study culture not because it was yet another factor that influenced economic outcomes. Rather, he championed greater understanding of culture as it lay at the heart of all social learning processes, the market process included.

Rather than a separate field within economics, Lavoie viewed the study of cultural processes in much the same way most economists view the study of political economy. Political economy is not so much an isolated field unto itself, but rather, lies at the heart of many sub-fields across the discipline. Political economy provides the foundation for much of the work in comparative economic systems, economic development, labor economics, public choice, industrial organization and economic history, just to name a few. Political economy asks foundational questions about why and how economic processes work the way they do. Similarly, Lavoie has helped to launch a closely related, though distinctly different field of inquiry, that of 'cultural economy'. Just as political economy seeks to reveal the fundamental connections between the economy and the political and institutional environment, cultural economy seeks to understand the connection between economic processes and the cultural context in which they unfold.

In keeping with the radical tone of his work in other fields, Lavoie's contributions to the field of cultural economy challenge the mainstream of the economics discipline to reconsider the very starting point of its analysis and its methodological approach. Drawing heavily from his work in philosophical hermeneutics, Lavoie's approach to understanding the connections between cultural and economic processes contrasts sharply with more mainstream efforts. By describing Lavoie's contributions to this research, this chapter seeks to articulate the foundational questions the field of cultural economy ought to be asking, as well as to articulate the potential advantages pursuing such an alternative approach holds for the economics discipline. After sketching out the scope of this emerging field of inquiry I suggest specific areas of research to which scholars interested in the field of cultural economy might turn their attention.

THE FOUNDATIONS OF CULTURAL ECONOMY

As a scholar schooled in the Austrian tradition, it was certainly no accident that Lavoie would pursue the connections between economic and cultural processes. At the center of much of Austrian economics is the question of how knowledge is generated, dispersed and used in society, a focus that tends to direct our attention to processes of cultural transmission. In his seminal works *Law, Legislation and Liberty* and *The Fatal Conceit*, for example, Hayek (1973; 1979; 1988) articulated the crucial connection between cultural transmission of knowledge and the advancement of the extended order. Whereas with a primitive or simple order, in which social coordination depends upon common ends (such as finding food or shelter) and a central authority (such as elders or headmen) to direct such initiatives, social coordination in an extended order depends on common rules. Social rules such as private property, money and contract carry with them the capacity for ever-increasing levels of social complexity, as individuals pursue a dizzying diversity of ends, all without the consent or direction of any central authority. Culture is the means by which such rules evolve, thus it is cultural evolution that is at the foundation of economic advancement. Or in other words, the market process is an outgrowth of the cultural evolutionary process.[1]

Lavoie was also influenced by interdisciplinary scholars working in economic sociology and economic anthropology, such as Brigitte and Peter Berger (Berger 1991) and their colleagues at the Institute for the Study of Economic Culture (ISEC).[2] As a comparative systems economist, Lavoie was naturally drawn to the question of how economic performance was related to cultural context. He encouraged young scholars to study communities known for their entrepreneurial character. Though he considered Austrian treatments of entrepreneurship to be the best that the economics discipline had to offer, he challenged his Austrian colleagues to take their investigations further – to go beyond general and abstract characterizations of entrepreneurship and to emphasize also the different ways in which entrepreneurship manifests itself cross-culturally.

Doing this kind of work well, Lavoie argued, requires economists to reduce the distance we customarily maintain between our subjects and ourselves (Lavoie 1990b). The habit within economics to privilege quantitative methods (such as econometrics) over qualitative methods (such as participant observation, interviews and case-studies) has sanctioned this distance under the guise of objectivity and rigor. Yet what we forfeit in the name of scientific rigor is a deeper understanding of how market participants understand their own circumstances. Certainly, there are times when that distance is an advantage – recognizing trends in cross-sectional and time series data, for example. But questions that require us to interpret how market participants are reading their own circumstances call forth a more qualitative approach. What are the survival strategies market participants might employ, for instance, when facing the austerity measures of a structural adjustment program? Will informal entrepreneurs change the kinds of goods they sell, or are there institutional or cultural barriers that keep this from happening? Will producers switch to domestic inputs, or does the local context not provide such an option? Will private entrepreneurs fill the void left by state owned industries in the wake of privatization and deregulation, or is the institutional environment too weak to gain the trust of potential investors? Do market participants expect the government to enforce laws and regulations pertaining to their business?

Do they expect the value of their currency to plummet in the near future, even if official inflation rates are low? These are questions that call forth qualitative methods as we seek to understand decision making from the particular cultural perspective of the market participants themselves.

It needs to be made clear that in promoting greater understanding of the relationship between cultural and economic processes, Lavoie was not interested in cataloguing a list of cultural traits that render a national economy more or less prone to economic development. He found the very concept of a 'national culture' deeply suspect, as it tends to privilege a whitewashed version of the dominant culture and ignores the contentious tugging and pulling within and among the many diverse cultures at work in society. Lavoie criticized the work of cultural conservatives such as Lawrence Harrison (1992) who assessed a homogenized version of entire national cultures on the basis of a list of cultural traits conducive for modernization and development. Harrison argues, for example, that a country is more development prone if its culture favors pragmatism, rationalism, empiricism and utilitarianism, and is more development resistant if the culture favors stability, solidarity, continuity and tradition. In contrast to this approach, Lavoie recognized the inherent heterogeneity within and among diverse cultures that make up any society, and wanted to explore the ways in which members of those cultures could create different sorts of opportunities from their specific cultural perspective.

> We are not trying to answer the question of which national cultures are most conducive to economic prosperity – whether, say, German culture, as a whole, is more or less likely to generate economic prosperity than American culture, as a whole. This approach obscures the heterogeneity of each culture, reducing cultural [analysis] to a crude sort of Values Nationalism, and ends up unhelpfully comparing apples to oranges. Nor are we arguing a position of cultural relativism, however…. Relativism also obscures the inherent heterogeneity within and among cultures. How can social scientists account for cultural differences, if we are banned from making any pronouncements about the effects of those differences? The position we are taking here is that each culture carries with it advantages particular to its own context, which might serve to advance economic development. Yet, those advantages will vary according to time and place. Thus, the question we need to ask is: which elements of American culture (or of this or that particular subculture of American society) constitute its 'comparative cultural advantages' and which (probably different) elements of German culture constitute *its* advantages? (Lavoie and Chamlee-Wright 2000: 63).

Rather than pursuing a checklist approach to cultural economy, Lavoie's approach is more foundational, investigating the fundamental relationships between culture, cultural perspective and economic engagement. Not only is the field of cultural economy interested in how a cultural context supports or deters entrepreneurs, it also investigates how culture shapes the very institutions and rules of the game in which we find ourselves – how, for example, property rights are legitimated within a particular cultural context (Chamlee-Wright 1997). As opposed to checking off a list of cultural traits, a more foundational approach to cultural economy would explore the ways in which culture shapes the character of entrepreneurship in a society. For instance, will women in a particular culture be systematically selected or inhibited in gaining prominence as entrepreneurs? Or, do child-rearing techniques within a given culture tend to foster particular styles of entrepreneurship? A foundational approach to cultural economy investigates how cultural perspective directs the attention and choices of entrepreneurs – for instance, how entrepreneurs plugged into an emerging urban youth culture are able to see profit opportunities others completely miss.

The foundational scope Lavoie attributed to culture is apparent in the very definition he employed.

> Culture is to be understood broadly as the complex of meanings that allows us to comprehend human action: it is the background context that renders purposeful action intelligible. Culture is the language in which past events are interpreted, future circumstances are anticipated, and plans for action are formulated. Although not a language in the sense of a static set of words and grammatical rules, culture is a discourse (Lavoie 1991: 34).

Lavoie's intellectual commitment to philosophical hermeneutics, which explores interpretive processes and human understanding in general, rings clear in his articulation of the foundational role culture plays in the evolution of market processes. [3] Culture is the framework of thought that allows us to attach meaning to the world around us. The 'interpretive turn' taken within hermeneutical philosophy recognizes that all thought is informed and shaped by the particular perspective of the thinker, and that that perspective is socially constructed. All thought, for instance, is generated through the medium of language. It is not possible even to form thoughts outside of a language. Even if an individual encounters the world around herself in isolation, the meanings she attaches to that world are inherently social, as her perspective has been shaped by the language in which she thinks. Similarly, one cannot encounter the world without seeing it through a cultural lens. Just as all our thoughts and actions are embedded within a particular language community, our thoughts and actions are also always embedded within a particular cultural context. The cultural context shapes the things we see, the things we gloss over, and the meanings we attach to events and circumstances. Yet mainstream economics is content to ignore the role culture plays in economic processes, as it treats the individual agent as if he is capable of existing outside of any specific cultural context, acquiring a sort of perspective-less perspective.

Mainstream scholars who do try to bring culture into economic analysis, tend to bring it in as a single factor, by asking questions like, 'Which matters more in economic performance: a society's culture or its institutions?' There may be some value in asking the question this way. Comparisons between North and South Korea, or Eastern and Western Germany before reunification, for example, reveal how important it is to get the institutions right, as culturally similar societies perform dramatically differently when subjected to different institutional regimes (Johnson and Sheehy 1996; Gwartney, Lawson and Block 1996). But such questions miss altogether the more fundamental relationships between cultural and economic processes – how, for instance, culture serves as the 'glue' that binds the formal rules of property or contract to the everyday actions and interpretations of people living under those rules (Boettke 2001). In a post-communist world, we finally seem to have resolved the question as to whether private property rights or government ownership is superior in terms of generating economic success. The more critical question now is how societies can adapt the right institutions to their particular context. In order to grapple with this sort of question, we cannot treat culture as a separate factor, but instead, need to explore the more fundamental relationship cultural processes have with economic processes.

Lavoie argued that an interpretive economics (one informed by hermeneutics and an understanding of cultural processes) challenges economists to rethink the very starting point of economic analysis. By starting from the 'individual rational mind', as if this were an unproblematic entity that is separable from the social realm, mainstream economics misunderstands the nature of the essential forces that drive the market process. By presenting entrepreneurial decision making as a purely calculative rather than interpretive and creative process, for example, mainstream economics has no way to explore the reasons why an entrepreneur is alert to some opportunities, but not others, or why two well-informed entrepreneurs reach different conclusions even when looking at the same data. In other words, many of the most interesting questions about the driving forces of the market process are ignored (Lavoie 1991).

Lavoie had no quarrel with methodological individualism – societies are made up of individuals. What he found objectionable was the treatment of the human, thinking, interpreting mind as if it were merely a brain existing in a culture-less, language-less isolation. Individual action would always be central to economic analysis, but for Lavoie it was cultural transmission that was the more interesting focal point for understanding the market process. Methodological individualism describes what takes place when an entrepreneur or other market participants act, but an analysis that emphasizes cultural transmission engages the question as to why the individual interprets the market context in a particular way, how she or he sees a particular action fitting into an overall plan, and perhaps why countless other alternatives that may have seemed obvious to a different observer were not pursued. As it is these interpretations that are the driving force behind the market process, the economics discipline ought to be eager to gain a more sophisticated understanding of how culture shapes those interpretations.

Though Lavoie's body of work took critical first steps in establishing the field of cultural economy, contained within that work are implicit suggestions for how the field might develop from here. Lavoie was interested in how the subject of culture could build bridges across academic disciplines. He was particularly interested in bridging the distance between the social sciences and the humanities and saw a collaborative effort between economics and the field of cultural studies as holding great promise in that regard. Secondly, he saw the potential for greater understanding of cultural processes to improve economic theory – Austrian and New Institutional theory in particular. Finally, in the years following the fall of the Soviet empire, Lavoie recognized that the practical challenges presented by policies aimed at economic reform and economic development also require greater understanding of cultural processes. It is to these areas of inquiry that we now turn.

RESEARCH AREAS IN CULTURAL ECONOMY

Cultural Studies, Markets and the Meanings of Everyday Life

Though a committed classical liberal, Lavoie harbored a deep and abiding respect for the radical left. He regularly sought the intellectual company of scholars such as Jurgen Habermas, Hannah Arendt and other leftists who, though deeply suspicious of market institutions, were just as critical of the intrusive powers of the state to crush the freedoms of ordinary people. Much of Lavoie's scholarship was an attempt to build bridges between classical liberalism and the academic left – both as a means of nudging classical liberals to take seriously what contemporary leftists were saying about the requirements of a healthy civil society, as well as to nudge the left in the direction of considering the power of markets to liberate ordinary people from poverty, state control and oppressive forces within the dominant culture. One such effort was the *Culture and Enterprise* (Lavoie and Chamlee-Wright 2000) project he initiated to bring together the fields of economics and cultural studies.

The interdisciplinary field of cultural studies represents the convergence of literature, ethnography and continental philosophy in the pursuit of understanding the meanings of contemporary everyday life. The field, which began in the late 1950s with the founding of the Birmingham Centre for Contemporary Cultural Studies (BCCCS), has its roots firmly planted in the soil of the leftist tradition. Early studies within the field were often categorized as 'cultural Marxism'. Richard Hoggart's *The Uses of Literacy* (1957), for example, celebrates 'authentic' elements of working class culture such as folk traditions, while criticizing those elements influenced by modern mass commercial culture. Cultural studies scholars were then, and largely remain, deeply suspicious of market forces. But as the field of cultural studies has advanced its central purpose – to reveal the ways in which ordinary people cultivate meaning in their daily lives – scholars within the field have become increasingly (and often uncomfortably) aware of the fact that markets represent one of the primary arenas in which cultural meanings are created, contested and reinterpreted.

The field of cultural studies developed as a response to both 'conservative' literary theory known as New Criticism, as well as radically left literary theory best represented by the Frankfurt School. Cultural studies challenged the analytical approach practiced within New Criticism, for example, to treat a text as if it could stand apart from any historical, economic, political or cultural context. Instead, cultural studies wanted to explore fully the many different ways in which a 'text' is embedded within overlapping, often contradictory cultural contexts.

As the field evolved, cultural studies also challenged the habit of literary theory, both radical and conservative, to privilege 'high culture' over the pseudo or popular culture of the masses. The Frankfurt School, for example, explained the inability of the masses to appreciate 'true art' as the result of the false consciousness from which they suffer within capitalist society. Cultural studies breaks down this distinction between high and low culture, arguing that it is the cultural engagement of everyday life – the reading of romance novels, watching reruns of Star Trek, or hanging out at the mall – that generates new meaning.

By adopting ethnographic research methods, what has developed within cultural studies is a deeper appreciation for how ordinary people interpret their own circumstances. Rather than treating 'the masses' as hapless dupes of commercial culture, subjects are allowed to express the ways in which they learn from and often challenge the meanings they interpret out of popular culture; how they actively choose to belong to certain sub-cultures, while disavowing others; how they use commercial icons for their own purposes, often in ways that are opposed to the corporate interests that financed them. Cultural studies recognized that while commercial culture has the power to shape and manipulate ordinary people, ordinary people also have the power to reread and reinterpret the meanings represented within commercial culture.

As the distinction between high and low culture broke down, cultural studies scholars began to treat the artifacts of popular culture – soap operas, fan communities, poetry slams, Internet chat rooms, television shows, youth fashion, and so on – with the same intellectual respect previously reserved for the opera, ballet and great works of literature. Given that what gains favor in popular culture is also often commercially successful, the legitimacy achieved by popular culture points directly to what may emerge as the next phase in the development of contemporary leftist thought: the idea that markets offer ordinary people the opportunity to creatively cultivate new meaning out of existing social structures, to redefine their own circumstances within society, and to challenge the dominant culture.

A few cultural studies scholars have cautiously ventured in this direction as they begin to articulate how a better understanding of market processes could enrich cultural studies, as market interaction plays such a vital role in our everyday lives (Willis 1990; During 1993). In *Culture and Enterprise* (2000), Lavoie and I wanted to help build that bridge by starting from the other shore. Not only did we hope to encourage cultural studies scholars to acquire a better understanding of market processes, we also hoped to convince economists to acquire a better understanding of cultural processes through the analytical and methodological tools of cultural studies.

A wide diversity of projects could help to fill in the pieces still missing in this bridge. Certainly, more work needs to be pursued to draw out the connections between popular culture and the market process. Tyler Cowen's (1998; 2002) work provides an excellent example of how close analysis of the historical record, as well as contemporary popular culture industries, can illuminate the ways in which the market process makes possible a thriving popular culture, one that allows for artistic expression of which the dominant culture approves, as well as art that offends, challenges, and brings to the surface assumptions that lie beneath our consciousness.[4]

In addition to overarching work like that of Cowen's, analysis that borrows the best of both cultural studies and cultural economy could be directed towards a deeper understanding of how sub-cultural movements are tied to, dependent on, and/or threatened by market forces. The cultural evolution of the feminist movement, skateboard culture, ethnolinguistic communities, fan communities, the environmentalist movement, gay and lesbian communities, and so on, is often intimately connected to the market process. Not only do activists' organizations make use of the commercial media to get their message to a wider public, sometimes becoming wealthy in the process, professional marketing strategists use the messages emerging out of such movements and emergent sub-cultures to their own advantage. In turn, it is important to consider how such messages are actually received by the consuming public, whether the meanings that are read out of this process are in line with or in opposition to the meanings that were intended. Up-close ethnographic research methods employed in cultural studies are particularly well suited to this sort of inquiry, as they allow the researcher to understand better the ways in which cultural meanings are presented, received and reinterpreted in the interplay of activist organizations, the popular media, target audiences, and those who just happen to be listening in.

The possibilities go well beyond the short list offered here, but the more general point is that collaborative efforts between cultural studies and cultural economy have the potential to enrich both fields of inquiry. In the effort to push the economics discipline beyond depictions of the market that suggest a cultureless arena, in which robotic decision makers march lock step towards a predetermined end, economists would do well to embrace the methodological and analytic tools of cultural studies. By the same token, by moving beyond traditional leftist depictions of the market and recognizing the market as an environment in which people creatively cultivate meaning in their lives, cultural studies opens up for itself a vast new territory to which they can bring their expertise.

New Directions for Austrian and New Institutional Economics

The fields within economics that best lend themselves to a cultural economic approach are those that already recognize the central role that cultural transmission plays in fostering social institutions, namely Austrian economics and New Institutional economics. Though they differ in their methodological approach, the Austrians and New Institutionalists share a common interest in how knowledge systems operate. Rather than seeing the price system and social institutions in parametric terms, for example, Austrians treat such phenomena as self-correcting systems of knowledge that have evolved over time (Hayek 1973; 1988). This insight was at the heart of the Austrian critique of central planning, as no central authority could ever gather the knowledge required to successfully plan a complex economic system. Similarly, New Institutionalists recognize that what is attempted, what is noticed, what is passed over, and what is learned in the market is shaped and directed by the mental models that market participants possess (Denzau and North 1994; North 2005). What people already know and the mental tools we use to make sense of the world play a major role in determining what we will learn in the future.

Given this emphasis on knowledge systems, both fields give rise to important questions that call for further investigation – inquiries that would naturally fall within the purview of cultural economy. For example, other than through the price system, how is information spread across dispersed market participants? What accounts for shifts in entrepreneurial perspective that drive economic change? What accounts for shifting mental models that drive institutional change? In turn, how does this institutional change redirect the learning process in the market? Particularly when one attempts to address these sorts of questions in the context of a specific setting, it becomes necessary to pay close attention to the local cultural context, thus cultural economic investigations along these lines offer a natural complement to both fields.

Both Austrian and New Institutional economics significantly improve upon neoclassical economics by recognizing the institutional embeddedness of economic processes. Yet until recently both fields have tended to characterize market decisions in instrumental, rather than interpretive terms. Austrians certainly recognize the subjective (and therefore interpretive) nature of the decision making process. But we often speak of the process by which winners and losers are selected in the market, or the process by which good (profitable) ideas win out over bad (unprofitable) ideas as if the rules by which such selections are made emerged out of a cultural vacuum. New Institutionalists have recognized that ideological commitments on the part of market participants matter in economic decision making, but the analysis has been forced into a cost–benefit framework, making adherence to cultural norms yet another sphere of instrumental calculation. More recently, however, both Austrian economics and New Institutional analysis have taken a more radical culturally informed turn. Douglass North's most recent book *Understanding the Process of Economic Change* (2005), for example, explores the connections between the human mind and the environment it seeks to understand, and how this relationship drives institutional and economic change. Similar to Lavoie's overarching project on social learning, North seeks to understand how cultural belief shapes what we know, how we learn, and how that learning shapes institutional and economic change.

Further, a cultural economic approach would consider the cultural norms that position a particular market participant or idea as being more or less persuasive. We would want to ask who is doing the persuading. How does her own position in society shape her thinking about the economic landscape, her chances of success, and her expectations of the future? Who is it that is being persuaded? How do his social position, cultural background and training help to define what he considers persuasive? How does his impression of the messenger influence what he finds to be persuasive?

Other social scientists consider economists to be pitifully naive when we characterize the market process as one in which better ideas tend to win out – period – without consideration for how the rules of the game might systematically favor some groups over others. Even when we temper our optimism with caveats about bounded rationality, incomplete information, non-robust feedback mechanisms, and promises about the long run, we are still presenting the market process as one that is culturally neutral. Though the rules of the market order may appear culturally neutral to a group of people who are mostly white, mostly male, mostly privileged, and who are all the beneficiaries of advanced education, many market participants experience them differently.

But the point behind examining the cultural embeddedness of the criteria by which market participants select one idea, profit opportunity, or product over another is not just about identity politics. The real point is to draw attention to the interpretive aspects of social coordination. Drawing from philosophical hermeneutics, Lavoie saw a fundamental similarity between the spontaneous order that emerges in a market environment and the meanings that emerge when a text is interpreted in a discursive process. The meaning a text takes on over time is not rigidly determined by some objective standard (like the meaning the author intended, for example). Every rereading of a text is a reinterpretation, as the reader's own history, place in society, and cultural perspective inform that reading and reveal new meaning out of the old text. But nor is the meaning of the text thrown completely open to, say, any old interpretation to come along. Rather, discourse around a given text allows people to offer their interpretation as to its meaning, argue for that interpretation, receive and respond to critique of that interpretation, and listen to counter interpretations. In this process, some ideas are dismissed as unpersuasive, others nudge the discourse in new directions, and new truths are revealed.

In turn, which interpretations are considered to be the most persuasive is itself the outcome of an interpretive process. The authority ascribed to the interpreter within a discursive community, the manner in which truth claims are presented, the rhetorical rules employed to convince one's audience, all influence the direction of the dialogue and the meanings that emerge as having the greatest force. This is not to suggest that it is an arbitrary matter as to which meanings 'win out'. Factors such as the (voluntary) authority ascribed to a particular speaker, or the rules of evidence are themselves subject to scrutiny and reevaluation. The point is that the process of creating intersubjectively shared meanings is based on a set of rules that is itself the outcome of an evolutionary cultural process.

Similarly, the market process is also discursive, generating not objective facts, but rather intersubjectively shared meanings. As Hayek (1948a; 1948b; 1948c) argued, market competition is not just price competition in the usual sense described by mainstream economics. Market competition is more fundamentally about competing interpretations of the market environment. Just as a particular cultural perspective shapes the interpretations a reader might have of a novel or play, so too does cultural perspective shape the readings market participants have of the economic landscape (Lavoie 1990c). Further, which interpretations are selected as more or less persuasive is itself an interpretive process. Though the market often provides useful feedback (like profit and loss statements) that tell us which interpretations were a good read of the particular market environment, and which were not, we do not always have the luxury of hindsight. A venture capitalist considering eight competing projects will certainly consider the 'authority' of the person proposing the idea (his track record with other projects, for example), the methods of market analysis, and the persuasiveness of the evidence. These criteria do not emerge in a vacuum, but rather are themselves the outcome of a cultural evolutionary process. A cultural economic research agenda that pursues this line of inquiry has the potential to move the economics discipline beyond what are often naive characterizations of the market process as culturally neutral.

Cultural Economy and the Road to Prosperity

On both a theoretical and practical level, the field of cultural economy also has the potential to make significant contributions to our understanding of how societies generate or fail to generate prosperity.

On a theoretical level, cultural economic analysis can add some much-needed flesh to the bare bones of entrepreneurship theory. The characterization of the entrepreneur purely as an agent of arbitrage leaves aside many of the most interesting facets of the subject. The successful entrepreneur is not just one who is alert to price discrepancies, but is also alert to ways in which the local context and his own placement within that context can be leveraged to his advantage. Research on entrepreneurial networks, for example, reveals the ways in which entrepreneurs employ, reinterpret, and sometimes break free of cultural norms they have inherited from their ethnic, linguistic and/or religious sub-cultures (Varese and Landa 1996; Kotkin 1992, Minniti 2005).

Further, entrepreneurs must also cultivate strategies that enable them to accumulate capital, but how one goes about this is not always obvious. What serves as the most successful strategy varies from one cultural context to the next. For example, Ghanaian women, known for their long history in market trading and relative financial independence from men, tend to employ strategies that reduce their husbands' involvement in their business activity. In Zimbabwe, on the other hand, where women have enjoyed far less economic independence, the most successful entrepreneurs tend to be those who are able to forge business partnership with their husbands (Chamlee-Wright 2002). The point is that capital accumulation strategies, wherever they are pursued, are culturally embedded and call forth the kind of thick descriptive analysis advocated here.

Cultural economic analysis of this sort also has the potential to reveal the path dependent nature of the entrepreneurial learning process. In other words, what is learned in the pursuit of entrepreneurial gain is not determined by some pre-existing profit opportunity. Rather, the learning process is embedded within a cultural and historical context, as the entrepreneur's gaze is focused and directed by that context. Virgil Storr's (2004) research, for example, suggests that the kind of learning Bahamian entrepreneurs acquire is shaped by the folklore, songs and stories that celebrate the pirate culture. Rather than acquiring knowledge that would improve productivity or enhance customer relations, the successful Bahamian entrepreneur tends to invest resources in acquiring the skills one needs to seek political favor and the rents that can be 'pirated' through such connections.

Cultural economic analysis is particularly important when it comes to understanding the process of economic reform. Kate Zhou's (1996) study of agricultural reform in China, for example, illustrates how women played a central role in the transition to private agriculture. Many women refused to marry unless their betrothed left the state farm for a private household farm. Further, when traveling to visit family, women served as information agents, spreading news of how life was better off than on the state farms. Abstract theoretical research on economic reform could never account for this type of phenomenon, and is therefore in need of complementary research that gains more intimate contact with the subjects responding to the newly reformed context.

Just as the cultural context can offer up 'solutions' as Zhou found, it can also offer up barriers to successful economic reform. Boettke (2001), for example, argues that the challenge facing the former Soviet Union is not just about getting the institutions right, it is also about getting the cultural norms right. Decades of a day-to-day existence within a shortage economy oriented entrepreneurial energy towards winning in the context of a zero-sum game. Soviet citizens were more than familiar with markets, but the markets they encountered tended to be difficult to navigate, with sellers almost always dictating the terms of exchange. Given this context, it is little wonder that most former Soviet citizens did not expect market reforms to improve their lot. Their suspicions were confirmed when they observed that only well-connected people willing to use the tactics of organized crime seemed to be prospering. In turn, this low level of expectations renders the polity weak, which generates a self-fulfilling prophesy.[5]

Once observations such as this are made, it is important to ask the practical question of 'what to do about it?' If significant cultural barriers are found to exist, is it possible to change that culture? How does a society set out to foster a cultural environment that is conducive to experimentation, that views profit as a legitimate reward for entrepreneurial activity, that favors productivity over rent seeking? And if it is possible to accomplish this, is it appropriate to recommend and pursue such changes? As classical liberals, shouldn't we worry about making recommendations that smack of academic elitism or at worst give marching orders to government policymakers to engage in social engineering? In short, what are the policy implications of cultural economic research of this sort?

It is on this point that Lavoie's appreciation of civil society is particularly relevant. When we are talking about cultural change, the principal role of academia is not that of preacher, nor that of government policy advisor. Rather, the proper role of academia is to serve as an integral part of civil society.

> Many institutional maladies are resistant to the top-down, Pass-a-Law mentality, and can only be overcome by a gradual change in attitudes and practices, but this does not mean that there is nothing we can do about them. Knowing what elements of a culture contribute to its economic prosperity is important, even if it cannot be directly translated into a bill in the Senate, or a constitutional amendment. Many of us spend a good deal of our lives in a different sort of 'policy activity', and perhaps it is this kind of policy work that is more likely to lead to lasting change. We attempt to pass along to our co-workers, our friends, our neighbors, and our children, the values we take to be conducive to the good life. Some of us spend hours in classrooms, clubs, temples, mosques, or churches conveying values to our students or audiences or congregations, whether we explicitly admit that we are doing so or not. Some of us write articles, letters to the editor, e-mail, or books, in which this or that value of our culture is encouraged or discouraged. Coaches of Little League teams and Girl Scout troop leaders who impart a work ethic, a pride in accomplishments, self-esteem, an ability to work with others, are perhaps more important policymakers in the end than legislators are (Lavoie and Chamlee-Wright 2000: 77).

By making markets and our attitudes about market exchange a more conscious part of our civil discourse, all members of civil society have the opportunity to nudge our culture (and various sub-cultures) in new directions. Economic reform cannot help but be intertwined with the cultural context in which it is pursued. Rather than avoiding the question of how or whether cultural change will take place, it would be far better if those of us who are involved in the debate about economic reform were more literate when it came to reading the cultural context in which such reforms are to be implemented.

CULTURE AND LIBERTY: CONCLUDING REMARKS

In articulating to his fellow economists the central role culture plays in the market process, Lavoie's primary motivation was scholarly. He understood cultural transmission to be the mother of all social learning processes, including the market process. He knew that the discipline of economics would be deeply enriched if economists moved out of the safe and comfortable confines of a rarified theory that assumes away all the complicating messiness of culture. He wanted to make economics relevant to scholars across the disciplines who might otherwise dismiss economic analysis for its relatively unsophisticated treatment of cultural processes.

Yet also behind Lavoie's scholarship on culture and economics was a desire to celebrate freedom. As a classical liberal, Lavoie understood that when human beings are allowed to live in liberty, not only do our markets prosper, our cultures prosper as well. He celebrated markets for their tendency to serve even the tiniest countercultural elements in society; for their tendency to bring together people from starkly different cultures for the purpose of peaceful exchange; for their tendency to subvert both political and cultural oppression. His frustration with mainstream economic theory was not that it misrepresented the nature of the market. He abhorred mechanical descriptions of the economy because they portrayed markets as lifeless, colorless and boring. He knew that, if the cause of liberty was to win hearts as well as minds, economists needed to do more than win the argument about which economic system was likely to produce more 'stuff'. We also need to talk competently about the ways in which a healthy civic life goes hand-in-hand with economic and cultural freedom, and how ordinary people use markets everyday in their pursuit of living a meaningful life. In short, by emphasizing the interplay of markets and culture, Lavoie was making the case for a free society.

NOTES

1. Lavoie pointed to the potential for the Austrian school to advance our understanding of cultural processes by editing a special volume of the journal *Cultural Dynamics* (1990a) on Hayek's theory of cultural evolution.
2. See also the work of scholars such as Janet Landa (1991), David Martin (1990), and S.G. Redding (1990). The work carried out at ISEC is now part of the Institute on Culture, Religion, and World Affairs (CURA).
3. Though hermeneutics originally focused on the interpretation of written texts, modern hermeneutics views 'text' as anything that calls forth interpretation, including complex human interaction, such as we see in a market economy.
4. See also Cowen (2002).
5. Cultural processes will also play a central role in recovery and rebuilding efforts following catastrophic disasters such as 9/11 and Hurricane Katrina. Early investigations of post-

Katrina recovery efforts suggest that community resilience depends on well worn patterns of social capital that communities enjoyed prior to the storm. Understanding the signaling mechanisms at work within the social capital structure will be an essential piece of explaining why some communities are more successful in their attempts to rebuild than others. The Mercatus Center at George Mason University has launched a major research program on the political, economic and cultural processes of resilience in the wake of Hurricane Katrina. It is no coincidence that several of the lead scholars on the project are former students of Don Lavoie.

REFERENCES

Berger, Brigitte (ed.) (1991), *The Culture of Entrepreneurship*, San Francisco: Institute for Contemporary Studies Press.

Boettke, Peter (2001), 'Why culture matters: economics, politics, and the imprint of history', *Calculation and Coordination: Essays on Socialism and Transitional Political Economy*, London: Routledge.

Chamlee-Wright, Emily (1997), *The Cultural Foundations of Economic Development: Urban Female Entrepreneurship in Ghana*, London: Routledge.

Chamlee-Wright, Emily (2002), 'Savings and accumulation strategies of urban market women in Harare, Zimbabwe', *Economic Development and Cultural Change*, **50**(4) 979–1005.

Cowen, Tyler (1998), *In Praise of Commercial Culture*, Cambridge: Harvard University Press.

Cowen, Tyler (2002), *Creative Destruction*, Princeton, NJ: Princeton University Press.

Denzau, Arthur and Douglass North (1994), 'Shared mental models: ideologies and institutions', *Kyklos*, **47**, pp. 3–30.

During, Simon (1993), 'Introduction' in Simon During (ed.) *The Cultural Studies Reader*, New York: Routledge.

Gwartney, James, Robert Lawson and Walter Block (1996), *Economic Freedom of the World: 1975–1995*, Vancouver, BC: Fraser Institute.

Harrison, Lawrence E. (1992), *Who Prospers? How Cultural Values Shape Economic and Political Success*, New York: Basic Books.

Hayek, F.A. (1948a), 'The use of knowledge in society', in *Individualism and Economic Order*, Chicago: University of Chicago Press.

Hayek, F.A. (1948b), 'The meaning of competition', in *Individualism and Economic Order*, Chicago: University of Chicago Press.

Hayek, F.A. (1948c), 'Socialist calculation III: the "competitive" solution', in *Individualism and Economic Order*, Chicago: University of Chicago Press.

Hayek, F.A. (1973), *Law Legislation and Liberty, Vol. I: Rules and Order*, Chicago: University of Chicago Press.

Hayek, F.A. (1979), *Law Legislation and Liberty, Vol. III: The Political Order of a Free People*, Chicago: University of Chicago Press.

Hayek, F.A. (1988), *The Fatal Conceit: The Errors of Socialism*, London: Routledge.

Hoggart, Richard (1957), *The Uses of Literacy*, Harmondsworth: Penguin.

Johnson, Bryan and Thomas Sheehy (1996), *Index of Economic Freedom*, Washington DC: Heritage Foundation.

Kotkin, Joel (1992), *Tribes: How Race, Religion, and Identity Determine Success in the New Global Economy*, New York: Random House.

Landa, Janet (1991), 'Culture and entrepreneurship in less developed countries: ethnic trading networks as economic organizations', in B. Berger (ed.), *The Culture of Entrepreneurship*, San Francisco: Institute for Contemporary Studies Press.

Lavoie, Don C. (1990a), Special Issue on 'F.A. Hayek's Theory of Cultural Evolution', *Cultural Dynamics* **3** (1).

Lavoie, Don C. (1990b) 'Hermeneutics, subjectivity, and the Lester/Machlup debate: towards a more anthropological approach to empirical economics', Warren J. Samuels (ed.) *Economics as Discourse: An Analysis of the Language of Economists*, Boston: Kluwer Academic Publishing.

Lavoie, Don C. (1990c), 'Understanding differently: hermeneutics and the spontaneous order of communicative processes', *History of Political Economy: Annual Supplement to Volume 22*, Bruce J. Caldwell (ed.), Special Issue on 'Carl Menger and His Legacy in Economics', pp. 359–77.

Lavoie, Don C. (1991), 'The discovery and interpretation of profit opportunities: culture and the Kirznerian entrepreneur', in B. Berger (ed.), *The Culture of Entrepreneurship*, San Francisco: Institute for Contemporary Studies Press.

Lavoie, Don C. and Emily Chamlee-Wright (2000), *Culture and Enterprise: The Development, Representation, and Morality of Business*, London: Routledge.

Martin, David (1990), *Tongues of Fire*, Oxford: Basil Blackwell.

Minniti, Maria (2005), 'Entrepreneurship and network externalities', *Journal of Economic Behavior and Organization*, **57**(1), 1–27.

North, Douglass (2005), *Understanding the Process of Economic Change*, Princeton, NJ: Princeton University Press.

Redding, S. Gordon (1990), *The Spirit of Chinese Capitalism*, New York: Walter de Gruyter.

Storr, Virgil Henry (2004), *Enterprising Slaves & Master Pirates: Understanding Economic Life in the Bahamas*, New York: Peter Lang Publishing.

Varese, Federico and Janet Landa (1996), 'Trust, ethnicity, and identity: beyond the new institutional economics of ethnic trading networks, contract law, and gift-exchange', *The American Journal of Sociology*, **101**(5), 1444–532.

Willis, Paul (1990), *Common Culture: Symbolic Work at Play in the Everyday Cultures of the Young*, Boulder, CO: Westview Press.

Zhou, Kate Xiao (1996), *How the Farmers Changed China: Power of the People*, Boulder, CO: Westview Press.

11. Innovation of cardio-imaging technology at Hewlett-Packard and HP/Philips

Don E. Kash

PREFACE

This study of the cardio-imaging technology (CIT) launched by Hewlett-Packard (HP) is part of a broader effort to understand the processes of innovation associated with contemporary complex technologies. Most successful innovations of complex technologies are characterized by patterns of development in which the technologies and the involved organizations co-evolve. The process of co-evolution commonly manifests three different innovation patterns. Each of the patterns has distinctive innovation goals and organizational structures and processes. This study uses a technology trajectory framework to investigate the different patterns.

For most technologies, the process of co-evolution associated with innovation produces increasingly complex technologies and organizational networks. The increasing complexity is evident in both the diversity of the components and the nature of their interactions with both the technologies and networks. Complex technologies and the organizational networks that produce them are appropriately seen as parts of cybernetic systems. With increasing complexity, commercial success commonly requires repeated changes in management strategies and public policy. Specifically, hierarchical planning and management become less and less effective and the organizational networks are characterized by self-organization.

Although industrial management and organizational processes in many companies have been responding to the complexity challenge, public policy and particularly technology policy, has been less responsive. The broader investigation of which this case study is a part has two goals. One is to seek insight into the processes whereby complex commercial technologies are successfully innovated. The other is to search for patterns that are common in the processes of innovating different complex technologies.

In Part I we introduce the framework of innovation patterns that structures this research. Part II provides an introduction to cardio-imaging technology, specifically the ultrasound echocardiography developed by HP. Using the innovation patterns framework, Part III examines the evolution of HP's CIT. Part IV examines the core capabilities and complementary assets, structure, strategy and learning characteristics of the network as it co-evolved with the CIT. Part IV also addresses when HP sought out a technical partnership with Philips to develop cardiac-MRI technology as a potential new platform for cardio-imaging technology. Part V briefly discusses the search for a new technology trajectory following the termination of the partnership. Part VII offers summary comments and conclusions.

PART I: INNOVATION PATTERNS FRAMEWORK

Innovation patterns are valuable conceptual references for the development and application of strategies aimed at stimulating the development of complex technologies.[1] The learning that is necessary for the innovation of complex technologies requires developing organizational *networks* that involve multiple firms and often other participants (for example, university or government laboratories).[2] Strategies and policies that successfully facilitate innovation must reflect the fact of co-evolution. The paths traced by co-evolving technologies and networks we label trajectories.[3] The three innovation patterns (that is, *normal*, *transitional*, and *transformational*) are shown on the trajectories in Figure 11.1.

The box symbol at the lower left of Figure 11.1 illustrates the fundamental innovations that characterize the transformation pattern. Innovations associated with the transformation pattern produce dramatically different technologies; they have fundamentally different characteristics than other technologies. A transformational innovation launches a trajectory, a co-evolving technology and network that then goes through the incremental innovations associated with the normal pattern. The process whereby a transformational pattern settles into a normal pattern is illustrated in Figure 11.1 by the incremental innovations at points 'a' and 'b'.

For complex technologies, in most cases the normal pattern is at some point replaced by a transitional pattern, illustrated in Figure 11.1 by the triangle symbol. The transitional pattern involves an innovation that produces a major change and improvement in the technology. Like the transformational pattern, a transition launches a new trajectory that then

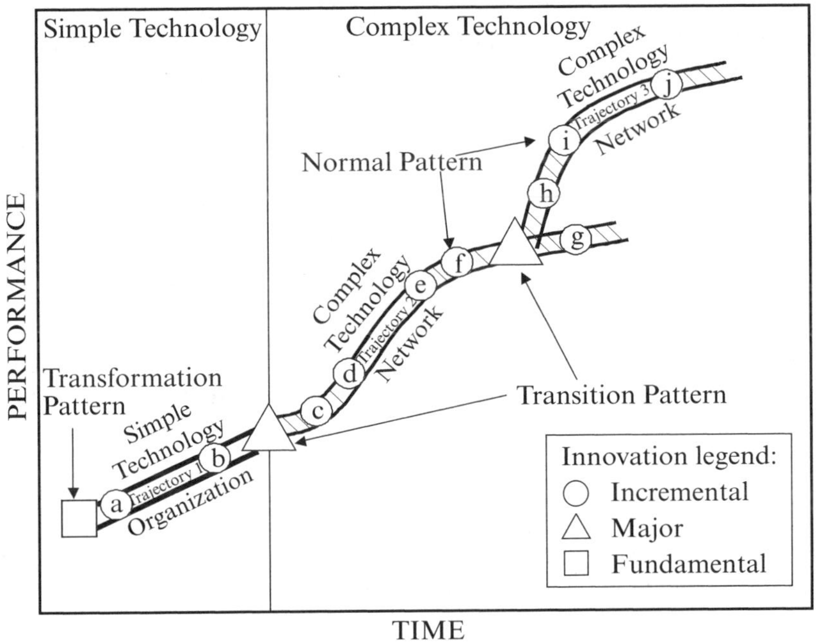

Figure 11.1 Three innovation patterns

settles into the normal pattern, illustrated in Figure 11.1 by the incremental innovations at points 'c' through 'f' and 'h' through 'j'.

Pattern Characteristics

The normal pattern is distinguished by the existence of a relatively stable network and a technology that has the same generic design before and after an innovation. Both the transitional and transformational patterns are associated with establishing new technology designs and networks. The new technologies may result from either major redesigns of established technologies (that is, transition) or from the creation of fundamentally new designs (that is, transformation). Similarly, new networks may have either the same participant organizations or new ones, but they always include new knowledge, core capabilities, and complementary assets.[4]

The normal pattern

The greatest profits from complex technologies are usually produced within the normal pattern. Specifically, it is the ability to incrementally innovate ahead of or parallel with competitors that produces success in the arena of complex technologies. The normal pattern is characterized by continuity. Incremental innovations occur within a network's current problem-solving model. Within the normal pattern, high levels of confidence exist regarding what the performance characteristics of the next increment will be, what problems demand priority, and what procedures should be followed in solving them. The dominant short-term uncertainties are about how long the problem-solving process will take and how much it will cost. Company and network strategies and structures are usually modified in small steps as each incremental technological advance takes place.[5] In the normal pattern, as technologies evolve along an established trajectory, network core capabilities tend to become more fixed. These capabilities commonly include increasing mastery of systems integration and architectural knowledge, and thus the growing capability to synthesize previously separate knowledge and complementary assets.[6]

Organizational learning in the normal pattern is predominantly internal to the network and normally becomes more focused with each incremental advance. As network routines become well developed, learning becomes ever more dependent upon what has been done in the past. Thus, as problems emerge, established networks know where to go for solutions. This makes problem-solving a less risky process than it is when more wide-ranging exploratory learning is required.[7]

The transitional pattern

Innovations that occur within the transitional pattern create new technology designs and networks as a result of major changes in what previously existed. Transitional innovations commonly deliver major advances in performance and qualitative changes in design by modifying established technologies in ways that overcome previously constraining boundary conditions. This often happens when previously separate technologies are integrated to produce a major redesign, for example mechanical technologies become electromechanical. When transitional innovations occur, networks face significant uncertainty about the design characteristics of the technology and about what the innovation will cost and when it will take place. Nonetheless, transitional innovations can usually rely – at least in part – on a reservoir of knowledge that has been accumulated while carrying out the incremental innovations associated with previous trajectories. Transitions may be generated by problems or opportunities, or a combination of both. When impending transitions are widely anticipated, there are substantial incentives for previously competing networks to cooperate. The great uncertainty associated with transitions is a powerful inducement to establish strategic alliances and other forms of cooperation.[8] As part of the transition to a new trajectory, even the most entrenched competitor networks are increasingly engaging in collaborative activities.[9] One factor that encourages cooperation is the belief that limiting the number of transition pathways through the use of voluntary standards setting has advantages for all the networks involved.[10]

Networks that carry out transitions become new networks because they must integrate new core capabilities to carry out the innovation. The most common occurrence is to integrate established core capabilities with core capabilities developed in other sectors. Because of the benefits of rapid innovation and because of the need to use significant amounts of tacit knowledge, new core capabilities are increasingly being accessed by adding new members to the network. That is because tacit knowledge takes too long to develop internally.[11]

The transformational pattern

The transformational pattern is the most chaotic of the three. Its innovations involve fundamental changes in technology and the creation of new networks. In this pattern major surprises and discontinuities are frequently encountered, and everything is subject to change. Thus, it is useful to think of transformational innovations as doing more than overcoming existing boundary constraints. Fundamental innovations establish previously unavailable technology paths.

Transformational innovations require creating new core capabilities. This often involves merging previously existing core capabilities, but sometimes it means creating them from whole cloth. In the arena of complex technologies, commercial opportunities seldom flow directly and immediately from scientific breakthroughs. Thus, the identification and development of entirely new core capabilities is a risky trial-and-error process. The learning critical to transformational innovations may be unrelated to the past learning of a network or company. Learning boundaries expand and become blurred. Thus, it is essential within this pattern that firms and networks learn to 'be at home anywhere'. No potential source of usable knowledge can be ruled out.[12] Success is usually associated with a general openness to redefining organizational strategy and structure, as well as existing routines and decision-making procedures.[13] For any particular firm or other organization, undertaking such broad learning may require memberships in multiple networks cutting across different industries, sectors, and economies.

The next section provides an overview of HP's CIT. With this understanding we then follow with an application of these patterns.

PART II: OVERVIEW OF HP'S CARDIO-IMAGING TECHNOLOGY

Hewlett-Packard in the early 1960s was recognized as a leader in innovations in electronic technologies. Company lore says that one of the influences that led to the focus on medical electronic technologies was that William Hewlett's father was a doctor. In 1961 HP purchased Sanborn, a Massachusetts medical technology firm that 'had 950 employees and annual sales of $16 million. Sanborn produced electrocardiographs and other test and measurement instruments used by the medical profession.'[14] Sanborn was the largest single HP acquisition up to that time and it started HP on a process that saw continuous expansion over the next several decades of its medical electronics capabilities and business volume. By the late 1990s HP's Medical Products Group was a worldwide leader in clinical measurement and diagnostic technologies with 5400 employees; in 1998, for example, it had revenues of more than $1.3 billion. Coupled with its core capability in information systems, HP's goal was to 'provide the technology that will enable clinicians to access patient data anytime, anywhere across the care continuum'.[15] In 1998 HP was acknowledged as the leader in the estimated $3.3 billion ultrasound market.

In an independent report published by New York-based Klein Biomedical Consultants, Hewlett-Packard was ranked the No. 1 medical diagnostic ultrasound provider worldwide for 1998 'becoming the first company to surpass $500 million in worldwide ultrasound revenues'.[16]

Cardiology accounted for 30 to 35 percent of the worldwide ultrasound market in 1998. HP specialized in cardiology, and it had a 55 percent share of the worldwide cardiology ultrasound market. Acuson had a 38 percent worldwide share. Philips, with the acquisition of ATL Ultrasound in the late 1990s had become a player along with Siemens.

HP SONOS 5000 Cardiovascular Ultrasound System

The evolution of HP's cardio-imaging technology, distinguishing capabilities and their benefits, network organization, and public policy relevant to the innovation process through its period of cooperation with Philips are outlined in Table 11.1. The initial innovation of the phased array CIT and five subsequent incremental innovations used ultrasound technology to create an image of the heart for medical diagnosis (Box 11.1). HP later joined forces with the Dutch electronics firm, Philips, to develop a cardio-imaging system using magnetic resonance imaging (MRI) technology that would offer capabilities not available with ultrasound (Box 11.2). A management decision at HP terminated this arrangement, and HP withdrew from the

MRI project in 1995. The evolution of HP's ultrasound echocardiography technology, and the attempted transition to the new MRI cardio-imaging technology trajectory are illustrated in Figure 11.2.

Table 11.1 Evolution of HP's cardio-imaging technology

Year	Technology	Model	Innovation	Benefit	Network	Public Policy
1980	Phased Array	77020A	64 channel transducer; sweep signal over 90° arc	Transducer, signal processing, system integration	HP Labs, HP Andover, Stanford	Health care policies encouraging high performance medical technology
1983	Doppler	Revision G	Enhanced signal processing	Measure blood flow velocity	SRI, Houston Memorial Hospital, Stanford, Duke, Mayo Clinic	FDA regulations
1986	Color flow	Revision K	Enhanced signal processing	Two-dimensional Doppler image	Duke University Medical Center, NOAA	Uncertainty regarding government–industry cooperation
1988	Transeso-phageal Probe	Revision L	Locate transducer in esophagus	Improved access	Oldelft, University of Aachen	Patents
1989	Linear Array	1000M	New transducer (Carotid–neck)	Diagnosis artery blockage; high resolution image of neck, entry into radiology	University of Massachusetts, Duke University	Patents
1991	Integrated Backscatter	2000	Distinguish among tissue types		Washington University (St. Louis), U. Iowa, Stanford	
1991 to 1995	MRI	n/a	MRI-based system	3-dimensional non-invasive image of heart and coronaries	Philips, Beth Israel, Washington University (St. Louis), Stanford	

BOX 11.1 BASICS OF ULTRASOUND CARDIO-IMAGING TECHNOLOGY[17]

Ultrasound echocardiography employs high-frequency sound waves to generate visual images of cardiac anatomy and function. A noninvasive procedure, ultrasound can image the body's soft tissue, organs, and blood flow in real time. It is a highly cost-effective medical diagnostic treatment and can eliminate the need for more invasive and expensive procedures. Ultrasound can be used to evaluate the repair of a vessel wall in surgery, check on the success of an organ transplant or evaluate the need for appendectomy and potentially avoid an unnecessary operation. It can be used in the most delicate conditions with minimal risk of side effects.

Echo sounding is also used by some animals to measure distance and has been employed by humans since shortly after World War I. The basic principles are similar to echo sounding used in sonar. After 1945 echo sounding began to find extensive applications in noninvasive medical diagnosis. When a rapid, fluctuating current is introduced into a piezoelectric crystal it vibrates, producing sound well beyond the range of human hearing, ultrasound. Each time a wave of this sound crosses the boundary or interface between two structures or tissues of different density, some of the energy is reflected at the interface and the echoes are picked up by the crystal and amplified as an electric signal. The position of the reflecting structures can then be plotted. This technology was enhanced in the 1950s to produce a two-dimensional view. Doppler capability was added in the 1970s and early-1980s enabling the detection of organ and blood motion within the human body. Ultrasound is used to diagnose numerous cardiac conditions such as valve disease, septal defects, and wall motion abnormalities. Nuclear cardiology is a complementary technology used to determine the blood supplied to various regions of the heart – a capability not presently available from echocardiography – however, advances in cardio-imaging technology have progressed significantly since its innovation, and echocardiography may soon present a competitive challenge to nuclear cardiology technology.[18]

HP phased array ultrasound technology involves using a transducer (that converts electric current into sound waves and echoes back into electronic signals) positioned on the skin between the ribs to gain an image of the heart by sending and receiving sound waves over a 90° angle). Electronic signals produced by the transducer (from the sound echoes) are transmitted to a computer where imaging software is used to create an image of the heart on the display monitor. This image is recorded on a video recorder and stored in a record monitor.

BOX 11.2 MAGNETIC RESONANCE IMAGING[19]

MRI is another mechanism for noninvasive medical diagnosis. When the human body is positioned within a strong magnetic field, certain nuclei – such as proton nuclei that have inherent magnetic properties – will align with and rotate around the direction of the applied field. If these nuclei are then subjected to radio frequency (RF) energy, they will absorb energy and move into an excited state. When the RF energy is turned off, the nuclei return to their equilibrium state, releasing a detectable RF signal. This signal is the basis for the three-dimensional diagnostic images produced by the magnetic resonance system. By varying the specific sequence of RF impulses applied to the tissue, differing magnetic properties in the molecular environment of the nuclei can be detected to differentiate tissue types and detect various dynamic processes that occur in the body. Thus, in cardiac applications, the RF signal from the heart tissue can be thought of as an amplitude-frequency plot from which the general outline and character of the tissue can be determined. A receiver antenna inside the scanner picks up these signals and a computer processes them to create an image. Used in cardio-imaging, MRI will provide an enhanced three-dimensional image of the heart and coronary arteries and allow doctors to determine the perfusion of blood in the heart muscle (this is not possible with current ultrasound cardio-imaging technology).

MRI Today

Magnetic Resonance technology dates back to 1945 and became a viable clinical technique in 1982. MRI has since become the primary imaging modality for investigations of the brain, spinal cord, spine, cancellous bone and joints. It is widely used for the identification and staging of tumors, investigations of large blood vessels, and in pediatric studies. Cardiac MRI, with its unique ability to provide simultaneous information about anatomy, function and tissue character, has become a primary or complementary modality in a wide range of pathologies, such as aortic disease, masses, congenital heart disease, ventricular function and cardiomyopathies. A few facts about the use of MRI in medicine today include:

- More than 11 600 whole-body MRI units are in operation today, at least 4000 of them in the US
- There are at least 20 million MRI scans performed worldwide each year
- Worldwide annual market demand is estimated at about 1300 systems, with the US, Japan, and Europe together requiring more than 75% of these
- In 1995, 44.3% of the total market revenues were generated in the US, though that share is expected to drop to about 38% by the year 2002
- A standard MR unit costs between $1.5 million and $2 million and requires about 400 sq. ft of isolated, shielded space plus another 400 sq. ft for computers, hardware and operating systems
- Standard MR systems have magnets with field strengths of 1 or 1.5 Tesla, though low-priced magnets with 0.1 to 0.3 Tesla are now available

Sources: Frost & Sullivan, Siemens Medical Systems, Philips Medical Systems, and *IEEE Spectrum*

Three distinct phases of network/technology co-evolution are distinguishable. The transformational phase (1973–1980) includes the initial emergence and lock-in of a dominant design. During this period the HP-centered network focused on innovating a first-of-a-kind technology. Lock-in occurred after the innovation of the phased array transducer.

The second or normal phase (1980–1991) saw the technology progress along a trajectory characterized by incremental innovations that enhanced the performance of the established design. Doppler and color flow imaging were early enhancements that emerged while HP had a stove pipe organizational structure. In this phase each HP business unit operated with autonomy. Later, additional enhancements such as the transesophageal probe, the linear array transducer, the integrated backscatter, and acoustic quantification were introduced. During this latter period HP adopted a

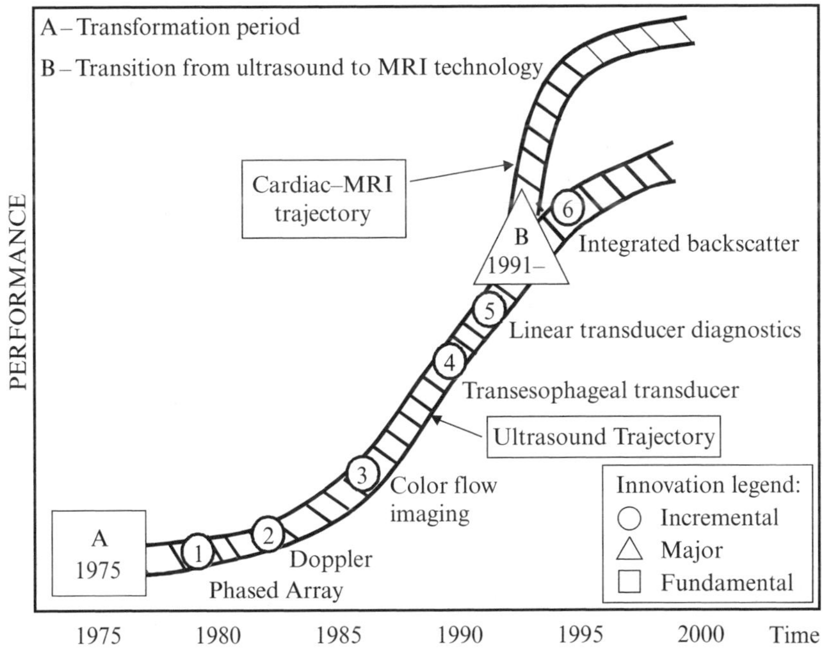

Figure 11.2 HP Cardio-imaging technology trajectories

matrix or 'rows and columns' organizational structure in an attempt to better integrate across business units.

Beginning in the early-1990s, HP Medical Products Group (MPG) began searching for a major redesign of the technology. The cooperative arrangement with Philips resulted from the search. During the period when the two companies were working on the development of an MRI-based technology HP reorganized around products and business areas (for example, PCs, servers, printers, cardio-imaging) and focused on three major technological areas: measurement, computation and communication (MC^2). In the mid-1990s it was evident that some HP managers saw the MRI-based cardio-imaging trajectory as incompatible with the new MC^2 strategy. Some opponents believed that the resources dedicated to innovation along the cardio-imaging trajectory could be used more profitably in other areas. With the termination of the cooperative agreement with Philips to innovate the cardiac-MRI, MPG explored a medical information/communications technology trajectory that was intended to align it with the communications focus of the HP corporate strategy.

PART III: INNOVATION PATTERNS APPLIED TO CIT

The transformational innovation pattern began when HP innovated the new technology in response to a perceived latent market demand. Lock-in on a generic design occurred when a significant segment of the medical community accepted the technology as an effective and practicable diagnostic tool. This occurred after HP's innovation of the phased array transducer component of the system.

The normal innovation pattern began when repeated incremental innovations of the generic design were carried out by a network of HP engineers, external suppliers and medical practitioners. HP underwent at least two organizational transitions during this phase.

The transitional innovation pattern began with HP's short-lived teaming with Philips to innovate a new line of cardio-imaging capabilities centered on magnetic resonance imaging (MRI) technology.

Fundamental Innovation: Basis for Transformation

Phased array ultrasound technology is an example of innovation that originates from a deliberate search for a new product to fulfill what Peter Senge describes as latent demand – 'what customers might truly value but have never experienced or would never think to ask for'.[20] By the early 1970s HP was well established as a leader in innovating medical technologies with a core capability in cardiac-related products. At this time Dean Morton, then the manager of MPG's R&D, became interested in imaging and computer technologies. Morton initiated a study by Arthur D. Little to examine the market potential for these technologies in medical applications. The study identified a strong potential for ultrasound technology. Morton then went to HP Central Research Labs in California and initiated an ultrasound cardio-imaging development project. Although ultrasound technology has other medical imaging applications, HP elected to concentrate on innovation of the cardio-imaging technology, a natural extension of HP's core cardiac business (Box 11.3).

Transformational pattern develops

Phased array ultrasound launched a new trajectory. Ultrasound using a movable transducer (transmitter-receiver) had been introduced in the 1960s. Attempts to expand the capability of a fixed transducer (A-mode) and one-dimensional motion (M-mode) machines to achieve two-dimensional imaging were attempted in the early 1980s. These initial experiments with two-dimensional ultrasound diagnostics were neither practical nor efficient. HP, therefore, did not produce a dominant design by displacing a previous

BOX 11.3 SYNTHESIS OF ULTRASOUND AND DIGITAL TECHNOLOGIES

Radiology and cardiology are two distinct medical applications of ultrasound technology. Radiology uses ultrasound to image objects such as a fetus or a liver. For these applications measuring motion is less important than obtaining a high-resolution image. In the cardiology application, ultrasound is used to diagnose heart disease by imaging blood and tissue in the heart, valves and vascular system. The cardio-imaging application is a more dynamic demanding system that can detect and display motion in real-time. The two ultrasound technologies have evolved along different trajectories. For example, digital technology offers expanded processing capability for both technologies. However, the optimal time for synthesizing ultrasound and digital computers varied between the two applications.

Radiology applications were able to synthesize digital technology at an earlier date. ATL Ultrasound introduced the first fully digital ultrasound machine in 1988.[21] At about the same time, HP experimented with digital processing and built a prototype to demonstrate the concept of a digital cardio-imaging machine. The computing performance state-of-the-art in the late-1980s was sufficient to process the volume of information needed for relatively static radiology applications, however HP found it was not adequate to process the larger volume of data needed to provide real-time images of the moving heart and blood at a reasonable price. The HP prototype required over $1 million in random access memory. HP did not consider digital technology practical and reasonably priced until the 1990s, and focused instead on incremental improvements along the CIT trajectory.

technology. Rather, lock-in of the phased array technology occurred when the technology was accepted by the medical community because it provided real-time moving two-dimensional images of heart functions.[22]

Ultrasound CIT reflects a synthesis of three technological systems: ultrasound, computer and video. HP sought to gain an advantage by focusing on three core capabilities: 1) phased array transducers, 2) signal processing capabilities, and 3) systems integration. Innovation of the initial technology was a cooperative effort between HP Laboratories in California and MPG in Massachusetts. HP Labs had experience with transducers and signal processing, and MPG had experience developing medical electronic systems.

Prior to the phased array innovation, ultrasound used for medical diagnostics involved either mechanically steered single beam transducers or linear array transducers that could not be steered (transducers could not be adjusted or moved while transmitting and receiving signals). The original A-Mode echocardiography machines, for example, looked along a single axis (sometimes referred to as an 'ice pick' view) and were limited to diagnosing valve disorders. The initial performance objective of the phased array innovation was to provide a two-dimensional real-time image of the pumping heart that clearly differentiated between muscle and blood. This is similar to radar identifying the moving boundary between an airplane and the atmosphere (Box 11.1).

Adequate performance required overcoming the problem that existing transducers were unable to 'look around' bone (ribs) and lung tissue to obtain a clear view of the heart. The phased array transducer surmounted this problem by sweeping signals over a 90° arc from a device that was small enough to be located between the ribs. In sum, the phased array transducer provided full surveillance of the heart from a single position. Initially, phased array technology was limited to 16 channels, thus it produced a relatively low quality image. Signals from the initial transducer produced 30 images of the heart every second.

Developing the phased array required overcoming major technical challenges. One was management of the returning echoes. Since the distance traveled by the signals varied over the sweep of the arc, HP needed to develop signal-processing capabilities to correctly interpret the incoming data. This involved extensive software development, and then the integration of the new phased array transducer and signal processing software with rapidly advancing computer hardware and video technology. Successful synthesis of these components, then, required innovations in systems design, development and manufacturing.

HP's first CIT machine was the model 77020A introduced in 1980. HP maintained the 77020 series nomenclature, and designated improvements as revisions until 1989. All series 77020 incremental innovations could be retrofit into older machines. This was a marketing decision to assure customers that they were not buying expensive capabilities that would quickly become obsolete.

Incremental Innovations Establish Normal Pattern

Once lock-in was achieved, the ultrasound cardio-imaging technology entered the normal pattern of incremental innovations along a trajectory that both guided and bounded innovation. Although there were many product upgrades and revisions to the technology, this section discusses the technological significance of five major incremental innovations that occurred between 1980 and 1991.

Doppler

The first innovation involved producing a two-dimensional Doppler image that provided a real-time picture of both the mechanical functioning of the heart and the flow of blood through the heart. Continuous and pulse Doppler sound waves allow use of frequency changes to generate information about blood velocities in the heart. Doppler technology makes it possible, for example, to see and understand the amount of blood leakage in a damaged heart. When a heart valve closes it produces back pressure and turbulence in the ventricle. In damaged hearts the result is substantial leakage around the valve. Since decisions concerning whether to replace heart valves rest, in part, on the amount of leakage, the Doppler innovation's picture of leakage was a major diagnostic contribution. The Doppler enhancement was commercialized in the model 77020Gl innovation in 1983.

Color flow

Color flow Doppler makes it easier for diagnosticians to read echocardiograms used to monitor the blood flow. The best analogy of the image provided by color flow technology is the rainfall map used on nightly weather broadcasts. These maps use different colors to show the intensity of rainfall (heavy or light) and provide a dynamic picture of changing intensity over time. This second incremental innovation offered a similar picture of blood flow in the heart. A commercially viable technology was developed and introduced in the market in 1986 with the 77020K innovation.

Transesophageal probe

The third incremental innovation involved the most direct and, in concept, simplest technological change. The initial goal was to place the transducer in the esophagus to accommodate a minority of the population with chest structures and/or heart locations that make it nearly impossible to get a clear image of the heart from between the ribs. Locating the transducer between the ribs also meant the ultrasound system could not be used when the chest cavity was open for surgery. HP postulated that locating the transducer in the esophagus would solve both problems. As with the Doppler and color flow technologies, a market developed immediately when this innovation was introduced with the 77020L in 1988.

Linear array transducers

The fourth incremental innovation occurred in response to HP's effort to expand the market from heart applications to diagnosis of vascular problems.

Previously the only way to see inside an artery involved an expensive and risky process of running a scope through the vascular system. HP's goal was to develop a linear array that would provide a real-time 'look' at the arteries without using invasive procedures.

The initial effort to use the phased array transducer for vascular diagnosis was not satisfactory because it was unable to differentiate clearly among tissue, blood and blockage material in the artery. It was quickly determined that a linear transducer several inches in length that could be laid along an artery and used to identify the quantity of blood flow was needed. HP innovated a 288 element linear array transducer with a steerable high-resolution beam and constant beam angle that provided enhanced color flow images. Improved signal processing software was developed to better identify different materials in the artery. The linear array technology was brought into commercial use in 1989. This product differed significantly from the 77020 series and was designated HP model-1000.

Integrated backscatter

The integrated backscatter innovation provided a way to distinguish among different tissues. Three kinds of tissue are associated with heart problems: (1) permanently damaged tissue with no capacity for regeneration, 2) damaged tissue with a capacity to regenerate, and 3) undamaged tissue. Each can be identified with the integrated backscatter technology enhancement. The integrated backscatter technology also provided a very precise definition of the boundary between flesh and blood that allowed for precise calculation of the size of the ventricle as the heart pumped. This technology makes it possible to measure the ventricle when it is at its largest and smallest, and gives the diagnostician a way to assess the efficiency of the heart. The integrated backscatter capability became commercially available in 1991 with the model HP-2000.

The Search for a New CIT Trajectory

HP began a search for a new CIT trajectory (that is, major technology redesign) in the early 1990s when it entered into an agreement with Philips to innovate a new mode of cardio-imaging technology centered on MRI. The cardiac-MRI technology would provide a three-dimensional image of the heart and coronary arteries allowing doctors to determine the perfusion of blood in the heart muscle. The MRI technology could replace two expensive and risky procedures for testing blood perfusion: the X-ray catheter and nuclear medicine. HP viewed development of this technology as a transition for two reasons. First, MRI is a different technology for gaining an image of the heart (Box 11.2). Second, the MRI innovation was a collaborative effort between HP and Philips that required the fusion of existing technologies and capabilities held separately by the two firms and the organizational networks they had developed around the different technologies.

PART IV: THE HP CIT NETWORK

The previous section described the core technology of the CIT innovation network. This section investigates changes in the core capabilities, complementary assets, structure, strategy and organizational learning associated with each of the three innovation pattern phases that occurred up to the mid-1990s.

Critical to the transformational pattern innovation that launched the CIT was HP linking with a group of suppliers of complementary assets and with cardiology lead users. As the holder of the core capabilities, HP became the center of an adaptive organizational network. If one thinks of the network as a web, the holders of complementary assets are appropriately seen as nodes of supporting capabilities located on the filaments of the web surrounding the core capabilities. Complementary assets were held both by other (non-MPG) HP organizations and by non-HP organizations. MPG developed the network strategy that provided the shared vision that guided incremental innovation along the technology trajectory. Strategy and core capabilities defined the path followed and bounded the network's learning ability. Structure is the architecture that linked the components of the network. Structure included everything from informal agreements, understandings, and communications links to contracts and patents. Finally, organizational learning refers to the process whereby the network acquired the knowledge and capabilities needed to achieve continued technological advance.[23]

Transformational Pattern and the CIT Network

The selection of the cardio-imaging technology and lock-in on the ultrasound design that characterized the technology trajectory coincided with an approach to organization known in HP as the 'integration period', 1973 to 1980. During this time, HP made choices concerning which core capabilities to nurture, and which complementary assets to seek from other participants in the nascent network.

Core capabilities and complementary assets

The interdependence among the technical components and the organizational network involved HP determining which core capabilities to develop in-house. For example HP management initially directed MPG to have its microprocessor developed by a sister division. This decision was influenced by broad company uncertainty concerning whether it should develop a microprocessor core capability and the immediate need for a 16-bit processor to handle the phased array signal processing at a time when merchant microprocessor companies offered only 8-bit technology. Ten years later, HP terminated production of its 16-bit microprocessor, and MPG adopted a Motorola chip. Even with the benefit of hindsight, people at HP remain uncertain whether it would have been more beneficial had MPG had either Motorola or Intel develop the first microprocessor.

Decisions involving other system components further expanded the network of suppliers. For example, HP chose to use the rapidly advancing video technology for its display component, but the monitor's standard at that time did not have a fast enough refresh rate to capture the desired images. MPG cooperated with a small business called Ball Brothers to build the necessary gray-scale monitor with a 60 Hz refresh rate. Similarly, MPG purchased Honeywell gray-scale paper strip recorders, but to meet performance requirements HP and Honeywell cooperated to develop an improved recorder.

HP, thus, used a variety of arrangements to provide the capabilities needed for CIT innovation. In contrast to its decision to develop a core capability in microprocessors, MPG elected to bring Ball Brothers and Honeywell into the innovation network through cooperative development of the required capabilities. Most other components were purchased at arm's-length.

Network structure

Upon completion of a prototype system at HP Labs, development responsibility was moved to the MPG facility in Andover, MA in 1976. Consistent with company norms HP Labs continued to provide its expertise in support of Andover's initial innovation process (for example, HP Labs served as a training facility for new employees hired by Andover to develop the ultrasound technology).

There were several competitors during the technology selection phase (that is, transformation pattern) including IREX (a subsidiary of Johnson & Johnson), ATL, Acuson, Diasonics and Varian (a pioneer in radar and radiation therapy linear accelerators).[24] Managers suggest that one HP competitive advantage was a network of forward-thinking practitioners at medical research centers and university hospitals. For example, Dr Don Harrison, chief cardiologist at Stanford, had developed a close relationship with HP's Dean Morton. Harrison provided a link with Dr Richard Popp at Stanford who became the lead-user for HP's first-generation ultrasound machines.[25] The Andover employees used their cumulative knowledge of medical technology and critical knowledge gained from Stanford to refine and enhance the prototype for introduction to the market. This included development of an enhanced 64-channel phased array transducer that provided considerable improvement in the electronic image of the heart. HP's relationship with Popp marked the beginning of a continuing series of arrangements between HP's engineers and scientists, and the medical community that facilitated each of the five subsequent incremental innovations.

Organizational learning

The significance of tacit knowledge in the innovation network is illustrated by development of the 64-channel transducer. Computer programs developed by HP to simulate the images that would be produced by a 64-channel transducer initially indicated that they would be of poor quality. John Hart, general manager of the MPG's Advanced Imaging Systems division, had worked with ultrasound technology for a number of years, and when he saw the computer simulated images he concluded that something was wrong. Hart could not articulate why he thought something was wrong other than to say the results did not feel right. Hart was drawing on his experience-based tacit knowledge, and after puzzling over the problem for some time he found that the assumptions being used in the computer program were incorrect. The gray-scale images being generated did not reflect reality. Modifications were made in the computer program and the 64-channel transducer was successfully developed. Hart notes that, 'What's interesting when you look back at it, to be honest with you, there is no invention here. All that stuff [I used] is in the radar books, what we were doing in the 1940s. And I think maybe that's where the intuition comes from'.[26]

Network strategy

During HP's integration phase, the company was small enough that Hewlett, Packard, and Barney Oliver (HP's Vice President for R&D at the time) personally integrated people and ideas. They were the central points through which ideas and virtually everything else flowed. During this phase HP focused on radical technology innovation and paid relatively less attention to marketing and management strategies. This was the strategy that worked for the company from its formation until John Young assumed the CEO position in the late 1970s.

From its earliest days HP maintained an organizational philosophy that encouraged self-organizing groups to achieve technology innovation goals. Packard writes,

> From the beginning we had the strong belief that groups of people should be given responsibility for specific areas of activities with wide latitude to develop

> their own plans and make their own decisions ... We feel our objectives can best be achieved by people who understand and support them and who are allowed flexibility in working toward common goals in ways that they help determine are best for their operation and their organization. The close relationship among HP people encouraged a form of participatory management that supported individual freedom and initiative while emphasizing commonness of purpose and teamwork.[27]

Another important element of HP's strategy was to establish clear technology targets and project objectives. This allowed individuals working in the HP innovation networks to focus their attention on how to achieve the next incremental innovation rather than what the innovation should be.

> No one operating policy has contributed more to Hewlett-Packard's success than the policy of 'management by objective'... Management by objective ... refers to a system in which overall project objectives are clearly stated and agreed upon, and which gives people the flexibility to work toward those goals in ways they determine best for their own areas of responsibility. It is the philosophy of decentralization in management and the very essence of free enterprise.[28]

Management-by-objective thus focused network learning on repeated incremental innovations along the locked-in CIT trajectory.

Public policy

The innovation of the ultrasound technology was pervasively impacted by public policy. Examples of the influence include patent protection, regulation by the Food and Drug Administration (FDA), and anti-trust policy. Health care policies that directly and indirectly supported the continued purchase and use of relatively expensive, high performance medical equipment also played an important role in the success of HP's ultrasound imaging technology. This included programs such as Medicare and Medicaid and their influence on a private health insurance system that reduced consumer sensitivity to health care costs.

Network Co-evolution and the Normal Pattern

Along with the five incremental innovations that evolved between 1983 and 1991, the CIT network expanded and adapted.

Core capabilities and complementary assets

With each innovation HP was faced with a decision whether to develop new core capabilities in-house, or use suppliers of complementary assets. Initially HP preferred in-house capability as illustrated by the 16-bit microprocessor.

During the first incremental innovation, HP sought Doppler expertise from Stanford Research International (SRI). SRI had accumulated substantial experience and tacit knowledge about Doppler from years of work with radar, but cooperation between HP and SRI soon broke down. At least one of the problems was the tendency for HP researchers to say to the SRI people, 'Look, we can go to the literature and find all of the knowledge on Doppler. Why do we need you?' The SRI people responded, 'We know things that you need to know and you won't find in any book.' Without SRI, HP had to adopt a trial and error approach and retrace some of SRI's Doppler learning curve. HP ultimately succeeded and emerged with a new core capability. HP people now believe they would have moved more rapidly in developing the Doppler innovation had they retained SRI involvement; even with hindsight, however, it is difficult to assess the ultimate costs and benefits of severing the SRI linkage. The uncertainty results from the degree to which the Doppler capabilities now in HP rest on the learning produced by severing the link with SRI. In retrospect, this knowledge and experience proved important for the innovation of the color flow technology.

HP appears to have been more receptive to expanding the network during development of color flow technology. HP initiated collaboration with the National Center for Atmospheric Research (NCAR), part of the National Oceanic and Atmospheric Administration. HP and NCAR discussed a joint development effort to better understand fluid flow. NCAR had modeling capabilities that used sophisticated software, while HP had unique hardware capabilities. NCAR researchers had been modeling the behavior of tornadoes in a water tank and those models were valuable to HP. In parallel, the HP transducer offered NCAR the ability to collect more accurate data from its experiments. Thus, HP proposed to provide NCAR with the improved transducers in exchange for access to NCAR's modeling and software capabilities. The relationship was never consummated, however, because NCAR was concerned that it could be perceived as favoring HP in a commercial relationship that would create political difficulties for this government-supported organization. As a result, HP once again nurtured a new capability in-house.

Color flow technology provided easily readable images on standard Sony monitors. The only problem with the Sony monitors was that they did not conform to Underwriter Laboratory standards for medical application. HP specified this requirement, and Sony complied. With the color flow innovation, MPG no longer needed the special 60 Hz refresh rate monitors produced by Ball Brothers, and that relationship was terminated.

In the later stages of the normal innovation pattern, HP appears to have become more receptive to relying on a network of suppliers to provide key components. In developing the transesophageal probe, for example, HP combined its own growing capability along with the clinical experience of Dr Hanrath of the University of Aachen in Germany, and the technology expertise of Oldelft, a Dutch company. Oldelft provided the scope (the instrument doctors use to look into the esophagus) to which the transducer was attached, and both firms cooperated in debugging the design.

Network structure

HP began the normal (incremental) innovation phase in a stove-pipe organization focused on individual business units. Coincident with the growth and evolution of the ultrasound technology, HP underwent a corporate evolution to a rows and columns or matrix organization (see Appendix A). This change in corporate philosophy influenced the nature of the relationships between HP's Medical Products Group and other nodes in the CIT innovative network.

Network strategy and organizational learning

Both the Doppler and color flow incremental innovations were products of enhanced signal processing capabilities and were essentially the next logical steps in the ultrasound technology trajectory. (The HP innovation network had in fact mapped out several of the incremental innovations before the first commercial product became available in 1980.) In both cases the new technology used had already been developed in other sectors (for example, Doppler was being used in radar systems, and color cardio-imaging displays were produced in Japan). Thus, the challenge for the HP ultrasound innovation network was to apply existing principles and knowledge to cardio-imaging technology. Consistent with HP's organizational norms in this period, these innovations involved few technology risks while allowing HP to gain a larger share of a growing market.

Although there was no broad demand within the medical community for the incremental improvements provided by the ultrasound CIT innovation process, in each case there was a doctor or medical institution lead-user with an interest in seeing the incremental innovation occur. The Doppler incremental innovation, for example, was carried out in Andover in cooperation with Dr Miguel Quinones at Houston Memorial Hospital. Dr Quinones had knowledge resulting from his earlier use of Doppler technology in another application. Color flow imaging had three lead-users: Dr Popp, Dr Quinones, and Dr Joseph Kislo of Duke University Medical Center. The color flow innovation resulted from a trial-and-error process involving HP Andover and the lead-users. Innovation of the transesophageal probe involved cooperative research with the University of Aachen (Box 11.4). HP collaborated with clinicians at the University of Massachusetts (who conducted clinical trials) and Duke University to develop the linear array technology. Most recently, innovation of the integrated backscatter technology was made possible by increasing signal processing capabilities and systems integration capability resulting from a cooperative effort with researchers at Washington University in St. Louis, MO (Box 11.5).

BOX 11.4 LEARNING TO INNOVATE THE TRANSESOPHAGEAL PROBE

The transesophageal probe innovation illustrates the ability of the ultrasound CIT innovative network to acquire new knowledge from a variety of sources. The idea of examining the heart with a transesophageal probe was first demonstrated by academics who placed a transducer at the end of a coaxial cable as early as 1976. In 1982 the product was presented to Diasonics, which produced about 50 probes before going out of business. The concept then lay dormant for several years until an HP scientist observed the potential of the transesophageal probe while examining with a laboratory model. Much of HP's early work was done in cooperation with researchers at the University of Aachen. Once the transesophageal probe was demonstrated, clinicians in the innovative network readily recognized its potential value, and actually provided HP with an old Diasonics probe. During the development phase, HP engineers were advised by gastroenterologists, who were experienced with the gastroscope. These practitioners were very concerned with the potential damage the probe could do, and the initial scopes were specifically designed to protect the esophagus. Cardiologists, however, were more interested in positioning the probe to get the best pictures, and subjected the probes to different stresses than anticipated from work with gastroenterologists. Several early probes were broken before they were redesigned by HP.[29]

Public policy

Public policy may alternatively either promote or constrain innovation. HP's relationship with NCAR during the development of the color flow innovation is an example of the latter. As a government agency, NCAR had a legal obligation to purchase all of its equipment by competitive bid and, thus, could not accept the HP transducers as part of an exchange. Furthermore, NCAR could not provide anything to HP that was not available to everyone else who might want it. Knowing a priori who might want knowledge, however, is difficult, so perceptions of impropriety had

BOX 11.5 INTEGRATED BACKSCATTER AND ACOUSTIC QUANTIFICATION INNOVATION

The integrated-backscatter (IBS) innovation is an example of an innovation resulting from a ten-year cooperative R&D project with Washington University in St Louis. Research was conducted by Jim Miller of Washington University's physics department and by MPG's Tom Shoup, a former student of Miller's. Much of the funding for the Washington University project was from National Institutes of Health grants. This project resulted in MPG developing a core capability in integrated backscatter.

Acoustic quantification (AQ) allows cardiologists to distinguish between blood and tissue. AQ was developed through the application of IBS and the serendipitous acquisition of Peter Melton from Diasonics, the company that developed the first transesophageal probe. Melton became interested in acoustic quantification as early as 1978, and early work was done in collaboration with the University of Iowa. Melton joined Diasonics in 1984, but left nine months later to join HP where he was assigned to work on tissue classification, a field distantly related to acoustic quantification. MPG's R&D policy, however, allowed researchers to exercise a considerable amount of individuality, and Melton worked largely 'outside' the system to pursue his interest in AQ.[30]

to be avoided. As a result the HP–NCAR cooperative relationship failed, and both parties were disappointed because each had lost an opportunity. The Federal Technology Transfer Act was signed into law in 1986, the same year that HP introduced color flow with Revision K of the Model 77020. This Act makes it a formal mission of all federal labs to transfer technology to industry, and establishes the Cooperative Research and Development Agreement (CRADA) as a way to conduct R&D of mutual interest.[31] One can only speculate, but it seems possible that HP and NCAR might have cooperated more freely had this act been in effect during the negotiations.

Conversely, public policy may stimulate innovation, whether intentionally or serendipitously. In the late 1970s and early 1980s the FDA was becoming more active in regulating medical technologies. The FDA's concern regarding ultrasound technology focused on the amount of energy emitted from the transducers. Since the depth of penetration of sound waves is a function of the energy level, the key regulatory question revolved around whether the energy levels needed to produce an adequate image of the heart were safe.

The FDA initially established one hundred milliwatts/cm^2 as a maximum limit for ultrasound technology. HP saw this as an arbitrary and overly simple standard given the lack of data to justify it. The arbitrariness was amplified by the fact that there was no equipment available to measure ultrasound energy emissions. Furthermore, the real risk from ultrasound energy was in fetal examinations, not in adult or pediatric applications. HP's reaction was to quickly innovate a reliable measurement technology that was rapidly transferred through a variety of professional and business networks. This technology provided a tool for gathering the data necessary to establish an informed standard. Based on measurements using this new technology, HP was able to convince the FDA to modify its standard to 800 milliwatts/cm^2 for cardiovascular applications. In sum, HP and the FDA ultimately collaborated to regulate HP's cardio-imaging technology.

Transitional Pattern: HP–Philips Cooperative Agreement

With the innovation of the integrated backscatter in the early 1990s, HP concluded that continued incremental innovations along the decade-old ultrasound trajectory were limited. Major emphasis was given to the search for a new cardio-imaging trajectory. The result was the cooperative agreement with Philips to develop cardiac-MRI technology.

MRI development at Philips[32]

As background to the cooperative agreement between HP and Philips, it is important to understand the complementary MRI technology development and evolution at Royal Philips Electronics of The Netherlands. Beginning in 1977, Philips began a research project in the area of magnetic resonance at its laboratory in Eindhoven. Philips had some idea that Magnetic Resonance Imaging (MRI) might be useful for medical purposes, thus its Medical Systems division in Best undertook a development initiative and by 1981 a prototype technology had been produced. At the same time, other groups around the world were investigating MRI systems. One of these was at Hammersmith Hospital in England. The work on magnetic resonance quickly accelerated. The early evidence was that it would have significant payoff in the medical area.

In 1981, Philips established a linkage with Delft Technical University to work on magnetic resonance. This was a very early and relatively primitive effort. The work with Delft involved Philips producing a prototype that it sent to Delft and said, 'See what you can do with it. Find out if it will work in any effective fashion.'

The initial technology used an energy level of 0.15 Tesla.[33] The magnetic field used for magnetic resonance systems was made by wrapped copper wires. In 1982, Philips decided to build MRI systems and the following year shipped the first MRI units for medical diagnostic purposes to Leighton University. In 1984–85, Philips began delivering commercial 'belts' (MRI machines). At that time brain imaging in the United States was the market MRI technology was being aimed at.

MRI technology moved rapidly because it was at the time the only diagnostic technology capable of identifying multiple sclerosis (MS). The technology could also identify other medical problems not identifiable by using other diagnostic technologies, but it was the MS capability that drove the technology. For example, in 1997 the brain (head) and spine represented the bulk (65%) of MRI usage (see Table 11.2).

Table 11.2 Principal applications of MR in 1997[34]

Spine	35%
Head	30%
Orthopedics	12%
Abdomen diagnoses	8%
Breast imaging	5%
Heart	3%

By the mid-1980s, the critical magnets Philips used in the magnetic resonance diagnostic technology were being purchased from other suppliers. In not producing magnets in-house Philips differed from some of its competitors (for example, GE). The magnets were bought from specialists in super-conductor technology. One of the suppliers was Inter-Magnetic General Corporation, a United States producer.

Siemens of Germany, a large producer of MRI systems, alternatively bought magnets from IPC, a UK supplier. Philips later moved to IPC, which became its primary magnet supplier. Over the decade of the 1990s, the cooperation between Philips and IPC in developing better magnets improved steadily and became a very close and intimate relationship. Philips understands enough about magnets to be able to participate with the magnet supplier in developing improvements. IPC, also, had a joint venture with a French company – thus some of Philips' magnets were produced in France – but the key relationship was with IPC.

Core capability and complementary assets

Though it does not produce magnets itself, Philips has a number of people who are very knowledgeable and sophisticated in the magnet area. This is key to the firm's ability to play a core capability role in the MRI network. Philips also outsources the big amplifiers used in its MRI equipment. Philips buys a large number of its components and sees its core capability role as MRI systems design and integration. With accumulated knowledge and expertise Philips can work intimately with subsystem suppliers while keeping its focus on the market and the search for applications. The heart of what Philips does is systems integration, which, in part, involves developing systems software.

Philips' transition to cardiac-MRI specialty

Around 1985, the question, 'What can you do with MRI in the area of the heart?' started to circulate within Philips. This inquiry led to Philips developing the first cardiac specialty with regard to MRI. As this specialty began to develop, Philips' US organization began to apply pressure to develop specialized designs for MRI focused on the heart. This is significant because Philips was following a strategy of having what was essentially a magnetic resonance platform from which it could develop specialized add-on capabilities for the brain, heart, spine, and so on. Demand in the US market was for machines totally dedicated to each of these diagnostic functions. This caused a good deal of stress within the Philips system.

Philips, in developing the cardiac-MRI machine, began to cooperate with Emory University. Philips' US organization made contact with a maker of a product that had been developed for cardiology and that machine was brought back and hooked onto the magnetic resonance platform (Philips refers to the platform as the core technology). The technology that was obtained from the US involved new software and hardware. This new technology could not only provide a picture of the soft tissue of the heart, it could also provide a moving image with different orientations of the heart. Essentially, this new technology was able to do everything ultrasound technology could do, and more. As an illustration, the MRI system would allow diagnosis of tumors in the heart and a variety of other soft tissue problems that ultrasound was not capable of providing.

HP/Philips collaboration

At this point, Philips began a related development in the area of angiology, the field concerned with diagnosing problems with blood vessels. Also about this time (1989), Hewlett-Packard envisioned a large market for MRI and wanted to develop cardiac-MRI technology. A contact between HP and Philips was made regarding collaboration on cardiac-MRI systems development. The initial discussions between Philips and HP involved trying to define what the substantive focus of the technology development would be. HP wanted a system that was focused solely on the heart whereas Philips was more interested in developing their magnetic resonance platform or their core technology for use across a variety of diagnostic techniques.

Expansion of HP CIT network

HP had considered various alternatives for developing cardiac-MRI technology, including developing an in-house MRI capability, acquiring a firm with MRI experience, and various cooperative arrangements. By electing to team with Philips, this relationship contrasts with HP's earlier unsuccessful relationship with SRI during development of the Doppler technology. In the former instance, HP elected to develop the new Doppler core capability in-house and discounted the need for SRI's tacit knowledge. In the MRI case, most of the specific components and subsystems used in the MRI systems were commercially available. In concept, HP could have bought magnets and various other components and integrated the system in-house. That HP did not take this approach reflected a recognition that Philips had developed substantial cumulative expertise in MRI technology that went beyond what was explicitly available. HP apparently recognized that cumulative tacit knowledge becomes critical as technologies and the socio-technical systems that innovate them become more complex. HP decided that it could not afford the cost, either in terms of dollars or time needed, to accumulate that tacit knowledge. Under the HP/Philips arrangement, Philips would provide the MRI system, and HP would focus on the specialized electronics and signal processing needed for cardiac-MRI innovation.

Throughout the evolution of the ultrasound CIT, HP had developed external relationships with cardiologists at Stanford and Washington University in St Louis. MPG also cultivated a relationship with Beth Israel Hospital in Boston. HP and Philips planned to capitalize on this network of professionals for the cardiac-MRI innovation. Researchers and physicians would serve as lead-users and provide the expert feedback needed to develop and refine the cardiac-MRI technology.

Philips' initial contact was with HP's research laboratory in Palo Alto, CA, but it soon linked to HP's Medical Systems Group in Andover, MA. The initial discussions with HP revolved around a machine that utilized a 4 Tesla magnet. Philips was, at that time, doing work on 4 Tesla technology, but the magnets were huge and it would not be possible to put a machine with that kind of energy performance into a hospital. Thus, a fundamental innovation objective was reduction in the size of the MRI technology.

Cardiac-MRI: a technical partnership

HP's partnership with Philips reflected an interesting backward movement for HP as it was driven by the technologists rather than the marketers. It was the technologists that saw MRI as the next step in imaging technology, thus HP concluded it needed a partner with MRI experience. The cooperative arrangement between HP and Philips involved HP gaining Philips' MRI technology and Philips, in return, receiving HP's ultrasound technology with the intent of modifying it for the non-cardio-imaging diagnosis market (Philips was already in this market selling other technology). Thirty to forty employees from each organization were involved in the collaboration.

For the cardiac-MRI development, HP and Philips agreed on a broad set of technological goals and a general division of labor consistent with their organizational core capabilities. Both firms agreed the innovation process should be guided by technical experts.

Management's role

Management's role was to provide broad guidance and to facilitate the resolution of disputes. A Statement of Principles provided the guidelines for collaboration and future negotiations. The overall effort was directed by a program committee composed of a small number of senior general managers in the two organizations. More detailed strategy was jointly developed in the policy team, composed of R&D and marketing managers, and the core project team, composed of senior R&D and marketing staff. These groups provided a mechanism for developing joint plans and for resolving disputes that naturally arise as inter-firm groups attempt to jointly develop a new technology system.

Partnership differences

There were obvious differences between HP and Philips in areas such as language, culture (both organizational and national), and even economic conditions that would create problems that management would need to address. More subtle issues emerged during the course of the relationship that provided additional challenges. These included conflicting corporate strategies and variations in program support within both firms.

Contrasting corporate cultures

HP's and Philips' cooperative agreement assumed a high level of trust. The companies, for example, agreed to wait and determine how to divide future profits based on an assessment of what each firm contributed to the ultimate product. Additionally, patterns of social interaction and the movement of tacit knowledge were important to the cardiac-MRI innovation. Compatible organizational cultures became major concerns in the effort to develop the network that would carry out the innovation. This is illustrated by the fact that HP initially had discussions with other companies in its search for a partner. Part of the reason for HP's preference for Philips was the belief that it could work well with the Dutch company even though it had a very different culture from that of Philips (Box 11.6).

BOX 11.6 TWO VIEWS OF TRUST

An interesting story about the consequences of the differing HP and Philips cultures and the challenges of building trust occurred in the early days of the relationship. HP was concerned with one of the components Philips was developing for the MRI system. HP engineers asked for drawings of this component. Initially, those in Philips who received the request said they could not comply since it was a violation of company rules. Before HP could get the drawings, it was necessary for HP's head of the joint project to intervene at a high level in the Philips organization and ask that the drawings be sent. After some discussions the drawings were sent to Andover. When the HP people working on the project looked at the drawings they discovered that they were not for the technology they were working on. The drawings were of a previous generation technology. The immediate reaction by the people at HP was to conclude that the Philips' people didn't trust them. At this point, a senior HP manager flew to the Netherlands. The Philips executives laughed and said that trust was not the problem. The person in charge of that particular group in the Philips organization did not know that the work his group was doing was aimed at developing a secret new generation technology. Rather, he thought all they were doing was improving the quality of the existing generation technology. He sent what he thought were the appropriate drawings.

From HP's point of view, this was simply an inconceivable way to operate. In HP's view, all managers and technical employees should be fully aware of technology and organizational goals. What is clear, however, is that HP and Philips developed a network based on the expectation that they would have a long-term, mutually beneficial relationship. The MRI technology was seen as the first innovation in what would become a pattern of incremental innovation. Under these circumstances the expectation was that only high-trust cooperation between the organizations would work.

HP at that point in time was often characterized as being like a Japanese company. The company's culture resisted hierarchy in the belief that lateral and informal relationships spawn creativity and rapid innovation. HP preferred teamwork. To encourage exchange of both tacit and explicit knowledge, HP sought to minimize hierarchy and encourage its people to talk to anybody in the network. HP was willing to make decisions on tacit knowledge, on 'gut feelings'. The company documented almost nothing. The way HP maintained tacit knowledge was to have long-term employees. Employee retention was highly valued at this point in HP's development. In contrast, Philips is a more traditional company in its approach to organization and interaction. Hierarchical boundaries exist between organizational units and Philips' management attempts to control the flow of information. In general the rule is that Philips' people only get information on a 'need-to-know' basis. Philips uses a matrix organizational scheme with cells in the matrix built around specific technologies, or subsets of technologies (for example, magnets). In general, employees are expected to know everything there is to know about that component and little about other parts of the system. Philips wants to understand the basics of everything, but that information/knowledge is not shared throughout the company. Philips documents everything. At Philips, explicit knowledge is very important and acting on intuitive knowledge is difficult.

The cultural differences between the two companies result in different styles of decision-making. While HP had collective decision-making, at Philips, decisions are often pushed from the level where the most knowledge exists to higher levels. At a minimum, decision-making in Philips was slowed by its structure and culture.

Philips people indicate that the cultural differences became quite clear almost immediately; there was a sense among some of its people that HP people were invading foreigners. For example, HP requested direct access to Philips' MRI innovation network including its complementary asset suppliers. The Philips people were very uneasy about this. They had acquired valuable knowledge in their innovation process that was embedded in these working relationships. Philips was unwilling, just because an agreement had been signed, to immediately give HP the direct benefits of those working relationships.

While HP emphasized that trust should come with the signing of the statement of principles, Philips viewed trust as something that had to be won. Phillips people had the view that 'you can't mandate it, you can't just sign contracts and assume trust exists'. This reflected a fundamentally different cultural perspective between HP and Philips. Within Philips, there was the general pattern of the Dutch approaching trust as something that you earn over long periods of time, while the HP people said trust is what you have to have to carry out tasks on a rapid basis. At that point in time HP was characterized as having its own cocoon. Within the HP organizational system there was lots of trust; everyone worked for the common good. HP was egalitarian; it had open communication. There was common profit sharing. The company didn't use profit sharing to reward high performers only. At Philips, people tend to work individually. One interviewee characterized Philips as a place where everyone has his/her own office, and it is difficult to communicate with other employees. The interviewee said 'every Dutchman is an independent shop'. The Philips people compete with each other for recognition.

Finally, differences in language, particularly in defining the terminology for innovation, required extra effort. Terms like *cardiac*, *radiation*, *angiology*, and *platform* each elicited different interpretations from Philips versus HP staff working on the project. The fact was that it took a fair amount of time to align the discussions between people in the two companies so that when people used words they meant the same thing on both sides of this partnership.

Skeptical management support

Although top management in both firms had agreed to support the decisions of the cardiac-MRI technical teams, on several occasions opposition was experienced. On the HP side, there was not a consensus regarding the value of the cardiac-MRI cooperation. Similarly, there was some distress within Philips regarding the relationship. Since HP would have the rights to market the cardiac-MRI technology worldwide, some within Philips viewed this as giving away a potentially very valuable large-scale technology. Thus, the cooperation between the two groups had to operate within an environment of skepticism.

Adding to the different interpretations of trust (Box 11.6) was the nearly inevitable uneasiness that resulted from the two firms being competitors in other fields. For example, some in Philips saw HP wanting a cardiac-MRI technology that was configured in a way that would cause it to be seen as an HP technology. To Philips, HP was applying pressure to change, modify, and jigger the technology so that it would look like a unique HP product as opposed to being a Philips product that was being marketed and sold by HP. Philips personnel worried that HP was trying to require a number of things that felt very unnatural to those in the Dutch company.

Some in Philips felt the joint development was a real potential threat to both the company's technology and its economic well-being. Those who felt this threat wanted to protect the unique tacit capabilities Philips had with regard to magnetic resonance technology. Similarly, some within HP felt the partnership was far more beneficial to Philips than HP. The agreement between HP and Philips involved calculating the relative contribution of the two companies to the innovation after it was commercialized, with the assumption that each would try to make a 50 percent contribution in terms of man-hours and effort. However, Philips' work was feeding not just the specialized cardiac-MRI product(s) that would emerge from this partnership, but the core platform magnetic resonance technology. Thus, in practice, the 50 per cent split became difficult, if not impossible, to measure, and it was a source of some friction between the two firms.

Philips' development environment

Other factors affecting Philips also impeded development. The first was that in the early 1990s Philips was dealing with a severe economic downturn contributed to by a weak world economy. Philips was under great pressure to cut expenditures on activities that were not absolutely critical. Giving priority to cardiac-MRI, as was required by the joint development with HP, at a time when the source of income was MRI focused on brain diagnosis created additional stress in the economically difficult environment.

Second, Philips' large corporate organizational structure presented problems of coordination, both internally and externally. The agreement between the companies involved HP providing Philips with its expertise in ultrasound for Philips' use in all areas other than cardiology; this involved an organizational relationship distinct from the MRI development. Philips had been motivated to enter the joint MRI development in part because it had been unable to refine its ultrasound technology and expected to gain major benefits from HP's expertise in this area, but the transfer of knowledge on ultrasound didn't solve Philips' problem. Thus, difficulties in the ultrasound relationship kept getting in the way of MRI development.

Conflicting cardio-imaging strategies

Perhaps the biggest impediment to a smoother relationship stemmed from how differently each viewed the scope of applications that the technology would be used for. Philips' view was that the agreement with HP involved solely a focus on the heart, on cardiology. Everything else to come out of the joint work was, from Philips' point of view, its property. At certain points in the process, HP argued that Philips should pay a larger share (more than half) because some work that was going on also had reference to angiology and other non-cardiac diagnostic techniques. From HP's viewpoint, Philips was essentially getting a dual-payoff from its work. Philips people indicated that there was a continuing tension with HP over the two companies' different priorities; HP was solely interested in machines dedicated to cardio-imaging, while Philips wanted to develop a general purpose MRI platform with diagnostic capabilities for the brain, blood vessels, heart and presumably a variety of other soft tissue areas. In sum, the Philips focus was on a generic MRI platform.

> Philips' interviewees characterized the differences in the HP and Philips approaches by drawing a horizontal line on the board. They characterized the horizontal line as the core or general purpose Magnetic Resonance technology (i.e., the magnet

> and associated equipment). On top of this horizontal line they then drew a series of peaks and each of these peaks represented a diagnostic focus: radiology; using Magnetic Resonance to look at a variety of organs such as kidneys, bladder, etc.; angiology; cardiology; and a number of other specializations.[35]

Philips people also indicated that its development of an MRI platform was heavily influenced by concerns about what user 'owns' the patient. That is, the cardiologist is one owner, the radiologist another, and the angiologist yet another. Innovation of technology within the medical community is heavily influenced by the division of labor (specializations) and the sometimes unpredictable reactions within the diverse community of users. These specialties, to some extent, have a pattern of demanding the technology be specifically for their use. Philips people told of one case where the sale of Philips Magnetic Resonance to an angiologist led a cardiologist to say he would throw all of Philips technology out of his hospital.[36]

Thus, Philips was, also, trying to develop a core magnetic resonance technology that had a lot of flexibility built into it to avoid patient 'ownership' issues.

The Philips strategy started with a focus on the largest volume specializations. Once the technology for the largest markets was successful, Philips would then be able to take the technology to smaller diagnostic markets. Philips indicates that each specialization has peculiar characteristics. For example, using MRI for brain diagnosis of multiple sclerosis doesn't require coordination with any other technologies. Alternatively, MRI use in cardiology requires coordination with electro-cardiogram diagnostic technology. Philips states that each specialized use involves a unique mix of different characteristics. With great uncertainty concerning where the MRI technology would be successful, Philips was trying to keep all of its options open and maintain flexibility in the initial period of the transitional pattern. HP, on the other hand, had a very narrow cardiac focus; it was going to succeed or fail solely on the basis of cardiology. Quite a difference of attitudes existed between the two companies.

HP-Philips agreement ends

In 1995 the cooperative agreement came to an abrupt end as a result of strategic and organizational changes at HP. The cooperative agreement was set up in 1989 by Ben Holmes, head of the HP medical group at that time. The turning point came in 1994 when Homes retired and Gary Eichorn took over.

Eichorn had a background in computer science. His goal was to use the leadership of the medical group as a springboard to becoming the CEO of HP. The medical group was a self-contained unit of 5000 employees at this time with capabilities that ranged from R&D to sales. It also had a record of producing CEOs for HP.

Eichorn's focus was on short-term projects that would offer the springboard needed for gaining the promotion to CEO. The five-to-ten-year lead-time for the development of the MRI was too long for the purpose of promotion. Eichorn, thus, decided to move the medical group into the computer business by providing technology for computer-managed medical information. In a meeting in which the HP CEO voiced support for the MRI project, Eichorn stated that he was brought in to run the medical group and that if they wanted him to run it, the company leadership had to let him make the key decisions. A key decision was to get rid of the MRI project.

Eichorn's focus on short-term projects was consistent with the more general philosophy HP had adopted after the departure of Hewlett and Packard from direct company management. The change in HP's general strategy had been led by CEO John Young. The most distinctive difference was the move from a long-term to a short-term focus. Eichorn headed the medical group for only 15 months, but that tenure was fundamentally to change the viability of the medical group for the long term. A problem with the focus adopted by Eichorn was that the medical group did not have enough expertise in the information area to successfully achieve the new goal of computer-managed medical information systems. The new strategy was inconsistent with the expertise of the people in the medical group.

When Eichorn decided to terminate the cardiac-MRI product development he agreed that HP would turn everything over to Philips. At this point the problems between the two companies had been worked out and they had a positive relationship. Thus, the negotiations that brought about the break-up of the joint development went smoothly. HP gave Philips its patents. HP also gave Beth-Israel hospital and Washington University hospital the experimental machines that were in place plus $1 million to each hospital to hire people to support the machines. Philips took over the development relationships with these three major medical school sites plus six others (for example, Johns Hopkins and Emory). Philips was especially delighted to get access to the relationships with the two major US hospitals. Philips viewed this as a unique opportunity to get access to the US medical community.

Philips emphasizes that it went into the cooperative endeavor with HP with the expectation that the cooperation would go on for a long period of time. Philips expected to be in the business of developing improvements and carrying out repeated incremental innovations for the foreseeable future. Thus, Philips sought to build a new self-organizing network that would continue along an innovation trajectory for the indefinite future.

Philips believes that the momentum it has developed with cardiac-MRI has benefited in major part from the cooperative project with HP. Because the benchmark location for these technologies is in the United States, Philips takeover of the HP project left it in a position of cardiac-MRI technology leadership. In sum, although this began as a partnership of two organizations with conflicting objectives and very different cultural characteristics, the view at Philips is that the cooperation with HP was a success. The success required a process of aligning motivations and working out problems. According to Philips, by 1995 most difficulties had been worked out and there was close, and by implication, highly trusting cooperation occurring. This was, in fact, the first cooperation of any significance between HP and Philips.

Philips after the break-up

Following the termination of the joint development, Philips proceeded with the development of the cardiac-MRI system. One element of this development involved Philips establishing its own commercial cardiac-MRI business organization. Philips now considers itself to be the leader in this field. It is important to note that with over 1800 MRI systems in use worldwide, Philips has the largest installed base and the most experience of any company.[37] In 2002 Philips had about 25 cardiac-MRI systems in place. The Philips' cardiac-MRI system had taken on some of the characteristics of a dedicated system and these systems are overwhelmingly located in departments of cardiology. Philips believes that it will take until about 2010 for the cardio-imaging MRI technology to be fully established. The reason is that the establishment process has to start by placing the technology in medical centers and teaching hospitals. Over a period of time, people learn to use the new diagnostic equipment in these teaching institutions. When the students go into practice, the market will grow. Part of the growth is because the technology is superior and part is because there is pressure within professional communities for practitioners to be at the state of the art. This is a takeoff process that requires building a core in the teaching hospitals and medical schools.

Philips is in the process of incrementally adapting and improving its technology based on the feedback it is getting from the teaching hospitals and medical centers. In addition, in late 1998 Philips acquired ATL Ultrasound, a US firm that is recognized as a leader in the ultrasound market.

Philips says the future of the diagnostic technology market is very unclear because of the restructuring in the medical community that is associated with the growth of health maintenance organizations (HMOs) and Preferred Providers. This consolidation may result, for example, in radiology and cardiology facilities being merged in pursuit of cost savings. Philips' strategy is one of trying to have a low profile while this restructuring shakes out; it wants to provide technology across the range of diagnostic activities when the restructuring is completed.

Philips believes that the pressure to blur the boundaries between the different medical and diagnostic technology specialties (for example, angiology, cardiology, radiology) is likely to continue. The Philips people say that at the hospital in Eindhoven, the radiology department and the cardiology department have decided to consolidate and quit fighting with each other.

PART V: HP'S CONTINUED SEARCH FOR A NEW TRAJECTORY

The end of the HP/Philips joint development marked the end of HP's involvement with cardiac-MRI technology (see Figure 11.1). With this decision, it appeared that MPG would focus its efforts on finding incremental innovations that would extend the mature ultrasound technology plus pursue the development of the new communication of medical information (CMI) technology initiative.

HP's pursuit of incremental innovations along the ultrasound CIT trajectory focused on at least three potential future innovations that had the potential for providing continued commercial success.[38] The first focus involved the development and use of contrast agents such as micro-bubbles that can pass through the microvasculature system and produce an ultrasonic contrast effect. This would improve measurement of blood supplied to various regions of the heart, and would directly compete with nuclear cardiography technology. The second area of potential innovation involved development of miniature probes for insertion into the heart through the microvasculature system. This technology could compete with angiography for detecting and localizing coronary artery disease. The third innovative area involved the use of ultrasound to identify tumors and scar tissue. An interesting aspect of these potential innovations is that, while prior innovations led user demand (technology push), these potential innovations appear to respond to generally recognized medical community needs (demand pull).

Fumio Kodama observes that firms engaged in high technology innovation must 'surf ride' so as not to miss a wave of innovation. Firms that miss a wave are likely to fall out of competition.[39] The MPG saw itself as having missed the MRI wave of innovation with the termination of the cooperative effort with Philips.

PART VI: HP MEDICAL GROUP SOLD TO PHILIPS

Shortly after the termination of the cooperative venture with Philips, HP spun MPG off as part of Agilent when HP was divided into two companies. Then in November 2000 Agilent sold MPG to Philips. At the time of the sale Agilent was facing economic difficulties and the leadership apparently held the same view that had characterized HP in that it did not want to devote the resources needed to help the medical group recover from the termination of the joint development and the short-term focus on medical information management that had occurred under the leadership of Eichorn.

Philips' decision to buy MPG appears to be one of the steps in a strategy aimed at both expanding its technological capabilities and gaining greater access to the US medical technology market. Earlier steps involved Philips' purchase of ATL and several other companies. Philips has given major emphasis to increasing its role in the cardiology/oncology market in the United States. Jouko Karvinen (who was previously with ABB) who became president of Philips Medical in 2001 has led the Philips expansion. Mr Karvinen had no medical experience, but he has executed an effort to expand the role in medical technology that began in 1997 under his predecessor. Philips' initiative in this area began, in part, in response to the effort by GE launched in 1996/1997 to buy NEMA members; NEMA is an association of companies that provide imaging maintenance and services. In the contemporary environment, money is made in the imaging industry by the maintenance/service providers. Increasingly the producers of hardware sell their technologies for very low profit to gain the maintenance service contracts. GE's purchase of NEMA member companies thus gave it access to existing maintenance contracts. Philips had to follow the same strategy to be competitive. Between 1996 and 2002 Philips spent \$5–6 billion buying a range of companies. By 2002 Philips had an \$8 billion business (up from \$1.7 billion in 1996).

Following the break-up with HP, Philips adopted a strategy that initially continued the development of the MRI cardiology technology as a 'package' that could be hooked to its generic MRI platform. Without the HP people to work on the user interface, Philips had no choice but to put the cardiology package on the platform. Philips took the technology it obtained from HP and continued to develop it along the lines that had been envisaged during the collaboration. Also, Philips continued to make progress in more basic research, consistent with its traditional strengths in long-term research based on a long-term view.

The Future

What is now Philips medical group in the United States is developing cardio-imaging technology with two distinct foci. The first, and relatively straightforward one is the development of an effective user interface. The second is much more complicated. It is associated with the development of genomics centers at major medical centers as the pharmaceutical industry is moving rapidly into the use of genomics.

As previously noted prior to its joint development effort with HP, Philips didn't have significant access to lead-users in the US. The new initiative came out of the cooperative endeavor that developed when the company gained the important lead-user access. Today, Philips holds MRI user group meetings yearly. In 2002 there were 500 people at the meeting. These people pay their own way and pay to participate in the user group meeting. Philips has come from essentially not having users integrated into its innovation network to the present situation where it has a very extensive system for interacting with users as it carries out its innovations.

Philips' most significant loss when the joint venture with HP was terminated was knowledge of the importance of and the skills needed to develop a sophisticated user interface for cardiologists. The lack of sensitivity to the importance of the user interface flowed in part from the original Philips' strategy of developing an MRI platform to which a full range of applications packages would be attached. To appreciate the problem it is important to recognize a key distinction. It is that non-cardiac uses of MRI involve getting static images. The cardiology uses require dynamic images. Recall that this difference in how the technology should be designed was an early point of tension in the HP–Philips relationship. The HP cardiology background had made the people in the MPG conscious that one had to be able to 'tune' the technology so that movement could be seen most effectively. Tuning required a capability to adjust the machine to achieve the optimal image. Put simply, to do that, you must give the medical people an interface that allows them to adjust knobs while watching the image. You can't optimize the image using keyboard control. GE and Siemens (Philips' competitors) have also not yet developed such an interface system. Philips has all the tools to do this, but hasn't done it yet. The user interface with adjustable knobs takes advantage of tacit knowledge. The way that optimization is done today is that the people in R&D optimize the machine for the average person. However, to get the best optimization, you really need to be able to optimize for each individual patient by using the adjustable knobs interface.

In 2002 Philips was trying to set up five lead-user sites in the US. This was a major challenge because whenever Philips tried to enter a medical center, its competitors (GE and Siemens) would attempt to block its entry. The competitors commonly do this by cutting the prices of their equipment. These competitors have usually had long-term relationships with the medical centers.

The genomics centers are collections of interdisciplinary capabilities. They are associated with an expected capacity to grow new blood vessels utilizing the rapidly expanding knowledge in genomics. The imaging technology will have to image proteins and molecules. It will have to be able to superimpose the distribution of veg F (the growth factor) that triggers angiogenesis, the growth of new blood vessels) on the picture of the anatomy. Philips US medical group is helping to establish a center that provides for molecular imaging. The group is working with Stanford, which is developing a $150 million Institute for Genomics. Its new building, funded with money donated by Netscape, is in the middle of many academic centers on the campus.

PART VII: SUMMARY AND CONCLUSIONS

As previously noted, this case is part of a broader effort to understand the innovation of complex technologies. A postulate of this research is that innovative networks co-evolve with complex technologies. In the HP case, a complex network of suppliers, users and government organizations converged around the CIT technology beginning in the 1970s. Several aspects of this case study illustrate the hypothesized co-evolution. First, the different network strategies reflected over time in HP's organization and management philosophy appear to have evolved and adapted to the increasingly complex cardio-imaging technology. Second, the significance of lead-users is repeatedly demonstrated throughout the CIT evolution. Third, the network strategy and organizational learning process appears to have evolved from a propensity for self-reliance, to a dependence on suppliers and competitors as essential members of the CIT network. Finally, public policy co-evolved with the CIT alternatively supporting and hindering technological advances during various phases of the innovation process.

Network Strategy

Although classical innovation theory has commonly linked new technology trajectories with radical innovations launched by 'exceptional individuals' or entrepreneurs,[40] contemporary experience indicates that directed research and learning-by-doing are more common sources of new technologies. HP's launching of both the ultrasound and MRI trajectories was preceded by periods of intense study aimed at identifying potential markets. Both cases resulted in a concentrated R&D effort to innovate a product to fulfill the latent demand.

HP progressed through four distinct management periods during the evolution of the CIT network. It began with an integration period, followed by a 'stove-pipe' period, a 'rows and columns' or matrix period, and finally a period focused on Measurement, Computation, and Communication (MC^2) technology development. These phases represent a movement away from organic norms and toward a 'professionally managed company', and starting in 1990 a movement back to organic norms and a greater willingness to accept technology risks in the innovation process.

The first ultrasound innovation emerged from an organic network focused on the innovation process. Marketing, for example, did not play a large role in the initial innovation process. Innovations in the 1980s reflected an increasing tendency to minimize technology risk and build market share in existing markets. MPG's cooperation with Philips to innovate an MRI-based cardio-imaging technology reflects a movement back to earlier organic norms and a greater willingness to accept technology risks in the innovation process. It appears reasonable to conclude from this case study that HP's cardio-imaging innovation network and technology were co-evolving over the last 20 years.

The ways groups functioned within this case study provides support for the view expressed by Ikujiro Nonaka who argues that organic, self-organizing teams that share both cognitive and tacit knowledge are effective vehicles for generating and integrating diverse knowledge within an organization. Nonaka views organizational knowledge creation as a synergistic process in which 'the enhancement of tacit knowledge has to be subjected to a continual interplay with the evolution of relevant aspects of explicit knowledge'.[41] This process enhances the individual's knowledge base and, in turn, the knowledge base of others in the group via a process of shared experiences. What is produced, in effect, is an upward spiral of knowledge creation in which tacit and explicit knowledge are converted from one to the other and back again in a process of social interaction. This upward spiral is often the product of synergistic processes.

The successful operation of the organic, self-organizing group depends on two key factors: mutual trust and a 'shared implicit perspective'.[42] Mutual trust is a product of experience and culture, and groups operating with strong mutual trust work in a high context environment in which communication has both intellectual and emotional content. Metaphors, descriptions, demonstrations, body language and feelings are all used to communicate. Mutual trust is especially important in communicating tacit knowledge because words and descriptions alone are inadequate in this process. A shared implicit perspective is often a product of sharing redundant information that enables one person to enter another person's area of expertise. Gateways among individuals are opened by redundant information fostering a synergistic process. What results, according to Nonaka, is often a dialectic process in which knowledge emerges from the sharing of points and counter points.[43]

HP adopted management strategies that generally encouraged the formation of mutual trust. HP has attempted to treat its employees as family. Packard writes,

> [W]e made an early and important decision. We did not want to be a 'hire and fire' – a company that would seek large, short term contracts, employ a great many people for the duration of the contract, and at its completion let those people go… We wanted to be in business for the long haul, to have a company built around a stable and dedicated workforce… The underlying principle of HP's personnel policies became the concept of sharing – sharing the responsibilities for defining and meeting goals, sharing in company ownership through stock purchase plans, sharing in profits, sharing the opportunities for personal and professional development, and even sharing the burdens created by occasional downturns in business.[44]

HP developed a number of personnel policies to retain employees who held knowledge critical to its core capabilities. These people, in part, held the tacit knowledge that is critical to the repeated incremental innovations of complex technology. James Collins and Jerry Porras write,

> To reduce the chance of layoffs, HP passed up large government contract opportunities – profitable as they might be – if they would lead to 'hire and fire' tactics. It required divisions to hire HP insiders first before looking outside, providing further secure employment across the entire company (not to mention keeping the culture tight). When facing company-wide turndowns, HP generally asked all employees to take every other Friday off and reduce their pay by 10 percent, rather than imposing a 10 percent layoff.[45]

Lead-Users

Eric Von Hippel describes a lead-user as one who recognizes a market need before the bulk of the market, and is in a position to 'benefit significantly by obtaining a solution to those needs'.[46] The CIT innovative network demonstrates a reliance on lead-users throughout the innovative process. A similar pattern is observed in examinations of the innovation networks of the Varian Clinac linear accelerator[47] and in nuclear cardiology technology.[48] This sample suggests that the innovation of complex medical technologies depends heavily on the tacit knowledge of medical practitioners.

A second common occurrence was that the lead-users in the CIT case were often unable to articulate specific needs. Instead, there was a general understanding of what incremental innovations were needed, and a process of trial and error where the manufacturer created an enhancement, and the practitioner evaluated it, and provided feedback that guided the next innovation. Ultimately the practitioner was able to say, 'Yes, this is what I need'. Philips appears to have successfully absorbed HP's cardiac lead-user network into the developing MRI network.

Network Learning

The CIT network illustrates movement from a vertically oriented organization and process toward a greater reliance on the network to provide needed knowledge. In the early days of the CIT network, HP chose to develop a core capability in fabrication of microprocessors rather than outsource to Motorola. Ball Brothers became an integral part of the ultrasound CIT network when HP required high-resolution gray-scale monitors. The innovation of color flow allowed standard Sony color monitors to replace special gray-scale units, and Ball Brothers was phased out of the network. HP similarly chose to learn how to use Doppler technology by developing a new core capability rather than relying on SRI. However, as the technology increased in complexity, HP's approach to acquiring new knowledge co-evolved. The unsuccessful attempt to cooperate with NCAR to develop color flow was followed by reliance on Oldelft to provide transesophageal probes. During the short-lived partnership with Philips, HP made a conscious decision to rely on another company to get the key MRI technology knowledge and experience.

Public Policy

The role of public policy is central in the HP innovation network. The expansive US health care system provided a market for expensive but efficacious machines. Secondly, the FDA was influential, but initially unable to establish realistic standards for the new innovation. In the CIT case, HP innovated a new measurement device enabling research that led to an explicit 800 milliwatts/cm^2 standard. Thirdly, public funding in the form of National Institutes of Health grants was a factor in the innovation of ultrasound phased arrays at Duke University in the mid-1970s, and again in the innovation of the integrated backscatter at Washington University in the 1980s.

Alternatively, public policy discouraged a mutually beneficial relationship between HP and NCAR. It is interesting to speculate how the HP–NCAR relationship might have developed if the Federal Technology Transfer Act had been enacted prior to negotiations. Public policy has also facilitated collaboration and standard setting by competitors. Forming joint research organizations such as the Andover Working Group may have been hampered by the threat of anti-trust prosecution prior to enactment of the National Cooperative Research Act in 1984.

This case study suggests that complex medical innovations present unique public policy challenges. Policies intended to regulate the introduction of pharmaceuticals require a lengthy certification process and reward innovators with strong patent protection. The CIT technology is associated with rapid advances in computers and systems integration. It is also clear that CMI will be affected by rapidly advancing information systems technology. Application of pharmaceutical type standards to the innovation of complex technologies may unduly deter the innovative process. The unique effects of public policy on complex medical technology innovation networks warrants further examination.

Conclusion

In conclusion, the CIT case study appears to support the contention that complex technology innovation occurs within a self-adapting network that co-evolves as the technology increases in complexity. It appears that technology policy intended to enhance a complex medical device should promote the association of manufacturers with lead-users at universities, medical centers and government laboratories. Case studies of other non-medical complex technologies support the notion of increasing importance of cooperation among competitors as complexity increases.

NOTES

1. Adapted from Robert W. Rycroft and Don E. Kash (1999).
2. Fiorenza Belussi and Fabio Arcangeli (1998); Richard N. Osborn and John Hagedoorn (1997).
3. Pascal Bye and Jean-Jacques Chanaron (1995).
4. David C. Mowery, Joanne E. Oxley and Brian S. Silverman (1998); Briance Mascarenhas, Alok Baveja and Mamnoon Jamil (1998); Brian J. Loasby (1998).
5. Riitta Smeds (1997).
6. Andrea Principe (1997), p. 1265.
7. Daniel Levinthal (1997), p. 172.
8. Shona L. Brown and Kathleen M. Eisenhardt (1997).
9. Kulwant Singh (1997), p. 334.
10. Chris DeBresson and Fernand Amesse (1991), p. 368.
11. C. Jay Lambe and Robert E. Spekman (1997).
12. John W. Slocum, Jr., Michael McGill and David T. Lei (1994).
13. Patricia W. Meyers (1990), p. 100.
14. Packard, David (1995), pp. 142–43.
15. 'History of HP Healthcare', available at http://www.healthcare.agilent.com/mpg/.

16. Press release dated 3 June, 1999, http://www.healthcare.agilent.com/mpg/.
17. DeMarre, Dean A., and David Michaels (1983), pp. 195–224.
18. Finkelstein, Stan N., Kevin Neels and Gregory K. Bell (1995).
19. Young, Stuart W. (1988) and Curt Werner (1998), p. 11.
20. Senge, Peter M. (1990).
21. ATL was founded in 1969 and by 1997 had achieved annual revenues of $430 million with 2600 employees. ATL pioneered the development of broadband digital ultrasound and software technologies, and became a leader in the high performance ultrasound market. In November 1998, Philips Medical Systems acquired ATL for $800 million and established ATL in Bothell, Washington, US as their worldwide headquarters for ultrasound business. http://www.medical.philips.com/what_new/releases/atl.htm.
22. Finkelstein, Neels and Bell (1995).
23. Rycroft and Kash (1999).
24. ATL subsequently refocused their ultrasound development from cardio-imaging to radiology applications. IREX and Varian withdrew from the ultrasound business. Today Toshiba, ATL and Acuson focus on radiological applications while HP continues to focus on cardio-imaging applications of ultrasound technology.
25. von Hippel, Eric (1988).
26. Personal conversation with John Hart, General Manager Advanced Imaging Systems, Medical Products Group at HP, 15 February, 1994.
27. Packard (1995), pp. 128, 147.
28. Ibid., pp. 152–3.
29. Finkelstein, Neels, and Bell (1995).
30. Ibid.
31. Christopher T. Hill, (1996).
32. Much of this section is derived from personal interviews at Philips in March 1999.
33. Tesla is the unit of magnetic field strength used for Magnetic Resonance systems. 1 Tesla (or 1 T) equals 20 000 times the force of the earth's magnetic field.
34. Source: Siemens Medical Systems in Curt Werner (1998), p. 10.
35. Philips interview, March 1999.
36. Ibid.
37. Philips Medical Systems, available at http://www.medical.philips.com/what_new/releases/mrnews.htm.
38. Ibid.
39. Fumio Kodama (1995).
40. Schumpeter as quoted in Freeman (1994).
41. Ikujiro Nonaka, (1994), p. 22.
42. Ibid., pp. 24–25.
43. Ibid., p. 25.
44. Packard (1995), pp. 129, 132.
45. Collins and Porras, p. 208.
46. von Hippel (1998), p. 71.
47. Lieberman, Stephen L. and Don E. Kash (1996).
48. Finkelstein, Neels, and Bell (1995).

REFERENCES

Belussi, Fiorenza and Fabio Arcangeli (1998), 'A typology of networks: flexible and evolutionary finns', *Research Policy*, **27** (4), 415–28.

Brown, Shona L. and Kathleen M. Eisenhardt (1997) 'The art of continuous change: linking complexity theory and time-paced evolution in relentlessly shifting organizations', *Administrative Science Quarterly*, **42** (1), 16–21.

Bye, Pascal and Jean-Jacques Chanaron (1995), 'Technology trajectories and strategies', *International Journal of Technology Management*, **10** (1), 45–66.

DeBresson, Chris and Fernand Amesse (1991), 'Networks of innovators: a review and introduction to the issue', *Research Policy*, **20** (5), 363–80.

DeMarre, Dean A. and David Michaels (1983), *Bioelectronic Measurements*, Englewood Cliffs: Prentice-Hall.

Finkelstein, Stan N., Kevin Neels and Gregory K. Bell (1995), 'Innovation in cardiac imaging', in N. Rosenberg, A.C. Gelijns and H. Dawkins (eds) *Sources of Medical Technology: Universities and Industry*, Washington, DC: National Academy Press.

Freeman, Chris (1994), 'The economics of technical change', *Cambridge Journal of Economics*, **18**, 463–514.

Hill, Christopher T. (1996), 'The evolution of United States federal government support for the development of industrial, energy, and environmental technology', Paper read at New Energy and Industrial Technology Development Organization of Japan, 4 March.

Kodama, Fumio (1995), *Emerging Patterns of Innovation: Sources of Japan's Technology Edge*, Boston: Harvard Business School Press.

Lambe, C. Jay and Robert E. Spekman (1997), 'Alliances, external technology acquisition, and discontinuous technological change', *Journal of Product Innovation Management*, **14** (2), 111.

Levinthal, Daniel (1997), 'Three faces of organizational learning: wisdom, inertia, and discovery', in Raghu Garud, Praveen R. Nayyar, and Zur B. Shapira. (eds), *Technological Innovation: Oversights and Foresights*, New York: Cambridge University Press.

Lieberman, Stephen L. and Don E. Kash (1996), 'The origin and evolution of the Varian Clinac radiation therapy accelerator', George Mason University: SPP Working Paper.

Loasby, Brian J. (1998) 'The organisation of capabilities', *Journal of Economic Behavior and Organization*, **35** (2), 139–60.

Mascarenhais, Briance, Alok Baveja and Mamnoon Jamil (1998), 'Dynamics of core competencies in leading multinational companies', *California Management Review*, **40** (4), 117–32.

Meyers, Patricia W. (1990), 'Non-linear learning in large technological firms: period four implies chaos', *Research Policy*, **19** (2).

Mowery, David C., Joanne E. Oxley and Brian S. Silverman (1998), 'Technological overlap and interfirm cooperation: implications for the resource-based view of the firm', *Research Policy*, **27** (5), 507–23.

Nonaka, Ikujiro (1994), 'A dynamic theory of organizational knowledge creation', *Organizational Science*, **5** (1), 14–37.

Osborn, Richard N. and John Hagedoorn (1997), The institutionalization and evolutionary dynamics of interorganizational alliances and networks', *Academy of Management Journal*, **40** (2), 261–78.

Packard, David (1995), *The HP way: How Bill Hewlett and I built our Company*, New York: Harper Business.

Principe, Andrea (1997), 'Technological competencies and products' evolutionary dynamics: a case study from the aero-engine industry', *Research Policy*, **25** (8).

Rycroft, Robert and Don E. Kash (1999), *Complexity Challenge: Technological Innovation for the 21st Century*, London: Pinter.

Senge, Peter M. (1990), 'The leader's new work: building learning organizations', *Sloan Management Review*, pp. 7–23.
Singh, Kulwant (1997), 'The impact of technological complexity and interfirm cooperation on business survival', *Academy of Management Journal*, **40** (2).
Slocum, John W. Jr., Michael McGill and David T. Lei (1994), 'The new learning strategy: anytime, anything, anywhere', *Organizational Dynamics*, **23** (2), 33–47.
Smeds, Riitta (1997), 'Radical change through incremental innovation: generic principles and cultural differences in evolution management', *International Journal of Technology Management*, **14** (1), 146–7.
von Hippel, Eric (1988), *The Sources of Innovation*, New York: Oxford University Press.
Werener, Curt (1998), 'Image is everything to thriving MRI system manufacturers', *Health Industry Today*, **61** (1).
Young, Stuart W. (1988), *Magnetic Resonance Imaging: Basic Principles*, New York: Raven Press.

PART 6

Appendix

12. Subjective orientation and objective wealth: entrepreneurship and the convergence of groupware and hypertext capabilities

Don Lavoie

This chapter will argue that certain specific classes of innovations in software engineering which arose in the 1970s – the development of two kinds of software capabilities that are often labeled groupware and hypertext – might be the primary source of the economic boom. Groupware is the name that has been given to software that is focused on helping work groups to coordinate their activities with one another. Electronic mail is the most ubiquitous and basic form of groupware functionality, but more advanced forms involve much more than email, including systems for workflow and the sharing of alternative ways of viewing information. Hypertext is the name given to software that improves our ability to work with electronic text. The World Wide Web at this point in time is the most ubiquitous and basic form of hypertext functionality, but more advanced forms involve much more than point-to-point jumplinks, including such markup tools as fields for categorizing, fine-grained annotations and embedded queries. These kinds of capabilities have been incorporated increasingly into the Internet and various corporate software programs, and they may be improving the ability of market participants to *orient* their complex activities more effectively toward one another. That is, software capital is markedly improving our entrepreneurial ability to coordinate our plans with one another, and one of the key elements in the software that is having its effect only recently is a convergence of hypertext with groupware functionality. The claim here, then, is that improvements in what Austrian economists such as Ludwig Lachmann called 'subjective orientation' may be what are behind the 'objective' (or at least real) improvement in living standards that is taking place in the new economy.

> There are at least two possible types of social process. (There may be more.) We may describe the first as 'mechanical', the second (for want of a better term)

> as 'orientative'. In the first, whatever men do within a period depends on the position they have reached. A 'feedback' mechanism in which each subsequent step depends on 'distance from equilibrium' is a special instance of it.... The other kind of social process, by contrast, leaves ample scope for divergent expectations. In it men's actions are neither determined by what happened in a past period nor by the distance of their present position from an imaginary equilibrium. No doubt, in making and revising their plans they will take account of these facts. But the latter serve them as points of orientation, and not as determining forces. (Ludwig M. Lachmann, 1994: 204–5)

What are the chief causes of the extraordinary economic prosperity in the so-called knowledge economy of the past couple of decades? In particular, is it possible that information technology tools that (merely?) help market participants to *subjectively* orient themselves to one another are among the crucial elements driving the real, *objective* improvements in standards of living that we have been witnessing?[1] Since Adam Smith, economics has been expected to help us to explain the real wealth of nations. Our models of economic growth have emphasized objective, material productivity. The production of larger amounts of physical stuff seems to be the very definition of wealth. But the Austrian school,[2] on the basis of what it calls its 'subjectivist' approach, contends that it is mainly our ability to coordinate with one another that enables us to make more stuff, to increase the objective standards of living of people around the globe. And our ability to coordinate with one another in turn may depend fundamentally on our capabilities for *mutual orientation*, to see not the things themselves, but to see how we are all seeing things.

The contemporary workplace and marketplace are increasingly enhanced by information technology capabilities that are improving, both within and between organizations, our ability to orient ourselves to one another's meanings. In the business literature can be found some enthusiastic proponents of the view that among the key capabilities that have been driving prosperity are what have been dubbed 'groupware' and 'hypertext' functionality in software systems.[3] I will return briefly at the end of this chapter to consider what these software capabilities are and what they may be doing. For now we might think of these capabilities as representing changes in the communications media we use for storing and retrieving information and sending messages. Has the shift in storage of information from file cabinets to the Web, or the shift in messaging from paper memoranda to email, made a difference? It seems that almost everyone who has lived through this transition would say yes, but exactly *what kind of difference* has all this really made? I'd like to approach these new technologies mainly in an indirect fashion, by seeing their impact in relation to previous technological changes in media, especially the revolution in writing and literacy brought on by the printing press. I will argue that the best way to think about what kind of difference these new changes in media are making now is to see them as adding more of the kind of capabilities that were added when Gutenberg's revolution transformed us from an oral to a literate culture. Printing, I will argue, altered our ability to add meaningful structure to the articulations we were trying to make. The information revolution is in many ways an extension of that revolution, and I will claim that, in a similar way, this one is bringing about real improvements in wealth.

In other words, our ability to make real objective wealth may depend primarily on our ability to orient ourselves to our distinct, subjective perspectives on the world. And our ability to orient ourselves to one another may, in turn, depend crucially on the technological media in which we are able to try to say what we mean. That is, the quality of the tools for working with words and other articulations has changed dramatically over time and is undergoing rapid change now, and this seems to be aiding precisely the entrepreneurial function, the coordination of plans.

The Austrian school's view of economic development identifies the entrepreneurial process, a process for the mutual coordination of plans, as a key factor in the creation of wealth. The theory of entrepreneurship studies the way the multiplicity of plans of market participants get oriented to one another. It could be that among the important effects information technology is having on the new economy are direct enhancements to this mutual orientation process. Tools that support the way we orient ourselves to one another directly aid in the entrepreneurial coordination of plans, the very process the Austrian school has identified as key to economic prosperity.

This chapter tries to get a preliminary handle, from an Austrian perspective, on the changing nature of entrepreneurship in the contemporary information-technology-enhanced workplace and marketplace.[4] The point here is not to resolve the empirical question of whether technology-based enhancements to entrepreneurship are among the primary wealth-creating forces of the 'knowledge economy' but to elaborate upon the theory of entrepreneurship to emphasize its relevance for such empirical investigations.[5] Indeed, the point will be to sprinkle into the Austrians' discourse a bit of empirical flavoring, drawing from historians of older media and practitioners of new media. The hope is to bring the Austrians' overly theoretical abstractions on entrepreneurship into closer contact with lived experience.

First I would like to try to say what is meant by a subjectivist and orientative approach to entrepreneurship, pointing to the idea that this sort of approach leads to a focus on the 'meanings' of the market, including the technological media in which meanings can be shared. Next, drawing from literature on the history of writing,[6] I will try to sum up the overall changes in the technological media through which market participants have been able to articulate meanings to one another. One way to look at the changes we've undergone as we went from an 'oral' to a 'literate' culture is to see the changes in terms of improvements in our ability to say what we mean to each other and thus our ability to orient our plans to one another. Then, drawing from the knowledge management literature,[7] I will argue that this is just the sort of thing software technologies are doing to the entrepreneurial process in the new economy. The new software capabilities, I claim, are enhancing the orientative processes that are at the core of entrepreneurship. Two specific kinds of software-enabled capabilities, groupware and hypertext, have been made increasingly available and affordable over the past couple of decades. These capabilities can be seen as enhancing our ability to structure our articulations, analogously to the way the printing press led to changes of this kind. Improvements to our ability to structure what we are saying may lie behind improvements in our ability to orient our plans to one another. And this in turn may be one of the main factors that is improving our ability to make ourselves objectively wealthier. If we pay attention to the orientative dimension of entrepreneurship, we may be able to see more clearly what is going on in the new economy.

A. ENTREPRENEURSHIP AS MUTUAL ORIENTATION

> The theoretical problem of the Austrian School can be summarized as the attempt to understand why the pursuit of subjective ends should result in situations that are objectively valid. In a perspective of this kind, the market (understood as a system for information transmission) and political society are none other than the consequences – at times unforeseen – of the meeting of different aims and bodies of knowledge that enrich society with their differentiation and evolution. (Raimondo Cubeddu, 1993, pp. xi–xii)

What does it mean to say that entrepreneurship should be understood as a process of mutual orientation? There has been some confusion about what the Austrian school means by its whole 'subjectivist' approach. When Ludwig Lachmann refers to an orientative approach to economics he is suggesting that economics ought to be seen as an interpretive kind of study, focusing on the ways in which market participants articulate meaning to one another. To him the principle of subjectivism means an interpretive study of the meanings of the economic world. Institutions are for him 'signposts' helping us to make sense of the world. Subjectivism should try to understand the processes for the articulation of economic meanings, and the *texts* that result from such processes. Texts in this sense are words and other articulations (including drawings, graphs, charts or prices) that have been 'written down' in some specific medium, whether on clay tablets, papyrus scrolls, or relational databases. Having been written down, texts are also available for future return, to be re-read, interpreted, worked upon, paraphrased, quoted, or even rearranged. The technological media through which we are able to say what we mean could be a crucial enabler of mutual orientation.

Lachmann's work has been more often noticed for what it was against than what it was for. To be sure he was against, or at least uninterested in, formal theoretical modeling. He vigorously resisted what he called 'formalism', the dominant conception of economics that sees it as a quantitative science of how measurable variables functionally relate to one another. But what was he for? The positive direction his work invites us to explore, in my view, is an inquiry into the way market participants come to make and share meaning with one another. What he called an orientative approach would ask *how meanings get conveyed*, how producers come to appreciate what consumers want, how investors come to understand what entrepreneurs want to do, and so forth.

1. Subjectivism: Pointing Inward or to Textual Interpretation?

The term 'subjectivist' may be unfortunate. To some proponents and to many critics the word seems to imply some sort of turn inward into the realm of the mind.[8] It sounds like it involves psychology or introspection, or some kind of privileged, internal observation, or even worse, some kind of mystical divination. So of course it must be even worse for those like Lachmann who call themselves 'radical subjectivists'. If things are subjective, it seems, they are not really of this world; they are purely mental phenomena residing inside the realm of the imagination. Surely, from this point of view, things of a merely subjective, inward nature couldn't possibly be what lie behind the dramatic increase in the real standards of living that have accompanied most of the last two decades. How can mere meanings make objective wealth?[9]

I think the Austrian response to this should be to answer boldly that what we are talking about is not inaccessible mental thoughts but human expressions of meaning, and that these meanings are fully *in* the real world. Indeed they are what make all the difference in economic development, the creation of real wealth. The view that the realm of the subjective is a private, inaccessible realm is an unfortunate remnant of earlier Cartesian and Kantian philosophical assumptions that we can dispense with today. Though the Austrians named their central philosophical principle 'subjectivism' they never meant what philosophers call by that name. As Raimondo Cubeddu says in the quote above, the Austrians were asking, 'why the pursuit of subjective ends should result in situations that are objectively valid'. Subjectivism in economics doesn't really point to some kind of solipsistic wonder about whether the real world exists or something. Even radical subjectivists, I would argue, are as focused on the real world of institutions, the markets and workplaces of the economy, as anyone.

Economics for the Austrians is neither objective nor subjective, in the usual philosophical senses of these terms. Or maybe the point is it is both, in some senses of the words. It is objective in the sense that it can be done in an openly self-critical and scholarly way; it can discover truths of the real world and not merely refer to opinions or things of the imagination. And it is subjective in the sense that its primary focus is on the intentions, purposes, meanings, plans, that is, the meaningful world of human affairs. But it is neither, in several of the other senses of these terms: it is neither a matter of impersonal detachment, as objectivism suggests, nor of private introspection, nor of complete relativism or solipsism, as the philosopher's term subjectivism suggests. Wealth, real tangible wealth, is created by improvements to mere mutual understanding, orientation and coordination.

The classic Austrian writings on subjectivism are partly to blame for this misreading. By sometimes pointing to 'knowledge from within', or 'introspection', or sometimes 'psychology', the Austrians sometimes trapped themselves in an unnecessary philosophical position. I prefer Ludwig Lachmann's wording when he refers to an economics of meaning. The realm of meaning is best seen not as an inner realm of the mind, but instead as a public realm of expressions, especially of *articulations* in language. The point of subjectivism is not to turn our attention to some kind of inwardness, but to turn to the reading of our cultural texts and other artifacts, the articulations being made out in the open in the marketplace and the workplace.[10] Subjectivism represents a turn not to the private inner consciousness, the introspective study of the mind, but to the public articulations (verbal, written, electronic, and so on) through which market participants attempt to communicate their meanings to one another.

As Lachmann (1971: 9–10) put it in his book on Max Weber,

> [T]he method of interpretation (Verstehen) … is nothing less than the traditional method of scholarship which scholars have used throughout the ages whenever they were concerned with the interpretation of texts. Whenever one is in doubt about the meaning of a passage one tries to establish what the author 'meant by it', i.e. to what ideas he attempted to give expression when he wrote it. This, and not an axiom of the philosophy of idealism, is the true origin of the method of interpretation. It is evidently possible to extend this classical method of scholarship to human acts other than writings. This is what all historians, whether philosophically minded or not, have always done.

Although I would argue that this way of defining meaning by reference to the author's original intention might not be the best way to put it, the main thrust of this passage is to point to an interpretive study of meaningful expressions. Taking the idea of meaning seriously obliges us to pay more attention in the theory of entrepreneurship to the way market participants engage in acts of articulation and of the reading of articulations. An orientative approach would attend to the talking or writing and listening or reading processes going on in the economy. Just as the successful market participant learns to orient herself to the articulations of the market, so the economist needs to attend to the communicative processes through which market participants orient themselves to one another.

2. The Kirznerian Entrepreneur and Lachmannian Orientation

There is something misleading in the prevailing work on the nature of entrepreneurship. The problem of social coordination is formulated as if it were a matter of an individual entrepreneur directly confronting reality. The entrepreneurial process is described without reference to the communicative processes through which market participants come to terms with one another, or to the institutional circumstances within which acts of communication are contextualized. The approach leaves the impression that modes of articulation, ways of expressing ourselves, are not involved.

In his important work, *Competition and Entrepreneurship*, Israel Kirzner developed a perspective on the fundamental nature of entrepreneurship according to which it is seen as involving alertness to opportunities to improve on the use of priced factors of production, but not as itself a factor of production in the ordinary sense.[11] The entrepreneur's alertness to market opportunities is what impels him or her to act, and through that action to improve on the market's coordination process. The diverse plans of separate individuals come to 'dovetail' with one another through the entrepreneur's coordinating actions. Entrepreneurship, in this perspective, is a sort of meta-factor of production: it is the alertness to how best to use factors of production. It is understood to be the essential driving force behind the process of economic development in that it improves the allocation of scarce resources, increasing the market's coordinative capacity, the ability of market participants to get more of what they want for less.

The point Kirzner makes about entrepreneurship as not merely a factor of production to be optimized along with all the others, but as referring to the capacity of the economy to coordinate its uses of all the factors, is an important contribution. But the concept of alertness as he developed it suggests that what is involved in entrepreneurship is primarily a matter of directly seeing something that physically exists in the world, not the communication of meanings among market participants within specific technological and institutional contexts. It is the ability to 'see' opportunities to take advantage of (and unintentionally improve upon) the market's pricing of productive inputs. The entrepreneur 'notices' inputs that are under-priced in relation to their (perceived) potential to produce outputs, and acts to rearrange factors of production into a pattern that tries to reap profit from the situation. This very effort to gain pure entrepreneurial profit has the effect of increasing market coordination.

The Kirznerian entrepreneurial act might seem to be the engagement by an isolated, cultureless individual to pre-existing objective circumstances.[12] The entrepreneur is the maverick who simply 'sees' objectively what others have so far overlooked. He is described theoretically first in the Robinson Crusoe context, as an isolated man directly confronting nature, and only secondarily, when Friday arrives, is 'society' brought into the picture.[13] Part of the difficulty may be in the preoccupation with the Crusoe situation, but even when the analysis explicitly advances to the social context, we find ourselves in a discussion of market prices as the only signals. It almost looks as if human actors were dumb and illiterate. It is not surprising that critics, such as Laslo Csontos, see the Austrian argument as one that necessarily makes the market exchange into 'the social relation *par excellence*' (1998: 83). The elaborations of the entrepreneurship in Kirzner's work are too abstractly described. They depict the entrepreneur as an intermediary in a world of (already somehow meaningful) price signals, almost as if these are peculiar agents who only communicate in money bids and offers, as if they were not involved in linguistic behavior, and a linguistically-constructed and institutionally contextualized world, but simply spotting numbers, price discrepancies, and making profits from exploiting differences between costs and revenues. There is no explicit place in the analysis where human articulations of meaning happen. Or rather it is as if the only things we ever say or write are the numbers we call prices, with which we silently 'signal' to one another. Even these price signals are somehow taken to already have their meaning ready-made.

From Csontos's reading of the Austrian's notion of subjectivism, it looks as if human actors were solipsistic agents who, since they have no access to the content of one another's minds, can only assume that others have minds like ours. This world does sound like the institutionless world implicit in a great deal of mainstream economics, where a price seems to be the solution to a set of simultaneous equations with variables for prices and quantities sold of abstractly named goods. Such isolated, alinguistic agents would seem to have little need for articulations of their meaning to one another. In such a world, tools that would merely help individuals in the economy to subjectively orient themselves to one another are unlikely to be responsible for real objective increases in wealth.

I don't think, however, that this is the friendliest or the most useful way to read what Kirzner and other Austrians are trying to do. He may be guilty of underemphasizing the important role of language that is involved in the entrepreneurial process, but we don't need to ignore that element of the process. The simplified world of Crusoe was a first, but not really an exemplary, case. The Kirznerian entrepreneur is properly understood to be thoroughly immersed in the already-linguistically-constituted world, where the social relation *par excellence* is not market exchange but the exchange of words, and other articulations. We are already engaged in acts of verbal articulation, where we are trying to say what we mean to one another, before anything like markets can come upon the scene.

Markets are an extension of language,[14] and they work through concrete acts of articulation, whether oral or written or electronic. You could say that markets simply add whole new kinds of texts, prices, profits, contracts, advertising, and so on, to the conversation.[15] The words are still a key part of market communication, but now there are these other kinds of texts such as prices circulating in our conversations that take numerical form and contribute to certain cognitive processes we call accounting, without which, as Mises was claiming in his famous challenge to socialism, modern technology could never have evolved. These articulations take place in a given political, social and technological environment. The 'seeing' of an entrepreneurial opportunity is best understood not as perception, but as a kind of reading of a meaningful situation in a language-constituted world. This is the kind of approach to entrepreneurship that has been usefully elaborated in Spinosa, Flores and Dreyfus (1997) as a process of disclosure of new worlds. The point is that the entrepreneur is not merely seeing what is there to be perceived, but rather opening up whole new ways of seeing. The entrepreneur is not Crusoe on an island, but a participant in social processes, in an institutionally rich context.

It is significant that in the calculation debate Oskar Lange accused Mises of being an institutionalist in that Mises seemed to be 'admitting' that specific institutional circumstances such as private ownership of the means of production played a crucial role in his argument. To the neoclassical participants in the debate such as Lange this admission that institutions matter makes Mises's position indistinguishable from that of the anti-theoretical historicists Carl Menger had challenged in the *Methodenstreit*. To Lange economic theory is universally valid and has no need to refer to institutional contexts. But Menger was precisely trying to weave together theoretical economics with institutional analysis. His account of the evolution of money is exemplary of this sort of approach. The choice is not between rejecting theory or abstracting from institutions.

Lachmann (1994: 283) pointed in this kind of direction when he called for an orientative or an interpretive economics. Like Menger and Mises he saw institutions as integral parts of economic processes. He points to the 'mode of orientation' through which individual actors coordinate their plans with one another.

> Institutions belong to the realm of culture, not that of nature. They are immersed in history. Although we can observe their operations, our observations cannot disclose to us what meaning their objects have to those enmeshed in them, a meaning that varies from group to group and over time. It is impossible to elucidate such meaning until we realize that the mode of existence of institutions corresponds to, and varies with, the mode of orientation of those who participate in them. Such a mode of orientation is an element of culture, a web of thought – open to interpretation but not measurable.

We need to remember that Lachmann uses the term 'institutions' to cover a remarkably wide set of phenomena. He includes organizations, but also regularized practices such as profit/loss accounting, or the use of mailboxes for posting letters. He also includes such phenomena as law, language, money and prices, and other evolved structures by which human action gets mutually oriented. He describes the orientative function of institutions in his essay 'On institutions' (1971: 49–50),

> An institution provides means of orientation to a large number of actors. It enables them to co-ordinate their actions by means of orientation to a common signpost. If the plan is a mental scheme in which the conditions of action are co-ordinated, we may regard institutions, as it were, as orientation schemes of the second order, to which planners orientate their plans as actors orientate their actions to a plan. …
>
> Whether we post a letter, wait for a train, or draw a cheque, our action is in each case orientated towards a complex network of human action of which we know enough to make it serve our ends, though we may know next to nothing about the internal working order of these institutions.

Unlike many who seem to only see institutions as constraints on the freedom of action, Lachmann saw them as indispensable aids to human action. They are 'signposts' which facilitate the mutual adaptation of plans. Lachmann ([1966] 1977: 59–62) had used this notion of 'second-order schemes of thought' when he concluded his article on 'The Significance of the Austrian School' by 'taking a look at the future tasks of "verstehende", or "interpretative" economics.'

> Economic agents orient themselves to plans. … But to what facts do the planners orient themselves when making plans? Partly to natural data, and partly to the actual or expected actions of other people. But there are also certain superindividual schemes of thought, namely, *institutions*, to which the schemes of thought of the first order, the plans, must be oriented, and which serve therefore, to some extent, the coordination of individual plans. They constitute, we may say, 'interpersonal orientation tables', schemes of thought of the second order. To them, praxeology, for which until now the plan and its structure have understandably occupied the foreground of interest, will increasingly have to turn in time to come.

Although Lachmann did not explicitly work out a distinct theory of entrepreneurship, the one that is implicit in his work depicts it as essentially a process of *mutual orientation*. By 'orientation' he meant not only, or even primarily, how we are oriented to the physical world, but rather how we are oriented to one another. He thought that key to the entrepreneurial function is the ability to interpret, to read the 'market signals'. Anybody can do the calculations of potential profit or loss but the profit/loss signals guide the market process through the selection of those who prove to be better readers of market signals. Lachmann ([1951] 1977: 102–3) put the point this way in a review of Mises's *Human Action*:

> Profits, those temporary margins between today's cost of complementary factor resources and tomorrow's product prices, are signposts of entrepreneurial success. In a symbolic form they convey knowledge, but the symbols have to be *interpreted*. …
>
> The market process … promotes the rise of those better equipped than others to wrest economic meaning from the happenings of the market-place…
>
> The essence of the matter is that the market process promotes the spreading of knowledge through the promotion of those capable of interpreting market data and of thus transforming them into market knowledge, and the elimination of those who cannot read the signs of the market.

Entrepreneurship is not an individual act of perception, a matter of looking at an already existing physical reality; it is an interpretive and communicative process involving efforts of different persons to communicate meaning about the future to one another. It is perhaps misleading to even present this coordinating process in terms of the activity of 'the entrepreneur', the single individual who is more or less alert to opportunities. What we have here is a coordination process that is taking place among persons who are oriented toward the future.

Lachmann (1956: 22–3) makes this point about the importance of the process of interpretation this way:

> In a market economy success depends largely on the degree of refinement of one's instruments of interpretation. On the other hand, every act is a source of knowledge to others.
>
> The formation of expectations is nothing but a phase in this continuous process of exchange and transmission of knowledge which effectively integrates a market society. A theory of expectations which can explain anything at all has therefore to start by studying this phase within the context of the process as a whole. … Its first task is to describe the structure of the mental acts which constitute the formation of expectations; its second task, to describe the process of interaction of a number of individuals whose conduct is orientated towards each other.

This wording in terms of the structure of 'the mental acts' is itself a bit misleading, in that it may sound too much like a matter of 'mind reading'. What we are really talking about here is not that mysterious; it is simply the reading of the texts of market-relevant articulations. Among the institutional forms to which Austrian economists ought to pay attention are the articulation processes and the resulting texts through which human actors communicate their meanings. And crucial to these articulation processes are the institutional and technological circumstances in which market participants act. As Lachmann suggests, the degree of refinement of the 'instruments of interpretation' is key to market success. In Kirzner the question can sometimes seem to be: how do entrepreneurs discover, or create, or share objective knowledge of the physical world? A better way to put the question might be: how do they orient themselves to one another's perspectives on the world, and in particular to one another's articulations?

The philosophical framework of Kirzner's entrepreneur seems to be one that takes 'seeing' to be central to the process of mutual coordination. An opportunity is 'seen' if the entrepreneur is sufficiently alert, or if not it is 'overlooked'. But looking and seeing are misleading metaphors for what is better rendered as a transaction of articulated meanings. It would be better to see what is going on here as a matter of what could be called a dialectic of 'seeing and saying'.[16] The entrepreneur gets at what is going on in the economy not by directly confronting the world itself, but indirectly, by way of an effort of interpretation of what is being said about the world. Seeing what opportunities are really there in the world is still the point. We are not interpreting what people say only because we somehow want to read their minds. We are trying to get at what opportunities for profit really exist, but it is just that our main way to get at real opportunities is indirectly through texts, through interpreting the efforts of others to say what they mean. The shared focus of those who are trying to articulate what they mean is the real world, the subject-matter of the texts, but it is crucial to bear in mind that we get at that reality via interpretations of articulations.

To get a handle on entrepreneurship we need to ask about the prevailing capabilities of the communicative media through which entrepreneurs are trying to orient themselves to the plans of consumers and producers. How, exactly, do market participants manage to convey their meanings to one another? Opportunities are not a matter of some kind of direct 'seeing' of reality in itself, but are a result of this dialectic of seeing and saying. An opportunity to improve the coordination of plans is not so much 'noticed' with the eyes as it is gleaned from conversations. The question shifts from how or why the entrepreneur sees an opportunity others have missed, to the question, how do market participants talk, write, show, in some manner *say* what they mean to their suppliers and customers, their co-workers, potential investors or stockholders?

The entrepreneur is situated within the context of a complex capital structure, where the market value of intermediate capital goods is a necessary guide to production decisions. Producers of capital goods several stages removed from the final consumer have no way of knowing what goods are more valuable than others than by the information contained in relative prices. The Misesian idea of economic calculation points to the necessity of the quantitative profit/loss calculation in order for the remote meanings of consumers to be translated, through the process of imputation of value, into a readable form. Producers of capital goods are suspended in this relative-price world, able to coordinate with consumers only because of this price information. But the point is not that prices alone, as numbers, are sufficient to accomplish this coordination. Permeating the market process are millions of efforts to communicate meaning. This is what I want, this is what I can do, this is how I could pay. The pricing of goods and services is a set of additional acts of articulation inserted into a world already buzzing with acts of talking and writing, of descriptions of products, of production possibilities, of alternative technologies, of contracts, and so on.

Because entrepreneurship fundamentally involves attempts to communicate, we need to inquire into the communicative-technological environment, the media, if you will, in which such communication can take place. A fundamental change in the tools for writing and reading, such as were provided by the printing press a few centuries ago, and by the Internet today, could utterly transform the workings of this sort of process for knowledge creation and sharing. The communicative media, within which ideas are brought into articulation and reinterpreted, have changed dramatically over the past several decades, and this could be expected to have significant effects on our orientative capacities. In other words, entrepreneurship should be conceptualized as a social process of mutual orientation in which tools for improving our ability to make and comprehend articulations would be expected to have a significant impact.

What tools like these do, I will claim, is make it easier for people who see the world differently from one another, to nevertheless make sense to each other, to orient their actions to one another.

When economics treats market exchange instead of language as the social relation *par excellence*, it obscures the market exchange process itself. It obscures the central role played in market transactions by various modes of articulation. The entrepreneur is not directly engaging with a language-less reality, but is coming to an understanding of a meaningful world through linguistic acts with others. In this context, looking at the technological media through which we articulate meaning to one another, makes sense. It seems reasonable to suppose that it helps the entrepreneurial coordination process when we develop new ways of saying what we mean. When we only have our vocal chords to work with there are certain kinds of things we can say. When we can also write words onto paper documents there are more kinds of things we can say. When we can also construct spreadsheets, databases and Web pages, there are more still. It matters for the coordination process how we are able to articulate. It matters what kinds of texts we are able to make.

3. Text and Its Structure

Lachmann's work *Capital and Its Structure* depicts the entrepreneur as involved in trying to mesh her plans with those of the ultimate consumers, by in some sense 'fitting' into an evolving structure of capital. This idea of fit is what Lachmann called 'complementarity'. The process of economic production involves the continuous adaptation of heterogeneous parts of the capital structure to one another. It is in this context that he sees the essential role of the entrepreneur as one of figuring out how to specify particular ways of using heterogeneous capital goods that in principle can be used in a multiplicity of alternative ways. Lachmann (1956: 16) identifies the key role of the entrepreneur in terms of deciding how to initially select (or later adapt) particular patterns of uses of capital goods.

> The entrepreneur's function as regards capital … is to *specify* and make decisions on the concrete form the capital resources shall have. … As long as we disregard the heterogeneity of capital, the true function of the entrepreneur must … remain hidden. In a homogeneous world there is no scope for the activity of specifying.

Early in that book Lachmann (1956: xv) says that he is not pointing 'towards the "objective" and quantifiable, but towards the subjective interpretation of phenomena'. Then he gives us an idea of what he means by a structure, from a subjectivist point of view.

> The generic concept of capital without which economists cannot do their work has no measurable counterpart among material objects; it reflects the entrepreneurial appraisal of such objects. Beer barrels and blast furnaces, harbour installations and hotel-room furniture are capital not by virtue of their physical properties but by virtue of their economic functions. Something is capital because the market, the consensus of entrepreneurial minds, regards it as capable of yielding an income. This does not mean that the phenomena of capital cannot be comprehended by clear and unambiguous concepts. The stock of capital used by society does not present a picture of chaos. Its arrangement is not arbitrary. There is some order in it.

Capital is a structure in the sense that it has a meaningful order. The order consists in more or less intricate patterns of complementarity among diverse, specialized capital goods. In the above passage I think Lachmann is essentially addressing the question with which this chapter opened: can a subjective process, a matter of human perspectives, and orientations, be what underlies an objective result, such as the creation of real wealth? We can comprehend capital, Lachmann insisted, 'by clear and unambiguous concepts', even while we insist that it is built out of subjective orientations, values and expectations. Like others in the Austrian school, Lachmann sees the process by which entrepreneurs adapt the structure of capital to the changing demands of consumers as central to the process of economic development. Enhancements to capital, which the Austrians sometimes misleadingly called a 'lengthening' of the structure of production, are for the Austrians what drive improvements in standards of living in growing economies.[17]

Howard Baetjer (1998: 22) refers to this notion of lengthening but I think he has a better way of putting it with the term 'complexifying'.

> When new capital goods are developed … what is generally involved is the development of new, more complex patterns of complementarity. The new capital must fit with the old (and other new goods) in order to be useful. The lengthening of the capital structure involves what Lachmann [1978: 79] calls a '"division of capital", a specialization of individual capital items.' We might call it a 'complexifying' of the capital structure, and increasing intricacy of the pattern(s) of complementarity among increasingly specialized capital goods, born in the ongoing growth and division of knowledge.

The adaptation and complexification of the capital structure can be thought of as a sort of social learning, where new knowledge is not only held in people's heads but comes to be embodied in our capital structure, just as it gets embodied in our institutions, practices, laws, prices, recipes and documents.[18] One can say that our capital structure 'learns' in the sense that Stewart Brand (1994) meant when he wrote the fascinating book, *How Buildings Learn*, that is, people working with these material things keep adding adaptations to them. Capital goods learn in the sense that people incrementally adapt them so that they come to better fit the environment into which they can be fit, and ultimately to the desires of the participants.

The reality in which entrepreneurial coordination has to take place is a complex, structured reality, in which parts have definite relationships to other parts. Capital goods are (subjectively) appraised as having the potential to earn a future flow of income because they are thought to be able to fit into the structure. The subjectivity of the structure, Lachmann is saying, does not change the fact that the structural relationships are real, and need to be taken account of. Entrepreneurs face the challenge of navigating within this complex structure of interconnected meanings, and to adapt elements of the structure so they fit into the whole. When that entrepreneurial process is working well, social learning in the form of rising standards of living can be the result.

It seems to me that texts should be thought of as possessing a kind of meaningful, evolving structure of this sort. Just as Austrians challenge those mainstream economists who mistake capital for a homogeneous quantity, so we can question those who tend to see 'information' as a homogeneous quantity, and media as nothing more than carriers of more or less information. Documents are not merely containers delivering a quantity of bits of information content, so that changes in technology would be nothing more than larger and faster trucks for delivering more such payloads to more distant locations. For the same kinds of reasons Austrians have wanted to discuss capital in terms of heterogeneity, complementarity, context and structure, we should look at texts in these terms.

Like capital goods, texts can 'learn' in the sense that those who work with them can add on improvements over time. Like capital, texts cannot be adequately appreciated apart from the institutional context within which they are used. Like capital, they are not understandable as an *amount* of something, say information, but as a heterogeneous structure with complex internal relationships. A text's parts stand in definite meaningful relationships to other parts, and to other texts.[19] It can be fixed in many different kinds of forms, or structures, and these can make it more readable. Thus we can differentiate the content of a text with the structure or form in which it is presented. What meaning a reader gets from a text will often depend greatly on the form in which the text is fixed, as well as the institutional context in which it is used. Different presentational structures can make the same underlying content convey meaning very differently. And yet the structure of a text is not strictly separable from its content. Understanding the content in part involves understanding that structure.[20]

What exactly the 'structure' of a text consists of will vary dramatically with different technological media, as the next sections will elaborate. For now I would like only to suggest that there is, within any given text, some kind of structure, and that this is, like the capital structure, a meaning-based order. There is at least a minimal amount of structure in any text, at least in the way the sentences are broken up into paragraphs and larger groupings. Structure does things like this; it helps us to do things with texts, to take the text apart and put it back together, to present the content of a message to an audience, to place it into some kind of larger context, to draw attention to the relationship between different parts of itself, to see one part of it in terms of a larger whole of which it is a part. Structural elements we now take for granted, such as spacing between words, and page numbers, were not always available to aid readers. The difference these added structural elements have made historically to the effectiveness of writing is very suggestive as we try to think about the knowledge economy. It may be that more complex kinds of production plans could not have evolved without accompanying structural features that made it easier for readers to work with texts. Improvements to our ability to add structures to texts may have had an important effect on our ability to communicate what we mean, especially by allowing us to increase the complexity of what we can say, and thus what we can do.

Complexity enters in two ways here. An articulation by one market participant to another is not just a description of a part of a complexly structured reality; it may also be a *complexly structured description* of a complexly structured reality. If the prevailing technologies for working with text permit, articulations can become structured in more complex ways that enrich our possibilities for conveying what we mean. In order to work with production plans that reach a certain level of complexity, it is necessary to have not only an exchange of unstructured content, an exchange of a linear, sequential string of words, but an exchange of complexly structured articulations of content.

Different media for articulation have differential advantages for conveying different kinds of content, which means that having available to us more alternative ways of articulating our meaning must help. We see this manifested in the way we feel the need to turn to verbal modes when writing seems inappropriate, or vice versa. In trying to express what we mean in market transactions or within the workplace we often find ourselves resorting to writing things down, or consulting a manual, or calling a face-to-face meeting. We find ourselves giving structure to the articulations in order to help guide the reader in how to read it. In such situations we are trying to help to provide the reader with a context in which the content of the message can be interpreted.

To characterize structures only as reading aids, however, would be to understate the scope of what they do. The structures in a text can include things that help the reader not just to read it, but also to *work with it*. The key to the knowledge economy, I will be arguing, is not primarily a matter of getting 'access' to quantities of data, it is more the revolution in ways of working with, and working together with, the data. We don't just possess information; we come to specific articulations in definite contexts, with questions in mind, with distinct purposes guiding our interest. Looking up information is not an unstructured search, but a question-driven process of looking for a certain kind of thing in a certain kind of situation. We don't just have information content, in a homogeneous lump, we have information that can be structured in order to contextualize the content, to guide the reader in how to see its significance, guiding differently depending on the question that is driving the look-up.

There is more going on here than an analogy between capital and texts. As Baetjer's book *Software As Capital* points out, a significant and growing part of the capital structure of the economy is in the form of software tools whose function is precisely the structuring of articulations. Entrepreneurs in the economy are appraising as very valuable the software that serves human efforts of articulation. They are judging that it promises to yield streams of future income. Such software is valuable, I think, for a reason. It may well be making improvements to our ability to structure our articulations with one another, and thereby our ability to mutually orient our plans with one another. It does seem reasonable to think that we might be enjoying such prosperity not only because our factors of production are more productive per se, but because of enhancements to entrepreneurship itself. Maybe we are, thanks to the tools, more able to discover, and coordinate our deployment of whatever productive factors we have. Something which had a substantial impact on the entrepreneurial coordination process would show itself as general prosperity, though it might be difficult to attribute this wealth to increases in the productivity of any particular priced factors of production.

Admittedly though, it is exceedingly hard to tell what is going on in technological revolutions one is in the middle of. I will return at the end to discuss what some writers think is happening in terms of electronic media, but it might be more useful to get at that question by first thinking through the technological transformations we have already been through. The text-structuring capabilities that emerged over the long course of the history of writing may help us to get a handle on the kinds of capabilities we are now beginning to see.

B. STRUCTURE IN PRE-ELECTRONIC MEDIA

> Contrary to the claims of historians in search of legitimacy, the backward glance is of little help in predicting what the future will bring. Because it is comparative, however, that backward glance can enable us to measure more accurately the changes that are revolutionizing our relations with written culture. It can also remind us that any comprehension of a text is necessarily dependent on a knowledge of the material forms it has taken. The historian's analysis is neither prophetic nor nostalgic: it has the dual task of pleading for the preservation and protection of the evidence of a written culture that for five centuries has been identified with the circulation of printed matter, and of making the revolution of the present moment more intelligible – a revolution as radical as the one that, seventeen or eighteen centuries ago, imposed a new form on the book. …
>
> The revolution of the electronic text will also be a revolution in reading. … While earlier revolutions in reading took place without changing the fundamental structure of the book, such will not be the case in our own world. The revolution that has begun is, above all, a revolution in the media and forms that transmit the written word. In this sense, the present revolution has only one precedent in the West: the substitution of the codex for the *volumen* – of the book composed of quires for the book in the form of a roll – during the first centuries of the Christian era. …
>
> [T]he codex undeniably facilitates organization and handling of the text. It permits pagination, the creation of indexes and concordances, and the comparison of one passage with another; better yet, it permits a reader to traverse an entire book by paging through. (Roger Chartier, 1995: 5, 18–19)

When the point of subjectivism is understood to be to turn our attention not inward to the mind, but outward to the texts, to the articulation processes in the economy, the issue of the *media* for working with texts forces itself into our attention.[21] The theory of entrepreneurship ought to attend more than it has so far to the technological media through which our articulations can be constructed and used. The meanings that subjectivism says we should pay attention to are not some kind of mysterious, inaccessible realm of the mental, they are all around us in the material form of spoken words and written texts, and are available for working with, and for interpretation. The fact that texts have a material reality to them tells us that they can't adequately be treated as pure content, but that particular forms in which they have been fixed, and the contexts in which they are used, can matter.

Entrepreneurship has been strengthened, I think, by fundamental improvements in the media in which we have been able to conduct our conversations. To get some perspective on the possible impact the latest technological media may be having on entrepreneurship it might be useful to review the kinds of transformations of media that have already taken place. There have been some fascinating debates in the literature on the history of writing from which the theory of entrepreneurship could benefit. The work of the historians of writing can help us to appreciate what textual structures have been in pre-electronic media, and how they have helped in the process of mutual orientation.[22] Most economists have paid scant attention to such questions, so that the Austrian school could take a major step forward by integrating ideas such as these into its analysis of the entrepreneurial process.

From the very beginning of the human species there has been an important connection between conversational media and economic advancement. How we are able to 'converse' makes an enormous difference in our ability to use, convey and generate economically relevant knowledge, and thus in our wealth and well-being. Our media technologies, from talking to writing to printing, to a whole variety of electronic tools, could all be called, in a broad sense, alternative ways of holding 'conversations' with one another.[23] We could refer to three overall *modes* of conversing, going from *verbal*, to (pre-electronic) *written*, to *electronic* modes. In all these media we are exchanging utterances, even though an 'utterance' could mean anything from a word or sentence verbally spoken, to a typed document printed, to a whole book published, and these days to an increasingly various set of electronic texts.

The point of the 'backward glance', as Chartier says in the quote above, is comparative. By considering what the transformation from a primarily oral to a literate culture has involved, we may get a comparative perspective that helps us to think about the new electronic technologies. I would like to suggest that before the arrival of computer-based media, our articulations were constrained by some fundamental trade-offs, and that a useful way to think about the potential of the new technologies is in terms of overcoming or relaxing these historical trade-offs. The trade-offs involve limitations in the possibilities for working with our articulations. Essentially I will be arguing that in a world where our articulation alternatives are limited to verbalizations or paper documents there are fundamental limits to the kinds of text-structuring activities we can engage in. Looking back historically can help us to get a better idea of what textual structure is by seeing how structural elements that have been introduced in the evolution of writing and printing have provided those working with texts to use them more effectively.

1. Talking and Listening

The literature on the history of writing does not say much specifically about economic processes, or entrepreneurship, but what it describes involves such profound transformations in the human condition that it is fairly obvious that they apply to the economic aspects of life. Oral culture and literate culture are fundamentally different, and the differences must have important implications for the process of entrepreneurial coordination.

Our ancestors developed the first fundamental mode of conversation, verbal talking and listening, long before our second, writing, got going. There is no doubt that verbalization has its power. Humankind emerged from competing primates on the strength of oral discourse. The original communicative technology, supplied by the biological evolution of vocal chords and eardrums and the cultural evolution of complex languages, is what made us human. The ability to communicate in language is apparently what gave our ancestors competitive advantages over their dumb rivals that were in the long run much more potent than claws or running speed. From language comes a profound enrichment of experience. The ability to communicate in words permits the passing along of work practices that embody gradually improving technologies of production. The extraordinarily complex technology, for example, that is involved in the sharpening of stone tools, which requires a sophisticated sequence of hundreds of precise movements, probably could not have been handed down to the next generation without talk. From the Stone Age to the computer age, high-tech advances have always been fundamentally dependent on our discourse media. To do more complex things, we needed to have increasingly sophisticated means of saying what we meant.

As Walter Ong and others have elaborated, an exclusively oral culture is strikingly different from the kind of verbal-plus-written culture we are in today, and many of the differences have to do with the challenge of preserving knowledge when texts cannot be written down. There is a need for complex procedures for the memorization of ritualized and formulaic verbalizations, sayings, narratives, epoch stories, 'old wives' tales', and so on, that today look to us like awkward ways to make up for the fact that nobody could preserve the 'texts' in written form. Ong suggests that values and ideas important to a society had to rhyme or follow a rhythmic pattern or take on other structural elements in order to be more easily committed to memory and passed along. Eisenstein (1979: 66) writes: 'As learning by reading took on new importance, the role played by mnemonic aids was diminished. Rhyme and cadence were no longer required to preserve certain formulas and recipes. The nature of the collective memory was transformed.'

The picture of oral culture in general that you get from the work of Ong, Havelock and others is a world that is in many ways alien to us today. We don't have to try to use memory tricks in our verbalizations to preserve knowledge we want to pass along, since it is so easy to write things down. The rise of writing does not so much substitute for talk; it makes whole new kinds of structured articulations possible while it lets talk specialize in what it is good for.

All this must pertain to the economy. The very nature of entrepreneurship must have been completely different in such a world. Market processes first emerged in strictly oral cultures, where transactions could only be conducted verbally and sealed with a handshake, and many types of market transactions today (informal deals between corporate executives, auctions, yard sales...) continue to occur primarily in verbal discursive modes. But the fact that we have changed from an oral to a literate culture has, of course, utterly changed the way market coordination takes place.

How an opportunity for mutual gains from trade can be 'seen' depends on how market participants are able to *say* what they want, what they can do, how they can do it, and so forth. In a strictly oral culture a deal essentially needs to be transacted face-to-face, without recourse to preserving in text aspects of the transaction that might be repeated in the future. Exchange thus tends to take the form of bazaar trading, with a premium on squeezing surplus out of the individual deal, as opposed to increasing the likelihood of future, repeated deals.

In terms of the notion of textual structure you could say that the oral medium has limits to its ability to present the content of the articulation in a complex structure. In verbal conversation, market participants can, to be sure, structure what they are saying through gestures, pauses, inflexion and so forth. But for the most part the words have to come out in a single, linear sequence, and cannot be rearranged or represented in different forms. Even in contexts where writing tools are not handy, we sometimes feel a need to express our meaning in a written, structured way; we reach for the napkin to sketch the idea. It may be that verbalization alone is too linear for some purposes. It has its strengths in a certain kind of direct interpersonal interactivity, but it has its limits as well. There are things we can do with written texts that we cannot do with spoken words alone. Our verbalized words come out in a single audio stream, structured by body language, pauses and emphasis, whereas we find we can give more and different kinds of structure to the content of our message if we can also make a visual presentation of it. Here, we say, look at it this way. Today in our literate culture we often find a need to express our meaning through the written articulation.

In other words, a verbalization-only culture faces severe trade-offs in its communicative efforts, which now, from the point of view of a literate culture, seem very limiting. This is not to say that the trade-offs are typically experienced by the speakers as limiting. The difficulty of seeing the technological limitations of our present media is that we do not have the distance from a verbal-and- paper-based-literate culture that we have from a strictly oral one. Although we are entering into a new medium, and have had a taste of some crude electronic capabilities, we are as yet in the dark ages of this medium, and it takes an effort of imagination to really see what electronic text, in its fully formed existence, will be like.

2. Writing/Reading

Talking and listening and writing/reading are all about the exchange of words and other articulations of meaning. Writing and reading as a new form of discourse comes on the scene after, and according to many interpretations of the prehistorical record, as a result of, markets. The fundamental advantages of writing over talking stem from the fact that things 'written down' can be returned to, re-worked, re-interpreted, or in some way worked upon. The persistence of the written text allows us in principle to make improvements upon what we are saying by revision.

The earliest forms of writing seem to have been accounting records, and these gradually complexify into written accounts in words of market transactions, contractual arrangements, and so on. The anthropologist Jack Goody (1987: 54–5) summed up the impact of the rise of writing this way:

> How did it change the world of man? Let me first touch upon the organizational changes. Writing, in the full sense, appeared with the growth of urban civilizations. Nor was it simply a consequence but also a condition of that development ... In Mesopotamia, the first written word appears to be that of the merchant and the accountant, though as part of the ecclesiastical organization of the temple city.
>
> What did writing facilitate? Clearly the identification of merchandise, the recording of types and quantities of goods, the calculation of the input and the output were much helped by the development of a script. None of these activities are impossible in oral societies. But without the written word the scale and complexity of the operation were limited.

Gradually written language spreads to all aspects of society and utterly transforms human civilization in all its dimensions. It may be no exaggeration to say that writing/reading gave us the flowering of Greek culture, the beginnings of philosophy, medicine, astronomy and mathematics. It had a profound effect in all the major religions, which became radically shifted toward an orientation to their key texts such as the Koran, Buddhist commentaries, or the Hebrew and Christian bibles. It restructured politics, since the ability to read and write bestowed enormous power onto the elite of literate culture. It led to the cumulative advance of technologies, whose complexities could be preserved in written form instead of in ritualized sayings.

The history of writing has been mostly written by and for literary scholars, and thus has not tended to emphasize the effects changes in media have had on economic processes. Often the focus is on the history of the book and of the activities of scholars, but as Landow (1994: 7) points out,

> First of all, not all printed text appears in books. An enormous amount of it comes to us as business cards and forms, order blanks, restaurant menus, advertising inserts in newspapers, posters, railroad and bus schedules, and the like. Even if one counts newspapers, magazines, and comic books as books, literature and the literary book turn out to occupy but a tiny proportion of print production: by far the greatest number and proportion of books are telephone directories and other institutional and public lists, repair manuals, merchandise and component catalogues and so on.

The evolution of writing, clearly, has had profound effects on the workings of market institutions. Prices that can be written down, accounts that can be recorded, are quite different from their precursors in oral culture. The possibility of written law stabilizes and clarifies property rights, and permits far more complex types of ownership arrangements. Money itself is writing, and all the various forms of monetary instruments are products of writing. Prices and other components of offers for exchange are not just written, but are posted in public places to attract buyers. Perhaps most importantly, written contracts and the whole apparatus of contract law become possible. Terms of incredibly complex transactions can be written out and consulted later in case of alleged breach of contract.

One of the key points Ong (1997: 21) makes about the difference between oral and written cultures is the separation in a literate culture between the expression and the reception of words.

> Oral utterance thus encourages a sense of continuity with life, a sense of participation, because it is itself participatory. Writing and print, despite their intrinsic value, have obscured the nature of the word and of thought itself, for they have sequestered the essentially participatory word – fruitfully enough, beyond a doubt – from its natural habitat, sound, and assimilated it to a mark on a surface, where a real word cannot exist at all.

There is a legitimate point in what Ong is saying here, though it sounds as if he is lamenting the written mode of communication as if it represents some kind of artificiality.[24] But as he clarifies in another work (1982: 82), he actually sees the artificiality of writing as something of an advantage:

> To say writing is artificial is not to condemn it but to praise it. Like other artificial creations and indeed more than any other, it is utterly invaluable and indeed essential for the realization of fuller, interior, human potentials ... Alienation from a natural milieu can be good for us and indeed is in many ways essential for full human life. To live and to understand fully, we need not only proximity but also distance.

Still, it can be said that in a world mainly limited to paper-based technology, writing and reading are alienated from one another, as compared with talking and listening, and in ways which are not all advantageous.[25] I like to think of the comparison Ong elaborates of oral and written culture in terms of a contrast between verbalization and writing/reading, where I deliberately express the first as one thing and the other as two distinct things separated by a slash. The slash, the cleavage between writing and reading, is important. Oral conversation is a far more integrated process where the talking and listening are in a concise and continuous dialectical interplay with one another. The subtle skills we have learned by which we engage in conversation involve a delicate sensitivity to such matters as when we should talk and when we should listen, a sensitivity we become acutely aware of when we use artificial conversational tools such as the telephone and feel the distinct lack of cues about when we are jumping in too quickly or not. By contrast, the writing and the reading of paper-based discourse are thoroughly separated components. The cleavage is both the source of the greatest strength of writing/reading and also the source of its greatest weakness. It is a strength in that the word cut loose from its original context can reach a wide range of future, disconnected readers, but it is a weakness in that we lose the immediate interplay of the saying and the hearing that is taken for granted in verbal conversation.

Historians of writing seem to broadly agree that a fundamental transformation has occurred over the course of the last couple of millennia, but differ over when the crucial turning points in this history took place. Some such as Eisenstein place primary emphasis on Gutenberg, or rather on the rise of the printing industry from the 15th to the 17th century which followed upon the invention of movable type. That is, this perspective puts the emphasis on the technology for circulating multiple copies of a work, which was dramatically altered at that time. This could be called a quantitative emphasis in that it looks for the change that had the most oomph, the most leverage and significance in shaping other changes.

Other historians such as Martin (1988: 208–12) back up a couple of centuries, identifying the key change as the technological advances in paper production that took place in Fabriano, Italy between 1240 and 1280:

> The importance of this movement can hardly be exaggerated. Before paper became available, the hides of a veritable herd of young animals were required to make a single in-folio volume. After the fourteenth century, when the West had access to a writing material in seemingly unlimited quantities, the way was open for printing.

Or you could date the crucial change as having already happened a thousand years further back. Several historians place the main emphasis on the rise of the 'codex'. This is an emphasis on the qualitative side of the transformation in that it focuses on the shift in the *form* of writing, its organizational structure. As Martin (1988: 59) said, 'The appearance of the codex – the work presented on pages written on both sides rather than on one side of a continuous scroll – was undoubtedly the most important revolution in the book in the Common Era'.

Indeed, one could go further back still. Chartier (1995: 7–9) points out that several 18th century contributors to the history of writing, including Giambattiista Vico and Marie-Jean-Antoine Condorcet, had located the key transformation in the shift from hieroglyphic to alphabetic forms. And there is something to be said for stressing the importance of the alphabetic form of writing, not only because it represents a more abstract form, but because, as is more clear today than it could have been then, it facilitates organization. When one is dealing with very large texts and collections of texts the ability to deploy alphabetic ordering has proven to be a powerful advantage.

If we characterize this debate as a question of determining when 'the' revolution took place, these differences appear irreconcilable. But from the point of view of this chapter, each of these epochal turning points has merit. These historians are drawing attention to the evolving possibilities for adding structure to texts, with some scholars telling us when such possibilities first appeared, and others telling us when they spread to become transformative in the culture as a whole. Both are highlighting crucial complementary elements of the transformation in media, and it is the combined effect of both the qualitative and the quantitative sides that constitutes the revolution.[26] But even though in a sense printing led to a quantitative shift, this in turn eventually had qualitative implications.

The shift Ong elaborates between an oral and a literate culture was not a single, dichotomous cleavage. The emphasis on the printing press in much of the literature on the history of writing is misleading in some respects. In some ways the more basic changes in the history of writing, from the point of view of the structure of the text, which is to say, the manner in which words and images were organized, were the shifts from hieroglyphic and cuneiform to alphabetic text, and from the roll or *volumen* to the codex, the book broken into pages.

The age between the rise of writing in the 4th century BC through the codex in the 2nd century AD, and the printing press in the 15th, was a gradual transition where Western culture was increasingly shaped by written texts, even though literacy rates were probably not high. Books, especially sacred texts, were crucial in cementing social community, and their ritualized reading aloud was a vital part of life for many, and not only for the scribes. The age of scribes is in a sense an oral age, but one increasingly shaped by texts.

The alphabetic form of writing had several advantages, but one of them that is particularly relevant here is that of permitting a straightforward method for organizing large amounts of text. Imagine the challenge of looking information up if it is written in hieroglyphs. The advantages of ordering lists alphabetically is an extraordinarily powerful structuring capability, but it only really came into its own after the printing press made the need for organizing large amounts of text necessary. Eisenstein (1979: 89) quotes from a compiler of a 13th century encyclopedia who still found it necessary to explain exactly how full alphabetic ordering works, and she points out that other, often idiosyncratic, ordering systems were widely used before the age of printing. With the explosion of texts and the spread of literacy it became all the more necessary to have catalogues, indices, bibliographic book lists, and so forth, and working with large complex texts demanded familiarity with alphabetical order to facilitate looking things up. The key here is structures that help us to work with text materials.

Organizing works by pages (and numbering them, and using Arabic and not Roman numerals) was similarly a powerful structuring capability, again helping those who needed to do work with texts to use them more effectively. Chartier (1995: 19–20) points out that the adoption of the codex format of text seemed to have been driven by the needs of early Christianity to work with texts, 'in particular, comparing the Gospels and mobilizing citations of the Sacred Word for preaching, worship and prayer'. This new technology took off, in other words, because the structure of the book in the form of numbered pages permitted a more complex ability to manage the word, as Ong puts it, than was convenient when text was in the form of a roll. For example, Chartier says,

> [T]o be read – in other words, unrolled – the roll had to be held in two hands. Thus, as frescoes and bas-reliefs illustrate, the impossibility of a reader's writing and reading at the same time, and thus, too, the importance of dictation. The reader was liberated by the codex. Resting on a table or a lectern, the book in quires no longer required participation of so much of the body. One might distance oneself, reading and writing at the same time, moving at one's own pace from page to page, from book to book.

It is widely agreed, in any case, that especially after the invention of movable type, society has undergone profound changes in the communicative media. Economic activity of all kinds must have been quite thoroughly transformed by the new media. And yet as Eisenstein (1979: 30) pointed out, it often appears that to economists the printing press mainly stands for an early example of a certain kind of technology, not a fundamental turning point in the ways of doing business:

> The relationship, if any, between expanding printing industries and the growth of capitalist enterprise during the early modern era still remains to be explored. Most surveys of economic history move from the later middle ages to early modern times without giving any indication of how the advent of printing might have affected commerce and industry in general, or methods of advertising, insurance schemes, stock market reports, and systems of currency in particular.

The printing press at first did not so much make a change in the forms of the texts, which retained the codex structure, but it so dramatically reduced the costs of the writing and reading process that it made writing and reading more central to all aspects of life. Though she admits the extraordinary difficulty of any estimates of the reduction in the cost of writing texts, Eisenstein (1979: 46) quotes one source that offers a useful comparison: in 1483, one copy of a translation of Plato's *Dialogues* copied by hand cost one florin per quinterno. A thousand copies of the same work done on a printing press at the time would cost three florins per quinterno.

Printing so dramatically lowered the costs of distribution of writing/reading that it universalized literacy.[27] Texts became standardized, enabling the spread of complex processes of interpretation and critique that used to be the privilege of the elite scribes. When in 1455 an obscure diamond polisher named Johannes Gutenberg brought together the different technologies necessary to make the printing press possible, he may have thought that the effect was going to be that more copies of the Bible would be circulated to his fellow Europeans. His invention certainly did that, but soon enough it did much more. Already by 1500 some 35 000 separate editions of books, amounting to somewhere around 15 million copies, were published. Eventually the printing press populated European discourse, which at the time had been focused on the Bible, with a bewildering variety of different texts, and eventually brought about an engineering and scientific revolution that transformed not only religion but almost everything else about the world. Writing/reading was now the basis of advanced conceptual thought.

One of the major changes as writing shifted from manuscripts to the age of printing is that the gradual decay of accurate information that had been taken for granted in the process of copying over manuscripts by hand was no longer the rule, and indeed was effectively reversed. With the printing press, came a gradual improvement of information, as the multiple copies of documents could accumulate criticisms from all directions that could be incorporated into the next edition. Maps, drawings of plants, technical manuals, and so forth could now be expected to improve with new editions.

Because of this feature of revisability, writing made more complex action possible, which in turn led to more complex forms of writing. Martin (1995: 486) illustrates this point with the example of the transformation of music as we changed from the predominately oral to the written mode of communication. He intended this example to make a broader point that complex production activities of all sorts were made possible by writing. At first writing down music only served a secondary mnemonic function, helping us to remember melodies or lyrics, but once music could be written, and musical notation became sufficiently complex, it began to change the possibilities for composition. Gregorian chant could be done without the aid of writing, but the great works for ensembles and orchestras of the Baroque and classical age could not have been composed without it. He writes:

> Polyphony brought another dimension to music, and because of it notation no longer functioned simply as an imprecise aid to memory and a prop to the oral tradition. The extreme complexity of polyphonic music made writing obligatory: only with written music could each independent voice line be coordinated with the other voices to form a harmonic whole and produce the desired effect ... A true writing system, musical notation ... furnished a working tool for composition that has never ceased to be improved.

Economic production, I would argue, has enjoyed the same kind of dynamic of increasing complexity through writing. At first writing down transactions was only an aid to memory in a fundamentally oral process, but having economically relevant texts available gradually permitted more and more complex types of transactions and production plans to be organized, and in turn led to more complex forms of texts to guide these activities.

The explosion of the printing press industry eventually led to major improvements in the kinds of structures available to readers and writers. Eisenstein (1979: 52) pointed out, quoting from Steinberg (1961: 28), that the focus of the process for the production of texts shifted 'from fidelity to scribal conventions and toward serving the convenience of the reader'.

> The highly competitive commercial character of the new mode of book production encouraged the relatively rapid adoption of any innovation that commended a given addition to purchasers. Well before 1500, printers had begun to experiment with the use of 'graduated types, running heads ... footnotes ... tables of contents ... superior figures, cross references ... and other devices available to the compositor' – all registering 'the victory of the punch cutter over the scribe.' Title pages became increasingly common, facilitating the production of book lists and catalogues, while acting as advertisements in themselves.

In spite of many differences among these historians in their emphasis on different moments and aspects of the transformation, all of them seem to refer to the idea of what we have called textual structures. Articulations became more powerful as we gradually came to find better ways of working with text. As a result of intense competition among master printers, new ways of structuring the text that had first appeared earlier increasingly became routine. Some of the kinds of structuring that had been necessary in verbal utterances only because we couldn't write things down could be dropped, while other kinds of structuring now possible in writing could be added. With writing and eventually the printing press, the possibilities for adding complex structure to the content have increased profoundly. With the modern book the structure includes its organization into paragraphs, pages, chapters, footnotes, tables, charts, and so on, and markers such as italics or underlining to draw attention to some words, and tools such as indices and tables of contents to help us find what we are looking for. The history of writing is constantly drawing attention to structures that serve as the 'hooks' to the text, allowing us to work with them more easily.

Not only has the printing revolution brought about a significant increase in the kinds of structures available to writers; it has also dramatically improved our ability to share these more complexly structured texts. Many of the kinds of structures we have mentioned were first invented in the scribal age, but it is because after printing far more readers came to read copies of the same text, and refer to it in their subsequent talking and writing, that the structures were found to be so useful. Structural hooks such as running heads, indices, tables of content, page numbers, paragraphs, and so forth, were really tools for sharing text. Conversations about a book could be precisely linked to texts in a manner that allowed a much more precise engagement with the ideas.

Having added complex forms of writing to our conversations, entrepreneurship can take place in new ways. Opportunities for mutually beneficial exchange can still get 'noticed' through the learning that occurs in the verbal conversation, but can now also arise in the process of reading texts. The dialectic of seeing and saying operates in such a manner that our sense of what opportunities are there to be grasped is continuously shaped by our efforts to express our meanings to one another in both verbal and written conversations.

Of course, the whole new ways of 'holding conversations' brought about by the rise of writing, printing and literacy have not supplanted the role of the previous technologies. As Martin (1988: 283) put it, although historians may mark the rise of printing in terms of stages, the age of the manuscript versus that of print, in fact 'a new procedure never eliminates its predecessor; it merely imposes a new division of labor'. Writing 'by hand' does not disappear after Gutenberg, but is able to settle itself into domains of practice for which it is better suited.[28] Nowadays handwriting has moved to the margins of printed documents, post-it notes, white boards, and so forth. Increasing our options with new technologies tends to permit us more often to use the right tool for the job.

In the same way, the increasing possibilities of writing in general have not supplanted the realm of the oral, but have allowed us to use the verbal media more for what they are good for. As Ong (1977: 82) points out, as important a revolution as writing/reading was for the progress of the human conversation, it could not be said to have replaced oral communication: 'A new medium of verbal communication not only does not wipe out the old, but actually reinforces the older medium or media. However, in doing so it transforms the old, so that the old is no longer what it used to be.'

The existence of all the books and magazines and newspapers in our culture does not in the least push back the role of oral communication, but on the contrary enriches it. As Ong puts it, once we had books we were encouraged to talk more, if only because we 'had more to talk about'. The verbal conversation remains, of course, a crucial mode of mutual understanding. Oral talking and aural listening in an ordinary conversation is the way we learn language and is our basic recourse whenever the more advanced communicative processes that have been invented since fail us.

The everyday uses of talking and writing illustrate the fact that they are complementary, both in that they each have different strengths, and in that they work better in combination. Even after the transformations of the printing press, corporate executives who could afford all the printed documents they wanted, when faced with certain kinds of situations, still resorted to the good old technology of face-to-face meeting. The immediate feedback of an oral discussion is still the best way to converse for some purposes, and the fact that we can do so *on the basis of* written texts only increases the potency of the talk. We can get more done in the talk when we bring some texts to the discussion, or when we've already read others before the meeting. In the fact that the corporate executives routinely ask participants to bring the documents to the meeting, or that professors ask students to bring the texts to class, we have evidence of the complementarity of oral and written technologies.

Having the more different modes of discourse available allows us to deploy each in the domains for which it is best suited. Talk is good for getting the immediate interplay of saying and hearing, but not so good at preserving and working, and re-working, with complex formulations. Writing is good for that kind of thing, but not so good for getting immediate, focused feedback.

3. Trade-offs in Talking and Writing

Verbal and written technological media have a tendency to disappear. Our practices with these familiar technologies have, so to speak, 'settled in on' their different comparative advantages, at least to some extent.[29]

These modes have become naturalized to us, to such a degree that paper documents and voices heard are often presumed to be somehow unmediated, to not involve technology at all. What is usually called technology are the media that are new and unfamiliar enough to draw attention to themselves. Technologies that have settled in are those that have come to be routinely used primarily in the situations where their strengths can kick in. New technologies are still being developed and experimented with, and often stand out all the more because they've been misapplied, used in a way that fails to take advantage of the medium's comparative strengths. But by looking closely at the dimensions in which these pre-electronic media are each strong, one can notice that there are imaginable combinations that would be valuable but that are not supported.

In an article entitled 'The open society and its media', Mark S. Miller, E. Dean Tribble, Ravi Pandya, and Marc Stiegler (1995) summed up, in a particularly sharp fashion, the different strengths of oral and written modes of conversation.[30] Like the historical literature just reviewed, the article does not talk specifically about economics; it refers to the impact of writing and printing on the scholarly and scientific worlds. And what they are saying again would seem to apply to issues such as the nature of entrepreneurial coordination processes. I reproduce (with some slight rewordings) a chart Miller et al. supply in their paper to illustrate the relative advantages of verbal and written (under paper technology) discourses.

Table 12.1 Strengths of each mode

Verbal	Written
Visibility of arguments (Can hear an absence)	Persistence of arguments (Cumulative)
Revision after publication	Revision before publication
Small expressions	Large expressions
Small audiences	Large audiences
Fast publication	Freedom of entry
Immediate feedback	Complex reputation systems

This formulation is of course a simplified one that passes over many of the subtle distinctions one finds in the literature on the history of writing, but it has the advantage of drawing attention to some of the essential issues. Verbal and written modes of communication, Miller et al. are saying, are good for different kinds of communicative tasks, as is borne out by our typical uses of paper documents and verbal discussions. Several of these contrasts are obvious enough, but a few of these phrases are a bit unusual, and to me thought-provoking. I think the point they are making when they call *visibility of arguments* a virtue of verbal discourse is that the contentions being made in any given oral discussion tend to be more out there in the open to those involved, whereas in the extended 'conversations' of books and scholarly journals, arguments can exist somewhere but can be hard to find. This can be put in the language of their intriguing phrase 'hearing an absence'. The advantage of verbal conversations is that both what is said in an argument and what is unsaid are out there for all to hear. 'Does anyone see anything wrong with this plan?' A silence has some force in a verbal discussion in a sense unlike the way typical written 'conversations' work. The very advantages of writing that allow texts to extend beyond the one room in which the discussion takes place, and to be duplicated and distributed to a large anonymous population of readers (the *large audiences* point), also has its costs: the back and forth of the dialogue is not all available in that one room, but is so dispersed that it is difficult to see which arguments are stronger than their rivals, or even to find all the rivals.[31] Corresponding to that visibility strength of the verbal, however, is a distinct strength of the written: the advantage of *persistence.* This is the characteristic that permits us to return to verbal formulations in different situations with different purposes in mind, in order to work with them. It is the condition that opens up the space for innovations in textual structuring of various kinds.

The contrast in the way revision occurs is also an interesting way to think about the differences between these media. Written discourse allows us greater opportunities than verbal discourse allows us, to deploy *revision before publication.* The writer can make several drafts in private, refining, crafting the text until she thinks it says better what she means. Verbal discourse permits and encourages *revision after publication* in the sense that as you talk, which is for this medium a kind of 'publishing', and you see from the immediate feedback that you are not being understood, or that you were in error, you can quickly reformulate your point. This leads to the phenomenon that written discussions often have more carefully formulated articulations in them than the kind of quick, off-the-cuff dialogue that tends to occur in oral discussions.

Our typical uses of talk and writing suggest that the former is better for the fine-grained dialogue on the smaller scale, both *small expressions* and *small audiences*, and that the latter is more suited to the larger expressions and audiences. There are advantages to the *fast publication* of verbal discussion, which for some contexts can help one to avoid misunderstandings by quickly spelling out what one means. Combined with the last strength, *immediate feedback*, it constitutes one of the key reasons to use the verbal mode of conversation. A writer could spend a year developing an argument that a reader will eventually refute, while if he floated it verbally he might be able to get the feedback needed to correct himself. The fact that writing lacks this feature is what was meant by the 'slash' in the writing/reading process. Talking and listening are not alienated from one another in the way that writing alienates the author from the reader. Typically in the age of printing the author doesn't see what reactions the reader has to the text.

The writing mode of discourse has a compensating advantage in that it can have a greater degree of *freedom of entry*, in the sense that any given verbal discussion has a limited supply of 'air time'. In verbal conversations it can sometimes be hard to 'get your words in edgeways' whereas when the expressions can be written down, more different voices can, as it were, speak at once. There is always some publication outlet, if nothing else, one's own, which will take an article, even if one can't break into the top journals of a certain field.

Corresponding in a way with the verbal mode's quick feedback is the strength that systems of writing have evolved of a kind of 'feed forward', the use of *complex reputation systems*. Getting published in this or that journal signifies the endorsement of this or that specialized community, offers assurance to potential readers that the text may be worth the work involved in reading it. Reputation systems can aid tremendously in the decisions one has to make about whose words to trust.

All these themes have their counterparts in the world of economic action. Our habits in market transactions suggest that we tend to deploy here more verbal, there more written conversational modes in distinct situations, corresponding to the kinds of trade-offs Miller et al. highlight. The advantages of verbal discourse redound to verbal-discourse-based markets. One can 'hear an absence' at an auction. One can get immediate feedback from the audience in a face-to-face transaction. One can make 'revision after publication' in verbal deals where the terms acceptable to both parties need to be explored tentatively and worked out dynamically. One can take advantage of 'fast publication' with verbal markets when, say, you want to just get rid of that old shovel quickly at the yard sale. For 'small expressions', that is, relatively simple, singular, and straightforward deals, the verbal agreement still works just fine.

And yet of course we know that since the printing press and the spread of literacy, the whole nature of the workplace and the marketplace has been transformed. All sorts of complex production plans and transactions are thoroughly involved with paperwork. The specific advantages of writing that Miller et al. are talking about (with science in mind) apply to the economy. Revision before publication has great advantages when one is trying to elaborate the precise terms of a complex transaction, or organize a complex production plan. Freedom of entry for authors is a virtue of writing-based markets in that anyone can get in by posting a better offer, and one does not have to get words in edgeways in the verbal discussions of dominant transactors. And reputation-based filtering is by now a rather advanced feature of markets where publications can facilitate a rapid communication of defects or virtues of particular products. Some industries such as banking are built around their own complex financial reputation systems.

By setting up this kind of contrast between the different strengths of alternative pre-electronic modes of conversation that have been familiar for centuries, Miller et al. are trying to provoke us to think about the combinations of strengths that are not easy to get in either mode. In the pre-electronic age, if one wanted to have a conversation that picked two from column A, and three from column B, it was difficult. There are situations, say, where we might like to engage in a relatively quick interpersonal engagement of the kind talk is good for, but also to make what we say persistent, which writing is good for. We are used to such trade-offs and routinely find ways to bounce back and forth between modes to make up for the shortcomings of each. What Miller and his collaborators are really getting at is that the possibilities of electronic media can be usefully thought about in relation to trying to reach new combinations of these kinds of strengths.

One could sum up the differential advantages of these media this way: the advantages, by and large, of the paper-based writing medium have been those related to persistence, and the ability to return to and revise what we are saying before we make it public, and afterwards in order to make improvements for the next edition. These persistence-based advantages involve the various kinds of *intertextual* structures that can be built into any one speaker's utterance. The advantages of the oral medium, on the other hand, have been those of *interpersonal* interaction, which is essentially our ability to alternate easily among speakers, and thus to use the feedback of interaction to revise what we are saying after we've made it public.

C. STRUCTURE IN ELECTRONIC MEDIA: THE CASE OF GROUPWARE WITH HYPERTEXT

> Knowledge comprises two components: knowledge structure and information content. Structure represents a framework used to arrange information to make it meaningful, while content represents the information itself. Knowledge structures therefore provide the context for making sense of information. …
>
> Information and knowledge can be acquired from many different internal and external sources. That knowledge is then subjected to value-adding processes such as labeling, indexing, sorting, abstracting, standardization, integration, re-categorization, as well as the process of making the knowledge explicit. …
>
> A well-structured repository allows for a high degree of viewing flexibility. If the repository is conceived as a knowledge 'platform', then many different

> knowledge views may be derived based on the particular content, format, and medium by which it is presented to the user. …
>
> Collaborative technologies such as Lotus Notes offer a natural environment within which to build a repository for rich, explicit knowledge. Input is captured by forms for assigning various labels, categories, and indices to each unit of knowledge. …The structure is flexible enough to create 'knowledge units', indexed and linked using categories that reflect the structure of the contextual knowledge and the content of factual knowledge of the organization, displayed as flexible subsets via customizable views. (Michael H. Zack and Michael Serino, 2000: 307–9)

It is commonly supposed within the business literature that the computer and telecommunications revolutions are *somehow* ultimately the engine driving much of this recent economic development, but of course the question is how. There is controversy about exactly what it is that these information technologies are doing that contributes to wealth. What is it exactly about the information technology revolution that has boosted economic wealth? Or to put it in terms we have been using, what is it about making text electronic that enhances our ability to orient our plans to one another?

These questions, however, are too big to do justice to here, and I think we are too early in the media transformations to be able to take a critical perspective on all the different ways computers and telecommunications are changing the way the economy works. What may have seemed like the crucial revolutions in electronic media a few decades ago, such as radio, electric typewriters, television, word processing software, or inexpensive laser printers, may no longer look so cutting edge by now. It is hazardous to venture a guess about which of the innovations going on now are the ones that will make a lasting impact.

What I'd like to do here is to illustrate one aspect of the change in media, the ability to make flexible the kind of shared textual structures that were emphasized by the historians of writing. I will review briefly the themes of the business literature on 'groupware' and 'hypertext' which claims that these key capabilities of telecommunications technology are the force that is transforming the new economy. Then I'd like to sum up how it is that these capabilities can be described as doing more of the same kind of thing the historians of writing were talking about, essentially, helping people to work with text by adding different kinds of 'structure' to what is written.

1. Knowledge Management and the Sharing of Structured Text

First of all it is important to appreciate the kind of scholarship involved here. Like most business literature, the writings in knowledge management are not typically trying to offer social scientific explanations of how the world works, but rather are trying to offer practical advice to practitioners. Their question is not so much to estimate the effects of groupware and hypertext capabilities on wealth as to try to explain how best to deploy such capabilities to improve the chances of making your organization successful. Several scholarly studies have had difficulty finding clear evidence that investment in information technology in general, or in knowledge management software systems in particular, contribute to worker productivity, and of course there are plenty of ways to waste money on information technology 'investments' which don't help productivity at all but which can mess up the statistics.[32] This skepticism about information technology's contribution to productivity has spawned in turn a large but somewhat unfocused management consulting literature purporting to show how businesses can overcome the 'paradox', such as Thorp (1998) and Lucas (1999).

But not all this literature is unfocused. The strand of knowledge management literature I am summarizing here offers some real insight about what it might be that software is doing for some businesses that could be driving the new economy. The strand I have in mind is perhaps best epitomized by the papers collected in the book *Knowledge, Groupware and the Internet*, edited by David E. Smith.[33] Among the contributors are Ikujiro Nonaka, author of an often-cited *Harvard Business Review* article 'The knowledge-creating company', John Seely Brown and Paul Duguid, co-authors of the book *The Social Life of Information*, and Michael Zack of the Lotus Institute.

Sometimes the terms groupware and hypertext are understood as synonyms, respectively, for intranets and the Internet, but this fails to identify the basic kinds of functionality involved. When this literature refers to software capabilities that they call 'groupware' and 'hypertext' they are generally pointing to the aspects of media that I have been calling, respectively, the interpersonal and the intertextual. The emphasis is on the ability of such software to help market participants to share knowledge. The so-called leading-edge companies according to these authors are the ones that have a better handle on managing their own intellectual resources, on using the knowledge they in some sense already 'had', but weren't using well, and on stimulating the growth of new knowledge. The knowledge management literature argues that improvements in 'knowledge sharing' have come from the convergence of these groupware and hypertext capabilities.

This phrase 'knowledge sharing' is a bit misleading. What we have here is not a matter of sharing some fixed thing called knowledge. It involves tools to enhance the kinds of work that groups of persons can do together. These authors are describing the same kind of 'social learning' process that I have been alluding to in the context of the history of writing.[34] Indeed as some of the authors explicitly acknowledge, what we have here is a form of knowledge-capital in which structured knowledge is the very essence of the usefulness of the capital goods.[35] The knowledge-creating process is usefully depicted in Nonaka (1994) as a spiral of writing and reading, of alternating between re-articulation and reinterpretation. That is, the potency of these new capabilities is said to be rooted in the process of a group of co-workers bringing tacit knowledge into explicit form, and reading off articulations to glean new tacit awareness. The 'seeing' of opportunities is enabled through the facilitation of the 'saying' of what is meant in texts.

These authors understand the point I have been making about understanding text in its context, both institutional and technological. There has been a tendency for some of the enthusiasts of new technology to ignore the role of social institutions or to treat them as mere constraints that will be overcome by the new capabilities of information technology. But in the knowledge management literature the role of institutions is often appreciated. Brown and Duguid (2000: 246) have been insistent, for example, in their claim that we need to see institutions as complementary with communicative technologies, and as not only fixed constraints to human action, but also as enablers of action:

> In an age that emphasizes individual freedoms, institutions are often portrayed merely as constraints on this freedom. In particular, they are portrayed as monolithic, static, even stagnant constraints. Yet, because they are human creations, they rarely are just that. They change as people change. And they adapt to serve social needs.

Similarly, the technological issues I have been calling textual structure, that is, the way structure facilitates the contextualizing of what is said, is widely appreciated by these authors. The shift from talking about 'data processing' to talking about knowledge management in fact signals a fundamental shift in thinking.[36] The issue is not the *amount* of information or data that can be stored, or how far or fast it can be transported. The issue is how meaningful data, that is, knowledge, can be obtained from raw information. Software capabilities are powerful because they allow participants to add more kinds of structure to texts and documents, to permit different views, different contextualizations of the information. Just as advances in writing led to structures such as paragraphs, headings, tables of contents, footnotes and indices, so these new electronic text advances are leading to new kinds of structures.

The functionality the knowledge management literature is talking about when it uses the terms groupware and hypertext consists of tools for the writing and reading of shared, structured, modifiable, electronic documents. Groupware and hypertext can be understood as different emphases on one kind of thing. I refer to a 'convergence' in the sense that although each of these aspects can be thought of in isolation from the other, the knowledge management literature is increasingly emphasizing their combination as the key to success. In principle these could be thought of as quite distinct kinds of capabilities. One can imagine a hypertextual repository of texts as a tool for an individual person to use. One can also imagine a groupware environment where the shared information is flat, unstructured content, with none of the textual structuring associated with hypertext. But in practice each of these kinds of capabilities is almost always found combined to some extent with elements of the other. Groupware is more powerful precisely when it incorporates more hypertextual capabilities, and vice versa. Groupware begins in a sense with the notion of individuals working together in a networked environment, and asks what tools, including textual structures, might enhance their work. Hypertext begins at the other end. It starts from the context of an individual confronting a structured text, and soon comes to take up the interpersonal context of shared access to the text.

Hypertext is not to be equated with the Web as it is now, in the early 21st century. We've all had experience, to be sure, with the basic 'hypertext' functionality that is supported in HTML, hypertext markup language, such as the simple jumplink where one clicks on something to go to another document. The term hypertext also refers to the kind of writing environment where access to written documents is not separated into access to distinct physical copies, but is concentrated upon a single electronic copy, as in the URL. But while somewhat suggestive, this familiar sense we have from current Web browsers can be misleading. It might be more useful in some ways to think about the use by corporations of complex relational databases that are available to co-workers over local area networks, or document depositories with built-in specialized markup and search functionality such as Folio Views. The kinds of hypertextual structuring capabilities that have become available within corporations often go way beyond the simple links most of us experience while browsing the Web, and we should expect significant advances in new kinds of structuring capabilities in the future that would make what we see now on the Web look as crude as the manuscripts of the early days of writing look to us today.

Some hypertext systems might seem to be only reversing the shift the historians of writing were describing when the codex, the book divided by pages, replaced the roll. But of course electronic text, even when, as in most word processors, it presents a text as a single, continuously scrolling document, is not at all like the scrolling paper document. Navigational aids can be added which allow instantaneous jumping around from one point in the scrolling document to another. Moreover if texts are broken up into discrete units they need not be the arbitrary divisions we are used to with paper pages, but can instead be chunked into meaningfully divided units. What some hypertext writers call 'lexias' are blocks of text which can be made whatever size is appropriate for the task at hand.

Much of the literature on the possibilities of hypertext has focused more on the world of science, literature and scholarship in general, rather than emphasizing the economic impact of such capabilities. Some of the literature focuses on the individual scholar using information on his own, as distinct from the collaborative work context of groupware. The earliest discussion of hypertext capabilities was the 1945 article by Vannevar Bush imagining a tool to help a single scholar work with information, and one of Doug Engelbart's pioneering articles on hypertext was entitled 'Special considerations of the individual as a user, generator, and retriever of information' (1961). Ted Nelson ([1974] 1987; [1980] 1990), who coined the term hypertext, was more oriented to the context of film and the humanities than that of collaboration in business organizations.[37]

The development of hypertext tools, and of the thinking about what they can do for us, has evolved, however, toward the kind of context groupware literature is talking about: collaboration within the workplace and coordination in the marketplace. The focus on the intertextual comes to embrace the context of the interpersonal.[38] Engelbart's work came to focus primarily on the context of groups of co-workers, and how to augment their ability to work together and share knowledge. The team of developers that attempted to implement Ted Nelson's vision came to increasingly emphasize practical business applications of the ideas.[39] Gradually both the thinking about hypertext and the practical systems involving these capabilities came more and more to turn to the world of business.[40] Even when academics focus on scholarly applications they often acknowledge that the capabilities they are describing are highly relevant to the contemporary workplace.

For example, although George Landow (1994: 7–8), like many commentators on hypertext, is primarily interested in literary and scholarly contexts, he has to admit that among its most important domains of application are those in the world of economic production:

> [S]ome of the greatest interest in these new information technologies arises in applications, such as aircraft repair manuals, in which the limitations of book technology have long been apparent. The repair manual for a modern airliner runs to 100000 pages, of which very many, say 25 percent, change each year. …[T]hey probably devote a greater portion of their work day to consulting books than does the average instructor in a department of literature, much of whose time is spent carrying out other activities in which professional reading plays little or no part. Some estimates claim that aircraft mechanics spend more than half their working day performing research in the form of consulting printed text. Therefore any improvement in the way maintenance workers can obtain information promises to save both the individual worker's time and also the

> enormous financial and ecological cost of producing frequently replaced paper documentation. Companies like Boeing Aircraft Corporation have therefore devoted great attention to hypertext repair manuals, which permit the maintenance worker to trace the history of a particular component or system and also to follow out its connections to other components.

Just as the historians of writing such as Eisenstein argued that printing reversed the tendency for information to decay (from errors in copying) and led to gradual improvements in printed editions, so electronic text holds the promise of accelerating that kind of improvement. Hypertext manuals permit a more rapid process of updating and adaptation than was possible in the age of printing whereby separate, identical copies accumulate hand-written markups to note improvements for the next edition. Just as Martin described the complexity dynamic in the evolution of music and (paper) writing, so Landow is suggesting that the increasing complexity of production such as that of modern aircraft is leading us beyond the printed text.

Similarly, groupware tools and the literature about them are converging from the other end toward hypertext themes. Although simple email may give us a general sense of what the interpersonal capabilities are evolving into, it can be misleading to focus on the limited capabilities of the kind of email systems most people are using today. The real potential of groupware may be more evident in the more advanced kinds of applications that permit work groups to collaborate more effectively, for example, networked calendaring, scheduling, and workflow applications. Products such as Lotus Notes Domino and its imitators (which include, but go beyond email) are closer to what the knowledge management literature is talking about than a basic email system is.

Zack and Serino (2000: 306) are getting at the issue of convergence of these kinds of capabilities when they differentiate *distributive* from *collaborative* applications.

> Distributive applications maintain a repository of explicitly encoded knowledge created and managed for subsequent distribution to knowledge customers within or outside the organization. These applications exhibit a sequential flow of information into and out of a central repository, structured to provide flexible access and views of the knowledge. Their primary focus tends to be on the repository and the explicit knowledge it contains, rather than on the contributors, the users, or the tacit knowledge they may hold.
>
> Collaborative applications are focused primarily on supporting interaction among people holding tacit knowledge. … These applications directly support interaction and collaboration within and among knowledge-based teams, enabling 'teams of teams' to form across knowledge communities.

Distributive applications in this terminology are repositories of texts with a complex and to some degree flexible structure, with links, annotations, categorizations or other tools to make it easier to 'navigate' around in it, mark it up, and so forth. But to some extent they may still be conceived of as tools for an individual researcher, as Vannevar Bush had in mind. The traditional focus of groupware, on the other hand, has not been primarily the texts, the documents with which the group works, but the coordination of a set of tasks and responsibilities. What tools such as these can help with is the organizing of the interdependent tasks of a workgroup.

When Zack and Serino (2000: 306) use the term collaborative applications, they are focusing on the way a repository within a collaborative environment becomes a different kind of thing from one conceived only as a store of information:

> In contrast to distributive applications, the repository associated with collaborative applications is a by-product of the interaction, rather than the primary focus of the application. This repository of messages is dynamic and its content emergent. The ability to capture and structure emergent communication within a repository provides a more valuable, enduring, and leverageable knowledge by-product than the personal notes or memories of a traditional conversation or meeting.

As a classic exposition of the idea of groupware (Lotus Institute, 1995) puts it, what is needed is an integration of what are called 'push' and 'pull' capabilities. Push is like email (or sending around paper memos). It is the ability to send somebody information, to alert someone of something. Pull is like the Web (or networked databases, or file cabinets). It is the idea of deliberately going after information. Where the power of groupware really shows itself is when these two modes can work in concert with one another. When the best we could do is tell someone in a memo that the information needed is to be found in a file cabinet on the third floor, we have not integrated push and pull enough to make knowledge-sharing work very well. The simple and now familiar act of sending an email with a URL in it constitutes a powerful kind of functionality that allows us to work with information far more effectively than we could when push and pull were disconnected. The combination of the interpersonal and the intertextual allows organizations to create new knowledge and share existing knowledge in different ways than are supported in a strictly paper-based communication medium.

But again, new media don't replace, but rather rearrange the uses of older media. Projections of the paperless office have been around for decades, while the use of paper continues to grow. But the kinds of things we do in paper documents are changing. Brown and Duguid (2000: 183) point to the misleading notion that paper documents are simply a way to deliver the 'payload' of information, so that electronic documents are to be seen only as an alternative delivery mechanism:

> It seems to us, however, that this information-payload view is the source of many wrongheaded confrontations between paper and information technology. The emerging, more sophisticated view of paper documents, revealing both how they structure information and even how they structure society, is making the old war on paper and paper-based institutions appear not only futile, but wasteful. Complementarity and compliments rather than confrontation and abuse seem more appropriate. In pursuit of better understanding and hence better technology, setting aside the view of documents as no more than information carriers is an important step.

Information technology is not best seen as something that simply delivers content faster and more cheaply and to all corners of the globe. Its most important capability is that of permitting more complex kinds of structures in the texts through which we orient our plans with one another. Fundamentally it is not the ability to rapidly move data across large distances, but the ability to contextualize our articulations through the use of meaningful structures, that constitutes the real promise of these technologies.

2. Flexible Structures for Navigation and Markup

The power of electronic media is in the paradoxical-sounding notion of *flexible structures*. Structure connotes fixity and persistence, but flexibility seems to connote the opposite. Miller et al. had argued that what gave *verbal* discussion its power was its flexibility. The interpersonal give and take of verbal conversation is what gives verbal conversation several of its strengths, what they call the capacity for Revision after publication, Fast publication, and Immediate Feedback. They also argued that one of the factors that has given *written* communication its power has been the opposite kind of strength, what they called Persistence of arguments. Writing is effective in helping interlocutors to express what they mean precisely because words 'written down', unlike words spoken, have the quality of fixity. Fixing what is written down leads to the development of textual structures that permit the strengths that Miller et al. called Revision before publication to improve on the usefulness of the text.

But electronic text is fundamentally a new kind of writing in that it also permits flexibility. Paradoxically you can save an original document in its pure, untouched form, and yet also add to it, say, a layer of markups or annotations of different kinds. What you write into the electronic space can stay; it can be fixed, and so it can be there to return to, to add things to, to re-order, or restructure, or whatever. Its fixity does not prevent it from being the site of a back and forth dialogue, at whatever pace one might prefer for the kind of discussion involved. To 'buy' the fixity and structure, you do not need to give up the valued capability of relatively quick interpersonal interaction.

It seems useful to look at what is going on now in electronic media as essentially an extension of the same sort of evolutionary dynamic that the historians of writing described. The real payoff of electronic media comes from tapping the advantages of the complex structuring of texts that had arisen in the aftermath of Gutenberg, but now in a context where multiple persons are involved in an interactive process with these structured texts.

How effectively we can structure (or restructure) what we say matters in the effectiveness with which we are practically able to work with information. What made innovations in writing effective were the changes that helped those who needed to work with texts to do their work. Just as the early Christians found the codex form of organization handier than the roll for the work they wanted to do with the Bible, so contemporaries working with electronic text are finding advantages in the text's flexible structuring capabilities. Just as it is easier to 'navigate' in a book with pages to quickly find a passage one is looking for, or to relate different portions of the text to one another, than to do so in a single scrolling paper document, so navigational aids in the new electronic media promise to help those who need to work with text to do their work. Just as the development of a navigational aid such as a table of contents, or a running head, or an index proved an advantage in the competition among master printers in the 16th century, so electronic versions of such tools are proving advantageous today.

Just as the real potency of the alphabetic form of writing only became clear when, as a result of printing, large quantities of titles had proliferated, and finding texts by alphabetically ordered lists of titles or authors proved its value, so some of the real potency of alphabetization is only becoming clear now in the age of electronic text. When alphabetized indexes appeared in the back of complex and large works, innovations in printing showed us some of the power of alphabetic text that had not been so apparent to the scribes. But then when full text indexing of electronic documents allows a 'type-ahead' feature to instantly search for any word in a massive document, the power of alphabetical ordering shows more of that same kind of power than had been apparent to the master printers.

We can think of the new flexible structuring capabilities in terms of navigation and markup. The potential for navigating, for finding one's way around in a large, complex electronic text, constitutes a fundamental advantage of the new media. What is written down not only gets shaped into a single form with structural elements that aid the reader, as happened with improvements to printing, but can get shaped into a 'meta-structure'. It can be given a form in which alternative structures can be selected, at the choice of the reader. The single hierarchical structure of a table of contents of a printed text can help a reader locate something, but an electronic text can offer the reader a choice of a variety of alternative hierarchical structures. Different readers approach texts with different questions in mind, so that equipping those who work with text with a flexible range of alternative ways of viewing the material can aid tremendously in the text's usefulness.

Think in this context of the limitations of file cabinets and folders as a way of storing corporate documents, as opposed to a networked database with software that offers the reader alternative hierarchies. A file cabinet takes advantage of the power of alphabetic ordering, but can only take advantage once, so to speak, in that it has to select one kind of order over other possibilities. Say we are keeping folders with information about both co-workers and the tasks they are working on. When we come to the file cabinet to look for information about a person, we would be hoping the filing system has ordered them by name. If we come with a different question, like 'Who is on this task?' we hope instead that the information is stored by task.[41] Paper documents force us to make a decision, to settle for one hierarchy as the least bad alternative, and stick with it. Clearly being able to have a networked database instead of a file cabinet to store information would make a major difference in our ability to get to it, to find what we are looking for, and to present it to others in ways that reflect our own meaning. Now we can say, let's view this list of documents in task order, or in order by name, or date, or whatever.

This capacity for re-structuring is not only an issue of how we manage to find information we are specifically looking for. It shapes our ability to convey information to others in a contextualized manner which helps us to orient ourselves to one another's meaning. If I am trying to convey something about the personnel working on several tasks, if I order the information by the last names of the person, and juxtapose to each name a task in the project that this person is responsible for, this helps the reader to focus on how the labor time of any particular person is allocated. But the same information in order by task, with names appearing under their tasks, conveys quite different meaning, and is useful in different situations. The structuring of the content makes a difference, a big difference, in how it can get read.

Electronic media open up the possibility for a wide variety of other navigational capabilities. Printed works often contain internal cross-references such as when we say something like 'see page 5 on this point', but the jumplink represents a dramatic reduction in the costs of following such connections. Convenience is not *mere* convenience. Electronic texts can make it so easy to follow links of this kind that in effect the reader's experience undergoes a qualitative shift. The typical experience in a book culture is that of the linear working through of a text in the author's order, from beginning to end. The typical experience on the Web is one of following the connections that look promising to the reader.

It is with markup capabilities that the distinctive differences of electronic media really become clear. Printed materials can of course get marked up. For a long time people have been inserting annotations into the margins, noting page numbers worth comparing, applying highlighter pens to key passages, and so forth. In a corporate context it is common to duplicate a document, encouraging a group of people to mark it up separately with comments, collect the marked-up copies, and then produce a new draft. The need to go through such a process reflects the need to bring the interpersonal and intertextual closer together. But the awkwardness of doing this in paper documents shows the potential of electronic media. Printing had the effect of separating the writing from the reading process. Markups in paper represent an attempt to introduce interactivity into an inflexible medium, leading to proliferation of parallel markups. The annotations in most scholars' personal copies of books and journal articles constitute a single further step of dialogue, a response to the original argument, but the dialogue only rarely includes a third step, a rejoinder by the original author. What I have been calling the slash between writing and reading cuts off the process from what might have been a fruitful, on-going interchange.

Silvio Gaggi (1997: 103) points to the potential for hypertext to remove the 'slash', to reconnect what paper writing had separated:

> In hypertext, as Landow and others describe it, readers can append their own comments and responses, add new nodes or lexias, to any parts of the text that they are interested in, and they can create new links among the various lexias. Thus, the distinction between reader and writer is attenuated, perhaps even dissolved entirely. The text is no longer a one-way communication system in which information and ideas proceed only from author to reader, but a communication system in which all participants can contribute to and affect the content and direction of the conversation.

Being able in electronic media to mark up a single shared text over a network opens up a crucial new kind of advantage. In effect it makes the text into a living forum, something more like words in a verbal dialogue, and yet without losing the advantages of fixity. One can view the original version without the annotations and other markups, or one can view a selection of markups that come from certain participants, or that raise certain questions. A hypertext document, for example, can be marked up with a categorizing tool that allows the reader to 'collect' the passages of the document that pertain to a certain issue, and then at a click, to view only those passages juxtaposed to one another. That view of selected quotations can be shared with others looking at the same document, and they can add other categories to it, yielding other selected representations of the document.

Moreover, the markups can themselves become additional navigational aids. We are already used to the way our marked up copies of printed text can become more useful when we've engaged with them, say, by marking the key passages with a red pen, or adding some marginalia. With electronic media it becomes possible to use the capacity of the computer to search the markups themselves, or to reorganize information in terms of the accrued layers it has accumulated from active readers.

The advantages of adding groupware and hypertext capabilities to our repertoire of kinds of articulation can be summed up by reference to the table I borrowed from Miller, Tribble, Pandya, and Stiegler for comparing talking with writing (Table 12.1). Electronic media are beginning to transcend the limitations of most of the tradeoffs identified in that table. The main purpose Miller et al. were trying to serve with this contrast was not only to reiterate the kind of analysis Walter Ong and others have undertaken to compare the two great pre-electronic discourse media we have had up to now, talking and (paper) writing, but to point the way toward the future. They set up these two columns depicting the relative advantages of pre-electronic media in order to illustrate the point that a fully-fledged groupware/hypertext system should be able to capture many of the advantages of both columns. Their point was that adding a third mode to our discursive repertoire would make an astonishing difference in society's capacity to work with text, a difference on the order of what happened with the inventions of writing and the printing press.

It seems natural to ask what kinds of effects such technological changes could be having on entrepreneurship. Might they be not only what are driving the wealth-creation process of certain organizations, as many authors in the knowledge management literature believe, but also what are driving the economic development of society as a whole? These kinds of technologies are bringing about a profound transformation of the nature of organizations and management, and they may be primary causes of the new economy's prosperity.

3. Conclusion: Mutual Orientation and Wealth

This chapter has tried to view the new electronic technologies through the lens of the literature on the history of writing and the printing press. That literature, in turn, has been viewed through the lens of the Austrian school's notion of subjectively meaningful structures. Significant changes in our ability to meaningfully structure what we are saying have transformed the workings of entrepreneurship in the past, in a manner that may be highly suggestive for thinking about the transformations we are undergoing today.

Entrepreneurship is not a direct 'seeing' of opportunities. The entrepreneurial process involves the mutual orientation of different persons to one another. Somehow a producer's perspective of what possible production methods might work needs to come into some degree of coordination with a consumer's perspective of what goods are most desirable. I see an opportunity mainly through coming to an understanding about what somebody is 'saying' about the world. This means that we need to attend to the economy's conversations through which we try to explain what we want, what we are trying to do, and so on. Entrepreneurship is fundamentally dependent on the media in which human communication takes place. Creating and sharing electronic information over a network is a fundamentally different communications medium from that of the creation and sharing of paper documents. The way co-workers and market participants are able to share articulations with one another has been profoundly transformed, especially over the past decade. The theory of entrepreneurship ought to be taking these changes into account.

Computers and modern communications media have undoubtedly contributed to the productivity of labor and other factors; however, it could be that the recent general prosperity is being driven as much by improvements in tools for the exercise of the general coordinative function of entrepreneurship as it is by measurable increases in the productivity of specific factors of production: labor, capital and land. This kind of orientative contribution of the tools would be difficult to measure in productivity studies, but may represent one of the main driving forces of wealth. The claim of the knowledge management literature is that certain innovations in information technology are transforming the contemporary workplace and marketplace, and I am arguing that these kinds of changes may be propelling the entrepreneurial process. One of the fundamental changes that information technology may be bringing about is enhancing the ability of market participants to subjectively *orient* themselves to one another and to their world.

In other words, something that sounds utterly subjective and mental, the way people orient themselves to one another, and in particular to one another's articulations, may be what underlies the very real, objective improvements in living conditions in the new economy. We make ourselves wealthier by making ourselves better understood.

NOTES

1. Estimates of the productivity of the American worker suggest that a dramatic shift has occurred in the last two decades of the 20th century. Using a productivity index based on 100 for the year 1840, labor productivity in 1980 was under 600, but by 2000 reached about 1000. In that 20 years Gross Domestic Product in the US went from around $5 trillion to over $8 trillion (in 1998 dollars). See United States Department of Commerce (1999).
2. I refer to the contemporary Austrian school in the sense elaborated in Karen Vaughn's book on *Austrian Economics in America*, spanning the period from the work of Carl Menger in the 1870s, through the writings in Europe of Ludwig Mises, Friedrich Hayek, and Ludwig Lachmann, all the way to the work of the contemporary American Austrians such as Kirzner, Rizzo, Garrison and Boettke. See for example, the journals *Advances in Austrian Economics* and *Review of Austrian Economics.*
3. These terms are intended to name capabilities that may be found in a wide range of different software products, not to refer to particular products. There are hypertext and groupware features in Microsoft Word, in the leading web browsers, in database programs, and other products that are widely used in contemporary organizations.
4. I focus here only on the issue of the impact of technological changes in media on entrepreneurship as a wealth-generating process. For a fascinating study of the impact of writing and printing on political power, see Dudley (1991).
5. That question will in all likelihood not be resolvable until future historians, with the advantage of historical distance and extensive interpretive investigations of historical documents, are able to weigh the relative impact of various elements of the current economic scene. Those who do take up this empirical question should look for changes in the economy that may have improved on our capacity for entrepreneurial coordination. This chapter is only trying to make clearer conceptually what is involved in entrepreneurial coordination.
6. I will be drawing from scholars such as Walter Ong, Jack Goody, Elizabeth Eisenstein, Henri-Jean Martin and Roger Chartier on the way the evolution of writing, the printing press, and the rise of literacy have transformed human society.
7. I am referring to a specific segment of the business literature associated with knowledge management and groupware technologies, to be discussed in Part C. This literature may look as if it has nothing to do with Austrian economics. The theoretical contributions to the concept of entrepreneurship within the Austrian school of economics on the one hand, have had little to say about information technology. The practical contributions to the understanding of knowledge management within the business literature, on the other hand, have had little to say about economic theory. Moreover, the economics I have been drawing from, such as the work of Kirzner and Lachmann, seems to have a completely theoretical concern: how to think clearly about the role entrepreneurs play in the market process. The knowledge management work has a completely pragmatic concern, how to help businesses who are deploying new information technologies to make the best return possible on their high technology investments. Yet in fact these scholarly literatures pertain to one another more than one might expect. Theoretical and practical concerns are not best understood as unconnected with one another, and in this case each of these literatures might benefit from exposure to the other. Both are really interested in what lies behind objective wealth creation.
8. The Austrian school has contributed to misunderstanding here. Friedrich Wieser called subjectivism a psychological method, and there are lapses to psychologistic language in all the Austrian writings on subjectivism. If taken seriously this psychologism would lead to the position Laslo Csontos (1998) calls methodological solipsism. For an attempt to sort out the legitimate from the illegitimate meanings of the words subjective and objective, see my 'The Progress of Subjectivism' (Lavoie 1991a).
9. Jean Baudrillard and some other post-modern philosophers seem to find the idea frightening that the whole economy might rest on nothing more solid than our own

subjective orientations and our mutual interpretations of one another's interpretations.... But we live in a world where survey reports on 'consumer confidence' are among the leading news items. Most of us, in these ironic and post-modern times, can learn to live with the idea that subjective points of view underlie the objective realities of markets. The point of this chapter is more to ask how such a process of mutual interpretation might depend on the communicative media in which it takes place.

10. The fact that the economy is ultimately rooted in subjective orientations does not imply, the Austrians insisted, that we need to abandon the idea of a systematic study of economics. They understand their subjectivism in a way that does not reject the sort of objectivity required for scholarship, but instead just identifies a limit to the scientists' ambitions. The principle says beyond this line (subjective preferences) we cannot go, as scientists. We cannot explain why a consumer prefers this to that, but we can work out the systematic consequences of such preferences. The Austrians see economics as a systemic study of the workings of this subjectively based but nonetheless systemic process. There can be systematic unintended consequences of purposeful action. Markets are in some sense an objective reality, in that they exhibit systemic patterns and regularities that can be studied. Yet this objective reality is founded ultimately on nothing more (or less) solid than human perspectives. For a discussion of objectivity in scholarship, see Lavoie (1995).
11. See Kirzner (1973; 1979; 1985).
12. In my paper, 'The discovery and interpretation of profit opportunities: culture and the Kirznerian entrepreneur', (Lavoie 1991b) I developed this point about the culturelessness of Kirzner's notion of the entrepreneur. See also Lavoie and Chamlee-Wright (2000).
13. Of course from this point of view it may be that indirectly, through communication with Friday, Crusoe will be able to see new objective opportunities for wealth creation, new ways of squeezing wealth from nature. When Friday knows an objective fact Crusoe doesn't yet know there can be wealth improvement via communication. But because Kirzner starts from the isolated individual and treats this as illuminating the very essence of entrepreneurship, his approach is apt to downplay mutual articulation processes.
14. One possible objection to the treatment of markets as discourse would be the argument that ordinary discourse is merely talk, the exchange of ideas, whereas market exchange is a form of action (or interaction). Two agents who talk to one another are not acting, are not actually doing anything, whereas two agents who engage in a market transaction are not just communicating, they are accomplishing something, in particular they are altering property ownership and thus shifting the whole framework in which future action can take place. They are, this argument goes, not simply enjoying some idle chatter; they are changing the world. But can we really maintain this distinction between communicating and acting? Is not the act of speaking or writing also an action? From the Austrian point of view a 'merely verbal' exchange is every bit as much a matter of *doing* something as an exchange of ownership. In other words, to describe verbal or market processes as communicative is not to claim that they are merely communicative (whatever that would mean). It is not to deny that any of these communicative processes involve doing real things in the world that can have lasting effects. The world of meaning, after abandoning the subject/object dichotomy, *is* the world of the real. To be sure, some human discourse is only 'small talk' and of little significance, just as some physical actions are of no consequence. But some discursive acts, say for example Martin Luther King's 'Free at Last' speech, are of profound importance, changing forever the shape of human affairs.
15. The point is not to belittle the differences between markets and other communicative processes. A culture in which these special kinds of texts we call prices are deployed in our conversations is as different from one without prices as a literate culture is from a pre-literate one. Some may object that prices are so different from words that it is misleading to call them texts at all. I do agree with the point that there are important differences here. Of particular importance, I think, is the fact that these kinds of texts make possible a process of economic calculation and the imputation of value appraisements across different stages of the structure of production. There is no way that non-price language can convey the

relative value of higher-order goods to entrepreneurs who are several stages away from those goods in the capital structure. I don't want to slight such differences as these, but I would insist that it can be very useful to think of market processes as a particular kind of linguistic communicative process whose similarities to verbal and written discourses are as important as the differences.

16. Brice Wachterhauser (1999) puts the point this way in his recent book, a summary of the work of Hans-Georg Gadamer's philosophical position.
17. Böhm-Bawerk ([1884] 1959) deployed this term in his classic work on capital, as did some other Austrians. It has been thought to be misleading in that it suggests that there would be a single dimension, length, in which to measure the extension of the capital structure. For a useful contemporary elaboration of Austrian capital theory, see Lewin (1999).
18. I get the idea of social learning if not the phrase from Hayek, and I have tried to elaborate the idea in my books on the critique of central planning: (Lavoie 1985a; 1985b).
19. As with capital, in a textual structure everything is shaped by the meanings things have to the participants, in this case, the writers and readers, but the structure is nevertheless real.
20. As Roger Chartier put it in his book *Forms and Meanings* (1995: 2): 'When the "same" text is apprehended through very different mechanisms of representation, it is no longer the same. Each of its forms obeys specific conventions that mold and shape the work according to the laws of that form, and connect it in differing ways, with other arts, other genres, and other texts. If we want to understand the appropriations and interpretations of a text in their full historicity we need to identify the effect, in terms of meaning, that its material forms produced.'
21. Walter Ong (1977: 46) points out that using the term 'media' to designate alternative technological ways of 'managing the word', such as talking, writing by hand, printing, and the Web, 'can be misleading, encouraging us to think of writing, print, and electronic devices simply as ways of "moving information" over some sort of space intermediate between one person and another'. But changes in media do not just help us transport words around; they open up whole 'new ways of thinking, previously inconceivable questions, and new ways of searching for responses'.
22. It looks to me as if this literature has been largely neglected by economists, and that the neglect goes both ways. The literature on the history of writing has said little explicitly about the impact of writing on economic processes per se, though often it is easy enough to see the implications of broader changes on economic phenomena.
23. The changes in our conversational media have been so profound that they transform the very nature of conversation itself, so that the thing that keeps undergoing these radical transformations is barely recognizable as a 'conversation' any more. Yet non-verbal communicative processes can be said to share with normal verbal conversation enough fundamental features that it makes sense to stretch the word 'conversation' to include them.
24. I am skeptical about what sounds like a privileging of the verbal over the written here, a point that the philosopher Jacques Derrida ([1967] 1974) has challenged under the label of phonocentrism. See also Ulmer (1985) for an application of Derrida's work to electronic media.
25. Ong sees great philosophical significance in this fact, attributing to the writing/reading mode of discourse the dominant attitudes of philosophical modernism: the exaggerated fondness for a kind of detached objectivity.
26. This way of putting the qualitative and quantitative dimensions of the transformation in media is suggested by Eisenstein (1979: 51).
27. The dramatic fall in the cost of computing in our own time comes to mind. There are good reasons to suspect that computer-based writing will have the kind of transformative effect on our ability to work with text that the revolution in printing had. The printing revolution changed us from a society in which readers were a minority, into a literate society, a society in which reading is almost universal, though authors are still a minority.

It is possible that the computer revolution, when it has fully exerted its effects, might make us into a society of authors.

28. For example, Martin (1995: 283–4) refers to estimates that the paper mills in 18th century France were producing about 2 million reams of paper per year, of which the printing industry was using about half a million. This suggests there was a very significant use of paper in hand-written documents in government and business.
29. Admittedly, we still err in this regard. The sheer fact that we have new capabilities does not mean we will deploy them in their best domains. For a valuable (if for my taste overly skeptical) view of the ways in which having new capabilities can lead to undesirable consequences, see Heim's ([1987] 1999) philosophical study of the effects of word processing on writing.
30. These authors are taking up the same questions the historians of writing were raising about the differences between oral and written culture; however, they are not historians. Like many of the writers in the knowledge management literature whom I will discuss in the next section, they are more practitioners than academics. They are a group of software engineers who have worked extensively on developing groupware and hypertext capabilities. Although this article emphasized the advantages to science and the growth of knowledge, their insights about the differential advantages of verbal and written media are also applicable to the changing nature of entrepreneurship.
31. The focus on the world of scholarship, as distinct from the economic focus of this chapter, makes this 'visibility' point misleading here. Business memoranda in paper have long played this role, where a definite, specific, audience is reached in a written medium.
32. See for example, Brynjolfsson's often cited paper 'The productivity paradox of information technology: review and assessment' (1993). See also the articles and books at the knowledge management website: http://www.strassmann.com.
33. The book includes a set of influential articles that were published in the 1990s in some of the leading organizational journals, such as *Organizational Science*, *Sloan Management Review* and *California Management Review*.
34. See Nevis, Dibella and Gould ([1995] 2000) and Powell ([1998] 2000).
35. See Cohen and Azzarello (2000) and Inkpen ([1996] 2000).
36. Several of the authors discussed earlier who have elaborated on the history of writing, such as Martin, when they do talk about contemporary technological media, use the language of information and data processing.
37. See also Eric Drexler (1991) for a summary of the implications for scientific work of a full hypertext publishing system along the lines of Nelson's vision.
38. Thus when Nonaka (1994: 35) coins the term the 'hypertext organization', trying to draw out aspects of hypertextual organization of text that have analogies in the organization of organizations, he is emphasizing this convergence. He draws attention not only to intertextual structures of text, but also the interpersonal advantages sharing structured text: 'Hypertext … links related concepts and areas of knowledge to allow a problem to be viewed from many angles. In many ways, this is analogous to the ability of individuals to relate stories in different ways according to the nature of the audience. The same knowledge might be used but in different formats, making it easier to draw relationships between different sets of information.

    The core feature of the hypertext organization is the ability to switch between various "contexts" of knowledge creation to accommodate changing requirements from situations both inside and outside the organization.'
39. By the way, the Miller et al. co-authors I have cited here were among the developers who were trying to implement Nelson's vision.
40. When Tim Berners-Lee (1999), who could be called the inventor of the Web, describes the early inspiration for the hypertext markup language, he places emphasis on the needs he and others at CERN had to try to facilitate collaborative work.
41. Or we duplicate copies of information into different filing locations in order to improve the odds of finding what we're looking for, but that leads to other serious problems, in trying to maintain changes in two different locations.

BIBLIOGRAPHY

Baetjer, Howard (1998), *Software As Capital: An Economic Perspective On Software Engineering*, Los Alamitos, CA: IEEE Computer Society.

Berners-Lee, Tim and Fischetti, Mark (1999), *Weaving the Web: The Original Design and Ultimate Destiny of the World Wide Web*, New York: HarperBusiness.

Böhm-Bawerk, Eugen von ([1884; 1889; 1912] 1959), *Capital and Interest*, South Holland, IL: Libertarian Press.

Brand, Stewart (1994), *How Buildings Learn: What Happens After They're Built*, New York: Penguin.

Brown, John Seely and Duguid, Paul (1998), 'Organizing knowledge' *California Management Review* **40** (3) (reprinted in David Smith, *Knowledge, Groupware, and the Internet* Boston: Butterworth-Heinemann, 2000).

Brown, John Seely and Duguid, Paul (2000), *The Social Life of Information*, Boston, MA: Harvard Business School Press.

Brynjolfsson, Erik (1993), 'The productivity paradox of information technology: review and assessment', *Communications of the ACM*, **36** (12), 66–77.

Bush, Vannevar (1945), 'As we may think', *Atlantic Monthly*, **176** (1), 641–9, reprinted in Theodor Holm Nelson, Literary Machines Sausalito, CA: Mindful Press, 1990.

Chartier, Roger, (ed.) (1989), *The Culture of Print: Power and Uses of Print in Early Modern Europe*, Princeton, NJ: Princeton University Press.

Chartier, Roger (1994), *The Order of Books: Readers, Authors, and Libraries in Europe between the Fourteenth and Eighteenth Centuries*, trans. Lydia G. Cochrane, Stanford, CA.: Stanford University Press.

Chartier, Roger (1995), *Forms and Meanings, Texts, Performances, and Audiences from Codex to Computer*, Philadelphia: University of Pennsylvania Press.

Cohen, Don and Azzarello, Richard (2000), 'Growing intellectual capital at IBM: more than technology', in David Smith, *Knowledge, Groupware, and the Internet*, Boston: Butterworth-Heinemann.

Csontos, Laslo (1998), 'Subjectivism and ideal types: Lachmann and the methodological legacy of Max Weber', in R. Koppl and G. Mongiovi, *Subjectivism and Economic Analysis*, New York: Routledge.

Cubeddu, Raimondo (1993), *The Philosophy of the Austrian School* (trans. Rachel M. Costa), New York: Routledge.

Derrida, Jacques ([1967] 1974), *Of Grammatology*, trans. Gayatri Chakravorty Spivak, originally published as *De la Grammatologie*, Les Editions de Minuit (1967), Baltimore: The Johns Hopkins University Press.

Drexler, K.E. (1991), 'Hypertext and the evolution of knowledge', *Social Intelligence*, **1** (2).

Dudley, Leonard M. (1991), *The Word and the Sword: How Techniques of Information and Violence Have Shaped our World*, Cambridge, MA: Blackwell.

Eisenstein, Elizabeth L. (1979), *The Printing Press as an Agent of Change, Communications and Cultural Transformations in Early-Modern Europe* New York: Cambridge University Press.

Engelbart, Douglas C. (1961), 'Special considerations of the individual as a user, generator, and retriever of information', *American Documentation*, **12** (2), April.

Engelbart, Douglas C. (1989), 'Bootstrapping organizations into the 21st century'. Paper presented at a seminar at the Software Engineering Institute, Pittsburg.

Engelbart, Douglas C. and Hooper, K. (1988), 'The augmentation system framework', in S. Ambron and K. Hoope (eds), *Interactive Multimedia*, Redmond, WA: Microsoft Press.

Gaggi, Silvio (1997), *From Text to Hypertext, Decentering the Subject in Fiction, Film, the Visual Arts, and Electronic Media*, Philadelphia: The University of Pennsylvania Press.

Goody, Jack ([1987] 1993), *The Interface Between the Written and the Oral*, New York: Cambridge University Press.

Heim, Michael ([1987] 1999), *Electric Language: A Philosophical Study of Word Processing*, 2nd edn, New Haven: Yale University Press.

Inkpen, Andrew C. ([1996] 2000), 'Creating knowledge through collaboration', *California Management Review*, **39** (1) (reprinted in David Smith, *Knowledge, Groupware, and the Internet*, Boston: Butterworth-Heinemann, 2000).

Kirzner, Israel M. (1973), *Competition and Entrepreneurship*, Chicago: University of Chicago Press.

Kirzner, Israel M. (1979), *Perception, Opportunity, and Profit: Studies in the Theory of Entrepreneurship*, Chicago: University of Chicago Press.

Kirzner, Israel M. (1985a), *Discovery and the Capitalist Process*, Chicago: University of Chicago Press.

Lachmann, Ludwig M. (1951), 'The science of human action', *Economica*, **18**, November, 412–27; reprinted in Ludwig Lachmann, *Capital, Expectations, and the Market Process: Essays on the Theory of the Market Economy.* Kansas City: Sheed, Andrews & McMeel (1977).

Lachmann, Ludwig M. (1956), *Capital and Its Structure*, London: Bell & Sons.

Lachmann, Ludwig M. ([1966] 1977), 'The significance of the Austrian school of economics in the history of ideas', translated from an article published in *Zeitschrift für Nationalökonomie* 26 (February 1966) by Robert F. Ambacher and Walter Grinder, in Ludwig Lachmann, *Capital, Expectations, and the Market Process: Essays on the Theory of the Market Economy*, Kansas City: Sheed, Andrews & McMeel (1977).

Lachmann, Ludwig M. (1971), *The Legacy of Max Weber*, Berkeley: Glendessary Press.

Lachmann, Ludwig M. (1977), *Capital, Expectations, and the Market Process: Essays on the Theory of the Market Economy*, Kansas City: Sheed, Andrews & McMeel.

Lachmann, Ludwig M. (1978), *Capital and its Structure*, Kansas City: Sheed, Andrews & McMeel.

Lachmann, Ludwig M. (1994), *Expectation and the meaning of Institutions: Essays in Economics*, London/New York: Routledge.

Landow, George P. (1994), *Hyper/Text/Theory*, Baltimore: Johns Hopkins University Press.

Lavoie, Don (1985a), *Rivalry and Central Planning: The Socialist Calculation Debate Reconsidered*, New York: Cambridge University Press.

Lavoie, Don (1985b), *National Economic Planning: What Is Left?*, Cambridge, Mass.: Ballinger.

Lavoie, Don (1991a), 'The progress of subjectivism', Mark Blaug and Neil de Marchi (eds), *Appraising Modern Economics: Studies in the Methodology of Scientific Research Programmes*, Aldershot, UK and Brookfield, US: Edward Elgar, pp. 470–86.

Lavoie, Don (1991b), 'The discovery and interpretation of profit opportunities: culture and the Kirznerian entrepreneur', in Brigitte Berger (ed.) *The Culture of Entrepreneurship*, San Francisco: Institute for Contemporary Studies; translated into French as *Esprit d'entreprise, cultures et sociétés* (Paris: Maxima, 1994).

Lavoie, Don (1995), 'The "objectivity" of scholarship and the ideal of the university', *Advances in Austrian Economics*, 2B: 371–403.

Lavoie, Don and Chamlee-Wright, Emily (2000), *Culture and Enterprise: The Development, Representation, and Morality of Business*, New York: Routledge.

Leonard, Dorothy and Sensiper, Sylvia (1998), 'The role of tacit knowledge in group innovation', *California Management Reviw* **40** (3) (reprinted in David Smith, *Knowledge, Groupware, and the Internet*, Boston: Butterworth-Heinemann, 2000).

Lewin, Peter (1999), *Capital in Disequilibrium: The Role of Capital in a Changing World*, New York: Routledge.

Lotus Institute (1995), 'Groupware – communication, collaboration, coordination', unpublished manuscript.

Lucas, Henry C. Jr (1999), *Information Technology and the Productivity Paradox: Assessing the Value of Investing in IT*, New York: Oxford University Press.

Martin, Henri Jean (1995), *The History and Power of Writing*, trans. Lydia G. Cochrane, Chicago: The University of Chicago Press.

Miller, Mark S., Tribble, E. Dean, Pandya, Ravi, and Stiegler, Marc (1995), 'The open society and its media', in James Lewis and Markus Krummenacker (eds), *Prospects in Nanotechnology: Towards Molecular Manufacturing*, New York: Wiley.

Mises, Ludwig von ([1949] 1966), *Human Action: A Treatise on Economics*, 3rd edn, revised, Chicago: Henry Regnery Company.

Moore, Stephen and Simon, Julian L. (2000), *It's Getting Better all the Time: 100 Greatest Trends of the Last 100 Years*, Washington: Cato Institute.

Nelson, Theodor H. ([1974] 1987), *Computer Lib/Dream Machines*, Redmond, Washington: Microsoft Press.

Nelson, Theodor H. ([1980] 1990), *Literary Machines, Edition 90.1*, Sausalito, CA: Mindful Press.

Nevis, Edwin, Dibella, Anthony J., and Gould, Janet M. ([1995] 2000), 'Understanding organizations as learning systems', *Sloan Management Review*, Winter, pp. 73–85 (reprinted in David Smith, *Knowledge, Groupware, and the Internet* Boston: Butterworth-Heinemann, 2000).

Nonaka, Ikujiro (1994), 'A dynamic theory of organizational knowledge creation', *Organizational Science*, **5** (1) (reprinted in David Smith, *Knowledge, Groupware, and the Internet* Boston: Butterworth-Heinemann, 2000).

Nonaka, Ikujiro and Takeuchi, Hirotaka (1995), *The Knowledge Creating Company: How Japanese Companies Create the Dynamics of Innovation*, New York: Oxford University Press.

Ong, Walter J. (1977), *Interfaces of the Word: Studies in the Evolution of Consciousness and Culture*, Ithaca, NY: Cornell University Press.

Ong, Walter J. (1982), *Orality and Literacy: The Technologizing of the World*, London: Routledge.

Powell, Walter W. ([1998] 2000), 'Learning from collaboration: knowledge and networks in the biotechnology and parmaceutical industries', *California Management Review*, **40** (3) (reprinted in David Smith, *Knowledge, Groupware, and the Internet*, Boston: Butterworth-Heinemann, 2000).

Smith, David E. (ed.) (2000), *Knowledge, Groupware, and the Internet*, Boston: Butterworth-Heinemann.

Spinosa, Charles, Flores, Fernando, and Dreyfus, Hubert L. (1997), *Disclosing New Worlds: Entrepreneurship, Democratic Action, and the Cultivation of Solidarity* Cambridge, Mass.: MIT Press.

Steinberg, S. H. ([1961] 1974), *Five Hundred Years of Printing*, Harmondsworth, UK: Penguin.

Thorp, John (1998), *The Information Paradox: Realizing the Business Benefits of Information Technology*, New York: McGraw-Hill.

Ulmer, Gregory L. (1985), *Applied Grammatology: Poste-Pedagogy from Jacques Derrida to Joseph Beuys*, Baltimore: The Johns Hopkins University Press.

United States Department of Commerce (1999), *Statistical Abstract of the United States*, No. 1382, Washington DC: Bureau of the Census.

Vaughn, Karen I. (1993), *Austrian Economics in America: The Migration of a Tradition*, New York: Cambridge University Press.

Wachterhauser, Brice R. (1999), *Beyond Being: Gadamer's Post-Platonic Hermeneutical Ontology*, Evanston, IL: Northwestern University Press.

Zack, Michael H. and McKenny, James L. (2000), 'Social context and interaction in ongoing computer-supported management groups', in David Smith, *Knowledge, Groupware, and the Internet*, Boston: Butterworth-Heinemann.

Zack, Michael H. and Serino, Michael (2000), 'Knowledge management and collaboration technologies', in David Smith, *Knowledge, Groupware, and the Internet*, Boston: Butterworth-Heinemann.

Bibliography of Don Lavoie's publications

Compiled with commentary by Bill Tulloh

PUBLISHED WORKS

1975

'MUSIM – Simulation of Music Composition Using GASP', *Proceedings of the 1974 Winter Simulation Conference, 2,* WSC/SIGSIM of the Association for Computing Machinery, Inc. (with Alan Aho and James Paprocki).

1977

'From Hollis and Nell to Hollis and Mises', *Journal of Libertarian Studies*, **1** (4), 323–36.

1978

'Austrian Economics Seminar, Part I: 1975–76', *The Austrian Economics Newsletter*, **1** (2), Spring.

'Austrian Economics Seminar, Part II: 1976–77', *The Austrian Economics Newsletter*, 1(3), Fall.

'Shackle: a critical sampling', *Journal of Libertarian Studies*, 2(2), 125–34.

'The relevance of the subjective', *Reason Papers*, **4**, 95–101.

1979

'Austrian Economics Seminar, Part III: 1977–78', *The Austrian Economics Newsletter*, **2** (1), Spring.

'Austrian Economics Seminar, Part IV: 1978–79', *The Austrian Economics Newsletter*, **2** (2), Fall.

1981

'A critique of the standard account of the socialist calculation debate', *Journal of Libertarian Studies*, **5**, 41–87 (translated into Japanese by Takeshi Hinata in *Journal of Management Information Science*, 4, February, 61–98).
'Introduction to special issue on "An Economic Critique of Socialism"', *Journal of Libertarian Studies*, **5** (1).
'Mises, the calculation debate, and market socialism', *Wirtschaftspolitische Blatter*, **4**.

1982

'Introduction to *Solidarnosc z Wolnoscia* [Solidarity with Liberty]', a collection of essays collected, edited and introduced by Don Lavoie, translated into Polish by Ewa Rurarz, Washington, DC: Cato Institute.
'The development of the Misesian theory of interventionism', Chapter 14 of Israel Kirzner (ed.) *Method, Process and Austrian Economics: Essays in Honor ofLudwig von Mises*, Lexington, Mass.: Lexington Books.

1983

'Economic calculation and monetary stability', *Cato Journal*, **3** (1) (Spring).
'Some strengths in Marx's disequilibrium theory of money', *Cambridge Journal of Economics*, **7**, pp. 55–68.

1984

'Review of T. W. Hutchison's *The Politics and Philosophy of Economics: Marxians, Keynesians and Austrians*', *Market Process*, **2** (1), (Winter).
'Two varieties of industrial policy: a critique', *Cato Journal*, **4** (2) Fall.

1985

National Economic Planning: What is Left?, Cambridge, Mass.: Ballinger.
'Reflections on the 1984 Mont Pelerin Society meetings', *Market Process*, **3** (1), Spring, reprinted in newsletter of Mont Pelerin Society.
'Review article: on *Rebuilding America* by Alperovitz and Faux', *Comparative Economic Studies.* **21** (3), Fall.
Rivalry and Central Planning: The Socialist Calculation Debate Reconsidered, first book in Cambridge series on 'Historical perspectives on modern

economics', New York: Cambridge University Press (translated into Japanese by the publisher Seizansh).

1986

'Euclideanism versus hermeneutics: a re-interpretation of Misesian apriorism', in Kirzner (ed.) *Subjectivism, Intelligibility, and Economic Understanding: Essays in Honor ofLudwig M. Lachmann on his Eightieth Birthday*, New York: New York University Press.

'Marx, the quantity theory, and the theory of value', *History of Political Economy*, **18** (1), 155–70; reprinted in J.E. King (ed.) *Marxian Economics, volume II*, Aldershot, UK and Brookfield, US: Edward Elgar (1990); reprinted in Mark Blaug (ed.), *Karl Marx 1818–1883*, Aldershot, UK and Brookfield, US: Elgar Edward (1991).

'Review of C. B. Macpherson's *The Rise and Fall of Economic Justice and Other Papers*', *Journal of Comparative Economics*, 10, June, pp. 195–7.

'The market as a procedure for discovery and conveyance of inarticulate knowledge', *Comparative Economic Studies*, **28**, Spring.

1987

'Polanyi's critique of objectivity', *Critical Review*, **1** (3), Summer, 109–16.

'Political and economic illusions of socialism', *Critical Review*, **1**, pp. 1–35.

'Reply to Mueller', *Critical Review*, **1** (2), Spring, pp. 78–82.

'The accounting of interpretations and the interpretation of accounts: the communicative function of "The Language of Business"', *Accounting, Organizations and Society*, **12**, pp. 579–604.

1988

'A political philosophy for the market process', *Market Process*, **6** (2) Fall.

1989

'Economic chaos or spontaneous order? Implications for political economy of the new view of science', *Cato Journal*, **8** (3), 613–35.

'Economic regulation: theory and history', *Market Process*, **7** (1), Spring, pp. 22–5.

1990

'Computation, incentives, and discovery: the cognitive function of markets in market-socialism', *The Annals of the American Academy of Political and Social Science*, **507**, pp. 72–9.

'Hermeneutics, subjectivity, and the Lester/Machlup debate: toward a more anthropological approach to empirical economics', in Warren Samuels (ed.) *Economics As Discourse*, Boston: Kluwer Academic Publishing.

'High tech Hayekians: some possible research topics in the economics of computation' *Market Process*, **8**, with Howard Baetjer and William Tulloh.

'Introduction to F.A. Hayek's theory of cultural evolution: market and cultural processes as spontaneous orders', *Cultural Dynamics*, **3** (1), 1–9.

'National defense and the public goods problem', in Robert Higgs (ed.) *Arms, Politics and the Economy: Historical and Contemporary Perspectives*, New York: Holmes and Meier: pp. 37–60, (with Jeffrey R. Hummel).

'Prefatory note: origins of the agorics project', *Market Process*, **8**.

Review Essay: Henry K. H. Woo's *What's Wrong With Formalization in Economics? An Epistemological Critique, Research in the History of Economic Thought and Methodology*, **7**, pp. 274–81.

'Understanding differently: hermeneutics and the spontaneous order of communicative processes', *History of Political Economy*, Annual Supplement to Vol. 22, pp. 359–77.

1991

'Coping with complexity: OOPS and the economist's critique of central planning', *Hotline on Object-Oriented Technology*, **3** (1), November, pp. 6–8 (with Howard Baetjer and William Tulloh).

'Increased productivity through reuse: an economist's perspective', *Proceedings of the Third Annual Workshop on Reuse*, Software Productivity Consortium, Herndon, VA (with Howard Baetjer and William Tulloh).

'Introduction to *Economics and Hermeneutics*', a collection of thirteen original essays commissioned, edited and introduced by Don Lavoie, London: Routledge.

'The discovery and interpretation of profit opportunities: culture and the Kirznerian entrepreneur', in Brigitte Berger (ed.) *The Culture of Entrepreneur ship*, San Francisco: Institute for Contemporary Studies, translated into French as *Esprit d'entreprise, cultures el sociétés*, (Paris: Maxima).

'The progress of subjectivism', Mark Blaug and Neil de Marchi (eds), *Appraising Modern Economics: Studies in the Methodology of Scientific Research Programmes*, Aldershot, UK and Brookfield, US: Edward Elgar, pp. 470–86.

1992

'Between historicism and formalism: the rise and fall of the Austrian school's calculation argument, 1920–1950', *Praxiology*, **6**.

'*Glasnost* and the knowledge problem: rethinking economic democracy', *Cato Journal*, **11** (3), Winter, pp. 435–55, translated into Russian under the title: 'Democracy, openness, and the knowledge problem: toward a democratic market economy', in Larisa Piyasheva and James A. Dorn (eds), *From Plan to Market: The Future of the Post-Communist Republics*, Moscow: Catallaxy.

1993

Component Software: A Market Perspective on the Coming Revolution in Software Development, Patricia Seybold Group Special Research Report, Strategic Technologies Series, April (with Howard Baetjer, William Tulloh, and Richard Langlois).

'Democracy, markets, and the legal order: notes on the nature of politics in a radically liberal society', in E. Paul, F D. Miller and J. Paul (eds), *Liberalism and the Economic Order*, New York: Cambridge University Press, pp. 103–20; also published in *Social Philosophy and Policy*, **10** (2).

1994

'Austrian models? Possibilities of evolutionary computation', in Peter Boettke (ed.), *Companion of Austrian Economics*, Aldershot, UK and Brookfield, US: Edward Elgar.

'Cultural studies and the conditions of entrepreneurship', in T. William Boxx and Gary M. Quinlivan (eds), *The Cultural Context of Economics and Politics*, Lanham, Maryland: University Press of America, pp. 51–69.

Introduction to *Expectations and the Meaning of Institutions: Essays in Economics by Ludwig M. Lachmann*, a collection of 21 essays by Ludwig Lachmann, edited and introduced by Don Lavoie, for the book series on 'Foundations of the market economy', edited by Mario J. Rizzo and Lawrence H. White, London: Routledge.

'Preface: the meaning of market process', in Peter Boettke and David Prychitko (eds), *The Market Process: Essays in Contemporary Austrian Economics*, Aldershot, UK and Brookfield, US: Edward Elgar.

'The interpretive turn', entry in Peter Boettke (ed.) *Companion of Austrian Economics*, Aldershot, UK and Brookfield, US: Edward Elgar.

1995

'The "objectivity" of scholarship and the ideal of the university', *Advances in Austrian Economics*, 2B: pp. 371–403.

1996

'Governments, firms, and the critique of centralized economic planning', in Paul Foss (ed.), *Economic Approaches to Organizations: An Introduction*, Aldershot, UK: Dartmouth Publishing Company (with Jerome Ellig).

1997

'On regrouping the intellectual capital structure of Lachmann's economics', *Advances in Austrian Economics*, **4**, pp. 219–26.

1998

'Preface to the Japanese translation' of *Rivalry and Central Planning*, Seizansha, Ltd.

2000

Culture and Enterprise: The Development, Representation, and Morality of Business, New York: Routledge (with Emily Chamlee-Wright).

'On the persuasive economist' in Laurence S. Moss (ed.), 'Remembrance and appreciation roundtable, Professor Ludwig M. Lachmann (1906–1990): scholar, teacher, and Austrian school critic of late classical formalism in economics', *American Journal of Economics and Sociology*, **59** (3), 399–404, July.

2002

'Culture and the Wealth of Nations', *Cato Policy Report*, January/February, **XXIV** (1) (with Emily Chamlee).

2004

'Subjectivism, entrepreneurship, and the convergence of groupware and hypertext', in Jack Birner and Pierre Garrouste (eds), *Markets, Information, and Communication: An Austrian Perspective on the Internet Economy*, London: Routledge.

'The subjectivist methodology of Austrian Economics and Dewey's theory of inquiry', in Elias L. Khalil (ed.) *Dewey, Pragmatism and Economic Methodology*, London: Routledge (with Peter J. Boettke and Virgil Storr).

SHORTER PIECES

'Austrian economics at New York University', *Austrian Economics Newsletter*, **1** (1), Autumn 1977.

'The spirit or the sword' (review of Loebl's *My Mind on Trial*) *Libertarian Review*, September 1977.

'The decay of radical socialism', *Libertarian Review*, **6** (6), October 1977, translated into Italian as 'Chi Sono I Veri Radicali', *Claustrofobia*, **2** (5), June 1979.

'Amnesty International: Enemy of the State', *Libertarian Review*, **7** (8), September 1978.

Interviewed by Patrice Bollon for Liberation (Paris), No 1522 (December 1978).

'Communists for Capitalism', *Libertarian Review*, **9** (8), August 1980 (review of Konrad and Szelenyi's *The Intellectuals on the Road to Class Power*).

'The strikes in Poland: workers against the workers state', *Policy Report*, **2** (11), November 1980.

'Industrial policy: son of central planning', *Heritage Foundation Backgrounder*, No 319, December 1983.

'How to profit from the coming class struggle', *The Wall Street Journal*, 3 October, 1985. (Review of Green and Berry's *The Challenge of Hidden Profits*).

'Editor's Note', *Market Process*, **4** (2), Fall 1986.

'Editor's Note', *Market Process*, **5** (1), Spring 1987.

'Editor's Note', *Market Process*, **5** (2), Fall 1987.

'Editor's Note', *Market Process*, **6** (1), Spring 1988.

'Editor's Note', *Market Process*, **6** (2), Fall 1988.

'Editor's Note', *Market Process*, **7** (1), Spring 1989.

'Editor's Note', *Market Process*, **8**, Spring 1990.

'Lessons from history on central planning and central banking', *Market Process*, **7** (1), Spring 1989.

UNPUBLISHED WORKS

The Interpretive Dimension of Economics, unfinished book manuscript: partial draft *circa* 1991, re-write of Market Process Working Paper

'The interpretive dimension of economics: science, hermeneutics, and praxeology', 1985.

Understanding Political Economy, unfinished book project. An attempt at synthesis between Austrian/Hermeneutic and Libertarian/Leftist lines of thought; partial draft circa 1991; more recent sketches.

'Mises and Gadamer on theory and history', paper presented at the 'Philosophers for Economists' session of the annual History of Economics Society meetings, Columbia University, New York, NY, June 1986.

'Beyond measuring rods: the contextual and multidimensional nature of rational judgment', comment commissioned for the Liberty Fund conference on Mancur Olson's forthcoming book, *Beyond the Measuring Rod of Money,* University of Victoria, Victoria, British Columbia, Canada, 2–5 June, 1988.

'S. H. Clark on Paul Ricoeur', book review prepared for the journal *Research in the History of Economic Thought and Methodology* in 1991.

'Order in complex systems: object-oriented programming and the economists' critique of central planning', with Howard Baetjer and Bill Tulloh. Paper submitted to the East European Conference on Object-Oriented Programming, 17–20 September, 1991, Bratislava, Czechoslovakia.

'A radical critique of socialism: a review of F.A. Hayek's The Fatal Conceit: The Errors of Socialism', prepared for book review section of *Public Choice*, but apparently not used. 1992.

'The use of knowledge in organizations: technologies of cooperation', with Bill Tulloh. Revised circa 1995 under the title, 'Boundaries and openness, markets and discourses: technologies for organizational learning'.

'Higher education, socialism, and the future of democracy', presented at the General Meetings of the Mont Pelerin Society, Cannes, France, September, 1994.

'Hermeneutics, hypertext, and the civil society: the big picture', working paper cited by Virgil Storr in his 'New Collaborative Learning Environments' paper, 1997.

'The electronic readings group: generating annotation dialogue streams with hypertext markup tools', with Theodor Holm Nelson and Mark Gilbert. Paper prepared for the Joint International Conference of the Association for Computers and the Humanities and the Association for Literary and Linguistic Computing, 9–13 June, 1999, University of Virginia, Charlottesville, Virginia, USA.

'Two steps beyond rational choice theory: Ludwig Mises and Hannah Arendt on human action', prepared for panel on 'Action and judgment: the significance of Hannah Arendt's work for political economy' organized by Kevin Quinn. Eastern Economic Association meetings, 2000.

'The Austrian critique of socialism: what it says and what it doesn't say', paper prepared for the *Cambridge History of Twentieth Century Political Thought,* edited by Terrence Ball and Richard Bellamy.

'Deciphering prices: the value theories of Marx and Menger as hermeneutical devices', updated version of 'Object and subject: the value theories of Marx and Menger as hermeneutical devices', paper presented at the History of Economics Society panel on 'New angles on Marx', at the annual Eastern Economic Association meetings, Philadelphia, Pennsylvania, April 1986. Also mentioned in 'The Progress of Subjectivism', 2001.

'Distinction or dichotomy: rethinking the line between thymology and praxeology' (with Virgil Henry Storr. Paper prepared for 71st Annual Meeting of the Southern Economic Association, 17–19 November, 2001; Tampa, Florida.

'Subjective orientation and objective wealth: entrepreneurship and the convergence of groupware and hypertext capabilities', Paper prepared for the third annual conference of the *Association des Historiens de la Tradition Economique Autrichienne* /*Association of Historians of the Austrian Tradition in Economic Thought,* to be held in Pisa, Italy, from 24–26 May 2001. This paper was drastically shortened (from 54–25 pages) by Bill Tulloh in order to meet space constraints for publication. Published as 'Subjectivism, entrepreneurship, and the convergence of groupware and hypertext', in Jack Birner and Pierre Garrouste (eds), *Markets, Information, and Communication: An Austrian Perspective on the Internet Economy,* London: Routledge 2004.

Index